INSIGHT GUIDES
IN THE SAME SERIES

ASIA	ISBN ASIA	ISBN USA, CANADA	ISBN BRITISH ISLES	ISBN AUSTRALIA, NEW ZEALAND
Bali	9971-925-62-1	013-056200-9	0245-54119-5	0-7018-1852-2
Burma	9971-925-71-0	013-090902-5	0245-54021-0	0-7018-1861-1
Hong Kong	9971-925-69-9	013-394635-5	0245-54019-9	0-7018-1860-3
Indonesia	9971-925-43-5	013-457391-9	0245-54129-2	0-7018-1836-0
Java	9971-925-63-X	013-509976-5	0245-54118-7	0-7018-1853-0
Korea	9971-925-66-4	013-516641-1	0245-54016-4	0-7018-1859-X
Malaysia	9971-925-64-8	013-547992-4	0245-54121-7	0-7018-1855-7
Nepal	9971-925-70-2	013-611038-X	0245-54020-2	0-7018-1863-8
Philippines	9971-925-65-6	013-662197-X	0245-54017-2	0-7018-1857-3
Singapore	9971-925-73-7	013-810710-0	0245-54120-9	0-7018-1854-9
Sri Lanka	9971-925-75-3	013-839944-1	0245-54025-3	0-7018-1866-2
Taiwan	9971-925-77-X	013-882192-5	0245-54128-4	0-7018-1867-0
Thailand	9971-925-67-2	013-912600-7	0245-54117-9	0-7018-1856-5

AMERICAS

American Southwest	9971-925-47-8	013-029521-3	0245-54176-4	0-7018-1872-7
Florida	9971-925-72-9	013-322412-0	0245-54022-9	0-7018-1862-X
Jamaica	9971-925-76-1	013-509000 -8	0245-54024-5	0-7018-1865-4
Mexico	9971-925-74-5	013-579524-9	0245-54023-7	0-7018-1864-6
New England	9971-925-50-8	013-612854-8	0245-54175-6	0-7018-1837-9
Northern California	9971-925-45-1	013-623562-X	0245-54173-X	0-7018-1869-7
Southern California	9971-925-46-X	013-823600-3	0245-54174-8	0-7018-1870-0

PACIFIC

Hawaii	9971-925-68-0	013-384651-2	0245-54018-0	0-7018-1858-1
New Zealand	9971-925-49-4	013-621111-9	0245-54177-2	0-7018-1871-9

GRAND TOURS

Australia	9971-925-48-6	013-291832-3	0245-54184-5	0-7018-1868-9
Western Europe	9971-925-52-4	013-053828-0	0245-54186-1	0-7018-1838-7

northern california

Edited by Jon Carroll and Tracy Johnston
Produced by Bret Reed Lundberg and John Gottberg Anderson
Directed and Designed by Hans Johannes Hoefer

APA PRODUCTIONS
PRENTICE-HALL • HARRAP • LANSDOWNE

THE INSIGHT GUIDES SERIES RECEIVED SPECIAL AWARDS FOR EXCELLENCE FROM THE PACIFIC AREA TRAVEL ASSOCIATION IN 1980 AND 1982.

NORTHERN CALIFORNIA

First Edition Published by:
© APA PRODUCTIONS (HK) LTD, 1984
All rights reserved ISBN 9971-925-45-1
Printed in Singapore by Singapore National Printers (Pte) Ltd

U.S. and Canadian Edition: PRENTICE-HALL INC. ISBN 013-623562-X	British Isles edition: HARRAP LTD. ISBN 0245-54173-X	Australia and New Zealand edition: LANSDOWNE PRESS ISBN 0-7018-1869-7

Photographs and text are also available for further use at special library rates from the Apa Photo Agency, Singapore, P.O. Box 219, Killiney Road Post Office, Singapore 9123.

APA PRODUCTIONS

Publisher and Managing Director: Hans Johannes Hoefer
Executive Director Marketing: Yvan Van Outrive
Financial Controller: Henry Lee
Administrative Manager: Alice Ng
Managing Editor: John Gottberg Anderson
Assistant Editor: Vivien Loo
Production Coordinator: Nancy Yap

Contributing Editors

Ravindralal Anthonis, Jon Carroll, Virginia Hopkins, Jay Itzkowitz, Phil Jarratt, Tracy Johnston, Ben Kalb, Wilhelm Klein, Saul Lockhart, Sylvia Mayuga, Gordon McLauchlan, Kal Müller, Eric M. Oey, Daniel P. Reid, Stuart Ridsdale, Kim Robinson, Ronn Ronck, Rolf Steinberg, Desmond Tate, Lisa Van Gruisen, Made Wijaya.

Contributing Writers

Edward Abbey, Ruth Armstrong, T. Terence Barrow, F. Lisa Beebe, Bruce Berger, Dor Bahadur Bista, Clinton V. Black, Star Black, Frena Bloomfield, John Borthwick, Roger Boschman, Tom Brosnahan, Linda Carlock, Jerry Carroll, Tom Chaffin, Nedra Chung, Tom Cole, Orman Day, Kunda Dixit, Richard Erdöes, Guillermo García-Oropeza, Ted Giannoulas, Barbara Gloudon, Harka Gurung, Sharifah Hamzah, Willard A. Hanna, Elizabeth Hawley, Sir Edmund Hillary, Tony Hillerman, Jerry Hopkins, Peter Hutton, Michael King, Michele Kort, Thomas Lucey, Leonard Lueras, Michael E. Macmillan, Derek Maitland, Buddy Mays, Craig McGregor, Reinhold Messner, Julie Michaels, Barbara Mintz, John Nichols, M.R. Priya Rangsit, Al Read, Elizabeth V. Reyes, Victor Stafford Reid, Harry Rolnick, E.R. Sarachchandra, Uli Schmetzer, Ilsa Sharp, Norman Sibley, Leslie Marmon Silko, Peter Spiro, Harold Stephens, Keith Stevens, Michael Stone, Colin Taylor, Deanna L. Thompson, Randy Udall, James Wade, Mallika Wanigasundara, William Warren, Cynthia Wee, Tony Wheeler, Linda White, H. Taft Wireback, Alfred A. Yuson, Paul Zach.

Contributing Photographers

Carole Allen, Roland Ammon, Ping Amranand, Walter D. Andreae, Ray Cranbourne, Rennie Ellis, Alain Evrard, Ricardo Ferro, Lee Foster, Manfred Gottschalk, Allen Grazer, Werner Hahn, Dallas and John Heaton, Brent Hesselyn, Dennis Lane, Max Lawrence, Bud Lee, Philip Little, R. Ian Lloyd, Bret Reed Lundberg, Kal Müller, Ronni Pinsler, Günter Pfannmüller, G.P. Reichelt, Dan Rocovits, David Ryan, Frank Salmoiraghi, Thomas Schöllhammer, Blair Seitz, David Stahl, Tom Tidball, Paul Van Riel, Joseph F. Viesti, Paul Von Stroheim, Rolf Verres, Bill Wassman, Jan Whiting, Rendo Yap.

Apa's editors direct the creation of all new titles and revisions of existing titles. In most cases, a project editor is assigned the task of coordinating a team of writers in his or her assigned geographical region, editing their work for publication, and supervising the selection of stock photography and historical materials.

MARKETING, SALES AND ADVERTISING

Insight Guides are available through the international book trade in 30 countries around the world as single copies or as complete collectors sets at discounts. Visit your nearest bookshop. Should any of the Insight Guides listed below be unavailable or out of stock, please refer to the ISBN numbers when ordering through the bookshop or direct through these distributors.

Distributors:
Australia and New Zealand: Lansdowne Press, 176 South Creek Road, Dee Why, N.S.W. 2099, AUSTRALIA. **Benelux:** Uitgevrij Cambium, Maliebaan 113, 3581 CJ Utrecht, The Netherlands. **Denmark:** Copenhagen Book Centre Aps, Roskildeveji 338, DK-2630 Tastrup, Denmark. **France:** Libraire Armand Colin, 103 Boulevard St. Michel, 75005 Paris, France. **Germany:** GEO Center Vertrieb, Neumarkterstrasse 18, 8000 Munich 80, West Germany. **Hawaii:** Pacific Trade Group Inc., P.O. Box 1227, Kailua, Oahu, Hawaii 96734, U.S.A. **Hong Kong:** Far East Media Ltd., Vita Tower, 7th Floor, Block B, 29 Wong Chuk Hang Road, Hong Kong. **India and Nepal:** India Book Distributors, 107/108 Arcadia Building, 195 Narima Point, Bombay-400-021, India. **Indonesia:** N.V. Indoprom Company (Indonesia) Ltd., Arthaloka Building, 14th floor, 2 Jalan Jendral Sudirman, Jakarta Pusat, Indonesia. **Jamaica:** Kingston Publishers, 1-A Norwood Avenue, Kingston 5, Jamaica. **Japan:** Charles E. Tuttle Co. Inc., 2-6 Suido 1-Chome, Bunkyo-ku, Tokyo, Japan. **Korea:** Korea Britannica Corporation, C.P.O. Box 690, Seoul 100, Korea. **Mexico:** Distribuidora Britannica S.A., Rio Volga 93, Col Cuauhtemoc, 06500 Mexico 5 D.F., Mexico. **Pakistan:** Liberty Book Stall, Inverarity Road, Karachi 03, Pakistan. **Philippines:** Print Diffusion Pacific Inc., 2135-C Pasong Tamo Street, Makati, Manila, Philippines. **Singapore and Malaysia:** MPH Distributors (S) Pte Ltd., 51 Lorong 3, Geylang #05-09, Singapore 1438. **Sri Lanka:** K.V.G. de Silva & Sons (Colombo) Ltd., 415 Galle Road, Colombo 4, Sri Lanka. **Spain:** Altair, Riera Alta 8, Barcelona 1, Spain. **Sweden:** Esselte Kartcentrum, Vasagatan 16, S-111 20 Stockholm, Sweden. **Taiwan:** Caves Books Ltd., 107 Chungshan N. Road, Sec. 2, Taipei, Taiwan, Republic of China. **Thailand:** The Bookseller Co. Ltd., 67/2 Soi Tonson, Nang Linchi Road, Bangkok 10120, Thailand. **United Kingdom:** Harrap Ltd., 19-23 Ludgate Hill, London EC4M 7PD, England, United Kingdom. **Mainland United States and Canada:** Prentice-Hall Inc., Englewood Cliffs, New Jersey 07632, U.S.A.

German editions: Nelles Verlag GmbH, Schleissheimerstrasse 3716, 8000 Munich 45, West Germany. Distributor: Geo Centre, Vertrieb, Neumarkterstrasse 18, 8000 Munich 80, West Germany. **French editions:** Less Editions Errance, 11 rue de l'Arsenal, 75004 Paris, France. Distributor: Librairie Armand Colin, 103 Boulevard St. Michael, 75005 Paris, France.

Advertising and Special Sales Representatives

Advertising carried in Insight Guides gives readers direct access to quality merchandise and travel-related services. These advertisements are inserted in the Guide in Brief section of each book. Advertisers are requested to contact their nearest representatives, listed below.

Special sales, for promotional and educational purposes within the international travel industry, are also available. The advertising representatives listed here also handle special sales. Alternatively, interested parties can contact marketing director Yvan Van Outrive directly at Apa Productions, P.O. Box 219, Killiney Road Post Office, Singapore 9123.

Asia and Australia: Martin Clinch & Associates Ltd., 20th floor, Queen's Centre, 58-64 Queen's Road East, Hong Kong. Telephone: 5-273525. Telex: 76041 MCAL HX. **Japan:** Media House Ltd., R. 212 Azabu Heights, 1-5-10 Roppongi, Minato-ku, Tokyo 106, Japan. Telephone: (03) 585-9571. Telex: 28208. **Europe:** Publicitas, 12 Avenue des Toises, 1002 Lausanne, Switzerland. Telephone: (021) 207111. Telex: 24986 PDG CH.

United States: Sfw-Pri International Inc., 1560 Broadway, New York, N.Y. 10036, U.S.A. Telephone: (212) 575-9292. Telex: 422260. **Hawaii:** The Brogden Group, 635 Pamaele Street, Kailua, Oahu, Hawaii 96734, U.S.A.

APA PHOTO AGENCY PTE LTD

General Manager: Sylvia Muttom
The Apa Photo Agency represents the work of photographers for publication rights. More than 150,000 original color transparencies are in the agency's picture files, including Southeast Asia's most complete photographic collection. All works are rented for commercial, cultural or educational purposes. Agency stock is given first consideration in choosing photography for Insight Guides.

CARTOGRAPHY

To complement **Insight Guides** and bring readers a more complete package of travel information, Apa Productions — in cooperation with cartographer Gunter Nelles of Munich, West Germany — has begun publication of a series of detailed maps on selected travel destinations. Initial maps cover Asian countries and cities:

INDONESIA MALAYSIA NEPAL PHILIPPINES SRI LANKA THAILAND

In sharp contradiction to Horace Greeley's 19th Century admonition to "Go West," Apa Productions—Asia-based publisher of the widely acclaimed *Insight Guides* series—set its sights east across the Pacific in the Olympic year of 1984.

Insight Guide: Northern California, released shortly after a twin volume on *Southern California*, was a "natural" for founder-publisher **Hans Hoefer** and his cadre of professional editors, writers and photographers. *Insight Guides* have long been regarded in Asia as the vanguard of travel literature for their sensitive cultural portrayals of leading destinations. Previous North American titles on *Florida*(1982) and *Mexico*(1983) were warmly received by readers and critics alike. But California was regarded as the crucial step in establishing *Insight Guides* in the awareness of the American traveling public.

Jon Carroll

Johnston

Lundberg

Hoefer

Whiting

Anderson

The lion's share of credit for *Northern California* goes to project coordinator **Bret Reed Lundberg** and editors **Jon Carroll** and **Tracy Johnston**.

Carroll and Johnston, a highly respected husband-and-wife team based in Oakland, were the key people in the San Francisco Bay Area. Together, they assigned, coordinated and edited the work of more than 20 different writers, arranged exclusive interviews with San Francisco Mayor **Dianne Feinstein** and novelist **Joan Didion**, and did additional yeomen's work in research and other aspects of production.

Lundberg coordinated photography and graphics for all of California from his Orange County studio, drawing most heavily upon the work of Marin County cameraman **Jan Whiting** for this book. Lundberg later assisted Hoefer and managing editor **John Gottberg Anderson** in final design and production of the book at Apa's Singapore headquarters.

Hoefer, a graduate of printing, book production, design and photography studies in Krefeld, West Germany, is a disciple of the Bauhaus tradition of graphic arts. He established Apa Productions in 1970, and that year published a guide to the Indonesian isle of *Bali*, thereby setting a new trend in travel literature.

The resounding success of *Hawaii* (1980) gave the company a firm foundation. There are now 18 books in the *Insight Guides* series, with several more due to appear by the end of 1984.

Hoefer assigned Anderson to appoint and supervise Apa's California project teams. Anderson knew California well, having traveled extensively in that state while a student at the University of Oregon and, later, as a reporter and editor for *The Honolulu Advertiser* and the *Seattle Post-Intelligencer*. He still maintains a home "just up Interstate 5" from California, near the Canadian border in the state of Washington.

Anderson joined Apa in 1981 upon completing the Gannett Fellowship program at the University of Hawaii. He has since overseen the creation of several new titles—including *Burma*, *Nepal* and *Sri Lanka*—and the revision of numerous others.

Lundberg operates a thriving photography business based in Newport Beach, California. In addition to his commercial work, Lundberg handles assignment work for photojournalistic markets worldwide. He has been published in more than 80 books, magazines and newspapers in over 20 countries, and his credits include *National Geographic*, *Time*, *Der Speigel*, *Paris Match*, *The New York Times* and the *San Francisco Examiner*.

Carroll, a native Californian, is a daily columnist for the *San Francisco Chronicle* and the former editor of California-based *New West* magazine. His work has appeared in such magazines as *Playboy*, *Esquire*, *New York*, *Psychology Today* and *Rolling Stone*.

Johnston, who has lived in California since she was two years old, is a free-lance writer and editor. She was the managing editor of *L.A. Weekly* and, for a time, an editor at *California Living*, the Sunday magazine of the

San Francisco Examiner. Her writing has appeared in many publications, including *The New York Times, New West, California Playboy* and *Redbook* magazines. A dedicated hiker and backpacker, Johnston also wrote this book's feature on "The Great Outdoors."

Tom Chaffin, who authored the introductory chapter on geological history and the travel piece on California's vast northeast, is a former staff member of *Esquire* magazine who moved to San Francisco in 1981. His articles have appeared in *Outside, The Nation* and *The New York Times Book Review.*

The extensive history section was written by **Tom Cole**, author of *A Short History of San Francisco*—published by Lexikos Press which, not coincidentally, he owns. Cole is a world traveler and an accomplished mountain climber: in 1981 he was a member of the first American expedition ever to trek the Tibetan approaches to Mount Everest. "I consider myself," he says, "someone whose obsessions have been treated kindly by fate."

"Californians" is essentially the work of three writers—**Lonnie Isabel** on Blacks, **Rick Rodriguez** on Hispanics and **William Wong** on Asians. Isabel, an Amherst graduate and former reporter for the *Boston Globe,* is presently covering City Hall for the *Oakland Tribune.* Wong, a native Californian, also works for the *Oakland Tribune* as assistant managing editor; he is a former *Wall Street Journal* reporter. Rodriguez, another California native, is a political reporter for *The Sacramento Bee.* In 1980, he took a year off to study the problems of illegal aliens and the farm labor movement at the Autonomous University in Guadalajara, Mexico.

The lengthy coverage of San Francisco was written by **Jerry Carroll**, who has covered the city for the *San Francisco Chronicle* since the late Sixties. Although born in Kansas ("an accident of birth for which I should not be held responsible"), Carroll was raised in California and has lived in the Bay Area since his college days. (Despite the fact that they have the same last name and work for the same newspaper, Jerry Carroll is no relation to Jon Carroll, co-editor of this book.)

Reporting on the communities surrounding San Francisco are **Karen Liberatore**, **Julie Smith** and **Philip Garlington**. Liberatore, who covered the Peninsula, is the author of four books, including *Complete Guide to the Golden Gate National Recreation Area* and *Under the Sun: A Guide to the Sonoran Desert.* She was also editor of a weekly paper in Marin County. Smith, who wrote about the East Bay, is a newspaper reporter-turned-mystery writer. She is the author of *Death Turns a Trick* and numerous published short stories. Garlington,

also a former newspaper reporter, has published articles in *Esquire, Outside* and *Plane and Pilot* magazines, and is the author of the novel *Aces and Eights.* He wrote this book's section on Marin County.

The Wine County chapter was scribed by **Don Edwards**, an expert on Sonoma County and the author of *Making the Most of Sonoma,* a detailed guide to the area. He is distantly related to the Boggs family, a pioneer Wine County family that came by wagon train to California in 1846, traveling part of the way with the ill-fated Donner Party.

Walt Wiley, author of the

Chaffin

Cole

Rodriguez

Liberatore

Garlington

chapter on Sacramento, spent his boyhood in California and currently writes a weekly column on Northern California geography and people for *The Sacramento Bee.*

De Vries

Rubenstein

Tom DeVries, who wrote on the Gold country, lived for 10 years in Mariposa at the southern end of the "Gold Trail," where he raised goats and peaches. He has published articles in numerous magazines and is currently a news producer San Francisco television station KRON.

Covering California's high country are **Steve Rubenstein** and **Kief Hillsbery**, two devotees of the mountains and their recreations. Rubenstein, who wrote about Lake Tahoe, is a reporter and columnist for *The San Francisco Chronicle.* Hillsbery, who covered Yosemite and the High Sierra, lived in Yosemite Valley for five years where he climbed, among other routes, the nose route on El Capitan. He has also climbed in the Cascades, Rockies, Dolomites and Himalaya. He writes: "I have

Lester

spent time in most of the world's great ranges and the Sierra to me is unsurpassed, be it for climbing or skiing or solitary contemplation." He was, until recently, a columnist for *Outside* magazine.

The southern part of Northern California was covered by two Pauls—**Paul Cohen** and **Paul Ciotti**. Cohen, who wrote the section on the San Joaquin Valley, was an associate editor of *California* magazine and is currently the editor of *Atari Connection* magazine. Ciotti, who wrote about the Monterey Peninsula area, has been a free-lance writer for 10 years and has published articles in *Time, People, Us, California* and *True* magazines.

Frank Robertson, who wrote the chapter on the North Coast, is a resident of Guerneville, a resort community on the Russian River 10 miles from the ocean. His articles have appeared in *California, Rolling Stone, Oui* and

wards

Wiley

Women's Sports magazines. Currently he is a reporter and columnist for the *Sebastapol Times.*

Four writers, in addition to co-editor Johnston,

tti

Robertson

Shilts

contributed to the book's feature section. **Ruth Reichl**, who discussed "The Gourmet's San Francisco," is the food critic for *California* magazine and the former co-owner of a Berkeley restaurant. She has also written a cookbook—*Mmmmmm:A Feastiary.* **Patrick Finley**, who wrote about the arts, is a poet, a translator, an actor, and one of the directors of the Pacific Poetry Ensemble, which stages theatrical revues about poetry for school-children. **Randy Shilts** has lived for eight years in the San Francisco gay community of which he writes, and has covered it extensively for television and newspapers, including the *San Francisco Chronicle.* He is the author of *The Mayor of Castro Street: The Life and Times of Harvey Milk.* **Les Cowan**, who covered Silicon Valley, is the author of *The Illustrated Computer Dictionary and Handbook* and articles for *PC, PC World, Popular Computing, Home Electronics* and *Entertainment and*

InfoWorld magazines. He also hosted his own television interview show on a Bay Area cable station.

The difficult and time-consuming task of preparing the "Guide in Brief" fell to **Michael Caleb Lester**, who for several years edited the "What's New" section of *New West* magazine. He has also written for *Esquire, Family Circle, Games, Women's Sports* and *Los Angeles* magazines.

Jan Whiting, who is represented in this volume by more than 70 photographs, is a native Californian who moved back to the Bay Area in 1983 after spending most of the previous decade living and working abroad. His work has been show-cased in several magazines in Australia and Asia, and he has contributed to previous *Insight Guides* on *Nepal, Burma, Mexico* and *Sri Lanka.*

Two other photographers, in addition to Whiting and Lundberg, had major representation in this book. **Mireille Vautier**, who operates the Photothèque Vautier-de Nanxe in Paris, France, traveled extensively through California and the American Southwest with

Cowan

her photographer colleagues in 1982, shooting 1,000 rolls of film along the way. Their vision of California through European eyes lends an important aspect to this book. **Lee Foster**, a photographer-writer who makes his home in Oakland, is the author of more than 10 books of travel, gardening, health, "how-to" and fiction. A former Stanford University graduate student, his most recent book was *Making the Most of the Peninsula* (Presidio, 1983). He is also a contributor to Apa Productions' soon-to-be-published *Grand Tour: Western Europe.*

Foster

Other photographic contributors include Bay Area photographers **Maxine Cass** and **David Ryan**; mountain sports specialist and Tahoe-area resident **Tom Lippert**; Southern Californians **G.R. Russell** and **John Sanford**; and veteran magazine photographer **Bud Lee**, now a resident of Florida. Additional photos were taken by Bill Bachman (Scoopix of Australia), Allen Grazer, Hans Hoefer, R. Ian Lloyd, Buddy Mays, C. Allan Morgan, Ronni Pinsler, Mary Robertson and Paul Von Stroheim.

Lundberg's office manager, **Kimberli Ann Campbell**, was also a photographic contribu-

Continued on page 350

TABLE OF CONTENTS

TABLE OF CONTENTS

IN THE BEGINNING, CALIFORNIA ...

In the beginning, California was without freeways and water covered the land. In the Mesozoic era, 200 million years ago, a trip to the West Coast would have ended in the mountains of central Nevada: the Pacific Coast paralleled the modern coastline but was 400 miles (650 kilometers) farther east.

The process by which California rose from the waters like some modern-day Atlantis was a slow one. But we'll speed up the clock.

Geologic Origins

Under the ocean off Nevada, something was happening. The Pacific's heavy rock floor began to slide under the lighter, granite core of the continent.

This oceanic rock, called basalt, was formed from magma, molten rock that originates deep in the earth's mantle. Far out at sea, magma rose toward fractures that marked the crests of mid-oceanic ridges. On either side of these underwater mountains, the magma solidified into basalt.

This new ocean floor was moved further away from the mid-oceanic ridge and toward the continental margin by convection currents in the earth's mantle. Geologists call this process sea-floor spreading, a notion that eventually led to a far-reaching revolution in the earth sciences.

Most geologists now envision the earth's crust as a series of some 20 solid plates — "tectonic plates" — that push under, over and against one another. Empowered by the mantle's convection currents, the plates, and the continents and oceans they carry, "float" on the mantle like bumper cars at an amusement park.

The Pacific Ocean plate ranges from three to 60 miles (five to 97 km) in thickness. As it bumped against the Mesozoic continental plate, offshore sediments were pushed upward and together to form sedimentary rocks. As this buckling continued, the new shoreline built to the west. Offshore, where it dived under the continental shelf, the Pacific plate scraped muds, other sediments and basalts together to form underwater

mountains that later rose to become the Coast Range.

In geology, one process does not wait for another. As mountains grow, they erode, subside and shift. At its core, California's Sierra Nevada range consists of granite that has been uplifted along giant fault blocks. While the Sierras were forming, they split along an east-west fault. About 140 million years ago, their northern half moved 60 miles westward. This prodigal Sierran section is now called the Klamaths. A thickly forested range, it covers the northwestern part of California.

During this entire period, internal pressures nudged the Sierras and the later Klamaths farther into the sky. In a process called subduction, oceanic basalts dived into the earth's mantle through offshore "trenches." Deep in the earth, the basalt became molten and rose toward the Sierras and Klamaths. Some of the molten rock erupted on the surface as volcanoes. Most of it solidified before reaching the surface. These solid emplacements – huge intrusions of granite – are call batholiths. Batholiths often "cook" surrounding sedimentary rocks, like limestone, and turn them into much harder metamorphic rocks, like marble.

About 25 million years ago, the granitic stuffing that created the Sierras and Klamaths ended. The offshore submarine peaks of the modern Coast Range, with nothing pulling them down, rose and broke the surface as an arc of offshore islands. Separating them from the Sierras and Klamaths was an inland sea — a 450-mile (725-km) trough that slowly filled with sediment to form California's Central Valley.

As the Klamaths-to-be moved westward, Pacific Ocean waters filled northeastern California above the northern end of the Sierras. Sediments eventually filled this seaway and created a plain under what is now the Modoc Plateau. About 30 million years ago, mantle convection currents stretched this new plain from the east and west. The pulling weakened the crust and allowed magma to rise to the surface. Volcanoes erupted, but not the towering piles usually associated with that word. Basalts instead flowed from long fissures in the strained earth, much as oceanic basalts ooze from deep submarine fractures. They were so fluid that geologists call them basalt floods; instead of piling up to create cones, domes and shields, they flowed laterally, covering hundreds of miles.

The basalt flooding eventually stopped but the stretching of the northeastern California crust continued. Ultimately, the crust broke into the giant fault blocks that pushed against one another, rising or sinking to form mountains like the Sierra Nevada and basins like the Nevada valleys east of northern Sierras.

Volcanic Violence

Before Mount St. Helens' 1980 eruption in the state of Washington, California's Lassen Peak ranked as the most recently active volcano in the continental United States. From the late 18th Century through the mid 19th Century, at least 11 other Cascade volcanoes were active.

Until recently, however, geologists viewed the Cascade range as a chain of dead volcanoes. Pioneer and Indian accounts of burning mountains were dismissed as just that — forest fires. Lassen Peak's smoke of 1914 was perceived as only the dying gasp of a moribund volcanism. Needless to say, since the St. Helens eruption, there has been an enthusiastic revisionism: geologists are giving many Cascade peaks, including majestic Shasta in north central California, a second look.

Mountains are often thought of as symbols of permanence, bulwarks against the vagaries of time. They are not. From 1914 to 1984 seems a respectable dormancy to man; a few million years seem quite permanent. In geology, such time frames mean little. Pacific Northwest coast continues to nourish the Cascades. More than any other California mountains, they are a range that is still becoming.

Convection currents cause more than mountains and lavas. While Northern California's mountains were rising, a piece of the southern Sierras hitched a ride northward. This slab of granite, called the Salinian Block, was once due west of Arizona. It carries the Point Reyes peninsula, which is currently north and west of San Francisco. This block is moving northward at about two inches (five centimeters) a year. In a sense, it is just one more California tourist, en route to Alaska. Its eastern boundary is the San Andreas Fault, the main cleavage of a system of faults that run parallel to California's coast.

It was a shift along the foreboding San Andreas that triggered San Francisco's traumatic 1906 earthquake. Geologists say it is only a matter of time before the same fault causes another devastating quake somewhere along California's west coast.

As mountains do not explain all geologic history, so subduction zones, lavas and fault blocks do not explain all topographies. One can speak confidently of the arid Modoc Plateau's topography in terms of past volcanism, because the Cascades to its west have blocked clouds that might have watered the Modoc and eroded the visible vestiges of its volcanic legacy. Thus, on the Modoc Plateau, there is a neat unity between geologic origins and modern topography.

Tensions that originate in the earth's mantle explain the elemental forms of continents and oceans, basins and ranges, and some local landforms — like those of the Modoc Plateau. But it is wind, water and gravity that usually have the last word in sculpting the actual surfaces that man looks upon.

Subduction explains the origins of California's Coast Range. But it was water from the Sacramento and San Joaquin rivers that eroded the range to open the passage to the sea known as the Golden Gate. And it was water from the rising Pacific Ocean, at the end of the last Ice Age, that drowned that ancient river mouth to create San Francisco Bay and its rich estuary environment. In turn, geologists predict, sediments from California rivers eventually will fill the bay and turn it into a low, foggy marsh that no boats will cross.

Similarly, subduction and fault blocks explain the circumstances of the Central Valley's birth. But it was river-borne sediments from the Sierras and Coast Range that filled the oceanic trough and created the rich farmlands of the valley.

The Klamaths and Sierras shared a common ancestry but they hardly look like brothers. The high Klamath peaks are jagged, those of the Sierras smooth. Origins do not explain the visible differences between the two ranges; glaciers do. The Klamaths are generally lower than the Sierras and glaciers never dominated them, as they did the Sierras. Glaciers gave those peaks a smooth, polished visage.

And all this will change; not in our lifetimes, but rather quickly in geologic terms. The serene California landscape of today is as temporary as the wildflower or the snowfall. Like everything else in nature, the mountains and the valleys pass this way but once.

Bubbling mud at Bumpass Hell in Lassen Volcanic National Park is a constant reminder that the Cascades are not dead.

par Franquelin d'après Choris.

Danse des habitans de Cal...

14

Pl. III

La mission de s. Francisco.

EVOLUTION OF A MYTH

Northern California is the product of a myth — a single, improbable myth of a land of gold.

For ages this region was the tranquil home of a race doomed by the myth. For less than a century it was dominated by a luckless people inspired by the myth. It was built and populated by a ragtag society of men and women who saw the myth spring to life.

In January 1848 a "half crazy or harebrained" man named James Marshall picked up a few bits of shiny material out of a millrace on the American River and started an explosion of greed, energy and longing called the Gold Rush. Marshall had at last found the country of old in the languid foothills of California's Sierra Nevada.

The world was changed by Marshall's discovery. California was created as a result of it. San Francisco was suddenly transformed from a droopy backwater into a bustling, world-famous dream city. Northern California today is streaked with memories of the Gold Rush. Marshall's discovery is the fulcrum of the California experience. But there is a history before it, however flooded it may be by what came later.

Northern California's peculiar destiny was shaped by its land. The same mountains that held the gold have long acted as a barrier — to immigration from the east, to weather from the west.

The Spanish came, fitfully, from the south, but it wasn't until the Transcontinental Railroad was completed in 1869 that the Sierra Nevada was partially tamed. Early immigration was hindered by the desert of the Great Basin, created by those moisture-blocking mountains.

Northern California is a watery place. Thirty-five to 50 feet (11 to 16 meters) of snow fall each year in the Sierra, and the runoff from the snowpack sustains the vast agricultural fields of the Central Valley. Gravity leads the Sierra meltwater down and westward toward the ocean. Along the way, the 250-mile (400-kilometer) Sacramento River collects most of those waters as it courses down the great valley from its source near the 14,000-foot (4,300-meter) volcano, Mount Shasta, close to the Oregon border. But Northern California's Coast Range, lower than the Sierra, though monumental in its own right, is a rampart against the inland water's seaward escape. The Central Valley might be a stupendous lake if it

weren't for a single breach in the Coast Range: San Francisco Bay's sublime Golden Gate.

San Francisco Bay is the keystone to Northern California's history. It was formed by the tilting and sinking of the earth caused by the San Andreas Fault, one of the many deadly rifts that marble the state. Those faults, and the vagaries of drifting continents, created a dip in the Coast Range and a valley behind it. The Sacramento carved its way through that valley canyon for millennia, reaching the sea some miles from what today is the Golden Gate. The Bay as we know it wasn't formed until the end of the last Ice Age (or during a pause in the glacial period: no one is quite sure). About 25,000 years ago the ice caps of the north began melting and the earth's sea level gradually rose. Decade by decade the ocean expanded until it overflowed into the fault and the river-created valley, filling it and making it into a bay.

The first tenants of this rich land were the tribes that through the centuries crossed the land bridge of the Bering Strait and slowly filtered down into the North American continent. Estimates vary as to the number of Indians in Northern California before European settlement. So many died so soon after their isolation was ended that anthropologists have had to rely on patchy mission records and informed guesses. A reasonable calculation is that 230,000 Indians inhabited the region.

The First Californians

Northern California's Indians were victims of their own quietude. The Spanish, and later the Anglos, considered the Native Americans ignorant, shiftless and godless. Late 20th Century man wears cultural blinders like his predecessors, but today the Indians are called wise, environmentally appropriate and suffused with spirit. They were less inclined to war than their relatives to the east. Their wanderings were shorter, the land's valleys being deeper and the mountains higher. Their country was richer than that of the plains and deserts, and their

Customs, talents and preoccupations varied from tribe to tribe — or more accurately from tribelet to tribelet. The Indians had divided themselves into thousands of small groups, many with distinct languages, all jealous guardians of separate identities. In the north, near Mount Shasta, the Konomihus, the Atsugewis and the Modocs melded themselves with the land in a singular way. Further south, around San Francisco Bay, the Miwoks and Ohlones were as different and as similar as the terrain.

When "the people," as most tribes referred to themselves, first arrived at the Bay by the sunset sea, it was still being filled by meltwater from the northern ice caps. The evidence for this lies in the middens left by the Indians. Great feasters, they created

age, nor how remote an event was that happened more than a dozen years ago." They valued changelessness. Nature, after all, changes slowly and a people wedded to nature change slowly, too.

The Bay's Indians moved in small nomadic spurts. From the ancestral shell mound they sometimes trekked up to the oak groves on what are now called the Berkeley Hills. There they ground acorns into "deliciously rich and oily" meal and socialized warily with other tribelets. Then they would pack up for the meadowland and its rich harvest

VII

Lith par Marle

des. par L. Choris

habitants de Californie

huge refuse heaps of shells and bones along the bayshore. The bases of some of these mounds lie below sea level, an indication that they were begun as the waters still rose.

Dissected middens testify to the Indians' fulsome diet. One investigator found, in addition to millions of shells, the remains of more than 18 species of mammals and the bones of countless fish and birds.

Northern California's Indians were little fixed in time or space. Anthropologist A.L. Kroeber wrote that "no one knew his own

Louis Storey renditions of 18th Century California Indians: preceding pages, dancing for Mission Dolores priests; and above, portraits of tribal members.

of deer and elk. At each stop, along each trail, the tribelet would greet and be heartened by ancient friends, landmarks: a venerable oak, a mossy boulder, a lively stream, a soft meadow.

The land around the Bay probably supported more humans than any other California locale. One area not much frequented was what is now the city of San Francisco. A sandy, windy, desolate place, it was an odd contrast to the lushness of the Berkeley Hills, the mild slopes of Mount Tamalpais, or the woods of the southern peninsula. In fact, San Francisco today has more trees and wildlife than at any time in its history. Before the Gold Rush (and for decades after), it was largely shrubs and sand dunes.

17

FRANCISCVS DRAECK NOBILISSIMVS EQVES ANGLIÆ AN° ÆT SVÆ 43

Habes Lector candide fortiß ac inuictiß Ducis Draeck ad viuum imaginem qui toto terrarum orbe, duorum annorum, et mensium decem spatio, Zephyris fauentibus circumducto Angliam sedes proprias 4. Cal: Octobr: anno à partu Virginis 1580 reuisit cum antea portu soluisset jd. Decem: anni 1577.

18

THE ARRIVAL OF THE EUROPEANS

For 1,000 years or so the Indians of Northern California enjoyed a calm and rich life. But in the second half of the 16th Century their fate was settled, first by an imperial reflex, then by a pirate's claim.

In 1542 Juan Rodriguez Cabrillo of Spain had explored the waters to the north of Mexico. He saw little and learned less, but his voyage inspired Spain to claim vast areas of the Pacific Coast, including what was called Alta, or upper, California.

The first European to set foot on this vague Alta California was Sir Francis Drake In 1579 Drake and his crew abroad the *Golden Hind*, exhausted after merrily pillaging Spanish settlements up and down the coast of South and Central America, landed somewhere near San Francisco Bay. Just where Drake made his landfall is the subject of much debate. Some claim the *Golden Hind* sailed through the Golden Gate itself; others insist it anchored further north, at Bodega or Bolinas bay. Most believe — June being a foggy month, and the Golden Gate being narrow — that Drake missed the great bay and landed on the Point Reyes Peninsula, 25 miles (40 km) to the northwest.

Once ashore, Drake unhesitatingly claimed what he called Nova Albion for "Queen Elizabeth and Herr Successors Forever." Drake posted a "Platte of Brasse" ashore to remind posterity, and perhaps the Spanish, who owned this delightful spot. That plate (or a wonderful forgery: no one is sure) now rests at the University of California's Bancroft Library.

The local Indians impressed Drake with their manners and gifts. But he was mystified by their self-flagellation and lamentation. He didn't know that the Indians saw his arrival as a sure sign that their world was ending — which it was, though it was two centuries before the process was complete.

Gold Paving, Soul Saving

England's days of empire were in the future, and Drake's visit had little effect other than to rouse Spain. The Spanish empire, long established as far north as Mexico, was already tottering and thinly spread. But

English explorer Sir Francis Drake, left, was received with great fanfare and crowned by native Indians, right, when his *Golden Hind* landed near San Francisco Bay in 1579.

Spain was never eager to give up its territory, however vaguely defined. Not only were the English in evidence; so, too, were the French and Russians on the lookout for new domains.

The Spanish were driven in their imperial way by two factors: a chronic hankering for gold (preferably lining the streets, as in the deathless legends) and a restless desire to save souls. Though Alta California was plump with gold, the Spanish would never find it. Heathen souls they would find in abundance.

Whatever conquering spirit still emanated from Madrid was enfeebled by the time it reached Mexico. It wasn't until 1769 that the Spanish flag was implanted in Alta California. After a horrible trek from Sonora, Mexico, in which half of the 300 men died, Gaspar de Portolá's Sacred Expedition arrived in San Diego. There, on July 16, Father Junípero Serra founded the first of California's 21 Franciscan missions.

From San Diego, Portolá continued northward toward Monterey Bay, discovered in 1602 by Sebastián Vizcaíno. Vizcaíno had written a glowing report on Monterey — so glowing, in fact, that Portola utterly failed to recognize it. In November, Portola sent a scouting group north under

19

the command of Sgt. José Ortega. The band followed the Pacific Coast along what is now Ocean Beach, made its way up the incline at today's Cliff House, came to the tip of the San Francisco Peninsula and gazed with awe at the magnificent Golden Gate and the vast bay beyond. Portolá's men had discovered a bay that made Monterey's look like a crabbed inlet, but Portolá had been sent to find Monterey. As he later wrote (with what one hopes was sarcasm), "Under all circumstances I shall always give preference to the Port of Monterey in order not to depart a jot from my blind and resigned obedience."

The next year Portola at last found Monterey. It had become something of an obsession and perhaps because of that was always the focus of Spanish and Mexican power in Alta California. Father Serra dedicated his second mission, a Presidio was built, and some eyes at least turned northward to San Francisco Bay.

The Founding of San Francisco

After Sgt. Ortega's discovery, Father Serra, a God-driven man, had announced his intention to found a mission "on the port of our father, San Francisco." He thought the great bay was the same one discovered by Drake, rediscovered, in 1595 by Sebastian Cermeño and named for the founder of the Franciscan order. There was a lush heathenland up there and Serra was ready to till its soil.

But Father Serra and his holy successors had to wait. It wasn't until 1775 that the Spanish finally decided to establish a settlement at San Francisco Bay. On March 28, 1776, after a six-month march from northern Mexico, an advance party of 14 men led by Juan Bautista de Anza planted a cross at today's Fort Point, overlooking the surging Golden Gate. Father Pedro Font wrote in his diary that if the site "could be well settled like Europe there would be nothing more beautiful in the world." On March 29, the expedition planted another cross three miles to the southeast. This would be the site of the sixth California mission, now known as Mission Dolores after a nearby stream. Today Mission Dolores, calmly proud, is San Francisco's only link with its colonial past. For though they had made inroads into an incomparably rich land, the Spanish were nearly finished as a power in what would soon be the American West. Typically, six months passed before the expedition was provisioned and work could begin on the Presidio and mission.

The gates to today's Presidio, now head-

quarters for the United States Sixth Army, boast that it was "Founded in 1776." That is true enough, although it was founded by troops of another country. But the Presidio languished from the beginning. It never played more than a slightly comic role in San Francisco's development.

The mission was of a sturdier aspect, but it too would soon be an irrelevancy. As Frederick Merk put it in his *History of the Western Movement*, the whole "California Mission program ended in failure. Its chief contribution was to leave attractive mission buildings to the future." Dr. Merk overlooked another legacy of the missions: the unwitting destruction of California's Indian population.

The Franciscan *padres* were operating under a number of handicaps in their dealings with the Indians. They suffered almost universally from epidemic, morally debilitating racism. They were unable to discern the slightest worth in the Indian way of life. And in saving souls, they went for quantity, they sent the Presidio's hapless soldiers into the hills and marshes in search of Indians. The *padres* herded the Indians into the missions, baptized them, segregated them by sex, taught them simple tasks, and tended to them with mounting exasperation while they died of foreign diseases and despair.

The concept of imperialism was never much questioned in the 18th and 19th centuries. Some parliaments, it is true, rang with debate about the wisdom of new conquests. Even the British had substantial numbers of "Little Englanders" who saw empire as a dangerous and costly game. But the governments of the day were caught up in a race for expansion, new markets, new souls and that old obsession, gold.

The Russian Threat

The Russians, for instance, were embarking on a colonial quest of their own, expanding into Siberia and Muslim Central Asia. In the early 19th Century they began edging southward from their base in Alaska, where they had massacred and been massacred in return. The immediate spur for the Russians were the pelts of the Pacific Coast's vast sea otter population. But when the Russians founded Fort Ross (named for Rossiya itself) in 1812, they were certainly interested in staking a colonial claim.

Fort Ross (today a state park, the old fort's onion domes and weathered wood buildings wonderfully restored) lies only 60 miles (97 km) north of San Francisco Bay. It was manned by 95 Russians and 84

Aleuts from Alaska. As a simple provisioning station for the Russian-American Company's ships, it posed little threat to Spain's hold on Alta California. But as a vanguard of Russian expansion, it was yet another worrisome indication to Spain that its Alba California would not be easily kept.

The Russians, like most of the other imperial powers, considered Spain senile and reactionary. Even in those days, Spain's treatment of its "charges" was looked down upon. Otto von Kotzebue, captain of the *Rurik*, visited the Bay in 1816. He professed disgust at the conditions he found in the mission: "The uncleanliness of these barracks baffles description and is perhaps the cause of the great mortality, for of 1,000 Indians at San Francisco, 300 die each year."

oppressed Indians were allowed:

Twice in a year they receive permission to return to their homes. This short time is the happiest of their existence, and I myself have seen them going home in crowds with loud rejoicings. The sick, who cannot undertake the journey, at least accompany their happy countrymen to the shore where they embark, and there sit for days, together mournfully gazing on the distant summits of the mountains which surround their homes. They often sit in this posture for several days, without taking any food, so much does the sight of their lost home affect these new Christians. Every time, some of those who have permission run away and they would probably all do it, were they not deterred

Similar stories were being enacted in the other Northern California missions: at Santa Clara (founded in 1777), Santa Cruz (1791), San Jose (1797), San Rafael (1817), and San Francisco Solano (1823).

The Indian culture was simple but delicate. By mixing the tribelets and tribes and forcing new and bizarre customs on them, the Franciscans undermined their very life force. Most poignant of all was their forced removal from the land that had cheerfully nurtured them for so long. Von Kotzebue wrote of the short vacations that these

The Presidio on San Francisco Bay was established by the Spanish in the early 19th Century. It is today an Army headquarters.

by their fear of the soldiers, who catch them and bring them back to the Mission as criminals.

The 10,000-year history of Northern California's Indians was now almost over. Hardy remnants of their culture still exist, but their civilization was crushed by the Spanish, and what was left of it by the Anglos.

In 1824 Mexico severed its flimsy link with Spain and declared itself a republic. Ten years later Governor Figueroa issued the first of the Secularization Acts. In theory, the acts handed the missions and their property over to lay administrators and the Indian neophytes. In practice, secularization drove the Indians out into a world of servitude and poverty.

THE MEXICAN YEARS

Republican it may have been, but fledgling Mexico was of no mind to renounce ownership of Alta California. The question of converts was now academic, but California was obviously a serendipitous land and there was always the nagging suspicion that a golden metropolis was awaiting discovery. Lacking the means to grasp the prize firmly, Mexico opened Alta California to colonization by issuing generous land grants. The promise of free land (the average grant was 23,000 acres, nearly 10,000 hectares) and unburdened freedom lured hundreds of settlers north.

For less than five decades Northern California was reigned over by a proud, newly landed aristocracy. Cattle ranching in the fertile inland valleys was a relatively easy way of life, especially with the help of dispossessed Indians and wandering citizens of nowhere in particular. The weather was mild, the grasses thick. Clear skies smiled on the hills and valleys. From the top of one of those hills a *ranchero* might have looked upon the Pacific Ocean as a perfect symbol of timelessness and permanency.

Those final years of quiet before the avalanche of the Gold Rush inspired wistfulness in latter-day Californians. Novelist Gertrude Atherton, among others, honed that nostalgia with books like *Before the Gringos Came* (1894) and stories like *The Splendid Idle Forties.*

Another admirer of early California was Julia Cooley Altrocchi. In her book *Spectacular Californians*, she celebrated the "joyous beautiful life" of the ranches. Then she identified the reason for their eclipse. That beautiful life "moved like a carousel all around the prosaic American settlement" at Yerba Buena Cove, a dingy mudflat on the northeast tip of the San Francisco Peninsula. In the 1840s, Yerba Buena was little more than a collection of shacks inhabited by a polyglot of traders and assorted birds of passage. Within two decades Yerba Buena, renamed San Francisco, would become a magnet that tugged at adverturesome souls around the world.

The first civilian habitation by the Bay of St. Francis was a "shanty of rough boards"

Left, General Mariano Vallejo, at whose Sonoma estate settlers declared California's independence in 1846. Today a statue, right, recalls the "Bear Flag Rebellion."

built in 1835 by an English whaling captain named William Richardson. Following the custom of the day, Richardson had married into a Mexican family, converted to Catholicism, and became a Mexican citizen.

Richardson had become acquainted with the great bay during his whaling voyages. Whalers frequented the bay for provisions throughout the early 1800s, but it was the hide and tallow trade that would support Don Antonio Richardson and the slowly growing population at Yerba Buena.

Northern California's hide-and-tallow

trade was opened in 1822 by the *Sachem* out of Boston. Hides and tallow — the rendered fat of livestock — were a valuable commodity, and the huge herds of the land grant ranches had a steady supply.

In 1835 a young man who was to have a great influence on Northern California's destiny arrived in the bay aboard a hide-and-tallow ship. Richard Henry Dana was a sickly youth who had left Harvard University to find his health at sea. When Dana sailed into the bay, the Presidio was already deserted and Mission Dolores was without the services of a full-time priest. Richardson's shanty was the only structure at Yerba Buena Cove. But Dana suspected that he was seeing a colossus in its infancy. And in his

23

book *Two Years Before the Mast* he shared his suspicions with his countrymen.

He described the bay's "large and beautifully wooded islands ... the abundance of water, the extreme fertility of its shores, the excellence of its climate, which is as near as being perfect as any in the world ..." The bay's climate may have appeared perfect only to someone from Cambridge, Massachusetts, but Dana's summation was delightfully accurate. "If California ever becomes a prosperous country," he wrote, "this bay will be the center of its prosperity."

'Living and Loving Together'

Hide and tallow alone would never bring that prosperity, but until Marshall's discovery 13 years later, it would be enough to attract a ragged stream of settlers to Yerba Buena. Years later an old timer, writing under the pseudonym "The Old Saw," remembered the village as it was in the mid 1840s. Perhaps 200 people — Yankees, Mexicans, Dutch, Indians and a few Kanakas from the storied Sandwich Isles — "lived and loved together, and their eternal routine of drinking, smoking, and dancing was never interrupted save by an occasional rodeo kicked up by the wild boys of the ranches, the periodical visitations of hide-droggers, or the rare appearance of a man-of-war or whale ship in the harbor."

Mexico made churlish attempts to monopolize the hide-and-tallow trade or to tax it out of existence. But florid edicts from Mexico City had a way of wilting in Northern California's air. In any case, however irksome an Anglo-dominated trading entrepôt on its prize bay, Mexico had other bigger worries.

By the 1840s it was already apparent that the United States had designs on Alta California. In 1839 the Russians, having hunted the sea otter to near-extinction, sold Fort Ross to a Central Valley land grant baron named John Sutter. But the English were nosing about, as usual. In 1843 the New York *Courier*, blithely ignoring Mexican sovereignty, wrote: "This idea that England is desirous to possess itself of the Californias seems almost as great a bugbear with the American people as the designs of Russia on India are to the English."

As the *Courier* made clear, the United States had little doubt that California would soon be part of the Union. As early as 1835 President Andrew Jackson had offered Mexico $500,000 for San Francisco Bay. Seven years later Secretary of State Daniel Web-

ster attempted to obtain it in return for settling damage claims by American citizens against Mexico.

In 1826 Jedediah Smith, legendary frontiersman, became the first non-Indian to cross the daunting barrier of the Sierra Nevada. Smith had entered California from the southern deserts. After spending some months exploring the state-to-be, sweet-talking nervous Mexican officials along the way, he made his historic crossing of the Sierra near the Stanislaus River.

The first party to cross from east to west was led by Joseph Walker in 1833. Walker's party stumbled upon one of the world's jewels, the Yosemite Valley. They were suitably impressed by the Yosemite's stunning precipices; but men of that age were more

stirred by the Central Valley.

In the 1830s and '40s Captain John C. Frémont, Kit Carson and numerous others pioneered new routes across the mountains. The crossing was never easy. The famous Donner Party of 1847 was trapped by early snow near Lake Tahoe and resorted to cannibalism. (John Muir later said they could have enjoyed a pleasant winter had they but known how to live off the land.)

By the mid 1840s, the stream of immigra-

Sam Brannan, left, was the leading civic voice in pre-Gold Rush Yerba Buena, right. By 1850, the town — now known as San Francisco — was the most prosperous on the coast (following pages).

tion had reached troublesome proprotions. Governor Paco Pico complained, "We find ourselves threatened by hordes of Yankee emigrants whose progress we cannot arrest."

The Bear ... Then Union

On May 13, 1846, President James Polk surprised no one by declaring war on Mexico. News of the war had not reached California by mid June when a covey of settlers stormed General Mariano Vallejo's Sonoma estate. Vallejo soothed the men with brandy and watched as they raised their hastily sewn Bear Flag over Sonoma's Plaza. The Bear Flag Revolt is sanctified in California history, but for all its drama, it was immaterial. Within a few weeks Commodore John Sloat

Aboard were 238 Mormons led by a fiesty 26-year-old named Sam Brannan. The Mormons found Yerba Buena wanting in two regards: not only did it lack the "soft airs of the Italian clime" that Frémont and others had promised; it was also devoid of fellow Mormons, other Latter-Day Saints having ended their migration at the Great Salt Lake in Utah. Brannan and his flock quickly made do. In short order Brannan had conjured up the town's first newspaper, the *California Star*; had performed its first American wedding; and was the defendant in Yerba Buena's first lawsuit (he was acquitted of a charge of misuse of church funds).

Brannan was Yerba Buena's preeminent pitchman. Where others saw shacks and mudflats, he saw a handsome metropolis.

arrived to usher California into the Union.

Most of the fighting in the War of American Conquest took place in the south. The war in the north effectively ended on July 9, 1846, when 70 sailors and marines from the ship *Portsmouth* marched ashore in Yerba Buena village and raised the stars-and-stripes in the central plaza. Northern California had thus long settled into American rule by the time the Treaty of Guadalupe Hidalgo was signed in February 1848, ending Mexican rule in Alta California.

Fewer than 300 people lived in Yerba Buena when the American flag was hoisted. Within three weeks the population almost doubled when the *Brooklyn*, six months out of New York, sailed into the muddy cove.

The little hamlet on the huge bay, he wrote "is rapidly improving and bids fair to rival in rapidity of progress the most thriving town or city on the American continent."

On Jan. 30, 1847, the town's military *alcalde* a mayor, Washington A. Bartlett, decreed that Yerba Buena henceforth should be known as San Francisco. Bartlett wisely wanted to link the budding town with its bay. Brannan fumed for three months against "our self-styled, unlimited prerogative *alcalde*" before he datelined the *Star* "San Francisco."

Its name had changed, but the village of San Francisco, remained sluggish, remote and unknown — for about one more year. For soon were loosed the argonaut hordes.

ON STONE BY F. PALMER.

Glackes Point.   Rincon Point.   Happy Valley.   Long Wharf (building

VIEW OF SAN FR

TAKEN FROM TELEGRAPH HILL, APRIL 1850, BY W^M B

Published by N.

D&P Court of the Northern Distr. of N.Y.
Appollo Warehouse   Elastic Warehouse   Sansome St   LITH. & PUB. BY N. CURRIER, 152 NASSAU ST. COR. OF SPRUCE N.Y.   Portsmouth Square

SCO, CALIFORNIA.

, DRAUGHTSMAN OF THE U. S. SURVEYING EXPEDITION.

Barton. San Francisco

Capt Sutter's account of the first discovery of the Gold.

"I was sitting one afternoon," said the Captain, "just after my siesta, engaged, by the bye, in writing a letter to a relation of mine at Lucern, when I was interrupted by Mr Marshal, a gentleman with whom I had frequent business transactions—bursting hurriedly into the room. From the unusual agitation in his manner I imagined that something serious had occured, and, as we involuntarily do in this part of the world, I at once glanced to see if my rifle was in its proper place. You should know that the mere appearance of Mr Marshal at that moment in the Fort, was quite enough to surprise me, as he had but two days before left it on purpose to make some alterations in a mill for sawing pine planks, which he had just run up for me, some miles higher up the Americanos. When he had recovered himself a little, he told me that, however great my surprise might be at his unexpected reappearance, it would be much greater when I heard the intelligence he had come to bring me. 'Intelligence,' he added; 'which if properly profited by, would put both of us in possession of unheard-of wealth—millions and millions of dollars, in fact.' I frankly own, when I heard this that I thought something had touched Marshall's brain, when suddenly all my misgivings were put an end to by his flinging on the table a handful of scales of pure virgin gold. I was fairly thunderstruck and asked him to explain what all this meant, when he went on to say, that according to my instructions, he had thrown the mill wheel out of gear, to let the whole body of the water in the dam find a passage through the tail race, which was previously too narrow to allow the water to run off in sufficient quantity, whereby the wheel was prevented from efficiently performing its work. By this alteration the narrow channel was considerably enlarged, and a mass of sand & gravel carried off by the force of the torrent. Early in the morning after this took place, Mr Marshal was walking along the left Bank of the stream, when he perceived something which he at first took for a piece of opal—a clear transparent stone, very common here—glittering on one of the spots laid bare by the sudden crumbling away of the bank. He paid no attention to this; but while he was giving directions to the workmen, having observed several similar glittering fragments, his curiosity was so far excited, that he stooped down & picked one of them up. 'Do you know,' said Mr Marshal to me, 'I positively debated within myself two or three times whether I should take the trouble to bend my back to pick up one of the pieces and had decided on not doing so when further on, another glittering morsel caught my eye. This one—the largest of the pieces now before you—I condescended to pick it up, and to my astonishment found that it was a thin scale of what appears to be pure gold.' He then gathered some twenty or thirty pieces which on examination convinced him that his suppositions were right. His first impression was, that this gold had been lost or buried there, by some early Indian tribe—perhaps some of those mysterious inhabitants of the west, of whom we have no account, but who dwelt on this continent centuries ago, and built those cities and temples, the ruins of which are scattered about these solitary wilds. On proceeding however, to examine the neighbouring soil, he discovered that it was more or less auriferous. This at once decided him. He mounted his horse, and rode down to me as fast as it could carry him with the news.

At the conclusion of Mr Marshals account, and when I had convinced myself, from the specimens he had brought with him, that it was not exagerated, I felt as much excited as himself. I eagerly inquired if he had shewn the gold to the workpeople at the mill and was glad to hear that he had not spoken to a single person about it. We agreed not to mention the circumstance to any one and arranged to set off early the next day for the mill. On our arrival, just before sundown, we poked the sand about in various places, and before long succeeded in collecting between us more than an ounce of gold, mixed up with a good deal of sand. I stayed at Mr Marshall's that night, and the next day we proceeded some little distance up the south Fork, and found that gold existed along the whole course, not only in the bed of the main stream, where the water had subsided but in every little dried-up creek and ravine. Indeed I think it is more plentiful in these latter places, for I myself, with nothing more than a small knife, picked out from dry gorge, a little way up the mountain, a solid lump of gold which weighed nearly an ounce and a half.

Notwithstanding our precautions not to be observed, as soon we came back to the mill, we noticed by the excitement of the working people that we had been dogged about, and to complet our disappointment, one of the indians who had worked at the gold mine in the neighbourhood of la Paz cried out in showing to us some specimens picked up by himself,— Oro!—Oro—Oro !!!—

'THERE'S GOLD IN THEM THAR HILLS!'

James Marshall's world-shaking discovery took place in the millrace of a sawmill set by the American River in the Sierra Nevada foothills. History usually races by at this point, not stopping to ask just what a sawmill was doing beside an often-raging torrent in the mountains. That sawmill was one of the screwier ideas of John Augustus Sutter — a man, one contemporary wrote, with a disastrous "mania for undertaking too much."

Born in Switzerland in 1803, Sutter arrived in San Francisco in 1839. Despite a disorderly career as a Swiss Army officer and dry-goods merchant, he somehow impressed Alta California's authorities enough that they offered him the largest possible land grant, nearly 50,000 acres (about 20,000 hectares) of the Central Valley. Sutter named his grant "New Helvetia" and, using Indians as serf labor, set out to create a semi-independent barony.

Sutter's Fort, at what is now Sacramento, was often the first stop for bedraggled overlanders after their harrowing Sierra crossing. Sutter gloried in providing majestical comfort and goods (at a price) to California's new settlers. He planted wheat and fruit orchards, bought out the Russians at Fort Ross, lent his aid to several of Northern California's jostling factions, and in 1847 decided to build the sawmill that was his ultimate undoing.

As John Bidwell, an astute early emigrant, wrote: "Rafting sawed lumber down the cañons of the American River (was such a) wild scheme that no other man than Sutter would have been confiding and credulous to believe it possible."

Sutter had hired Marshall to oversee the mill's construction. (Today a recreation of the fabled mill stands at Coloma, 50-odd miles east of Sacramento.) On Jan. 24, 1848, Marshall peered into the millrace and noticed a bit of shiny material, one of the millions of smithereens of gold that had been gaily tumbling down the streams of the Sierra for millennia.

Marshall took the nugget to Sutter. The two "applied every test of their ingenuity and the American Encyclopedia," and de-

cided that it was indeed gold. They raced back up to the sawmill, poked and panned awhile, and looked each other straight and clean in the eye. They had found the country of gold.

Sutter realized that New Helvetia would be overrun if word of the discovery leaked out prematurely. He swore his mill hands to secrecy. But Sutter's Fort was probably the worst place in California to keep a secret, and nuggets kept popping up in bars and stores at the Fort and in the mission towns. John Bidwell wrote that "as a lumber enter-

A GOLD HUNTER ON HIS WAY TO CALIFORNIA, VIA, ST. LOUIS.

prise, the mill was a failure, but as a gold discovery, it was a grand success." Sam Brannan shooed away the last scraps of silence. On May 12 he strolled down Montgomery Street in San Francisco, beaver hat cocked, a vial of gold dust held high, shouting "Gold! Gold! Gold on the American River!"

Gold Fever

The Western world had been waiting for the myth to come to life for centuries. The Spanish had uprooted and discarded more than one civilization looking for the country of gold. The rest of the world had watched and waited and looked for itself. The myth

Left, John Sutter's personal account of the discovery of gold at his sawmill. Right, an Eastern publisher's tongue-in-cheek view of a California-bound fortune seeker.

had grown into a prophecy.

The news spread as rapidly as the times allowed. San Francisco was left nearly deserted, its shops stripped of axes, pans, tents, beans, soda crackers, picks and whatever else might conceivably be of use. Monterey, San Jose, all of Northern California's mission towns and farms joined in the scramble. Gold fever worked its way on happy sufferers in Utah and Oregon, where "two-thirds of the state's able-bodied men were on their way to the diggings."

Ships in the Pacific spread the word to Peru, Chile, Hawaii and Australia. Lt. L. Loeser carried a "small chest ... containing $3,000 worth of gold in lumps and scales" back to Washington, D.C., where it was exhibited at the War Office, irradiating the boy's map. ... The Sacramento River was reported as abounding in alligators. ... The general opinion was that it was a fearfully hot country and full of snakes."

Dodging snakes and alligators was a small price to pay for instant wealth. In the first three years of the Gold Rush more than 200,000 men, a few women, and fewer children came to California in one of the greatest peaceful mass migrations in the history of the world.

The farm boys, sharpies, bored clerks and solid citizens who comprised this horde known as "The '49ers" were plucky and young — more than half were in their 20s. Almost all were male, though as always there were some bemused wives, indomitable cultural missionaries, and more than a

Capital with cheery greed. On Dec. 2, President Polk told Congress that the "extraordinary accounts" were true. A few days later the *New York Herald* summed it up: "The El Dorado of the old Spaniards is discovered at last."

Westward Ho!

In 1848, despite the ruckus of the Mexican-American War, California was still popularly thought of as somewhere tucked away behind the back of the beyond. Young Prentice Mulford of Sag Harbor, New York — who later became one of San Francisco's literary stars — remembered that "California was but a blotch of yellow on the school-

few of those tough ladies who could turn a profit from the company of men. The '49ers needed all their pluck to survive the diggings, and before that the toilsome journey to California and its heady boom town of San Francisco.

About half of the '49ers chose the overland route to the gold country. Many were Eastern and Missouri Valley farmers who already owned the necessary wagons and stock. In April and May of 1849, the jumping-off towns of St. Joseph and Indepen-

Left, "Life at the Mines" from a late 19th Century book. Pick-and-shovel work was hardly a romantic concept; neither was the perilous voyage around Cape Horn, right.

dence, Missouri, and Council Bluffs, Iowa, were choked with eager gold seekers. There they formed into caravans for the long, still-mysterious trek west. There were a number of routes, but most followed the shallow, weaving Platte River across Nebraska, their scouts calling back with news of the famous landmarks ahead — Courthouse Rocks, Chimney Rock, Scotts Bluff, Independence Rock, talismans of fortune to come.

The overlanders crossed the Rockies at South Pass near the forbidding Wind River Range in Wyoming, then dropped down to Salt Lake City. After reprovisioning at the Mormon capital, the worst part of the journey — the crossing of the Great Basin — began. Cholera was widespread. Indian attacks were a constant fear. In some places

waterholes were 30 to 40 miles apart. A broken axle, a sick animal, a lost trail could and often did mean bottomless disaster.

By the time the trains reached the eastern slope of the Sierra, what one chronicler had called "a mighty army" more often looked like a strung-out collection of stragglers. After the bitter dryness of the Humboldt Sink, the climb up the mountains began. Whispers and rumors spread through the wagons: no one had forgotten the fate of the Donner Party. But finally the crest was reached, and beyond it, after five or six months of work and heart and campfire dreams, the long view over the green western slope, down to the foothills and the country of gold itself.

The sea routes to California were simpler,

sometimes shorter, and usually less exhausting. The quickest route was by way of the Isthmus of Panama, long before construction of the Panama Canal. Ships from the Eastern seaboard, crammed with gold seekers, sailed to the Atlantic port of Chagres, a "50-hut cesspool of matted reeds." From Chagres the '49ers made their way by canoe, foot and mule across the mosquito-infested and disease-drenched isthmus. (Their deeply rutted trail had been built centuries earlier by the Spanish, who used it to transport Peruvian gold to the Atlantic and back to Europe.) At the end of the trail lay "another tropical excrescence," the town of Panama. There the argonauts piled up, madly bidding for tickets on San Francisco-bound ships.

The Panama route took six to eight weeks. The voyage around Cape Horn was cheaper but took four to eight months, sometimes much longer. It was alternately boring and dangerous (between 1851 and 1853, 11 ships were lost at the icy cape); the rations were wormy and meager, the captains dictatorial, the quarters impacted with would-be millionaires. But like the overlanders at their campfires, the Cape Horners sugared their voyage with dreams.

Those hundreds of thousands of reveries were fixed on the fabled Mother Lode, which ran for 120 miles (193 km) from north of Sutter's Mill to Mariposa in the south. Forty-niners worked the streams of the Klamath Mountains in the far north early on. Later, the southern deserts had their share of miners and boom towns. But the Mother Lode's wooded hills and deep valleys were the great centers of the raucous, short-lived argonaut civilization.

Aurophiles, argonauts, '49ers, panners, eccentrics, trollops, gamblers, wanderers and adventure-drunk youths tramped the foothills in search of the claim that would make them rich. Gold Rush mining, especially in the early days before the streams were panned out, was a simple affair. The Mother Lode was owned by the federal government, and claims were limited to the ground a man and his fellows could actually work. Stockpiling of claims was thus impossible. Hiring a work force was unlikely, as there was little reason to make another man rich when one's own wealth-spouting claim was so easily got.

The Sierra streams did much of the miner's work for him. The rushing waters eroded the hillsides and sent placer gold (from dust to nugget size) rushing downstream. A miner crouched by the streambank, scooped up a panful of gravel, muttered, sighed, shifted and turned his pan, letting the gold sink to the bottom as debris washed out. Later, sluices — in effect, pans made large — were built, holes were dug, and finally hydraulic mining took over. (It was banned in 1884 after causing dramatic ecological damage to the foothills.) But the '49ers never needed much more than grit, enthusiasm and the youthful notion that luck was on the lookout.

California was rushed into the Union on Sept. 9, 1850. In November 1849, it had already formed a state government and drafted a constitution which guaranteed the right to "enjoying and defending life and liberty, acquiring, possessing and protecting property, and pursuing and obtaining happiness," a typically Californian mix of the sublime and practical.

weaved their way through the Mother Lode, gaping at dance hall epics, peering at nuggets, adding to the legend. The '49ers themselves knew they were part of a phenomenon. Their correspondence bristled with extravagant myth-making.

There was money to be wrung out of those hills. The problem lay in keeping it. In 1849, $10 million of gold was mined in California; the next year, four times that. In 1852, the pinnacle of the Rush, $80 million wound up in someone's pocket.

The men who started the Gold Rush, John Sutter and James Marshall, were only two of the many losers in the great game. Marshall ended his days in 1885 near the site of his discovery, broken-down, weepy, nattering at fate. Sutter, whose barony was overrun

But government and politics were of little interest to the '49ers. They formed what government there was in the hills. Elected "recorders" and impromptu juries settled claim disputes, chastened over-greedy merchants who fattened on the supply-starved miners, and kept a semblance of order in the gambling "hells" and ramshackle brothels.

The Gold Rush was a world marvel. After all, the country of gold was a legend even before it was discovered, and once it was found it sold newspapers and books, rail, ship, coach and barge tickets, and enlivened imaginations in every corner of the globe. Authors like Alexandre Dumas, Mark Twain and Bret Harte spun romantic tales of life in the diggings. Countless reporters

just as he'd feared, kept a brave front for some years. But history had swept him aside, too, and he died in 1880 after years of futile petitions to Congress for restitution.

As easy as it was to find, the Mother Lode's gold was easier to lose — to rapacious traders, in the gambling hells and bawdyhouses, to the simple unwisdom young men are prey to. But for most it was a grand advanture. Many returned home, sheepishly perhaps, but well-stocked with stories for grandchildren to come.

Remnants of the Gold Rush persist in ghost towns like Bodie, east of the Sierras. Left, some of the old mine buildings and equipment; and right, another reminder of the past.

LATE 19TH CENTURY: BOOM AND BUST

The Gold Rush's magic was nowhere more powerful than in San Francisco, immediately and forever after the capital of the country of gold. When Sam Brannan ambled down Montgomery Street with his vial of gold, the town's population was less than 1,000. By early 1850, when the madness was in full swing, upwards of 30,000 souls were in residence.

Bayard Taylor, a doughty reporter for the *New York Tribune*, witnessed the explosion of San Francisco into a "perpetual carnival." When Taylor arrived in September 1849, the town was still "a scattering of tents and canvas houses with a show of frame buildings on one or two streets." After four months in the diggings, he returned to find "an actual metropolis, displaying street after street of well-built edifices … lofty hotels, gaudy with verandahs and balconies were met with [everywhere], finished with home luxury and aristocratic restaurants presented daily their long bills of fare, rich with the choicest technicalities of Parisian cuisine."

For those who could afford it, the cuisine was indeed technical, but for most of the '49ers it was rough, ready and slightly less expensive. Eggs from the Farallone Islands off the Golden Gate sold for $1 apiece. Water from Sausalito across the Bay cost 10 cents a bucket during the dry season. Real-estate speculation was epidemic. As the city burst from the boundaries of Yerba Buena Cove, "water lots" sold for crazy prices on the expectation they could be made habitable with landfill. Much of today's downtown San Francisco is built on landfill.

Commodity speculation was a dangerous game. Whereas ever-crafty Sam Brannan might succeed in cornering the tea market, a fellow like Joshua Abraham Norton might be wrecked trying to corner the rice market. Norton's ruin in 1853 scrambled his senses. After laying low for a few months, he put on a tatty uniform and proclaimed himself Emperor of the United States and Protector of Mexico. Emperor Norton I went on to enjoy a quarter-century reign as San Francisco's leading eccentric, a living reminder of the gleeful lunacy of the Gold Rush.

None of California's new towns, much less

San Francisco, were built with much care or foresight. Pre-Gold Rush street plans, based on tight grids, were expanded out from flat Yerba Buena Cove with a flick of pen on ruler, jauntily ignoring the city's hills — which is why San Francisco's streets barge up and down those hills, rather than gracefully following their contours. Most buildings were hasty wooden edifices, and between 1849 and 1851, six major fires ravaged San Francisco. Sacramento, smaller, marginally quieter, also had its share of blazes.

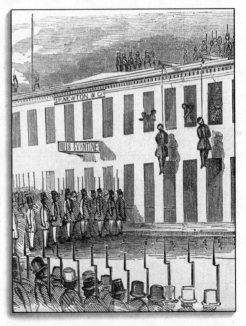

Most of California's new tenants — fixed on their golden dreams — had little desire to pour the foundation for the orderly society that would surely follow the Gold Rush. The popular conception was that the foothills were crammed with gold. "Ages will not exhaust the supply," Bayard Taylor wrote.

In the end, the winners in the great money-scramble were those who took the time to sink roots by establishing businesses and buying land, taking advantage of the '49ers' disdain for tomorrow. So each fire was an opportunity for the arising bourgeoisie to build new, more solid buildings. Each boatload of grinning '49ers represented another batch of customers.

In 1851 the forces of social stability

Vigilantes took the law into their own hands in the 1850s. Left, a vigilante committee membership certificate; and right, a graphic recreation of an 1856 execution.

asserted their constitutional right to "acquire, possess and defend property" by warring against the criminal elements that feasted on California's plentiful lack of tranquility. In San Francisco, hoodlums (a word coined in late 19th Century San Francisco, by the way) had organized themselves into gangs like the Sydney Ducks and the Hounds. At least some of the city's fires were set by these gangs, in addition to their run-of-the-mill robberies, beatings and generally ugly behavior.

Rise of the Vigilantes

The robbery and beating in early 1851 of a merchant named C.J. Jensen inflamed the righteous, especially Sam Brannan — a man

for awhile. But within two years a resurgence of outlawry threatened the state's fragile social order.

In 1853 the Gold Rush began to wind down. Gold production dropped by $30 million. Real-estate values fell 20 to 30 percent. Immigration slowed to a trickle and merchants were cornered by massive oversupplies ordered during the heady days.

But the city's growth had been phenomenal. At decade's end it had a population of 50,000, a level it had taken New York 190 years to reach, Boston 200, Philadelphia 120. California's capital had been in Sacramento since 1854, but San Francisco presided without rival over a rapidly settling, coalescing state. Agriculture in the Central Valley had grown fantastically in response to

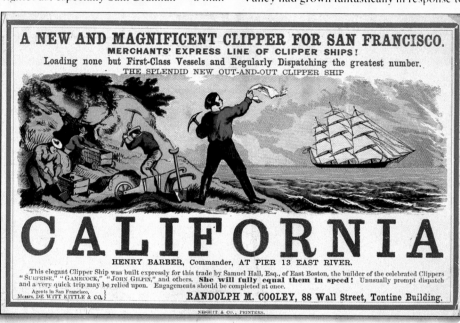

who, according to historian Josiah Royce, was "always in love with shedding the blood of the wicked." Newspapers like the *Alta* brought up the specter of lynch law, and Brannan shouted that the time had come to bypass "the quibbles of the law, the insecurity of the prisons, and the laxity of those who pretend to administer justice". A Committee of Vigilance was formed; soon a Sydney Duck named John Jenkins was hanged for attempting to steal a safe. (He dumped it in the Bay, but the absence of evidence didn't deter the vigilantes.)

Within two weeks Sacramento had its own vigilante corps. Scores of Northern California towns followed suit. California's first bout of vigilantism put a damper on crime

the needs of the state's exploding population. In the decade of the 1850s, for instance, California's cattle herds grew from 262,000 to more than 3 million. Towns like Stockton, San Jose and Monterey were thriving as '49ers set up their shops and sank their roots.

Whatever chance California had of becoming placid, however, was swept away in 1859 by yet another torrent of riches flowing down the Sierra slope. This time it was silver, not gold, that geared up the rush.

Left, 19th Century travel agents encouraged tourists and immigrants alike to travel to San Francisco by sea. Those who arrived in 1865 found Market Street bustling, right.

The Rush for Silver

One of the most comfortless outposts of the Gold Rush had been centered around Nevada's Sun Mountain on the dry eastern slope of the Sierra near Lake Tahoe. There was a little gold up in the Virginia Range, enough for an occasional "$10 Gold Rush" as the crusty denizens ruefully put it. But eking a living out of the area's irritating bluish clay was wicked work. In June 1859 a sample of that "blue stuff" found its way to Melville Atwood, an assayist in Grass Valley. Atwood found an astounding $3,876 worth of silver in that sample of Sun Mountain ore.

At first it appeared that the Silver Rush would mimic the Gold Rush of a decade

for capitalists, men with the money to dig tunnels, buy claims, install the expensive machinery and mills that transformed the blue stuff into cash. They were men like William Ralston of the Bank of California in San Francisco, and the four legendary "Bonanza Kings," James Flood and William O'Brien — former saloon keepers — and James Fair and John W. Mackay — old miners — whose Consolidated Virginia regularly disgorged $6 million a month.

As usual, the treasures of the Comstock Lode (named for a gristle-brained old timer who, in traditional fashion, ended up broke) flowed downslope from the boomtown of Virginia City to San Francisco. By 1863, $40 million of silver had been wrested out of the trembling tunnels in, around, and through

earlier. "Our towns are near depleted," wrote one spectator. "They look as languid as a consumptive girl. What has become of our sinewy and athletic fellow citizens? They are coursing through ravines and over mountaintops," looking for silver.

One of the athletic young men who rushed up to the Virginia Range was Mark Twain. In his marvelous book *Roughing It*, he describes how he and his fellow almost-millionaires "expected to find masses of silver lying all about the ground." The problem for Twain and the thousands like him was that the silver was *in*, not *on*, the steep and rugged mountains. And getting it out was no matter of poking and panning.

The Silver Rush, it turned out, was a game

Sun Mountain. Two thousand mining companies traded shares in San Francisco's Mining Exchange. Fortunes were made and lost in moments as rumors of bonanza or *borasca* (profitless rock) swept into town. At one time, more speculative money was wrapped up in Comstock mining shares than existed in real form on the whole Pacific Coast.

The Comstock lasted until the 1880s. The $400 million the Virginia Range yielded had plumped up California's economy. In San Francisco, Billy Ralston, the Comstock's greatest mine owner, had taken over from Sam Brannan as the city's top booster. (Sam by this time was going broke trying to make his resort at Calistoga into "The Saratoga of the West." He died, dollarless, in 1889.)

Ralston poured his Comstock money into a myriad of grand schemes: he built the Palace, America's largest city hotel; he bought sugar refineries, lumber, stage and water companies; and as the 1860s drew to a close, he happily prepared for what he and his fellow plutocrats thought would be the capstone to the state's greatness — the long-awaited completion of the Transcontinental Railroad.

Advent of the Railroad

Plans for a railroad linking the coasts had been floating around for many years. When the Civil War broke out Congress, intent upon securing California's place in the Union, at last stirred itself. In the winter of 1862, the Pacific Railroad Act granted vast tracts of Western land, low-interest financing and outright subsidies to two companies — the Central Pacific, building from Sacramento, and the Union Pacific, building from Omaha. As it happened, the Civil War largely by passed California, but it nonetheless prompted the building of a railroad that brought unexpected havoc to the state.

The genius of the Central Pacific was a young engineer named Theodore Dehone Judah. Judah had built California's first railroad, the 22-mile Sacramento Valley line, in 1856. He spent years crafting the crucial route across the Sierra at Donner Pass. Unfortunately for Judah, the Central Pacific's other partners were uncommonly cunning and grabby men.

Charles Crocker, Mark Hopkins, Collis Huntington and Leland Stanford, who became known as "The Big Four," were Sacramento shopkeepers when they invested in Judah's scheme. Shortly after Congress dumped its largesse in their laps, they forced Judah out of the Central Pacific. He died, age 37, in 1863, still trying to wrest control from his former partners.

The Central Pacific made the Big Four almost insanely rich. The ex-dry goods merchants moved to San Francisco's Nob Hill and began a merry mansion-building jamboree. The government's haste to get the railroad built, and Stanford's political maneuvering, made the Central Pacific the virtual dictator of California politics for years. When Frank Norris wrote *The Octopus* in 1901, no one had to guess at the reference: the Southern Pacific (as it was renamed in 1884) had its tentacles in every corner of the state.

In the beginning, at least, carping at the Big Four's use of the railroad's treasury as a kind of private money preserve was a game

for malcontents and socialists. In the mahogany boardrooms of San Francisco's banks, on the editorial pages of its newspapers, in the overheated stock exchange, up and down Montgomery Street, the verdict was the same. The railroad would bring firm and fabulous prosperity to California.

The Golden Spike

In April 1868, five years after construction had begun on Sacramento's Front Street, the first Central Pacific train breached the Sierra at Donner Pass. (With typical cheek, the Big Four had convinced the government that the Sierra slope began a few miles outside of Sacramento, thereby netting millions in hardship allowances). Once the historic ram-

part was crossed it was downhill work. Thirteen months later, on May 12, 1869, the Golden Spike was driven at Promontory Point, Utah, and the coasts were linked.

"San Francisco Annexes the Union" read one San Francisco headline. The city and state were seized with glee. But the onrush of prosperity failed utterly to materialize. Only a few deep thinkers — none of them ensconced in board rooms — had understood the financial calamity the railroad

The domination of the railroad by "The Big Four," left, was a target of protest for the press; while they became very rich, Chinese laborers toiled for sparse wages, right.

would bring.

One of the deepest thinkers of all was Henry George, a journeyman printer and passionate theorist. In 1868 George, whose idea of the Single Tax is still important in socialist thinking, outlined the catastrophe to come. In an article in the *Overland Monthly*, he predicted that California's immature factories would be undersold by the Eastern manufacturing colossus. He predicted that the Central Pacific's ownership of vast parcels of land along its right-of-way would drive prices of much-needed agricultural land shamefully high. George even saw the racial tensions that would result from the railroad's importation of thousands of Chinese laborers. "Crocker's Pets," as they were called, flooded the state's job

California in San Francisco, he had presided over the endless boom mentality that was a legacy of the Gold Rush. He was, a friend said, a man "with a passionate, almost pathetic love of California." In the mid '70s the full bloom of depression was on the state. On "Black Friday," April 26, 1875, a run on the Bank of California forced it to slam shut its huge oaken doors at Sansome and California streets. Driven into debt by Comstock mining losses and by the failure of the railroad to bring prosperity, Billy Ralston drowned the next day while taking his customary swim in the Bay.

Ralston's death symbolized the end of California's booming affluence. Those hurt most by the great shrinkage of capital in the 1870s were the state's working men. During

market in the 1870s and became targets for bitter discontent.

George's prophecies began arriving with the first train. In San Francisco, real-estate dealings of $3.5 million a month fell to $1.5 million a month within a year. In the winter of 1869-70 a severe drought crippled the state's agriculture. Between 1873 and 1875 more than a quarter of a million immigrants came to California. Many were factory workers and few could find work. The "Terrible Seventies" had arrived.

'The Terrible Seventies'

For William Chapman Ralston the 1870s were a calamity. As head of the Bank of

the Gold and Silver rushes California's laborers had enjoyed a rare freedom to move easily from job to job and to dictate working conditions. Now, however, with massive unemployment, unionization began to take hold. For the next 60 years California would suffer recurrent bouts with labor strife.

The depression was slow to disappear, but California was too rich to suffer permanently. In the next few decades it slowly built its industrial strength up to the point where it could compete with the East. After decades of depending on the land to deliver riches in the form of gold or silver, the state developed its agricultural lands as never before. In the Central Valley, wheat, rice and cotton became major cash crops. The splendid Napa Valley began to produce fine wines in earnest in the late 1870s.

From 1860 to 1880, despite the depression, Northern California's population expanded at its greatest rate until the mid-1900s. The six Bay Area counties (San Francisco, Marin, San Mateo, Contra Costa, Alameda and Santa Clara) grew from 84,000 to 350,000. Though San Francisco accounted for most of that growth, its neighboring cities of Oakland (the terminus of the Transcontinental Railroad), Berkeley and San José were growing apace. The Central Valley's population doubled in those years, as did Napa and Sonoma counties'. The rise of agriculture was responsible for the creation of new inland towns like Redding (an arti-

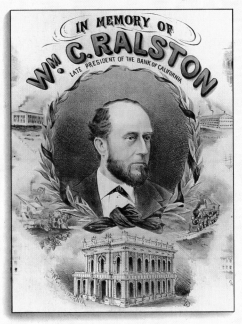

fact of the Big Four) and Modesto (originally to be named for Billy Ralston; when he declined the honor it was named for his modesty).

San Francisco's boomtown mentality may have taken a beating, but as the century wore on, its historic prediliction for high living remained. Rudyard Kipling, visiting during the Gilded Age at the end of the century, called it " a mad city, inhabited for the most part by perfectly insane people whose women are of a remarkable beauty." San Francisco's society had "a captivating rush and whirl. Recklessness is in the air."

As the rough frontier democracy of the Gold Rush was replaced by order and stratification, the middle classes sought recreation

at places like Woodward's Gardens, a kind of pre-Disneyland near the Mission, and Sutro's heated baths at Ocean Beach. Weekend trippers ferried across the Bay to picnic in the Berkeley Hills or on the bountiful slopes of Marin's Mount Tamalpais.

Increasing population and the emerging middle class gave rise to the mass building of Northern California's trademark Victorian houses. Beautiful redwood Victorians rose all over the North, but the decades-long building boom nearly transformed San Francisco, where subdivisions spread out over the city's 45 square miles (116 square km).

The city's steady expansion from its historic center at Yerba Buena Cove dictated new ways to transport people and materials up and down its daunting hills. In 1873 a Scotsman named Andrew Hallidie unveiled the first of his ingenious cable cars. In the years that followed cable cars opened the city's hills to development. Men like Crocker, Fair and Stanford installed their own cable up Nob Hill and used it to transport the grand pianos, Greek statuary and teakwood for their immoderate mansions.

The country of gold always attracted eager wordsmiths to its shores. In the latter half of the 19th Century its literary tradition flowered in magazines like Bret Harte's *Overland Monthly* and less elegantly, but no less rambunctiously, in scores of newspapers like the De Young brothers' *Chronicle* or William Randolph Hearst's *Examiner* (the flagship of the Hearst chain and the laboratory for his seamy, successful variety of yellow journalism).

One of the surest ways to launch a circulation war in those days was with a fresh expose of the political corruption rampant in San Francisco. Northern California's politics were firmly in the tentacles of the Southern Pacific. But San Francisco enjoyed a limited autonomy. Political bosses like "Blind Chris" Buckley kept close to the railroad's platform in state matters and thus were free to run San Francisco much as they pleased. Kickbacks and protection money from the thrillingly odious Barbary Coast and the cribs and opium dens of Chinatown fattened the Buckley gang's coffers and bought off the authorities.

The Gilded Age, with all its extravagance and corruption, continued right up to an April morning in 1906, after which nothing was ever the same again.

Low points of "The Terrible Seventies" were the death of financier William Ralston, left, and violent discrimination against Chinese immigrants, right, regarded as job threats.

VOL. 2 — THE SAN FRANCISCO — № 71

ILLUSTRATED WASP

PUBLISHED EVERY SATURDAY.

PRICE 10 Cts.

OFFICE: 602 CALIFORNIA ST. N.W. COR. OF KEARNY ST.

San Francisco, December 8th 1877.

RECORDED AT SACRAMENTO CAL. BY THE PUBLISHERS OF THE WASP.

STEAMPRINT BY F. KORBEL & BROS. S.F.

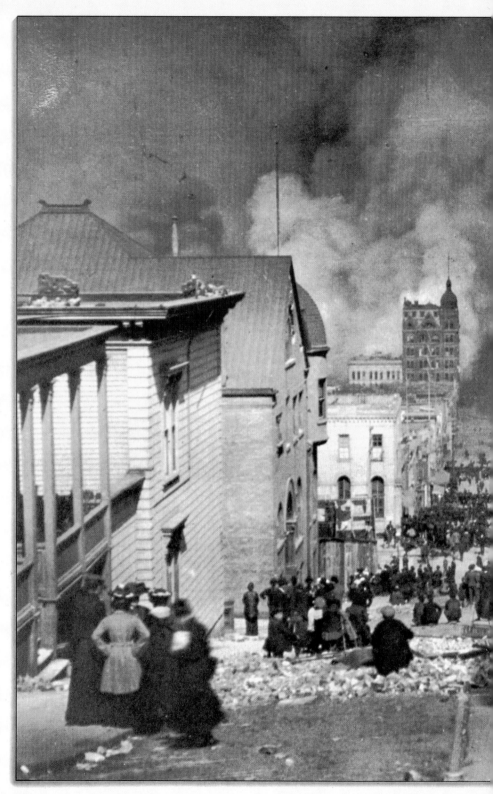

EARTHQUAKE, FIRE, RENAISSANCE

Old San Franciscans talk about "The Fire of 1906," but it was an earthquake that started the fire that first shook Northern Californians from their beds at 5:12 a.m. on April 18, 1906. When the deadly San Andreas Fault lurched that morning it sent terrifying jolts through an area 210 miles (338 km) long and 30 miles (48 km) wide, from San Juan Bautista in the south to Fort Bragg in the north. Other towns like San José and Point Reyes Station near Drake's Bay suffered more from the initial shock than San Francisco. As it was, few lives were

bound feet were carried to safety. The streets were jammed with carts and carriages, and with dazed men and women carrying heirlooms and caged birds, old paintings and squawking children.

For three days and nights the fires raged. Three-quarters of San Francisco's homes, businesses and hotels were destroyed. From Oakland and Marin, from atop the city's hills, San Francisco appeared a single maw of flame. The fire's westward advance seemed inexorable. As it approached broad Van Ness Avenue, Mayor Schmitz, forget-

lost in the quake itself. Elaborate moldings crashed onto the early morning streets, dishes fell, windows shattered, dogs barked, Enrico Caruso (appearing locally in *Carmen*) was scared voiceless, and San Francisco's new City Hall crumbled.

But as the city nervously started assessing the damage, a scourge of fires began in the Financial District. San Francisco was still a wooden city, and the fires quickly melded and began a sickening westward march. By mid-afternoon the Financial District was enveloped in flame. Billy Ralston's proud Palace Hotel was engulfed. Refugees gathered up what seemed important at the moment and trekked up the hills away from the firestorm. In Chinatown, women with

ting the indictments being readied for him, consulted with Gen. Frederick Funston of the Presidio. They decided to halt the fire by dynamiting houses on the west side of Van Ness. The effort was grandly impromptu, and many (especially those whose Victorians were being blasted away) thought the dynamiting encouraged the fire. But a blessed shift in the wind ended the shouted debate, and the fire was driven back on itself.

Preceding pages, terrified San Franciscans watched helplessly as the fire of 1906 engulfed Sacramento Street. The city appeared as a veritable wasteland, left, on the day following the disaster; but that didn't dissuade hungry diners, right.

In the end the destruction of San Francisco's hub was almost total. Buildings on Telegraph Hill were saved when they were draped with wine-soaked burlap. The Old Mint at 5th and Mission streets was rescued by the heroic efforts of the Appraiser-General and his men. But when the fires at last burned out, more than half of the city's 400,000 residents were homeless. Some 28,000 buildings, four-fifths of San Francisco's property, had been destroyed. More than $400 million had gone up in smoke.

The Fire of 1906 was more horrifying than

the state's industries, farms and banks. The Port of San Francisco was still one of the world's busiest. San Francisco's historic business of making business was unstoppable.

A long and spicy series of trials cleared the most noticable crooks out of government. In 1911 San Francisco elected a new mayor, James "Sunny Jim" Rolph, a shiny purveyor of good will and government with a wink, an ideal compliment to flush times.

Sunny Jim's reign encompassed some of San Francisco's giddiest times. There was for instance, the Panama Pacific International

any before it, but San Francisco gathered up its Gold Rush spirit and immediately set to work rebuilding itself. For many months the city's parks were taken over by tent cities. In the unaffected areas all cooking was done in the streets while gas mains were carefully checked. Construction began, photographer Arnold Genthe wrote, "while the ruins were still smoking. On top of a heap of collapsed walls, a sign would announce: 'On this site will be erected a six-story office building to be ready for occupancy in the fall.'"

San Francisco's renaissance was indeed plucky. It was also inevitable. The new, improved, taller buildings of Montgomery Street, the Wall Street of the West, were needed to process the money churned out by

Exposition, cranked up in 1915 to celebrate the city's rebirth. Still considered one of the greatest of world's fairs, the Panama Pacific was built on 600 acres (244 hectares) of reclaimed land in what is now the Marina. The magnificient Tower of Jewels loomed over the fairgrounds while the Palaces of Agriculture, Industry and Education enlightened and thrilled millions of visitors. Today only one vestige of the flamboyant celebration remains. The Palace of Fine Arts, intended by its architect, Bernard Maybeck, to impart a certain "sadness modified by the feeling that beauty has a soothing influence," was saved from gradual decay by civic benefactors in the 1960s.

During the Roaring Twenties, the state

fully entered its incarnation as a tourist mecca. Towns like Monterey and Carmel polished their charms. The mountains of the northern state, especially at Lake Tahoe and the Yosemite Valley, drew easterners and Californians alike.

As a state created by a myth, California knew how to enjoy its dances with fortune. In San Francisco, Sunny Jim Rolph presided over a delicate mixture of discreet lawlessness, mild corruption and high times. But Rolph, like just about everyone else in America, was floored by the shocking Crash of '29.

As historian T.H. Watkins has written, "The disaster cut through the underpinnings of California's economy like a scythe." Montgomery Street's great institutions trem-

Bridge was completed three years later at a cost of $80 million, "the greatest expenditure of funds ever used for the construction of a single structure in the history of man," according to one historian. In May 1937 the last rivet was driven in the wondrous Golden Gate Bridge and 250,000 people walked to and from San Francisco and Marin County. The Golden Gate was more than an aesthetic and engineering triumph. It and the Bay Bridge would be important intermediaries in Northern California's growth after World War II.

In 1939 San Francisco was host for its second world's fair. The Golden Gate International Exposition was organized in celebration of the bridges and California's links with the Pacific. Built on "Treasure

bled; some fell, all grasped to stay alive. Agricultural revenue in the state dropped from $750 million in 1929 to $327 million in 1930. The old game of land speculation came to a sickening halt. By 1934 nearly 20 percent of the population was on welfare.

Despite the Depression, Northern California in the 1930s embarked on some of its grandest building projects. In 1934 the long-debated Hetch-Hetchy water project, which brings water and hydroelectric power from the Sierra to the Bay Area, was completed — at the cost of flooding the gorgeous Hetch-Hetchy Valley, once compared with the Yosemite.

In 1933 construction began on San Francisco Bay's two great bridges. The Bay

Island," 400 acres (162 hectares) of reclaimed land adjacent to Yerba Buema Island, midway between San Francisco and Oakland, it featured a gaudy melange of exhibits, arcades and entertainments like Sally Rand's "Nude Ranch." It was all gloriously brash, but Treasure Island was stalked by war. When it closed in September 1940, Europe was already embroiled in battle and the Japanese attack on Pearl Harbor was little more than a year away.

Left, the Panama Pacific Exposition in 1915 helped revive city spirits. Right, the Bay Bridge linking San Francisco and Oakland was a wonder of engineering in the 1930s.

© ASSOCIATED OIL COMPANY

47

World War II plunged Northern California into a spasm of activity. Twenty-three million tons of war supplies and 1½ million men and women passed through the Golden Gate during the war's 46 months. As historian Oscar Lewis wrote, the war "had as great an impact on [San Francisco's] economy as any event since the Gold Rush."

The ports of San Francisco, Sausalito, Oakland, Vallejo and Alameda were busy 24 hours a day, building and repairing ships, loading supplies for the war machine. The federal government spent $3 billion on shipbuilding in the Bay Area. A dramatic new wave of immigration swept into the region as new factories needed new workers — 100,000 at the Kaiser Yards in Richmond, 90,000 at Sausalito alone. Between 1941 and 1943 the number of wage earners in San Francisco almost tripled, an increase mirrored around the Bay.

In some ways the great influx of workers into Northern California is the war's lasting legacy. The six Bay Area counties nearly doubled their population from 1,462,000 in 1940 to 2,783,000 in 1960. The explosion was felt all over the state, most spectacularly in the south. In the Central Valley, Sacramento County's population increased from 170,000 to 502,000 in 20 years, with Fresno County showing a similar increase.

Following the war, the great suburban sprawl began in earnest as war workers and their families settled down to enjoy post-war prosperity. It was in large part the children of those families who were to play such a significant role in Northern California's (and the nation's) disordered 1960s and 1970s.

There is something of the over-indulged child about California. In the south, the warm air cools anxiety and drives it deeper into the psyche. In the north, the Gold Rush legacy of hit-or-miss experimentation, of untrammeled freedom, created a luxuriant field for every kind of new idea, nutty scheme and political upheaval.

As a new, almost instant society, California has always felt free to tinker with its fundament. Many of its newcomers, from the "Anglo hordes" of the 1840s to Sam Brannan's Latter-Day Saints to present-day arrivals, have come to the state to escape some kind of irritating conformity elsewhere. The great majority of Californians have always been settled, straight, and to one degree or another God-fearing. But the anti-conformists — the colorful, sometimes crazy minority — have given California its reputation for verve and drive.

The Beatniks

It was in San Francisco that the first stirrings of post-war protest and florid eccentricity were felt. While the American nation was settled into a prosperous torpor, the city's historically Italian North Beach area became the haunt of a loosely defined group of poets, writers, declaimers and pavement philosophers who became known as the beatniks (a word coined by San Francisco's great newspaper columnist Herb Caen).

By today's standards the beatniks were rather bland. But in the 1950s they seemed titillating and somehow significant, a tempting combination for the nation's press. Latter-day Bayard Taylors ogled at their rambling poetry readings, sniffed at the light marijuana breezes drifting out of the North Beach coffee houses, and wondered if civilization could stand such a limpid assault.

As San Francisco novelist Herbert Gold has proudly written: "The beatnik begat the hippie and the hippie begat a life style that touches us in ways that extend from fashion and drugs and sexuality to politics and race and a sense of what America might be." The beatniks, it seems, mostly wanted America to go away. But it wouldn't, and before long "beat" had become a fashion and North Beach a tourist attraction.

The beats, though, had struck a nerve of dissatisfaction and alienation in America. Though it was never a coherent movement, it produced juice-stirring works like Allen Ginsberg's *Howl* and Jack Kerouac's *The Dharma Bums*. That inspired alienation gave rise to two parallel, dissimilar, but oddly congruent movements: the angry politics of the New Left and the woozy love fest of the hippies.

The first great protest of the protest-rich Sixties took place in San Francisco in the decade's first year. In mid-May, the House Un-American Activities Committee opened a series of hearings in City Hall. When hundreds of demonstrators met the Committee in the Rotunda, the police reacted

Pro-drug, anti-military protests are a reflection of the New Left and hippie movements which wielded great influence in the Sixties.

furiously, turning water hoses and billy clubs on the crowd. Dozens of battered protesters were carted off to jail, but the angry shouts in City Hall that day were heard around the world. Abbie Hoffman, who shouted aplenty in coming years, announced: "A generation has cast its spirit into the crucible of resistance."

The locus of dissent was the University of California at Berkeley. There the Free Speech Movement kept up a steady assault against racism, materialism and the stifling "multiversity" itself. As the war in Vietnam grew in horror, the New Left spread across America and the world, tilting at governments, bombing, marching, indeed changing the way America looked at itself.

The hippies attacked their target with raggedy, long-haired young men and women. The movement reached its apogee in the massive Be-In that year and the celebrated Summer of Love the next. It was at the Be-In that Ginsberg first attempted to alter earthly consciousness by the mass chanting of the puissant mantra *om*. Golden Gate Park was given over, one "flower child" remembered, to "a lot of stoned people wandering around blowing their minds on how many others were there. It was like awakening to find you'd been reborn and this was your new family."

At first San Francisco was amused by the hippies. But as altogether too many sons and daughters of respected citizens took to stoned meanderings, as the LSD hysteria took flight, cross-generational solicitude be-

gentler weapons. While the New Left ranted at the evils of an affluent, smug, hypocritical society, the hippies tried to undermine that society with glimmering love and peace. In the mid-1960s, San Francisco became the center of the Hippie Revolution. The city was a natural refuge for the spacey idealists. It had, after all, been created by youthful myth-chasers. Many former beatniks like Ginsberg, Neal Cassady and Ken Kesey slid easily into the hippie style. The Haight-Ashbury neighbourhood, which became the hippie encampment, was well-supplied with funky, cheap Victorians, and nearby Golden Gate Park was handy for roaming and wondering.

By 1967 the Haight was thronged with

came scarce. Then, too, the hippies suffered as had the beatniks from their own outlandishness. Hippie became a world fashion. Busloads of tittering tourists drove through the Haight. Some of the self-consciously guileless men and women fell prey to the likes of Charles Manson, who recruited much of his awful "family" in the Haight. Others cracked their brains with drugs, while psychedelic impresarios like Timothy Leary looked on, smiling.

Gay rights marches, left, symbolized the emergence of the homosexual population in the Seventies. Moscone Center, right, is a memorial to the mayor assassinated in 1978.

Legacy of the '60s

But the hippie movement and the New Left have, as Herbert Gold wrote, left lasting marks on America. In Northern California the two streams of thought still exert a strong influence on the region's life today.

Sometimes they intertwine, as in the ecology movement, where a concern for beauty and joy in creation is helped along by no-nonsense politics. The Bay Conservation and Development Commission of 1965 and the California Coastal Commission of 1972 are two examples of idealism with a hard nose. Northern California is in many ways the center of the ecology movement, home for such groups as the Sierra Club, Friends of the Earth, and the whale-savers of the

Greenpeace Foundation.

Activism extends to the man-made ecology, as San Franciscans fight a long battle against "Manhattanization" by grim skyscraper. Towns like Petaluma have passed no-growth ordinances, and throughout the region a narrowed eye is cast on the old shibboleth of progress.

Sometimes the legacy of political activism creates bizarre mutations, like the Symbionese Liberation Army, which kidnapped and brutalized William Randolph Hearst's granddaughter Patricia in 1974. Northern California has been wracked with political upheavals like the 1978 assasination of San Francisco's mayor and first homosexual supervisor by a disgruntled ex-supervisor.

But the activism that causes tensions has a logic and life of its own. Confronted with America's full range of urban and rural problems, Northern California struggles in its own inimitable way. The banners of gay, Black and Asian rights continue to be waved high and proudly. Historic wrongs, like the forced imprisonment during World War II of more than 100,000 Japanese, three-quarters of them American citizens, are not forgotten: redress is sought.

Political tumult is hardly peculiar to Northern California (however often it seems to have originated here). The region's reputation rests more exactly on its innovative approaches to late 20th Century life.

In Pursuit of the Future

A national newsman from New York recently said: "Think what you like about California, but the wave of the future is moving west." Many think, in fact, that the wave has already arrived in Santa Clara's Silicon Valley, the nation's spawning ground of high technology. While the center of California's political power has moved south, Northern California maintains its place of pride as the historic nest of inventiveness and a financial giant in its own right.

Northern California was the product of the myth of a country of gold. As its robust history shows, that myth came to life. The state's first constitution promised the right not only to acquire, possess and protect property, but to pursue and obtain happiness. For the rest of America the pursuit was enough but California, even in 1849, wouldn't settle for less than obtaining it.

Northern California of the 1980s exhibits mysterious and multifarious ways of obtaining happiness: in the wide-ranging interest in Eastern philosophy; in the fascination with health and exercise; in the consciousness expanding, raising and exploding movements; in the delight in food (San Francisco has enough restaurants to seat every resident of the city at the same moment); in the historically apt rush after dollars. There are literally hundreds of ways in which Northern Californians feel free to explore and create their lives.

And there is no better stage in the world to act out this continuing, sometimes troubling, but usually happy drama. The country of gold delights the senses. The deep-dyed charm of its small towns, the liveliness of its cities, its mountains, forests and soaring sea cliffs, have always been fuel for happiness seekers.

CALIFORNIANS

It is fashionable just now to make a distinction between tourists and travelers. Tourists are the people who go from hotel to souvenir stand to overpriced restaurant and never really understand the place they're visiting at all – they want their experiences sanitized, second-hand, pre-tested. A traveler likes to understand the place he's visiting directly; he wants to go where the tourists don't go. He likes surprise; he relishes a soupcon of danger.

Here's one thing a traveler understands: a place, any place, is more than vista points, monuments and museums. It is people. A traveler knows that all the best experiences on the road come from other human beings, the natives and the long-time residents, and from the culture they collectively define.

For that sort of traveler, Northern California is as rich and varied as any place on earth.

There are ranchers in Modoc County, for instance, who believe that they are living the last bastion of Old West, the final home on the last real range. And there are gay men in San Francisco, scarcely 400 miles (650 kilometers) away, who believe they are living within the cutting edge of an entirely New Society, the final frontier of tolerance and experimentation.

There are aging hippies on the Mendocino coast who think that Northern California is final enclave of the Sixties, and farm workers near Salinas who believe that Northern California is still mired in the dark days of the 19th Century. There are many who think that San Francisco is the most sophisticated and cosmopolitan city in the United States, and others who think that it's a precious, narcissistic throwback, as irrelevant to the realities of 20th Century life as the horseshoe or the Home Guard.

Of course, they're all right. Northern California is a large elephant, subject to as many interpretations as there are blind men to grope and define.

History created this diversity. Northern California was settled all at once, a child of greed and restlessness. The Irish came early to San Francisco, along with the Jews, the Italians, the Chinese and any other ethnic

group that was having a hard time making it on other coasts and other continents. Blacks, Hispanics, Japanese, Filipinos, Vietnamese – each followed in their turn. San Francisco was an international city before it was 100 years old.

With its roots in the Gold Rush, Northern California was also settled late. Some of the people on the streets today had grandparents who were children when San Francisco was a muddy little village of fewer than 10,000 souls. The history and the flavor of the earliest days of this region can still be

relished today, in the conversation and recollections of its people.

In the following pages, this book relates the stories of three leading cultural minorities – Blacks, Asians and Hispanics – told by members of those groups themselves.

Blacks: A Heroic History

Clues and reminders found all over California monumentalize the 500 years that Blacks have lived on this lush land.

Every workday, thousands of San Franciscans clad in business suits and carrying briefcases pass by one of those reminders. Leidesdorff Street, two blocks long, in the shadow of that symbol of the city's prosper-

Preceding pages, the Oakland Women's Rowing Club on Lake Merritt. Left, a multi ethnic college band plays at a football game in Berkeley. Right, father and adopted son.

ity, the TransAmerica Pyramid, bears the name of a Black man — a man who built the city's first hotel and had enough civic pride to work toward opening its first public school.

Another reminder is in a pastoral setting. In Napa's Tucolay Cemetery is the grave of a true San Francisco personality, a fiery, strong-willed Black woman named Mammy Pleasant. She detested slavery and discrimination and was became known as the mother of civil rights in California.

Still another clue is in the extreme southwestern corner of Tulare County on the edge of Southern California. Signs along State Highway 43 show the way to Col. Allensworth State Historic Park, where one former slave's dream of a haven for other Blacks fleeing poverty and discrimination temporarily became a reality.

In every period of California history, since the arrival of the first Europeans, there have been Black faces in the passing panorama. Blacks have cashed in on the state's wealth as farmers, gold miners and shipping magnates. They have fed its industries with their labor as shipbuilders, fishermen, cowboys and machinists.

The Golden State has not always welcomed Blacks nor has it been a refuge from racial hostility, prejudice or even slavery. But it has always been an arena in which Blacks have attained levels of power and influence. The go-for-it-all spirit of the Blacks who came to this then-uncharted land with the Spanish conquistadors is a legacy that is still evident.

Nowhere is this spirit more discernible than in politics. California Blacks, comprising 1.8 million (7.6 percent) of the state's population, flex more political muscle than perhaps any other racial minority in any of the other 49 states. For the first time since the Reconstruction era that followed the Civil War, a Black man, Los Angeles Mayor Tom Bradley, came within a few thousand votes of being elected governor in 1982. Had he won, Bradley would have joined San Francisco's Willie Brown, a brash and flashy-dressing politician, in the highest rung of state political power. Brown is the nation's only Black speaker of a state assembly or house of representatives. Bradley today remains one of 30 Black mayors from Berkeley to Long Beach.

Oakland, across the Bay Bridge from San Francisco, is perhaps the best example of Black political, economic and cultural success. There the mayor, five of nine members of the city council, the city manager, museum director, superintendent of schools,

fire chief and publisher of the city's only daily newspaper are Black.

What seems like a proliferation of Black faces doing things previously reserved for Whites is a development of the past 15 years. Its roots, however, are in the beginnings of recorded California history.

The Earliest Settlers

When Spain first colonized California in 1535, there were already Blacks living there. They had relocated with others from Baja California and further south. Blacks were in almost every early Spanish expedition into the American Southwest and South America. They came with Balboa, Pizarro, Coronado and Cortez.

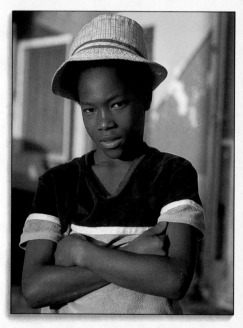

During the Spanish colonial era, several of the largest settlements had significant Black populations. San Jose, the first civic pueblo, was 24 percent Black and mixed-race in 1790. Monterey, the Spanish capital, was 18.5 percent Black and San Francisco 15 percent. When Los Angeles was founded in 1781, a majority of its original settlers — 26 of 42 — were Black.

At the time of Mexican independence in 1821, about one-fifth of California's population was Black. Some were slaves; others

Portraits of Black youth: left, a young resident of an inner city district; and right, a sidewalk chewing-gum sales promoter is her own advertisement for whiter teeth.

had been exiled to the colony because of a criminal past. But the majority were free men and women.

During the 27 years of Mexican rule, California became more open to foreigners, particularly those seeking trade. Adventurers began to trickle in from all over. French, British and Russian settlements that had been illegal under the Spanish were given legitimacy under the Mexicans.

The Wizard of Yaws

No newcomer made a more dramatic and conspicuous entrance than William Alexander Leidesdorff, a native of the Virgin Islands. Finally reaching his destination after a long journey from New Orleans. Capt

Leidesdorff cruised his 106-ton schooner *Julia Ann* into San Francisco Bay in 1841. It was the first time a steam-powered vessel had ever chugged through those waters.

Then 31, Leidesdorff was to become one of the city's richest and most dominant citizens in just seven years. A wizard at business, he established a lucrative shipping company. At first, he piloted *Julia Ann*, later rechristened the *Sitka*, from San Francisco to the Hawaiian Islands and back. As business grew, he hired others and bought more ships.

Having freed himself, Leidesdorff had more time at his disposal and so started investing in real estate. He purchased a large warehouse at the foot of California Street

and two parcels that are in the center of what is now the financial district. Leidesdorff Street is the sole hint of his former holdings.

At another parcel at Clay and Kearney streets, Leidesdorff built the city's first hotel, long since leveled. He also purchased a ranch that is now a large part of the mostly White and affluent East Bay city of Lafayette. His other ranch, obtained through a Mexican land grant, was the 35,000-acre "Rios de los Americanos" in the Sacramento Valley. Today, this is the site of Folsom, a Gold Rush town known primarily as the location of a formidable state prison.

Leidesdorff was also a civic leader. He was appointed American vice-consul at Yerba Buena in 1845. Later, he was also a member of San Francisco's first school committee where he worked diligently to open California's first American public school.

At the time of his death from "brain fever" at 38, his estate was worth about $1 million. Capt. Joseph Libby Folsom, a White man, got himself declared administrator of the estate by making a questionable cash deal with Leidesdorff's mother in the Virgin Islands. Thus the town of Folsom in the Sacramento Valley bears his name.

Leidesdorff was buried beneath the floor of the old Mission Delores chapel. A crypt plate was set among the tiles. On the day of his funeral, the city's businesses were closed and flags were flown at half-mast.

'Mammy' Pleasant

Another leading Black personality in 19th Century San Francisco was Mary "Mammy" Pleasant, born on a Georgia plantation. Pleasant had a number of successful business ventures in the city. A confidante of San Francisco's empowered elite, she was a major conductor on the Underground Railroad which assisted escaped slaves. She personally hid thousands of fugitives and placed many of them as servants in the homes of the city's leading White citizens.

Mammy Pleasant had strong anti-slavery feelings and acted on them openly. It was she who financed John Brown's ill-fated raid at Harpers Ferry, Maryland, a legendary act of armed opposition to slavery. Pleasant gave Brown $40,000; he used most of it to buy 15,000 condemned army rifles.

Mammy Pleasant also used an innovative tactic to battle discrimination, one that was used successfully for generations afterward. In 1865, she sued the San Francisco Omnibus Co. for rude treatment of Black passengers. The company promised courteous service and the suit was dropped.

Although Mammy Pleasant amassed a fortune, she died penniless in 1902. Her lifetime was a period of intense change for many Blacks in the state. Segregation began to become the law of the land under American rule. The state Constitutional Convention in 1849 excluded Blacks from the militia and denied them the right to vote. One of the ideas that was debated and rejected would have excluded Blacks from the state altogether. Laws were later passed that encouraged Blacks to leave. The legislature also prohibited Blacks from testifying in court against Whites or even being witnesses in any case involving Whites. Slavery was prohibited in the state constitution but the provision was often not enforced.

Gold Rush Successes

Even during the gold rush, that mad scramble for a taste of riches, Blacks were not allowed to work or own a claim. About 5,000 came anyway and some became wealthy. Albert Callis, a runaway slave, struck gold and became one of the first residents of Downieville. A Black man known only as "Dick" mined $100,000 worth of gold in an 1850 strike and then hastily lost it all at the notorious San Francisco gaming tables.

Others had more prudent use for the money. The *Grass Valley Telegraph* reported in 1855, for example, that 54 Blacks in Nevada County had that year purchased their freedom for a total of $112,750 in gold.

Other Blacks succeeded in more traditional ways. Mifflin Gibbs came to San Francisco during the Gold Rush and ran a shoeshine stand in front of the old Union Hotel. Later he operated the city's only boot store on Clay Street. A resourceful and politically minded man, Gibbs started the *Mirror of the Times*, the first Afro-American newspaper on the West Coast. In 1897, Gibbs was appointed U.S. Consul to Madagascar by President Rutherford B. Hayes.

William Shorey, a navigator who once sailed around the world on a whaling ship, started his own shipping company and became a leader in the politics and culture of the city.

George Washington Dennis, who opened the city's first coal yard and livery stable, once owned the block bordered by Post, O'Farrell, Hyde and Larkin streets and another block where Mount Zion hospital is now. Dennis constructed a home for his wife and 10 children at 2507 Bush Street.

After statehood, Blacks began to establish a separate society with their own financial institutions, funeral homes, fraternal orders and schools. Jim Crow had arrived in the Golden State.

Near the turn of the century, Allen Allensworth, a former slave who had risen to the rank of Lt. Colonel in the U.S. Army (at that time the highest military rank of any Black man in America), dreamed of a town that would be a refuge for Blacks. He established his haven in 1908 on land he bought in the fertile San Joaquin Valley.

Allensworth, the town, grew to have 35 buildings, including a school, a church, a general store, post office and hotel. The town thrived until the 1930s, long after the colonel's death, when a combination of the Depression, unemployment and a shortage of water led to its downfall.

Just before World War II, California's Black population began to multiply exponentially. The pre-war economy was booming. Plants were turning out airplanes and ships at unheard-of speed. From Louisiana and Texas, Blacks left the dying rural economy to join the assembly lines. They came by Greyhound bus or by train, some with only a few coins in their pockets, a sack lunch and cardboard luggage.

It was a wave of Black immigration that

Football and Christianity are two focal points in the life of the Black man at left, above. Colorful traditions are important to other Blacks, like the man at right.

transformed some areas almost overnight. In Alameda County, for example, where Edgar Kaiser's shipyards were churning out vessels for the war effort, the Black population increased 15-fold between 1940 and 1944.

Many of the newcomers were soldiers or sailors stationed at bases in Oakland, San Francisco, Vallejo and Alameda. Once their military tenure ended, they settled in the Bay Area, some bringing their families with them.

With this explosion Black population came hundreds of social problems, not the least of them lack of acceptance from Whites. There were poor housing facilities, inadequate health care, unemployment, increased crime and more pressure on the educational system.

The new and vibrant residents also brought with them the rich Black cultural heritage. Seventh Street, now a ragged line of sad-faced buildings beneath a rapid-transit station in West Oakland, was the center of West Coast blues. Soul food restaurants, barbecued rib joints and gumbo houses sprang up in predominantly Black communities.

The newcomers from Texas celebrated June Tenth, a Black holiday that goes back to the Emancipation Proclamation. The story goes that some Texas Blacks weren't told slavery was over and continued to labor in bondage until June 10 — hence the celebration, usually a family barbecue.

The Black church also blossomed. Store-front holy rollers, huge and powerful churches for the more sedate middle class, and churches that broadcast over the radio waves were in every big city.

With the 1960s came a new social and political consciousness. In Oakland the Black Panther Party, a self-proclaimed socialist revolutionary group, clashed with the police. The Panthers, with their black leather jackets and rifles, caught the imagination of an idealist segment of young America.

Battles with the police and dissension from within crippled the effect of groups like the Panthers. Soon the Blacks began to turn to the ballot. The result was a new-found power to determine the future political direction of several cities.

As California heads into the next decade it will likely become a state in which Blacks, Asian Americans and Hispanics outnumber Whites. Minorities as individual groups, but a near-majority as an ethnic conglomerate, they may well determine the future directions of the state of California.

The Hispanic Influence

The Hispanic influence in Northern California is everywhere, pervasive and real.

It's in the names of streets and cities — San Francisco, Sacramento, Monterey, San Jose, Alameda and a host of others.

It's in the spicy, flavorful food that is part and parcel of Western Americana — *tortillas, tacos, tamales, enchiladas* and *burritos.*

It's in the blood of a fifth of the population — long-established citizens and recent immigrants with roots in Mexico, El Salvador, Honduras, Peru, Chile, Guatemala and other Latin American countries. About 1½ million Hispanics, roughly one-third of all Latino people in California, live in the northern half of the state.

Hispanics once ruled Northern California from lofty social, economic and political perches. They were the masters of the land for part of the 19th Century, building missions and enslaving the native Indian populations. They were the owners of great *ranchos,* huge land grants from Mexican authorities who considered California little more than an isolated outpost.

They were the judges, the generals and the politicians who attended opulent *fiestas* dressed in silver-buttoned suits and who courted elegant *señoritas* adorned with gold-braided jewelry.

The period of Hispanic prosperity in Northern California was short-lived, however. The annexation of California by the

United States and the discovery of gold in the mountains cast of Saeramento in 1848 attracted ambitious and aggressive Anglo-Americans.

By the turn of the 20th Century, the landed gentry had lost its *ranchos* and with them, its political clout and social standing. The early Mexican-Spanish settlers, known as Californios, slowly became Americanized. Yet they never really blended with the American culture. They were set apart by their dark hair and brown skin, by their family-oriented culture, and by the Spanish language they spoke.

Even today, Hispanics continue to exist as a separate culture in large cities such as San Jose and San Francisco, as well as in certain rural areas. They often live in their own neighborhoods, known as *barrios*. Many are afflicted by severe poverty. Some speak Spanish to friends and relatives and English to the rest of the world. Some speak no English at all.

The Hispanic culture in Northern California is not likely to perish soon. Even as the sons and daughters of farmworkers, gardeners and restaurant workers become lawyers, doctors and accountants, a steady stream of illegal and legal immigrants from poverty-stricken Mexico and politically unstable Central America pours into the state.

Ranchos and Gringos

In early Northern California history, Hispanics were anything but apathetic. After Mexico became independent from Spain and took control of California, the Mexican-Spanish settlers sought secularization of Catholic missions and division of the church's land holdings.

Between 1833 and 1840, their wishes were granted in an ostentatious way. The mission lands were parcelled out, thousands of acres at a time, to political cronies of Mexican government officials. This land-grant spoils system reached its zenith in Northern California, where great *ranchos* spread as far as the eye could see around Monterey, San Jose, Napa, Sonoma, Petaluma and other cities.

The *patrones* (bosses) of these *ranchos* were few in number, but were very powerful. The majority of the Mexicans were semi-skilled or unskilled laborers; they often worked at the *ranchos* herding cattle or running errands.

Even though northern and southern Californios were quarreling among themselves, their Mexican patriotism never disappeared completely. In the Mexican War with the

United States in 1846, some Californios fought under the Mexican flag. The defeat of Mexico and consequent loss of California to the Americans in 1847 signaled an end to the Californios' reign.

Slowly the Yankees — or *gringos*, as they were less politely known — began to assume power. Some tried to promote a smooth transition by naming prominent Californios like Mariano Vallejo of Sonoma to government positions. But in some settlements, like San Jose, the old ruling class never stopped fighting the new authorities.

Legal Discrimination

The Gold Rush brought 100,000 newcomers to California, including 80,000 Yankees,

8,000 Mexicans and 5,000 South Americans. American businessmen attempted to discourage Hispanic and other prospectors by successfully pushing through the state legislature a law taxing foreign miners. Vigilante groups added violence as a means of ridding themselves of foreigners' competition, although citizens' groups in several cities came to the defense of the Hispanics.

While a battle for control of the gold mines went on, so did one for control of the *ranchos*. Acting under a law approved by

Embroidered fashions and hand-crafted jewelry make up the wardrobe of the Hispanic lady at left. Cesar Chavez, right, is the spokesman for migrant farm workers.

Congress in 1851, hundreds of squatters laid claim to Californios' *ranchos* throughout Northern California, despite guarantees in the Mexican War Treaty of Guadalupe Hidalgo that resident Mexicans' property rights would be respected.

The Mexicans were required to prove ownership before a lands commission. But in old California, deals were often sealed with a handshake rather than the stroke of a pen. More often than not, evidence heard by the commission came down to the Mexicans' word against the claims of the Americans, more experienced in U.S. legal practices.

As the Gold Rush wound down, many Hispanics left the Sierra Nevada mines to take up residence in large American cities. This new urban movement, coupled with the

friction over gold rights and *ranchos*, spawned a period of "Hispanophobia," a brand of virulent racism exacerbated as Mexican bandits gained widespread notoriety.

Among the most infamous *banditos* was Tiburcio Vasquez. Although he became something of a Robin Hood-type folk hero to his Mexican countrymen, this was more a commentary on the state of relations between Mexicans and Americans than a tribute to Vasquez. He had a long career as a cattle rustler and stagecoach robber; lawmen captured him in Los Angeles in 1876 and convicted him of a murder near Tres Piños, a small community east of Salinas. A few days before he was hanged, Vasquez told journal-

ists what led him to a life of crime: he was angry that Americans pushed Mexicans aside at *fiestas* and monopolized *senoritas*.

Californios continued to dabble in local politics but lacked clout statewide. Vallejo, the mayor of Sonoma, was the only Northern California Hispanic to participate in the state's constitutional convention of 1849.

But Romualdo Pacheco, an aristocratic San Luis Obispo rancher, succeeded where most failed. After serving as an assemblyman, senator and state treasurer, Pacheco was elected lieutenant governor of California in 1871. When Governor Newton Booth resigned to become a U.S. senator, Pacheco finished out Booth's term, serving 11 months as governor.

Although Pacheco's success gave great pride to the Spanish-speaking population, it can be partly attributed to the fact that Pacheco was different from most Mexican-Americans of his time. Educated in Hawaii, he had forgotten much of his native Spanish tongue by the age of 12. He married an Anglo-American woman and belonged to the Republican Party while most Mexicans were Democrats.

As the Californio influence declined, Hispanics gradually faded out of the limelight. For the most part, they became the menials, the forgotten, an almost invisible culture. They clustered in large-city *barrios* in San Jose, San Francisco and Sacramento, or in shanties on farms. Life was marked by poverty.

"We cut out the ends of tin cans to make collars and plates for the pipes and floor molding where the rats had gnawed holes," Ernesto Galarza, a respected Hispanic author, wrote of his childhood days in Sacramento, circa 1920s. "Stoops and porches that sagged, we propped with bricks and fat stones ... Such repairs which landlords never paid attention to were made *por mientras*, for the time being or temporarily. It would have been a word equally suitable for the house itself or for the *barrio*."

Rise of the UFW

Mexican nationals were brought to the state *por mientras* to work on farms during both world wars. These *braceros*, as the workers were known, were shipped back to Mexico annually as the harvests concluded. Following World War II, the program continued at the urging of farmers who contended there was a shortage of labor. It stayed intact until 1964, when it was ended following a barrage of criticism which charged massive exploitation of the laborers.

The death of the *bracero* program gave life to a series of new attempts to organize farmworkers, Cesar Chavez, a well-taught community organizer in San Jose with boundless energy, finally succeeded. His efforts to upgrade the lives and working conditions of farmworkers, primarily Mexicans, caught the attention of the nation and even the world.

Chavez's organization became known as the United Farm Workers (UFW). After years of hard-fought victories in the southern San Joaquin Valley, the UFW's rallying cries of "*Huelga!*" ("Strike!") and "*Viva la causa!*" ("Long live the cause!") shifted to the lush Salinas Valley. There, the UFW's drive to organize field hands evolved into more than a union-versus-management issue. It became the focal point for a larger social movement, and helped to bring about a heightened cultural awareness among Hispanics throughout California.

El Teatro Campesino was one of many theater groups born on the picket lines. Its founder, Luis Valdez, has won widespread acclaim for productions such as *Zoot Suit*. The UFW used Teatro Campesino's biting, satirical skits to capture the imagination and build cohesiveness among striking workers, while the theater company saw the flat-bed trucks on which they performed as a forum for art and self-expression.

The UFW, although still relatively small, today is the most powerful Hispanic political force in California. It has contributed about $1.2 million to statewide political candidates since 1980. Without exception, they have been Democrats.

As a whole, Hispanics have not fared well politically in Northern California. There are currently no Hispanic state assembly representatives or senators from Northern California. However, Hispanics are now making some inroads on city councils and as county supervisors.

Both Democrats and Republicans are beginning to court Hispanic voters, having recognized that the state's fastest-growing minority could one day be a powerful voting bloc. The battles of the streets and fields are increasingly being fought at the ballot box, where the increasing number of Hispanics may be translated into increasing power.

The Asians of 'Gold Mountain'

Ever since the mid 19th Century, when reports of nuggets that cobbled the streets circulated back to the Orient, California has been known to the people of China and Hong Kong as *Kum Saan* — the "Gold Mountain."

Word spread quickly through Chinese communities, and soon thousands of fortune-seekers from Kwangtung province of southeastern China joined the flood of immigrants looking for Lady Luck in California. The Cantonese people of the time were lashed by political upheaval and natural disasters, and it didn't take much to convince them to pack onto crowded ships for the treacherous journey across the Pacific Ocean in search of a fortune that might buy them peace and prosperity.

The hearty men of Kwangtung were the forebears of 1.2 million Asian Americans who today enrich the California landscape. The state's reputation as *Kum Saan*, the

land of opportunity, is but one reason why Asian newcomers of all races have made it a favorite place to settle. Its temperate climate and geographic location are others.

Today, Asian Americans make up more than 5 percent of California's population of 23 million. The growth in the state's Asian population between 1970 and 1980 has been an astonishing 140 percent. More than a third of the United States' 3½ million-plus Asian Americans live in California, with the San Francisco Bay area accounting for about 400,000.

Colorful festivals are an important aspect of life for the Hispanic community. Left, a stylish celebrant smiles amidst the frenzy. Right, a Mexican Aztec Indian dancer.

In San Francisco itself, more than one in every five residents is an Asian American. In the East Bay, in Alameda County (Oakland), Asian Americans make up 8 percent of the population. They comprise a similar percentage in the two counties immediate south of San Francisco, San Mateo and Santa Clara.

The Migration Cycle

Despite their increased numbers and spreading impact, Asians are hardly newcomers to the American scene. They have contributed to the building of the United States for at least 130 years. And unlike western and northern European migration, which was heavy in the 19th and early 20th

centuries but has now receded to a standstill, Asian migration continues today.

Laws aimed at stopping or discouraging Asian immigration, integration and assimilation are now mostly matters of historical curiosity. Yet they form the core of the Asian American experience. They explain the continuing isolation of portions of the Asian American community, as well as the cyclical nature of migration patterns of Asians.

Traditionally, Asian families have moved to *Kum Saan* for greater economic opportunities. The first generation works hard, but the children stray from old-country ways. The first generation born in the United States struggles to maintain one cultural identity while learning to adapt to another. Later generations experience the schizophrenia of trying to maintain both group harmony and individual freedom.

The recurrent cycle means a repetition of the immigrant experience in the Asian American community — poor English, menial jobs and psychological dislocation. But the fact that Asian immigration began more than 130 years ago, then stopped, then started again, means there is a history, a tradition: a culture that is distinctly Asian American.

Later generations of Asian Americans are proficient in English. Some may be biliterate and/or bilingual. Many live outside of all-Asian neighborhoods and work with Whites, Blacks and other Americans in a countless variety of jobs. They may not maintain much of an interest in the land of their ancestors. They may prefer a vacation in Europe to one in China, Japan or the Philippines. They may eat Asian food only occasionally. Their entertainment dollars generally go to a Hollywood movie, a football game, a ballet, a symphony or theater. Sociologists have a neat phrase for this: the "Americanization" of Asians.

The truth is rather more complex. At the same time that second, third and fourth-generation Asian Americans assert their "American-ness," they wonder about their heritage. They may feel slightly uncomfortable in all-white settings — or in all-Asian ones. But they retain certain cultural values passed on by their elders, particularly the belief in the importance of the family.

The Chinese Experience

Different Asian ethnic groups have had slightly different immigration experiences. The early Chinese were mostly men, merchants at first, then laborers (by the thousands) who mined gold, built the Central Pacific and Southern Pacific railroads, tilled the rich California soil. Restrictive laws kept their wives and families in China. Many of the early Chinese never wanted to stay in the United States; they sought a fortune to bring back to China. But fortunes were rare, and they were forced to stay out of poverty or shame, or both.

Nonetheless, the lure of *Kum Saan* was intoxicating. The early Chinese found loopholes through immigration barriers, creating elaborate schemes to continue the flow of immigration despite the law. Other laws forced them into segregated districts which grew into today's Chinatowns. There, they formed an intricate society very little dependent upon the outside world. That was the bachelor society of early Chinese America.

When China became an ally of the United States during World War II, conditions improved for Chinese Americans. More women were allowed to enter and contemporary Chinese Americans began to take deeper roots. The liberalization of immigration laws in 1965 resulted in a resurgence of Chinese immigration, especially from Hong Kong.

Filipinos and Japanese

Filipino American immigration history also includes a bachelor society element. Early Filipino immigrants were mostly men; they came as laborers, mainly in agriculture. They formed communities in various central and northern California farm towns. Some settled on the edges of San Francisco Chinatown. The recent surge of Filipino immigration differs from the early pattern in that today's Filipino immigrant is likely to be a professional: a doctor, nurse, engineer or accountant. These modern arrivals have settled in San Francisco and surrounding communities — Daly City, South San Francisco, Oakland, and the tiny East Bay community of Hercules. Some have moved to cities further inland.

For Japanese Americans, the galvanizing experience was the World War II internment, one of the most shameful episodes in American history. Some 110,000 Japanese Americans and Japanese nationals were herded into the American equivalent of concentration camps shortly after the Dec. 7, 1941, Japanese bombing of Pearl Harbor. War hysteria fed the U.S. government policy; like most hysterical actions, it was unjust. The interned Japanese Americans were not saboteurs and spies; most were not even pro-Japan.

In a way, the internment experience destroyed an American subculture. It tore Japanese Americans from their American roots, broke up families, undermined their beliefs in their country, and dispersed them to harsh and hostile environments. To this day, the internment is a difficult subject for many Japanese Americans to discuss. But details of the myriad human stories of coping, adjusting and resisting in the camps are emerging. Japanese American organizations are still seeking reparations from the U.S. government.

The sorry treatment of early Asian immigrants didn't deter millions more from coming after the U.S. Congress lifted strict quotas on Asian immigration in 1965. Their presence in certain Northern California cities is highly noticeable. They crowd into San Francisco's famous Chinatown, which already bulges with residents, businesses and tourists.

Life in Chinatown

San Francisco's Chinatown is a peculiarity of American culture. It is at once a tourist attraction and a ghetto. Tourists stream into Chinatown, strolling Grant Avenue's gaudy souvenir emporiums, restaurants, bars and grocery stores; while on the upper floors and side streets, thousands of Chinese Americans live in crowded and substandard conditions. The tuberculosis and suicide rates in

Chinatown far exceed the national averages.

Chinatown is a truly self-contained complex community with networks of businesses, social and political organizations, newspapers, religious and financial institutions. Politics in San Francisco's Chinatown is intricate. Some factions maintain loyalty to the nationalist regime in Taiwan; others favor the communists in Beijing; still others prefer to concentrate their political energies on winning more power within the American system.

The old and the new in the Asian community: left, an elderly Chinese man strolls down Stockton Street in Chinatown; right, a Korean girl flips over her modern dance class.

San Francisco's Chinatown doesn't have enough space to accommodate all the newcomers, so a second Chinatown of sorts has sprung up several miles to the west in the Richmond district. Along Clement Avenue and Geary Boulevard, scores of Asian restaurants (Chinese, Vietnamese, Korean, Japanese, Filipino and Thai) have opened over the past decade. Some San Franciscans believe this new center is the place to find the finest Asian cuisine.

Oakland's Chinatown is also bulging at its more compact seams. New shops and restaurants are ranging farther from the core blocks centered at Eighth and Webster streets. On one edge of Oakland Chinatown, Hong Kong developers are building an

office-rental complex that promises to make the community more tourist-oriented.

Vietnamese Refugees

Vietnamese refugees, even newer and poorer than their Chinese counterparts, have found a temporary home in one of San Francisco's worst neighborhoods, the Tenderloin. They have also moved into some of the more rundown sections of Oakland. Forty miles (65 kilometers) to the south, Vietnamese refugees work and live in the heart of Northern California's semi-conductor and high technology industry; many are assembly workers putting together miniature circuit boats and numerous other electronic

components.

The tiny community of Locke in the Sacramento Delta, about an hour's drive from San Francisco, is facing other problems. Locke is a living example of a rural Northern California Chinatown. Built in the 1870s, it is a quaint, compact community of rickety old buildings reminiscent of a Hollywood Western set. It draws a fair number of visitors during the summer. But it is threatened with extinction if a Hong Kong developer gets his way. In the late 1970s, the developer sought to buy out Locke and turn it into a full-fledged tourist attraction. He is being opposed by Chinese American groups, but the issue is undecided. Anyone interested in Asian American history should plan a trip to Locke — now.

Today's Asian American is a different breed from the early Chinese of Locke, or from Japanese and Filipino farm workers. There are still Asian American laborers, farm workers, gardeners, waiters and laundrymen. But there are now more bosses, bureaucrats and businessmen than there were in the early days of Asian immigration, and more doctors, lawyers, scholars, artists and entertainers.

Problems Persist

For all the success stories, however, problems persist for those Asian Americans who speak little or no English. Many older Chinese, Japanese and Filipinos — those who have lived in the United States for many years — live in poverty, alone. They are victims of past discrimination, never having had the opportunities that some better educated immigrants of today have. There are problems with younger Asian Americans, too; gang violence is a fact of life in every Asian ghetto.

Anyone who doubts the ethnic cohesiveness of Asian Americans has only to spend a Sunday in San Francisco or Oakland Chinatown. Restaurants and tea houses overflow with families. Hundreds of Asian Americans who live outside Chinatown spend part of their day eating, shopping and visiting in Chinatown. Pink boxes filled with Cantonese *dim sum* (tea pastries) are found everywhere.

The interaction between Asian Americans and other Americans isn't always smooth. Some Asian Americans get along well professionally and personally with White, Black and brown Americans. Others choose to remain relatively isolated. One trend that is noteworthy is the high rate of "outmarriage" by young Asian Americans; some estimate that more than half of the Japanese American youths in California marry outside their culture.

Religion plays a central role for many Asian Americans in Northern California. Christian churches dot the Chinatowns in both San Francisco and Oakland and are important social centers for many Asian American young people. Chinese temples play an important role in the lives of older Chinese Americans, and elderly Japanese observe religious rites in Buddhist and Shinto temples. Some small Northern California towns still have Chinese temples. The most notable is one in Marysville, north of Sacramento. In addition, many Chinese Americans continue an ancient rite of worshiping ancestors. For the most part, Filipino Amer-

icans remain very much the Roman Catholics they were when they or their parents lived in the Philippines. A good many Korean American newcomers belong to Christian churches.

Asian Americans love to gather for Asian holidays. For Chinese Americans and Vietnamese newcomers, Chinese New Year (or Lunar New Year) is the major event of the year. On the Gregorian calendar, it usually falls sometime between late January and mid February. Chinatowns are transformed into explosions of red paper, firecrackers, cherry blossoms and pyramids of oranges. The grocery stores are very crowded and very cheerful. Extended families come together for huge feasts during the celebration.

One of the biggest public celebrations for the Japanese American community is the Cherry Blossom Festival during spring San Francisco hosts a major Cherry Blossom Festival in the city's Japan Town, which is a largely tourist-oriented showcase of shops and restaurants a few miles west of Chinatown, at Geary Boulevard and Laguna Street.

The sharp rise in Asian immigration that began in the late 1960s has deepened the involvement of Asians in the United States. Nonetheless, according to the 1980 census, Asian Americans account for but 1.7 percent of the 230 million residents of the United States. In political terms, those numbers are inconsequential. This fact leads to a profound irony of Asian American life. Certainly, they are no longer trapped in laundries, restaurants, vegetable farms, fish beds and fruit orchards; their influence on American culture is becoming more evident; their scholastic achievements are impressive, particularly in mathematics, computer sciences and other sciences.

But their presence in politics is hardly noticeable. To be sure, some Asian Americans serve in important political roles. Among them is March Fong Eu, California's elected secretary of state who grew up in Oakland's Chinatown. Asian Americans supported her election, but her victories were achieved because non-Asians voted for her. The same can be said of other Asian American political figures: Robert Matsui and Norman Mineta, members of the U.S. House of Representatives from Sacramento and San Jose, respectively. The political invisibility of Asian Americans is best illustrated by the fact that San Francisco, a city with a very significant Asian American population, does not have a single Asian American on its chief governing body, the Board of Supervisors.

There is a burgeoning political movement among Asian Americans throughout California. Those in Northern California are organizing to pull together the disparate interests of the various Asian American communities. In November 1983, the city of Monterey elected the U.S.A.'s first Chinese American woman mayor, Lily Chen. But becoming a political force in the state that has the most Asian Americans remains the last frontier for the beneficiaries of the Gold Mountain legacy.

Left, a Vietnamese immigrant earns a living harvesting pickles near Gilroy. Right, Japanese fan dancers await their turn on stage during the Aki Matsuri festival.

PLACES

Okay, maybe there just isn't enough time. That's understandable. Northern California is not Paris or the Pyramids, compact and easy to explore. But don't let that get in the way. Make a little time; take a few chances. The upper half of California has more places than Gallo has grapes. The Golden Gate Bridge and Fisherman's Wharf and the Wine Country are nice, but they're not all there is.

Within the arbitrary boundaries this book has assigned to Northern California — the southern edge is an utterly imaginary line drawn north of San Luis Obispo and south of Paso Robles, over the mountains and through the central valley just south of Fresno, with a dip down to the southern tip of the Sierra then up to Lone Pine and so on to the Nevada border — are more things, and more kinds of things, than exist in any similar territory anywhere in the world.

There are the austere glacial cirques around Desolation Valley and the small peaceful tidepools on the Monterey Peninsula. There are the windswept meadows on the Mendocino coast and the hurried crush of San Francisco Chinatown. There are rich bottomland and high desert plains, raging rivers and sweeping freeways, roller coasters and ski runs and lava caves and granite cliffs. And as if that weren't enough, there is Yosemite, quite simply the most beautiful valley anywhere.

A person can be where the action is, or he/she can be utterly alone. He can drink the best wines made in America, eat the best seafood, take the best mudbaths. He can play the best golf courses, climb the highest mountain, see the oldest tree, immerse in the hottest hot tub.

Or he can just take a walk and discover things the authors of this book don't even know about.

Northern California, more than any other place in America, is an area where people live by choice. The climate is temperate, the vistas are extraordinary, the people friendly. Robert Louis Stevenson lived here for a while, and so did Ronald Reagan. Jack London spent most of his life here; Jack Kennedy went to school here. George Lucas lives here; so does Francis Ford Copolla. One city just to the east of San Francisco boasts more resident Nobel Prize winners than any other community in the world.

Certainly, this is a place worth exploring, a place with secrets worth discovering by foot, bicycle, bus, car, train or plane. But be forewarned: one visit may be all it takes to turn another visitor into a resident.

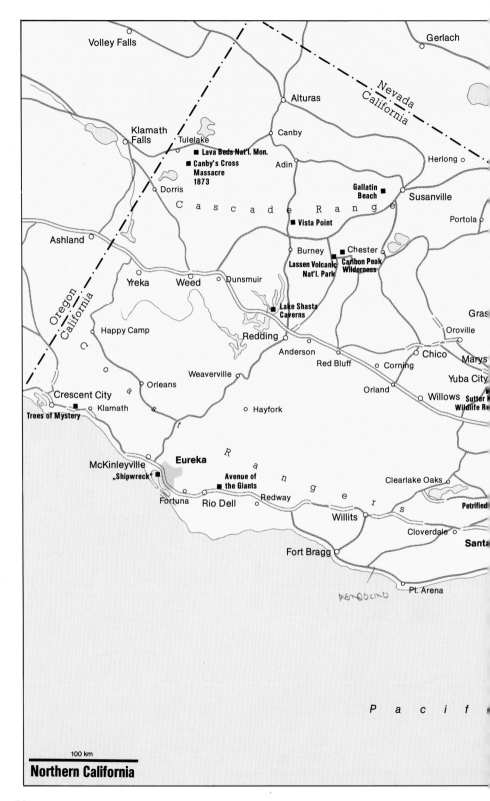

Volley Falls

Gerlach

Nevada
California

Alturas

Klamath
Falls   Tulelake   Canby
■ Lava Beds Nat'l. Mon.
■ Canby's Cross   Adin
Massacre
1873
Dorris

Herlong

Gallatin
Beach ■   Susanville

Portola

Cascade   Range

■ Vista Point

Ashland

Burney   ■ Chester
Lassen Volcanic   Caribon Peak
Nat'l. Park   Wilderness

Yreka   Weed   Dunsmuir

Lake Shasta
Caverns

Gras

Happy Camp   Redding   Oroville

C   Anderson   Chico   Marys

Red Bluff   Corning   Yuba City

Weaverville   Orland   Willows   Sutter
Orleans   Wildlife R

Crescent City
Klamath   Hayfork

Trees of Mystery

McKinleyville   Eureka   R
„Shipwreck"   Avenue of   n   Clearlake Oaks
the Giants   g
Fortuna   Rio Dell   Redway   e   r   s   Petrified
Willits   Santa
Cloverdale

Fort Bragg

MENDOCINO   Pt. Arena

P   a   c   i   f

100 km

Northern California

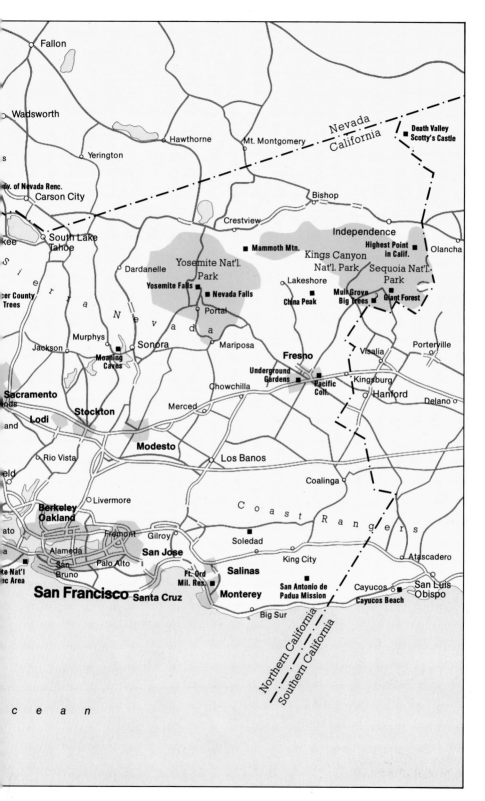

SAN FRANCISCO: CITY BY THE BAY

Every man should be allowed to love two cities, his own and San Francisco.
—*Gene Fowler, author, journalist and screenwriter (1890–1960)*

The United States has cities that trigger responses nearly as predictable as those in Pavlov's dogs. New York gains respect as a power place where the energy level always borders on overload. Cleveland is pitied because of its sad decline from regional eminence to municipal neediness. Some cities are amusing, like New Orleans; or dull, like Philadelphia. One, Los Angeles, defies comprehension because of its vast sprawl.

Only San Francisco wins visitors' love, straight away and effortlessly. It is a pastel city for lovers and pleasure seekers, soft and feminine and Mediterranean in mood. Foghorns and bridges, cable cars and hills, Alcatraz and Fisherman's Wharf, Chinatown and North Beach — all invite feelings of fascination or enchantment. Scores of movies and television programs have made use of the remarkably beautiful natural setting.

San Francisco is comfortable with contradiction. It jealously preserves the past and delights in anachronism, yet rides the latest wave of fashion, whether in *haute couture* or computer chips. Haughty but humane, the city may fleece the tourist; but it maintained soup kitchens for the poor long before Reaganomics revived that custom elsewhere in the land. San Francisco is passionate about its views, but is always willing to lend a sympathetic ear to the latest corporation wanting to erect another high-rise slab.

San Francisco sits like a thumb at the end of a 32-mile (51-kilometer) peninsular finger, surrounded by water on three sides and blessed by one of the world's great natural harbors. It is joined to the mainland by two of the acknowledged masterpieces of bridge design and construction, which blaze at night like strings of priceless jewels. In the daylight, San Francisco's profile of mighty towers and home-girt hills look from a distance like some place a prince would take a princess to live happily ever after.

Elegant and cosmopolitan, San Francisco is a sleek courtesan among the cities of the world, narcissistic and proud of it.

The Sacred and the Profane

Poll after poll acclaims San Francisco as the city Americans most like to visit, while nine out of 10 people who come to the United States on foreign-exchange programs ask to be taken here. As a result, more than 3 million visitors a year come to the city and leave behind more than $1 billion annually, making tourism San Francisco's most profitable industry.

Certainly, there is no appetite, licit or otherwise, that need go ungratified in this sacred and profane queen city of the west, and no option that need go unexplored for lack of opportunity. With a population of 705,000 packed into 46.6 square miles (125 square km), San Francisco has a density of nearly 15,000 people per square mile, and 10 times that number in Chinatown. Elsewhere in the nine-county Bay Area (population: 5.1 million), the density

ceding
es: State
way 1,
Sur;
kee River
inter;
ell Street
ecars;
Francisco
ine.
the
den Gate
ge.
it,
strel on
els in
den
e Park.

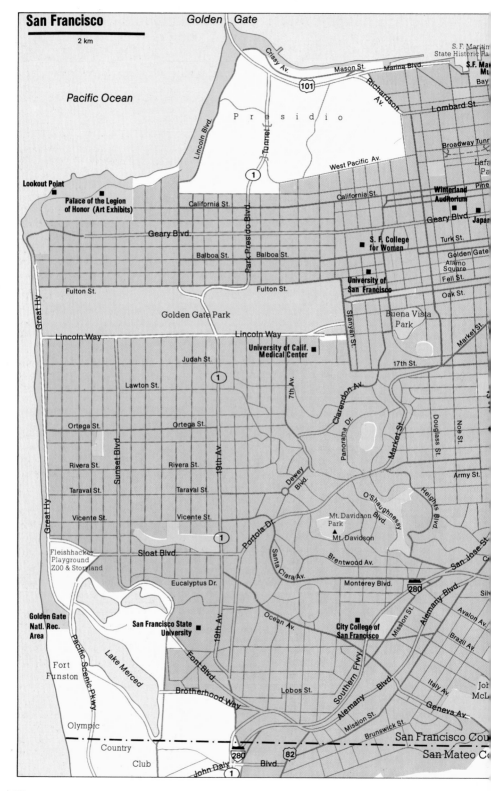

San Francisco

2 km

Golden Gate

Pacific Ocean

S. F. Maritim
State Historic Pa
S.F. Ma
Mu

Bay

Crissy Av.

Mason St.

Marina Blvd.

Richardson Av.

Lombard St.

101

Broadway Tunr

Presidio

Lafa
Pa

West Pacific Av.

Pine

1

Lincoln Blvd

Tunnel

California St.

California St.

Winterland
Auditorium

Lookout Point

Palace of the Legion
of Honor (Art Exhibits)

Califprnia St.

Geary Blvd.

Japan

Geary Blvd.

Turk St.

Golden Gate

S. F. College
for Women

Balboa St.

Balboa St.

Alamo
Square

Park-Presidio Blvd.

Fell St.

University of
San Francisco

Oak St.

Fulton St.

Fulton St.

Great Hy

Buena Vista
Park

Golden Gate Park

Market St.

Lincoln Way

Lincoln Way

Stanyan St.

University of Calif.
Medical Center

Judah St.

17th St.

7th Av.

Lawton St.

Chardon Dr.

Ortega St.

Ortega St.

Panorama Dr.

Market St.

Douglass St.

Noe St.

Sunset Blvd.

Rivera St.

Rivera St.

Taraval St.

Taraval St.

Army St.

Dewey Blvd.

Heights Blvd

Vicente St.

Vicente St.

O'Shaughnessy

19th Av.

Mt. Davidson Blvd.

Fleishhacker
Playground
ZOO & Storyland

Portola Dr.

Mt. Davidson
Park

Mt. Davidson

San Jose St.

Sloat Blvd.

Santa Clara Av.

Brentwood Av.

Eucalyptus Dr.

Monterey Blvd.

280

Silv

Golden Gate
Natl. Rec.
Area

Ocean Av.

Alemany Blvd

Avalon Av.

San Francisco State
University

City College of
San Francisco

Mission St.

Brazil Av.

Fort
Funston

Lake Merced

19th Av.

Pacific Scenic Pkwy

Font Blvd.

Italy Av.

Joh
McL

Brotherhood Way

Lobos St.

Southern Frwy.

Alemany Blvd.

Olympic

Mission St.

Geneva Av.

San Francisco Cou

Country

280

82

Brunswick St.

San Mateo C

Club

John Daly

Blvd.

1

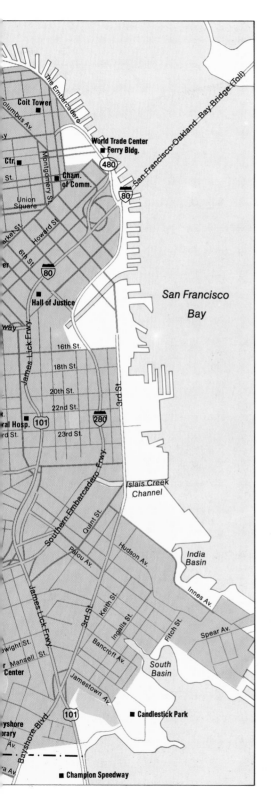

averages 1,500 per square mile.

This compression is one of the city's great charms. Instead of long, bland blocks of transition, San Francisco's neighborhoods change with vivid suddenness, like a tightly edited film. Only a resident Dickens could do justice to the rich complexity of the city, the vast social chasm that separates the rich living atop Nob Hill from the poor who live a short stroll away in the crime-ridden squalor of the notorious Tenderloin district.

Elegance brushes shoulders with the sordid, the exotic with the commonplace. Couples in formal evening dress parade past doorways reeking with the ammonia stench of urine. Slippered feet tread sidewalks etched with stomach acids. Stately homes, raised in an age when mineral and merchandising fortunes built with a lavish hand, ascend and descend the slopes of Pacific Heights. Lesser mansions stare out at the Golden Gate from Seacliff, or regard one another in the hushed precincts of Presidio Terrace and St. Francis Wood. Across town, where the weather is better, are the vandalized public housing and mean streets of Hunters Point and Bayview.

An Ethnic Bouillabaisse

The residents of this charmed city, the nation's 13th largest, form a demographic bouillabaisse not found elsewhere on the North American continent. Although the descendants of early Italian, German and Irish families are still found in snug neighborhood enclaves, their numbers have been greatly diminished over the past couple of decades by the lure of suburbia with its cheaper land and bigger houses. Their place has been filled by an influx of Asian and Hispanic people.

The city's population stands at 45 percent White, 21 percent Asian, 12 percent Black, 12 percent Hispanic, and a rainbow assortment of "others." By contrast, in the rest of the state, Whites comprise 76 percent of the population.

The city in recent years has become a mecca for Filipinos, the fastest growing minority; refugees from Southeast Asia; and both wealth and people from jittery Hong Kong. One consequence has been that the colorful 23 square blocks of Chinatown haven't been able to absorb the new arrivals. So they have spread their cultures west through the avenues into the formerly all-White Richmond and Sunset districts.

San Francisco is to an extraordinary degree a city for young singles. Between 1970 and 1980, the number of single persons 25 to 34 years of age jumped an astonishing 40 percent to more than 150,000. The traditional family was meanwhile decamping. During the same decade, the number of children below 18 in San Francisco dropped by 27 percent.

Many of the new singles were homosexuals fleeing hometown disapproval for San Francisco's famed easy-going tolerance. Only New York City can claim a great concentration of gays. During the past 15 years, San Francisco's gays have emerged from a guilt-ridden existence "in the closet" to play a major role in the city's political, cultural and economic life. They have even been elected to the 11-member board of supervisors, which governs the city along with the mayor. The police department now actively recruits both gay men and women to carry guns and badges.

No one knows how many homosex-uals live in the city. The most frequent estimate heard is 100,000, which would mean an improbable one in every seven residents. That figure is based on highly unscientific guesswork done some years ago by the police intelligence squad at a time when gays were seen as a law-enforcement problem and the squad lobbied to beef up its budget. The questionable figure has nonetheless been since treated with the respect accorded revealed truth.

The Earthquake Next Time

Not everyone lives happily ever after in San Francisco. Alcoholism and the incidence of cirrhosis is greater in San Francisco than in any other major city. And the Golden Gate Bridge has been a magnet for the suicidal ever since it was completed in 1937. To date, more than 700 persons have jumped to their deaths from the span, most while facing the glittering city they believed had in some way failed them.

No one can predict when the next earthquake will come and lay waste to the great beauty of San Francisco as it did (coupled with fire) in 1906. People

Reflectio in a Uni Square boutique window.

don't talk about it much, but the fear is always there, lying just below the surface like the treacherous San Andreas Fault itself. One day the earth will move underfoot again, the tall buildings will sway, and death and destruction will rain down. It's just a matter of time.

It can be argued that this underlying tension is what gives San Francisco its special zest; that this may explain why it abandons itself so to self-indulgence. Tomorrow may never come, so why not live it up while you can? In San Francisco, having fun is what counts most.

Fun is easy to find in San Francisco, thanks to the happy accident of geography. Few cities reveal themselves as easily to the pedestrian. An unhurried 15-minute stroll will take one from the pinstriped heart of the financial district into the center of Chinatown. The contrast in cultures is so sharp, one feels as though he should have had his passport stamped.

Union Square

Union Square is within easy walking distance of most of the city's hotels. Regarded during pioneer days as the city's geographical center, it was deeded to public use in 1850. It got its name a decade later from meetings held to demonstrate solidarity for the union of American states, then threatened by Southern secession.

Apart from the shaft supporting the winged statue commemorating Admiral George Dewey's naval victory over the Spanish in 1898, there is not much to be said for the square itself. Its main denizens are multitudes of pigeons and indigents seeking small contributions toward the purchase of potable fluids.

On the south of the square, facing Geary Street, are two major department stores — **Macy's** and the swanky **Nieman-Marcus**, featuring a glorious rotunda saved from its predecessor on the site. To the north, on Post Street, are the **Hyatt Union Square** hotel, its detailed fountain by sculptress Ruth Osawa demanding minute inspection; the distinguished **Bullock & Jones** store, purveyors of traditional men's clothing since 1853; and the posh **Saks Fifth Avenue** store.

To the west of Union Square, the somber dignity of the **St. Francis Hotel**, the city's second oldest, faces Powell

ling the
in
nt of
Westin
Francis
tel.

Street. The St. Francis was built in 1904 by Charles T. Crocker when he and a few of his robber-baron friends decided the city lacked enough first-class accommodations. Queen Elizabeth stayed here, President Gerald Ford was fired upon by a would-be assassin as he left the hotel, and silent-screen comedian Fatty Arbuckle killed a beautiful young woman here in romantic horseplay that got too rough. It is, to be sure, a place with a lot of history. Looming behind the hotel like an eavesdropper is a new tower that brings the inn's room total to 1,500. The tower has glass elevators that offer an excellent view of the city.

To the east of the square, beyond Stockton Street, rising in the distance above all other buildings, is the dark square hulk of the 52-story **Bank of America**, headquarters of the country's biggest bank and the city's tallest structure. The plaza in front of it features a polished hunk of black marble known locally as "the banker's heart." On the top, the **Carnelian Room** — an expensive restaurant by night, a bankers' club by day — offers a spectacular blimp's-eye view of the whole Bay Area.

A cable-car line runs north from Union Square up Powell Street, almost immediately beginning an ascent of Nob Hill. (The cable-car system was shut down temporarily in 1983 for renovation; it was scheduled to begin operation again in July 1984.) Before boarding the cable car, locals and visitors alike frequently get the morning wrinkles out of their bellies with a stop at **Sears Fine Foods,** 439 Powell St. This cafe is famed for its tiny pancakes and French toast. At the corner of Sutter Street is the **Holiday Inn at Union Square,** a misnomer as the square is really a block away. The 30th floor boasts the **S. Holmes Esq. Public House and Drinking Salon,** which recreates the Baker Street digs of the master sleuth and offers fine views from tall windows that actually open.

Nob Hill and Beyond

Only cable-car passengers and Olympic-class athletes will not be winded by the time they reach the top of 376-foot (115-meter) **Nob Hill** at California Street. Here runs another cable-car line linking Van Ness Avenue with the financial district. Men used to say that

Left, the Fairmont Hotel on Nob Hill; right, a view tow. Russian Hill.

San Francisco women had great legs from walking up and down the city's 40-or-so hills. Now that the last sexist has been shamed into silence, comments like that aren't heard any more.

The top of Nob Hill has clustered three of San Francisco's best-known hotels — the **Stanford Court,** the **Fairmont** and the **Mark Hopkins** — as well as the small, exclusive **Huntington Hotel,** where quiet old wealth stays when it pays a visit. Across the street from the Huntington is the stuffy **Pacific Union Club,** built in 1886 by James Flood at the then-stupendous cost of $1.5 million. Today it is an ultra-exclusive club for the wealthy and well-connected. The big neo-gothic pile next to the "PU" club is **Grace Cathedral,** started by the Episcopalians in 1928 but not finished for nearly 40 years. The church frequently hosts weekend concerts, charging nominal admission. It's worth a visit even if nothing is going on.

The next hill north, before descending toward the waterfront, is **Russian Hill.** This was once the habitat of impecunious writers and artists enslaved to their muse. The muses have moved on to less costly neighborhoods. The

only reminder is the **San Francisco Institute of Art,** founded in 1871 at 800 Chestnut Street. It has four galleries and a tower said to be haunted. A one-block section of **Lombard Street** weaving down Russian Hill is ballyhooed as "the crookedest street in the world."

The Waterfront

The 24-mile (39-km) waterfront can properly be said to begin at **Fort Point,** the grand old Civil War fort built in 1853 to defend the entrance to San Francisco Bay. It is now dwarfed by the Golden Gate Bridge, where traffic rumbles overhead; but it still presents an appearance sufficiently gallant to scare off any Confederate privateers that may still be lurking in the fog. A sharp wind almost always blows at this spot, so visitors should dress warmly. In fact, a jacket or sweater is almost always a necessity wherever one goes in San Francisco. With that perversity of people who must endure nature's quirks, Bay Area natives love to quote Mark Twain's famous line that the coldest winter he ever spent was a summer in San Francisco.

Water always dashes against the sea-wall at the beginning of the 3½-mile (5½-km) **Golden Gate Promenade.** Joggers and romantics favor this bracing walk which gives a panoramic view of San Francisco, Alcatraz, Angel Island, the Marin shoreline and the East Bay.

Part of the promenade goes through **Crissy Field,** an airfield belonging to the 1,400-acre (567-hectare) **Presidio,** another of San Francisco's graces. Established by the Spanish in 1776 and owned by the United States Army, the Presidio is the least warlike of any military installation. Only heaven ranks higher when servicemen and officers list their preferred posting. Lowly lieutenants occupy quarters with a view a millionaire would prize, and generals' housing is better sited than the home of San Francisco's resident billionaire, Gordon Getty, son of late oil tycoon J. Paul Getty. The Presidio's beautifully manicured grounds include stands of pine and eucalyptus, a museum, a hospital, a golf course, even a lake. The spit-and-polish home of the Sixth Army, it is open to everyone except the people who live at the Soviet consulate on nearby Green Street, a third of

whom are presumed to be spies by the FBI agents who maintain a circumspect surveillance.

Further down the promenade is the **Marina Green,** beloved by kite flyers, joggers, sunbathers and others who specialize in looking upon same. The big yachts moored in the harbor belong to the wealthy members of the **San Francisco Yacht Club,** whose handsome Spanish-style clubhouse looks out on the Bay.

The Plaster Palace

Across Marina Boulevard to the south is the classic rococo rotunda of the **Palace of Fine Arts.** It stands above a reflecting pond where ducks and swans glide. Designed by Bernard Maybeck, the Palace was originally built of plaster of paris for the Panama-Pacific Exhibition of 1915. It wasn't meant to last, but somehow it did. Not until 1967 was it strengthened and made permanent, thanks to the generosity of a millionaire who lived in the neighborhood. The Palace houses the **Exploratorium,** a museum with more than 500 exhibits to awaken even the most dormant interest in science. There is strong local opinion that this is the best science museum in the world.

The promenade continues past **Gas House Cove,** a middle-class yacht club, to **Fort Mason,** a former Army installation that has been turned over to the U.S. Department of the Interior. The government administers the fort, part of the vast **Golden Gate National Recreation Area,** which extends north along the Marin County coast to include 20 miles (32 km) of beaches, timbered ridges and sylvan glades. Fort Mason has many interesting little nooks and crannies, ranging from **Green's** — a fine vegetarian restaurant run by Zen Buddhists — to museums, art galleries and the *S.S. Jeremiah O'Brien,* a lovingly restored World War II Liberty ship. It fires up its boilers once a year for a ceremonial tour of the Bay, and can be visited most weekends.

Beyond Fort Mason is **Aquatic Park,** a terraced greensward that leads out to a small beach and curving municipal pier usually crowded with local fishermen. It includes the **National Maritime Museum,** which has all kinds of nautical displays and photographs, and is adjacent to the Hyde Street Pier, where the

The Palace of Fine Arts.

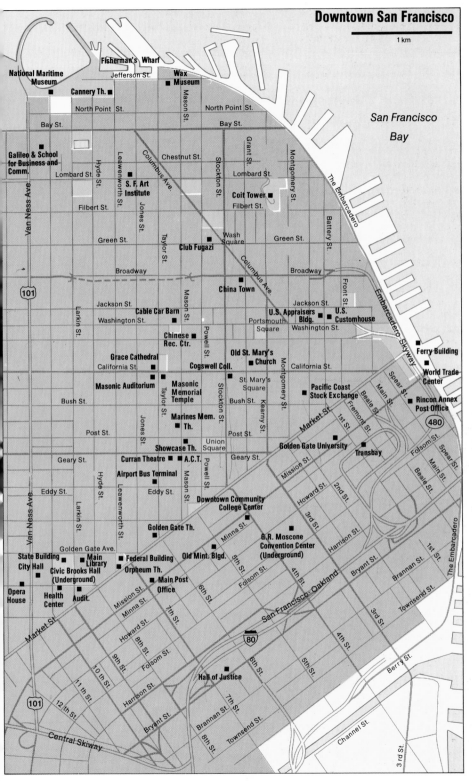

Downtown San Francisco

1 km

San Francisco Bay

National Maritime Museum

Fisherman's Wharf

Jefferson St.

Wax Museum

Cannery Th.

North Point St.

North Point St.

Bay St.

Bay St.

Galileo & School for Business and Comm.

Chestnut St.

Lombard St.

S. F. Art Institute

Lombard St.

Coit Tower

Filbert St.

Filbert St.

Green St.

Club Fugazi

Green St.

Broadway

Broadway

China Town

Jackson St.

Jackson St.

Cable Car Barn

U.S. Appraisers Bldg.

U.S. Customhouse

Washington St.

Portsmouth Square

Washington St.

Chinese Rec. Ctr.

Ferry Building

Grace Cathedral

Old St. Mary's Church

World Trade Center

California St.

Cogswell Coll.

California St.

Masonic Auditorium

Masonic Memorial Temple

St. Mary's Square

Pacific Coast Stock Exchange

Rincon Annex Post Office

Bush St.

Bush St.

Marines Mem. Th.

Post St.

Post St.

Showcase Th.

Union Square

Golden Gate University

Transbay

Geary St.

Curran Theatre

A.C.T.

Geary St.

Airport Bus Terminal

Eddy St.

Eddy St.

Downtown Community College Center

Golden Gate Th.

Minna St.

G.R. Moscone Convention Center (Underground)

State Building

City Hall

Main Library

Federal Building

Old Mint. Bldg.

Civic Brooks Hall (Underground)

Orpheum Th.

Opera House

Health Center

Audit.

Main Post Office

Market St.

Hall of Justice

Central Skiway

Channel St.

Van Ness Ave.

Hyde St.

Leavenworth St.

Columbus Ave.

Jones St.

Taylor St.

Stockton St.

Grant St.

Mason St.

Montgomery St.

Battery St.

The Embarcadero

Embarcadero Skyway

Larkin St.

Powell St.

Kearny St.

Front St.

Spear St.

Beale St.

Main St.

Wash Square

Union Square

Mission St.

Howard St.

1st St.

2nd St.

3rd St.

Harrison St.

Bryant St.

Brannan St.

Townsend St.

Folsom St.

5th St.

4th St.

6th St.

7th St.

8th St.

9th St.

10th St.

11th St.

12th St.

Harrison St.

Bryant St.

Berry St.

Golden Gate Ave.

Mission St.

Minna St.

Howard St.

Folsom St.

San Francisco=Oakland

101

480

80

101

87

museum's floating displays are docked. These include a sidewheel ferry and three schooners that carried freight in the days of sail.

Across the street from Aquatic Park is the fanciful **Ghiradelli Square,** a superb example of putting the past to work in the present. Ghiradelli Square was built as a woolen mill during the Civil War era and later became a chocolate factory. When the chocolate business moved elsewhere, it could easily have been torn down to make way for something modern. But William Matson Roth, a financier with a keen aesthetic sense, saw the possibilities for rebirth. Over a five-year period, starting in 1962, it was transformed into a brilliant showcase for retail shops, restaurants, bookstores and bars. There is usually some free entertainment going on somewhere in the Square, likely including tomfoolery by mimes, who are nearly as common locally as gulls.

Down the street east of the Square, across from a cable-car turnaround, is a durable attraction — the **Buena Vista Cafe.** The owners make so much money selling Irish coffees to locals, who stand elbow-to-elbow with tourists at the bar, one wonders why they bother serving food. But those lucky enough to get a table are glad they do. This is not primarily one of the body shops where singles gather to swap telephone numbers, but many a romance has had its start here.

The restoration of Ghiradelli Square has triggered another miracle in this part of town. Near the Buena Vista is **The Cannery,** where once hundreds of tons of peaches were canned in season and shipped out by rail to market. When the Square proved its profitability, a similar job of marketing a then-and-now marriage arose here. Among its attractions is **Ben Jonson,** a restaurant that features a 17th Century interior bought in England by newspaper tycoon William Randolph Hearst. He couldn't find a place for it at his San Simeon castle, so it ended up here.

Fisherman's Wharf

The Cannery abuts tangy **Fisherman's Wharf.** Tourism surveys claim this is what 84 percent of all San Francisco visitors have come to see. Although the fishing boats look like

Jogging along Ma Green be Pacific Heights.

parts of a quaint set designed in the Walt Disney studios, they are actual working vessels that put out before dawn to fish the abundant waters outside the Golden Gate. The catch they bring back often determines the "special of the day" at the numerous restaurants clustered around the wharf. Italians historically skippered and manned the boats and also ran the restaurants. A glance at the names of the restaurants — **Sabella's, Tarantino's, Alioto's** — indicates that not very much has changed.

Chances are Fisherman's Wharf will be where visitors have their first encounter with one of the city's proudest legends, its crusty sourdough bread. It is quite unlike any found anywhere else. Natives swear the secret ingredient rolls in with the fog, working a mysterious influence on the bacteria in the sourdough starter. The best way to enjoy this bread is with sweet butter, Dungeness crab and a crisp Chablis.

The Wharf has catered to generations of tourists and knows how to do it with skill. At sidewalk concessions, strollers can watch crabs being steamed and can buy shrimp or crab cocktails as take-away treats. There are numerous shops selling low-budget souvenir items for friends and relatives who are not excessively encumbered by good taste. There are also an assortment of carnival midway-type attractions on Jefferson Street.

The **Wax Museum** presents nearly 300 wax mannequins in costumes that sometimes bear a passing resemblance to those of the great people in history they purport to represent. **Ripley's Believe It or Not! Museum** assembles under one roof a collection of some 2,000 peculiar things once belonging to the late cartoonist Robert Ripley. The **Guinness Museum of World Records** offers a gallery of biggest, smallest, fastest, slowest and other such pacesetters from the pages of the Irish brewer's best-seller.

A short walk east at **Pier 39** is a popular but missable tourist attraction. This 45-acre collection of shops, arcades, fast-food restaurants and other diversions reproduces a cutesy past that no one in San Francisco remembers. Why, the critics asked, have they reproduced a turn-of-the-19th Century Cape Cod whaling village? The only thing authentic at Pier 39 is the **Eagle Cafe,** a water-

irardelli
uare.

front fixture favored for decades by fishermen and longshoremen before it was moved intact from its original site a couple of blocks away.

The tall masts and rigging at water's edge nearer to the main Wharf belong to the graceful Scottish-built clipper **Balclutha,** a 265-foot (81-meter) beauty open to the public. It put to sea in 1886 and made many voyages around Cape Horn. Two piers away is one of the Wharf's newest draws, the **Pampanito,** a World War II submarine whose narrow passageways may awaken claustrophobia. The yellow choppers taking off at intervals from near the *Balclutha* belong to **Commodore Helicopters.** The price is steep, but the ride they offer around Alcatraz is unforgettable.

Flying over the Bay is fun, but skimming across its waters is even better. For those with the time and money, chartering a sailboat is the best way to go. For those with less time and money, hopping aboard a big tour boat is nearly as good. **Red and White Fleet** at Pier 41 and **Gold Coast Cruises** at Pier 45 offer regular trips. They have snack and liquor bars on board. The usual route takes passengers out along the Marina Green and under the Golden Gate Bridge before heading back for a circuit past Angel Island, Alcatraz and the Bay Bridge.

The Golden Gate

When sailing under the **Golden Gate Bridge,** it is interesting to consider that at one time there was a respectable body of engineering opinion that held it would be impossible to build a span at this point because of the depth of the water (318 feet, or 97 meters, at the deepest point) and the powerful tidal rush in and out. The city authorized the first studies in 1918, but not until 35 years later was the first shovelful of earth turned under the gaze of master engineer Joseph B. Strauss, no relation to the Waltz King. Four years later, it was finished at a cost of $35 million and the lives of 11 construction workers.

The bridge is seven miles (11 km) long, including its freeway approaches. The suspension section alone is 6,450 feet (2,320 meters) long. The towers stand 746 feet (228 meters) above the water, and the span is 220 feet (67 meters) above the water at low tide. There are two piers supporting it, the biggest of which extends 100 feet (31 meters) below the water. They poured 693,000 cubic yards (520,000 cubic meters) of concrete and used more than 100,000 tons of steel in its construction. There are 80,000 miles (128, 700 km) of cable helping to support it. Crews are continually sandblasting rust off the bridge and repainting it its international orange color, using 10,000 gallons (38,000 liters) of paint a year. More than 17 million southbound cars cross the bridge each year, paying a toll to do so. (Nobody counts the northbound cars because no toll is collected from them). The bridge was built so sturdily that it has been closed only three times due to high winds.

Naturally, these figures only begin to hint at the inspiring beauty of the bridge, which has to be seen to be appreciated. No commuter from Marin ever grows so jaded that the sight of the bridge doesn't lift his spirits. Sometimes, when the fog rolls in off the ocean, only the tops of the towers are visible, like islands in a gossamer sea.

Alcatraz Island

Another tour boat outfit, the **Blue and Gold Fleet,** has headquarters at Pier 39 east of Fisherman's Wharf. There is a colorful rivalry between Blue and Gold and Pier 41's Red and White, sometimes manifested in the maneuvering that goes on between the boats off **Alcatraz.** Each tries to sail closest to the island to give its passengers the best view.

The island's famous prison, however, is falling apart. Its steel bars are being eaten away by salt air and its pastel buildings are slowly giving way to the ravages of time. What is it about ruins that make them so appealing?

In the case of Alcatraz, part of the explanation lies in its location. Just over a mile offshore of San Francisco, it is windswept and scoured by swift tides. When it was first sighted in 1775 by Spanish Lt. Juan Manuel de Ayala, the only occupants were pelicans. Ayala accordingly named it *Isla de los Alcatraces,* or the Island of Pelicans.

Its strategic location in the Bay obviously suited it to military purposes and it was garrisoned with soldiers in the 1850s. Because escape from the island was a remote possibility, renegade servicemen were incarcerated on Alcatraz, to be followed by Apaches taken prisoner in Arizona during the 1870s Indian wars and prisoners from the Spanish-American War at the turn of the century.

Alcatraz evolved into a federal prison that housed such case-hardened criminals as Mafia leader Al Capone and the notorious Machine Gun Kelley. Those few desperate inmates who managed to escape their cells in bids for freedom perished in the frigid waters surrounding the island.

The prison was finally closed in 1963 when the costs of repairing the constant ravages of wind and weather grew too great. Since then, proposals have surfaced from time to time to put the island to some sort of use, but all have come to nothing. A band of American Indians occupied the island for an 18-month period in the 1970s to dramatize their differences with the Bureau of Indian Affairs, but they were only too glad to finally leave.

So the prison buildings crumble away bit by bit as people increasingly think the best thing to do with Alcatraz is just to leave it as it is, a symbol of "man's inhumanity to man." Park rangers give one-hour guided tours of those parts of the island safe to traverse, including a peek at some of the cell blocks. Ferries leave from Pier 41. Warm clothing is essential.

North Beach Nightclubs

Broadway is the heart of the city's nightclub district, a stretch tawdry enough for the most jaded tastes. On weekend nights, the streets are thronged with people who come to ogle the hookers and be lured into dark joints by cold-eyed barkers with smiles as dazzling as real zircons. Inside, these patrons sip liquor-flavored water sold at larcenous prices and watch naked ("totally nude" is the preferred usage on street posters) women dance in a manner meant to seem erotic.

But there is an undeniable excitement to the street. The neon lights are bright and live music blares from inside many clubs. There are also some nice restaurants and a variety of wonderful coffee shops where midnight snackers can sip expresso or *caffe latte*, fork down pastry, and eavesdrop on some first-rate conversations at neighboring tables. This area, known as **North Beach,** has

Waterfror transport, Pier 39.

always been congenial to writers, artists and other deep thinkers. At the same time, it has retained the flavor of an old-fashioned Italian neighborhood whose dual anchors are the **Church of Sts. Peter and Paul** on grassy **Washington Square** and the little working men's bars where elderly Italians sip red wine and consider the affairs of the day.

The outside tables at **Enrico's** on Broadway are a good place from which to study the passing scene. Many interesting local characters and home-grown celebrities drop by at night, including entertainers from up and down the street who are taking their breaks between shows. The man in the beret is the excitable owner, Enrico Banducci. The sizeable bartender is named Lucky, and no prudent man would dream of giving him any trouble.

Most people find a visit to **Finocchio's** fun — it's one of the world's best drag shows. There are four shows a night and busloads of tourists from all over the world troop in to gape and rub their eyes. Indeed, it is hard to believe at first that all those beautiful entertainers are men — until they yank their wigs off.

A few steps away is the **Condor Club,**

the p," adway, th Beach.

where a waitress named Carol Doda peeled to the waist one night in 1964 and ushered in the topless boom. The venerable Doda still descends nightly from the ceiling atop a piano. She is clad only in a G-string and shows her debt to silicone technology.

Those with their hair dyed magenta, or who perhaps have a nostril pierced with a safety pin, fit right in with the punk-rock crowd that lines up outside the **Mabuhay Gardens** on Broadway to catch the first show at 11 o'clock nightly. Talk about schizophrenia: this is a staid Filipino restaurant by day.

A word of warning — parking is near impossible in North Beach at night, and police are very strict on illegally parked vehicles. It is best to walk or take a taxi.

As one might expect, there are a raft of good Italian restaurants in this neighborhood. The busiest is probably the **North Beach Restaurant** on Stockton Street. The food is at least as good, however, at **Mama's** on the same street two blocks away. **Vanessi's** on Broadway always has a line, and most of the time it's worth it. The same can be said of **Little Joe's** just down the street; Joe's chefs juggling pans over the leaping flames are worth an admission charge. The **Caffe Sport** on Green Street may be the best of them all, as the long lines will testify.

The **Washington Square Bar and Grill** is a hangout for lawyers, politicians, writers and others who make their livings from words. Rugby experience is helpful in getting a drink from the small crowded bar. Another favorite North Beach haunt of the wordsmiths is the **City Lights** bookstore on Columbus Street. For some 30 years it has been operated by poet Lawrence Ferlinghetti, one of the literary lights of the 1950s beat era. Across the alley is **Vesuvio's,** a wonderfully atmospheric bar where intellectuals in rimless glasses sip aperitifs and think long thoughts. And nearby, on Columbus, is the **Tosca Cafe,** where the cappucino is delicious and where off-duty cops and society swells play pool and listen to opera records on the jukebox.

Above North Beach, at the end of Lombard Street, is **Telegraph Hill.** The *moderne* tiara crowning the hill is **Coit Tower,** built in 1934 by Mrs. Lillie Coit in memory of her husband and other city firefighters.

Chinatown

Standing on the corner of Broadway and Columbus Avenue, surrounded by the glitter and sleaze of North Beach, one is near enough to the Grant Avenue entrance of exotic **Chinatown** to hear the clacking of *mahjong* tiles. If Chinatown were the only attraction San Francisco had to offer visitors, it would still be worth the trip.

San Francisco's Chinatown is the biggest Chinatown outside of Asia, and the steady influx of immigrants keeps it growing. Its streets are narrow, crowded, alive with color and movement. It extends for eight blocks, far enough to make visitors feel after a time that they might be walking the teeming, traffic-choked streets of Hong Kong or Shanghai. Mysterious alleys abound. Tiny cluttered herb shops offer powders and poultices promising everything from rheumatism relief to the restoration of sexual powers.

In Chinatown's dozens of hole-in-the-wall shops, one can buy anything from cheap trinkets to exquisite screens and massive hand-carved furniture costing thousands of dollars. Silken clothing, hand-painted vases, paper lanterns, rattan furniture, and many other Asian articles are for sale.

Some of the world's finest Chinese restaurants can be found in this quarter. It would be supreme folly for visitors not to take advantage and have at least one meal here. **Johnny Kan's** and the **Empress of China** are the best known of the fancy restaurants, but there are any number of obscure restaurants and tiny cafes where diners can sit down with the Chinese locals and eat well and cheaply.

Veteran gastronomes have been known to cry out in ecstasy after a meal of *dim sum*. These delicious pastries, filled with meat, chicken, shrimp or vegetables, are a favorite Chinatown lunch. Waitresses push them from table to table on carts like peddlers. Diners select the dishes they want; the number of empty dishes on the table at the end of a meal determines the charge. Best bets for *dim sum* are the **Tung Fong, Hong Kong Tea House** and **Asia Garden,** all on Pacific Avenue, and **Louie's** on Grant Avenue. Those who like friendly insults with their food can climb the stairs and thread their way through the kitchen at **Sam Wo's,** where Edsel Ford Song will oblige them.

Intriguing though it is, Grant Avenue should not be the sole focus of Chinatown exploration. Grant is the face Chinatown wears for tourists. One block over is Stockton Street, where the real business of life is carried on. Tiny Chinese women, ancient enough to have had their feet bound many decades ago, totter on shopping errands. Old men smoke cigarettes and read Chinese-language newspapers. Bright-eyed children chatter on their way to or from school. Crates of fresh produce and meat are unloaded from double-parked trucks as staccato bursts of Chinese dialect are exchanged.

The **Chinese Cultural Center** in the Holiday Inn on Kearny Street is worth a visit. It offers art shows, entertainment and guided tours.

It's only a couple of blocks west from Union Square to San Francisco's **theater district,** focused on Geary Street. The 1,768-seat **Curran Theater** and the 1,300-seat **Geary Theater** stand side by side. The Geary is the home of the American Conservatory Theater, one of the nation's best repertory companies. The Curran offers some of the biggest hits from New York's Broadway. Incidentally, San Francisco also has more than 50 cinemas offering everything from the raunchiest hardcore pornography to the artiest and most obscure foreign-language import.

Across the street from the Geary and Curran theaters are a couple of dark little bars which alert patrons when intermission is coming to a close at the theaters.

Other theaters in the general area are the 800-seat **Theater on the Square,** 450 Post St.; and the experimental **One Act Theater,** 430 Mason St. A little further afield is the **Golden Gate Theater** at 25 Taylor St. This ornate 2,400-seat theater, formerly a movie house, hosts a lot of out-of-town musicals.

Continuing west on Geary, it's eight blocks from Union Square to Van Ness Avenue, a broad north-south thoroughfare with a planter strip in the middle. This is one of the city's main arterials, serving as the gateway via Lombard Street to points north across the Golden Gate Bridge.

The Civic Center

Abutting Van Ness at McAllister Street is **City Hall,** one of the most

ant
enue,
inatown.

beautiful public buildings in the United States. It was designed by Arthur Brown, an architect so young and so unknown that he figured he might as well shoot for the moon in the early 20th Century competition to select the building design. To his surprise, Brown and his partner, John Bakewell, won with a design that called for the lavish use of costly marble and a dome patterned after St. Peter's Cathedral in Rome.

Built in 1914, City Hall is honeycombed with municipal offices and both civil and criminal courts. The full effect of the building is best felt from its Polk Street entrance, which faces a plaza. The magnificent stairway inside leads to the second-floor Board of Supervisors chambers. This is the building where in 1978 Supervisor Dan White shot Mayor George Moscone for refusing to reappoint him to the seat White had resigned. White then shot gay Supervisor Harvey Milk for smirking at him. After White was convicted of manslaughter and given a wrist-slapping sentence, howling mobs descended on City Hall and were only narrowly prevented from breaking in.

Across the plaza from City Hall is the stately main branch of the **Public Library,** built in 1916. The south end of the plaza is occupied by the **Civic Auditorium** (1913) and the north side by a **State Office Building** (1926). Together, they present an appearance of order and harmony. This comprises San Francisco's Civic Center. The brutal federal building standing behind the state building on Golden Gate Avenue is a reminder of how badly the Civic Center could have turned out had it been planned less carefully.

Opposite City Hall on Van Ness Avenue are a series of distinguished buildings. The **Veterans Auditorium Building** (1932) at the corner of Van Ness and McAllister Streets houses the 915-seat **Herbst Auditorium** and the **San Francisco Museum of Modern Art.** The latter includes works by such 20th Century masters as Picasso and Matisse as well as noted American artists. Next to it is the 3,535-seat **Opera House** (1932), one of the world's greatest. It has a summer opera festival and a regular season running from September to December. The opera company, which draws the foremost artists of the day to its stage,

Interior of City Hall, left; and its No. 1 resident, Mayor Di Feinstein, right.

MAYOR FEINSTEIN: 'I'M SO LUCKY'

Nostalgia does a big business in San Francisco, where old-timers insist the city was a much nicer place to live in the past, when the pace was slower and pedestrians didn't have to crane their necks to take in the big buildings downtown.

But Dianne Feinstein, the 54th mayor in a line dating back to 1834 and the first woman to hold the office, doesn't buy it. She was born and raised in San Francisco and knows it intimately.

"I find a lot about the city now is really nicer," she said in an exclusive interview for this book. "There's a great deal more variety in terms of fine restaurants, places to go, things to do."

In a city where tourism brings in $1 billion a year and ranks as the leading industry, the Mayor naturally is not neutral on the subject. But Feinstein won't deny there have been some losses.

Take Fisherman's Wharf, for example. When she was a girl it was "more authentic," less given to cute shops dealing in T-shirts and glazed seashells. "I remember the crabs cooking in pots," the Mayor fondly recalled.

But there is much that offsets this small decline in authenticity. "There was no Ghiradelli Square when I was a girl, no Cannery, no Pier 39." She says the museums are better today, and Golden Gate Park has never been in better shape, boasting such attractions unknown in Feinstein's girlhood as the Academy of Sciences.

There are some critics who claim San Francisco has abandoned itself so utterly to playing host to the millions of annual visitors that the people who live here get shortchanged.

The Mayor doesn't buy this, either. "This is our blue-collar industry," she said of tourism. Where it not for the tourists, countless numbers of retail clerks, hotel workers, restaurant help and other employees in the service industries would be out of work. "Fifty percent of these are minorities," she pointed out.

Every recent mayor of San Francisco has been in favor of continued growth, and the reason most often stressed is the need to provide jobs. Feinstein is no exception, but she has been more sympathetic than others to the desire of those elements who want to restrain growth before San Francisco loses that special quality which makes it such a magnet to tourists. The upshot of this has been her endorsement of greater controls over new skyscrapers planned for the financial district.

Her favorite tourist attractions — the sights she advises out-of-town friends to see — include Chinatown, Ghiradelli Square and Golden Gate Park.

Feinstein said that she has discovered when she travels across the United States or abroad, being Mayor of San Francisco carries a cachet undreamed of by her counterparts in Los Angeles, say, or Des Moines.

"'San Francisco!' people tell me, 'Why, that's my favorite city!' They tell me they can hardly wait to go back. They tell me it's so beautiful, then they tell me I'm so lucky."

97

shares quarters with the highly regarded San Francisco Ballet. Across the street from the Opera House is the lavish 2,958-seat **Louise M. Davies Symphony Hall,** which was finished in 1980.

Davies Hall is the new home of the San Francisco Symphony, which some critics feel has improved so much in recent years that it is ready to break into the elite circle occupied by the New York, Philadelphia, Boston, Cleveland and Los Angeles orchestras. Davies Hall has greatly increased the city's cultural capacity, permitting longer opera and symphony seasons and a separate ballet season.

The symphony also offers special attractions like "Mostly Mozart" and "All-Beethoven" festivals, a Summer Pops Concert where music lovers can bring picnic dinners, and Sunday afternoon summer concerts at Sigmund Stern Memorial Grove south of Golden Gate Park.

Davies Hall has triggered quite a boom in the Civic Center area. Expensive condominium buildings are rising to the north, hotels are being smartened up, and excellent restaurants like the **Hayes Street Grill** are opening. The **Opera Plaza** complex, where apartments begin at around $240,000, is a good example of the quality. It has a street-level bar with a European flavor. Its **Modesto Lanzone** cafe, like its sister restaurant in Ghiradelli Square, draws raves over its lighter-than-air pasta.

The Western Addition

West from the Civic Center is an area known as the **Western Addition,** a neighborhood of public housing and derelict Victorians just beginning to feel the first touches of restoration. Gays have been the shock troops in "gentrification," the spread of affluence into slum areas. The process works something like this: One or more gays buy a house in a rundown block of old Victorian homes. They lavish time and money restoring it to its former glory. Other homes in the neighborhood change hands and renovation begins. Speculators enter the picture and property values soar. In time, the whole block is reclaimed from neglect and the excrescences of modernity. Then the process begins all over again a few blocks away. The chief victims of all this have been Blacks, whose numbers have declined over the past decade in San Francisco.

It is not wise to linger in the Western Addition, even in a car. Every summer brings its tales of tourists who wander naively into the area and are robbed. Even the buses are sometimes stopped and boarded and their passengers forced to surrender their valuables.

At the corner of Geary and Gough streets is a huge building that looks like a washing-machine agitator. This is **St. Mary's Cathedral,** built by the Roman Catholic Archdiocese in 1971. Just down Gough at the corner of Eddy Street is the far handsomer **St. Paul's Lutheran Church,** built in 1894.

A short distance further west on Geary is the **Japan Center,** otherwise called *Nihonmachi*. This five-acre (two-hectare) complex, spread over three blocks, is the center of Japanese culture in San Francisco. It contains the 14-story **Miyako Hotel,** first-class restaurants, Buddhist temples, movie theaters showing Japanese-language films, community baths, the Japanese consulate, a nightclub, retail shops and offices. Those who have never tasted the delicacy known as *sushi* might find

St. Mary'
Cathedral

Japan Center the place to do it.

San Francisco has always been preeminently a restaurant town, back even before the Gold Rush. Visitors marveled over the "perfectly mad people" who ate and drank at all hours of the day and night. At last count, the city had nearly 4,300 dining establishments — more than 92 per square mile, or one restaurant to every 164 residents. In 1982, $870 million was spent in San Francisco on eating and drinking in restaurants, compared to $345 million on clothes and $226 million on gasoline. That prompted a U.S. Department of Commerce analyst to observe: "San Franciscans are willing to lavish more money on having a good time eating out than on taking care of themselves."

'The Avenues'

One of the densest concentrations of restaurants in the city is on Clement Street in the **Richmond district,** where in a one-mile stretch there are nearly 100 restaurants. With six major culinary schools in San Francisco, including the respected **California Culinary Academy** founded in 1977, scores of new chefs

seek employment each year. Many of them find jobs in this area.

The Richmond district, fogbound much of the summer, is an area of orderly streets, tidy homes and manicured lawns. These allow it to blend well into the neighboring **Sunset district,** which is equally middle class and conservative. One can easily become lost in this grid of streets, so the best thing drivers can do is to follow the signs that guide them along the city's 49-mile (79-km) **Scenic Drive.**

The drive snakes past the **Cliff House,** which overlooks the Pacific Ocean and peers down upon barking seals clinging wetly to the rocks below. This is worth a stop, as generations of San Franciscans have testified since 1863. The present Cliff House is the fifth to have been built here. Its predecessors have all burned down or suffered some other

North of Cliff House is verdant **Lincoln Park,** whose 270 acres (109 hectares) include an 18-hole municipal gold course and the handsome French-style **California Palace of the Legion of Honor.** The palace is really a fine museum. At the entrance is one of five existing bronze casts of Rodin's famous statue,

"The Thinker." The museum also has 18th Century paintings and tapestries as well as works by impressionists like Monet, Renoir and Degas. Also within the palace is the **Achenbach Foundation for Graphic Arts,** the largest collection of prints and drawings in western America.

Golden Gate Park

South from the Cliff House, the Scenic Drive leads past the pounding surf of **Ocean Beach** (too dangerous for swimming) into **Golden Gate Park,** one of the great urban parks in the world. It is three miles long and half a mile wide, and consists of groves of redwoods, eucalyptus, pine and countless varieties of other trees from all over the world. It is dotted with lakes, grassy meadows and sunlit dells. There can be thousands of people within its borders, but Golden Gate Park is so large that one can easily find solitary tranquility in a misty forest grove or by a peaceful pond. More than a century ago, the park was painstakingly reclaimed from sand dunes through the herculean efforts of a crusty Scottish landscape architect named John McLaren. Park superintendent for 55 years, McLaren so disliked statuary that he shrouded all human likenesses in dense vegetation. Most park statues remain "lost" today.

The park has myriad attractions. There are baseball and soccer fields, horseback riding trails, tennis courts, lawn bowling and horse pitching areas, flycasting ponds, even a polo field. Visitors can rent bicycles to tour the park from any of a number of adjacent shops, as well as roller skates from vendors who keep their stock in the back of trucks. Part of John F. Kennedy Drive, which runs through the park, is closed off on Sundays so that skaters can strut their stuff. Some of their routines, accompanied by recorded music, are quite spectacular.

The park has feasts for the mind as well as the eyes. The **California Academy of Sciences** comprises three museums in one. The natural history section incorporates displays of anthropology and ethnology with dioramas of North American and African animals. The **Morrison Planetarium** has a whiz-bang laser light show about our tiny, undistinguished corner of the universe under its 65-foot (20-meter) dome. The **Steinhart Aquarium** has nearly 16,000 specimens of marine and shore life on display in its 190 tanks. The latest attraction is a gang of appealing warm-water penguins; there is also a simulated swamp and a unique doughnut-shaped "fish roundabout." The aquarium was recently paid the highest compliment these times can offer: the Saudis asked for the blueprints so they can duplicate the Steinhart in detail.

Across the Museum Concourse, past the Music Concourse where Sunday afternoon concerts are given, is the **M.H. De Young Memorial Museum.** Blockbuster traveling exhibits are presented here, but even without these shows, the De Young — which opened in 1921 — is the city's best museum. Its collection includes Renaissance and medieval paintings and tapestries, sculpture and suits of armor, African and Polynesian galleries.

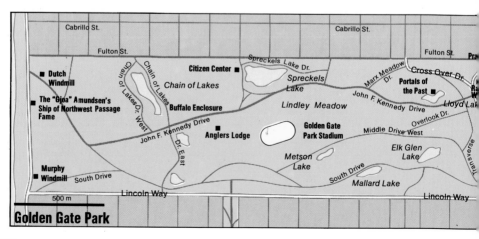

Golden Gate Park

An adjunct of the De Young is the **Asian Art Museum,** donated to the city by the late Avery Brundage, the iron-willed millionaire who dominated the international Olympic movement for half a century. The Brundage collection has some 10,000 items, making it the largest of its kind outside of the Orient. It includes precious jades, ceramics, sculptures, bronzes, vases, figurines and a host of other examples of Chinese and other Asian art, some dating back 3,500 years. Brundage bought his pieces during his global travels, paying top dollar at a time when there was little Western interest in Asian art.

South of the museums is **Stow Lake,** a pleasant body of water where sporty types can rent rowboats or pedal boats and work up a sweat before quenching their thirst with a beer at the snack bar. The island in the middle of the lake is called Strawberry Hill.

The **Conservatory of Flowers,** half a mile east of Stow Lake, was built in 1878, modeled after the Palm House at London's Kew Gardens. It was shipped piece by piece around Cape Horn from Dublin. It has permanent displays of many plants and features spectacular seasonal displays of blooms.

The **Japanese Tea Garden,** built in 1894, is a harmonious blend of architecture, landscaping and pools. It was here, many years ago, that fortune cookies were invented. The custom spread to Chinatown, then traveled throughout the Chinese food industry in the Western world. The garden was disassembled during World War II, then restored to its former grace when the threat of wartime vandalism had passed.

Stanyan Street borders the eastern edge of the park and intersects with **Haight Street,** one of the world's most famous thoroughfares in the 1960s. That was when long hair, tie-dyed fabrics, hallucinogens and a belief in the power of love and peace persuaded a generation of alienated young people that they could create an alternative lifestyle.

They were called "hippies." They openly smoked marijuana, took up forms of Eastern mysticism, declined to be sent overseas to fight in foreign wars, and otherwise were a thorn in the sides of their elders, who sometimes sent police in riot gear to the middle of the Haight-Ashbury district to scourge them. Haight Street was once so gaudy and bizarre that tour buses ran up and down it with their windows full of goggle-eyed tourists. Like most such radical departures from the social norm, the hippie experiment fell victim to time and fashion. Hippies now maintain only tenuous footholds in rural communes of Mendocino County and the Santa Cruz Mountains. After its moment in the hot glare of the media, Haight-Ashbury has returned to a quiet existence as a faintly down-at-the-heels neighborhood.

The Financial District

From Union Square, the most interesting approach to the **financial district** is by foot down Post Street. An elegant series of shops includes the **Alfred Dunhill of London** smokeshop on the corner of Stockton Street; **Gump's,**

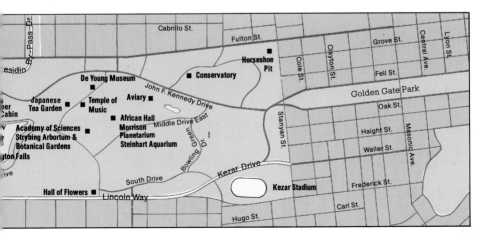

famous for its crystal and jade and *objets d'art;* **Eddie Bauer,** the outdoors clothier and outfitter; **Shreve & Co.,** jewelers; **Gucci,** maker of costly footware and other leather goods; and **Brooks Brothers,** the classy conservative tailor to those with button-down tastes.

Upon crossing Kearny Street, one is properly in the financial district, sometimes called "the Wall Street of the West." Buildings are getting taller and taller with each passing year. A few years back, fears were expressed that a "Manhattanization" of San Francisco was underway, that the city's wonderful views were being obscured by immense windowed slabs. After noisy political campaigns a few paltry controls were imposed, but the erection of behemoth office towers continues unabated.

Pedestrians appear to walk more briskly in this sector of the city. Perhaps avarice quickens the step. Or perhaps these monster buildings really do capture the chill winds aloft and circulate them down to street level to blow at gale force.

The financial district is roughly bounded by Kearny Street on the west;

Washington Street, a quaint neighborhood of tasteful antique shops and interior decorator showrooms, on the north; and Market Street on the southeast. After the Bank of America colossus, which is so tall its top sometimes disappears in the fog, the most distinctive building is the **Transamerica Pyramid** on Montgomery Street. At first, a lot of people were appalled by its, well, unorthodox appearance. But now most everyone has come to like it for the architectural eccentric it is.

The **Ferry Building** at the foot of Market Street was built in 1896 along the lines of the cathedral in Seville, Spain. Before the bridges were built, the Ferry Building was the portal through which ferry-borne commuters arrived and departed the city. Today it is partially hidden by the ugly Embarcadero Freeway that was suddenly stopped when the citizenry rose up in aesthetic revolt. Ferries still operate from the Ferry Building — rakish **Golden Gate Bridge District** vessels carry passengers to Sausalito and Larkspur, while the **Red and White Fleet** provides transportation to Tiburon.

In the nearby $300 million **Embar-**

Near the Conserva of Flower left, an ol salt casts his fishin line in a pond at Golden G Park, righ

cadero Convention Center is the **Hyatt Regency Hotel,** which boasts a spectacular 20-story atrium lobby. This is the sort of newcomer that has elbowed the venerable **Sheraton Palace Hotel,** a few blocks further west on Market Street, from the ranks of the city's premier hotels. The Palace, opened in 1875, is San Francisco's oldest luxury hotel. Its 150-foot Palm Garden, with its leaded-glass dome roof bathing diners in light, remains as striking as ever. Its Pied Piper bar with its beautiful Maxfield Parrish mural is a fine place to have a drink. Seven American presidents have stayed here, from Ulysses S. Grant to Franklin Roosevelt. One of those presidents, Warren G. Harding, died at the Palace in 1923 while still in office.

Market Street is a thoroughfare of contrasts. In the financial district, it's comfortably interesting. But it turns seedy down toward 5th Street, and stays that way for four blocks before beginning to revive. It finally ends at the multi-intersection that includes 24th and Castro streets, one of the busy hubs of gay action. Broad, tree-lined and well-lit at night, it has all the elements needed to become one of the world's great avenues. The city even spent millions of dollars building a tunnel beneath Market Street to eliminate the clutter of streetcars. But somehow the street has never achieved its potential.

South of Market

South of Union Square, Powell Street passes near the eastern fringe of the **Tenderloin district,** a neighborhood of sleazy bars, porn parlors and residential hotels where the poor are ruthlessly exploited by the owners and their agents. Drag queens traipse coquettishly, drug dealers sell their stepped-on cocaine and sugared heroin, hookers beckon, and street-wise Vietnamese children offer bags of garlic to passersby. It's a good area to avoid after nightfall.

Hallidie Plaza — named after Andrew, inventor of the cable car — is located where Powell meets Market Street. The cable-car turnaround near here is a wonderful place for people-watching. Some days it looks like something adapted from an Ionesco script. Bible thumpers shout salvation, street musicians and performers compete for available spare change, merchants hawk

their wares, glassy-eyed bums hustle dimes and quarters, pickpockets work the crowd, tourists look on astonished, and (perhaps) a brassy military band blasts away down in the plaza in front of the entrance to BART — the **Bay Area Rapid Transit.**

No visitor to San Francisco should miss an excursion aboard a high-tech BART train. It's the fastest way to give the Bay Area a once-over. The system has 71 miles (114 km) of track and 34 stations. The line ends in Fremont, a swatch of American suburbia, after passing through a 3.6-mile (5.8-km) trans-bay tube buried 135 feet (41 meters) beneath the water.

When people talk about **"South of Market,"** they refer to the hodgepodge of businesses and rundown residences that once ran to China Basin and the waterfront. Land has become so valuable in San Francisco, however, that even this area is beginning to put on airs. The Southern Pacific Co. owns a large tract of land and has proposed an entirely new community of office towers and high-rise apartments to completely transform the area.

The catalyst is the new 11-acre (4½-hectare) **Moscone Convention Center,** completed in December 1981 at a cost of $126 million. Constructed largely underground, the center has a six-acre exhibit hall without columns to obstruct the view, 41 meeting rooms and a grand ballroom that can accommodate 30,000 people.

At the moment of its completion, the new convention center was within walking distance of 8,000 hotel rooms. Within two years, another 2,100 rooms were completed; an additional 3,000 are projected by 1987. This feverish building is designed to accommodate the masses of convention delegates expected to be lured to San Francisco by the new center. The city hosted 631 conventions and 775,000 delegates in 1982; industry sources say those numbers are bound to increase dramatically.

Before the Moscone Center, perhaps the only attraction to draw the visitor South of Market was the **Old Mint** at 5th and Mission streets. Completed in 1874, it survived the 1906 earthquake and fire. Its classic facade today houses a museum, a collection of gold nuggets worth more than $1 million, exhibits that tell the story of the Gold Rush, and

the U.S. Treasury Department's numismatic operations.

Latinos and Gays

Mission Street heads due south into the heart of the **Mission district,** San Francisco's great melting pot of Latin American cultures. **Mission Dolores** (Dolores Avenue near 16th Street) was founded less than a week before the American Declaration of Independence was signed in 1776, and its four-foot adobe walls still form what is the oldest building in San Francisco. The graves of many of the city's earliest pioneers, and thousands of native Costonoan Indians, can be found in the mission cemetery. The 16th mission in the chain, the church was originally known as Mission San Francisco de Assisi. It was renamed by *padres* after a nearby lagoon, the Laguna de Nuestra Senôra de los Delores (Lake of Our Lady of Sorrows).

The Mission district oozes Hispanic culture. Red-tile roofs predominate on public buildings, palms and utilitarian shops line the streets, and restaurants offer the gamut of Latin-American cuisine — from Mexican to Chilean,

dining
e
Golden Court
e
aton
ce Hotel.
t,
dly
ersation
de the
century-
Mission
res.

Cuban to Salvadorean. Cruising the streets are gentlemen whose cars seem to scrape the ground; they are known as "low riders." Latinos are not the only residents, however; there are many Blacks living in the Mission district, along with Italians, Irish, Russians and other European immigrants.

Colorful murals, many of them done by amateur artists, brighten nearly every corner of the urban environment from Mission to York streets, 14th to Army streets. They are found on the exposed outer walls of public and private buildings of all types. Tours of these murals are offered the first Saturday of every month by the **Mexican Museum,** 1855 Folsom St. (at 15th Street), beginning at 10 a.m.

The macho Latino culture sometimes clashes with the neighboring gay culture of **Noe Valley.** The concentration of gays here and around the **Duboce Triangle** is so great it is said a homosexual can lead a full life and never come in contact with a heterosexual. He can do his banking at a gay bank, buy his croissants at a gay bakery, have his television fixed by a gay technician, get his teeth capped by a gay dentist, and so forth.

The busy promiscuity that once characterized the gay scene in San Francisco has been chilled by the sudden phenomenon of the baffling AIDS (acquired immune deficiency syndrome) plague. It has threatened with bankruptcy the bathhouses that specialized in anonymous sex, and sparked a revival in bingo nights and evening recitals. But the restaurants are still crowded, the bars are still hopping, and eternal friendships are still being pledged nightly and repudiated in the morning.

Much the same can be said for nearby **Union Street,** the straight equivalent of the brilliant Castro and Polk streets body-shop scenes. On Union, the specter that chastens is herpes, a resurgent venereal disease for which no cure has been discovered. People are more cautious, but still — when the hour is late and someone hasn't scored after a night of never-fail icebreakers that fail and inspired raillery gone flat — the desperation can almost be tasted in the air of the singles bars. By day, Union Street is a chic stretch of boutiques, antique stores, gourmet shops, delicatessens and classy restaurants.

West of this district are the **Twin**

Market Street a the Fina District.

Peaks, a pair of steep grassy knobs that provide a broad panorama of the city. In Indian legend, these two hills were once united in marriage, but their constant quarreling provoked the Great Spirit to separate them with a clap of thunder. To Spanish explorers, they were the "Breasts of the Indian Maiden." They later provided a windy vantage point from which Adolph Sutro conceived the city's post-fire urban plan in 1907. A little further south is **Mount Davidson,** the highest point in San Francisco at 938 feet (287 meters) elevation.

The residential southwest corner of the city features some lovely parkland. Highlights include the **Sigmund Stern Memorial Grove** (Sloat Boulevard at 19th Avenue), a grove of redwoods, eucalyptus and fir trees where free summer Sunday jazz and opera concerts are held; **Lake Merced** (Harding Way), popular for boating and trout fishing in season; and the 70-acre (29-hectare) **San Francisco Zoo.**

Sports fans flock to famed **Candlestick Park** on a rocky promontory in the Bay at the southeast corner of the city. The San Francisco '49ers football team, winners of the 1982 Super Bowl

symbolic of American football supremacy, and the San Francisco Giants baseball team both make their homes in this stadium. Up to 60,000 spectators can be accommodated.

Not far to the west, amidst the look-alike boxes of **Daly City** suburbia, the **Cow Palace** has hosted everything from rock concerts to basketball games to livestock shows. Seating capacity at this arena varies up to 14,300.

San Francisco is not a city where goods are produced, steel forged, minerals processed or machinery made. San Francisco deals in the sensory and trades in memories.

Every visitor takes a different memory away from San Francisco. There is the street that drops off steeply toward the whitecapped bay, where sailboats heel before the wind. There is the fog drifting through the Golden Gate, blurring the lights bejeweling the bridge. There are the savory dishes that magically blend to make the perfect meal. There is the shared sense of fun from a cable-car ride.

Indeed, San Francisco — the city that may be gone tomorrow — has mastered the good life.

cisco
ts'
eball at
dlestick
.

THE PENINSULA: HIGH-TECH LIVING

In the early 1870s, railroad mogul Leland Stanford, one of the earliest of the well-heeled residents of the San Francisco Peninsula, hired flamboyant photographer Eadweard Muybridge to take photos of his prize race horse, Occident, running at full gait.

Stanford was not interested in pretty pictures. A man of industry, he was trying to settle a gentlemanly wager among members of the horsey set: were all four legs of a horse ever off the ground at one time when it ran? Stanford claimed they were. It's been said, though never confirmed, that Stanford had $25,000 riding on his side of "unsupported transit."

In order to prove Stanford right, the photographer set up 12 cameras in a row alongside the race track. Attached to the shutters of each camera was string, which was pulled taut across the track. As the horse ran past, the shutter was tripped, and Muybridge ended up with a sequential portrait of a horse in motion — with all four feet off the ground.

This anecdote is noteworthy because of the historical complement it provides. Muybridge, with the financial support of Stanford, continued his experiments with motion photography and is recognized today as the granddaddy of the modern motion picture.

New technology — from Muybridge and the movies, to Silicon Valley's computer chips — is a natural, perhaps fated, by-product of the Peninsula, thanks in large part to Stanford and the university he founded nearly 100 years ago. And just as the Peninsula was in the late 19th Century, it remains today an enclave of the wealthy. Here, a $25,000 bet may not seem so outrageous now.

Where the Money Is

The Peninsula is a 55-mile (89-kilometer) swath of high hills, tall trees and beautiful estates, located between the Pacific Ocean and San Francisco Bay. To its north is San Francisco city. At its southern end lies the sprawl of the **Silicon Valley**. There, the highlands of the Peninsula glide head-on into the newly affluent, high-technology communities of Los Altos, Sunnyvale, Santa Clara and San Jose. Sales by Silicon Valley firms have set records at $40 billion a year, and the $100,000-plus suburban homes spread like a heat rash across the ample flatlands. (See this book's feature, "Playing the Game in Silicon Valley.")

The style of the Peninsula is sophisticated and current. Six thousand residents have doctorate degrees and Stanford University is the hub of much academic and cultural activity. Mixed in with the high-mindedness, however, is a great deal of new money (millionaires made from scratch are as common as tennis courts) and old (San Mateo is one of the four wealthiest counties in California, with a blue-book list of locals including the Hearsts, the Crosbys and the Caspar Weinbergers).

Along with prosperity, modern technology has brought modern problems, among them subdivision sprawl, fast-food outlets and convenience stores on land that once supported a bounty of fruits and vegetables. Until the Sixties, Santa Clara County counted agriculture as one of its major industries. Today, rush-hour traffic is bumper to bumper.

Stanford University

A farm — a blue blooded horse ranch — is exactly what **Stanford University** was a little over a century ago when Leland Stanford and photographer Muybridge began their experiments. Today, it is the cultural heartbeat of the Peninsula. It is located in the northwestern corner of **Palo Alto**, a comely city of 55,000 known for its environmental policies and praised as one of the "model little cities of the world."

When Stanford first proposed his plan for a private university in the 1880s, the response ranged from curious surprise to vituperate criticism, with one East Coast academician claiming that there was as much need for a new university in the West as there was for "an asylum for decayed sea captains in Switzerland." But a Yale of the West it became. Today it is an acclaimed center for the study of science, engineering and medicine. Ten Nobel laureates are among its 1,200 faculty members as well as 75 members of the National Academy of Science and three Pulitzer Prize winners.

eeding
es, the
on Point
house.
, a
t
er of
Stanford
ersity
pus.

Architecturally, Stanford's handsome, rough-hewn sandstone buildings are Romanesque in styling, though the red-tiled roofs, the burnt adobe color of the stone, and the wide arches give the university a Spanish mission look. The effect is one of uncluttered calm.

Stanford lacks the greenery associated with Ivy League schools on the East Coast. The entrance, along Palm Drive (off University Avenue via U.S. Highway 101), is basically unlandscaped (some say bleak), consisting of dirt, scrub oak and tufts of wild grass. Designed by Frederick Law Olmsted, it is meant to reflect the landscape of the West.

The exception to the overall prosaic quality of the university is **Memorial Church**, which dominates the **Inner Quad**, or central courtyard. It is resplendent in stained glass and richly colored murals, with a domed ceiling, broad transepts and scripture from the Bible etched into its marble walls.

Also open to the public is the **Hoover Institution on War, Revolution and Peace**, housed in a 280-foot (86-meter) tower next to the Quad. A famed research center, it contains a myriad of political and historical documents including the enormous collection of former U.S. President Herbert Hoover, one of the first Stanford graduates.

The campus also contains the very fine **Leland Stanford, Jr., Museum**, featuring paintings and sculptures dating back as far as the Renaissance. Its *pièce de résistance* is the original Golden Spike driven in 1869 in Utah to complete the Transcontinental Railroad.

On the northern border of Stanford University is the town of **Menlo Park**, founded in the late 1880s by two Irish immigrants as an outpost to serve the needs of Leland Stanford. Victorian quaint, with awnings on downtown store fronts and lots of antique shops, Menlo Park has two classic attractions — the **Allied Arts Guild** and the headquarters of *Sunset* magazine.

Lunch or tea is a fashionable occasion at the Arts Guild, a collection of fine art and crafts stores plus an indoor and patio restaurant. All are nestled within the beautifully landscaped, sylvan creekside grounds of an 1885 Spanish Revival ranch house located at the corner of Creek Road and Cambridge Avenue.

The Memorial Church, Stanford University

Since 1898, *Sunset* magazine has been the bible of western living and hospitality. In that spirit, the offices of **Sunset/Lane Publishers** (Middlefield and Willow roads) are open to the public Monday through Friday, 10 a.m. to 4:30 p.m., for organized tours of unescorted sightseeing. The buildings are of Spanish mission styling with high ceilings and wood beams; the southside building opens onto a lawn so manicured and flowerbeds so perfectly tended and delightfully colored that this showcase garden could be an illusion. Happily, it is not.

Along the Bayshore

The busiest artery in the Peninsula is the Bayshore Freeway, a section of U.S. Highway 101 that skirts the edge of the bay from **South San Francisco** to San Jose. It is along the Bayshore that industry has settled, notably the more than 1,000 electronics firms that are crushed within the 25-mile (40-km) stretch of Silicon Valley.

Coming south from San Francisco, the Bayshore Freeway provides the principal access to all of the Peninsula's major settlements, as well as to **San Francisco International Airport**, a few miles south of the city on the Bay side of **San Bruno**. Moving south, the bayshore towns include:

—**Hillsborough**, 15 miles (24 km) south of San Francisco, one of the world's most exclusive communities. Although residents disdain sightseers, Forest View Avenue and many other drives wind past its luscious homes and manors. Railway heiress Harriet Pullman Carolan, for whom a train car was named, built a 99-room mansion in Hillsborough's hills.

— **San Mateo**, a fashionably trendy city of 80,000. Its premier attraction is **Marine World/Africa USA**, a 65-acre (26-hectare) animal entertainment park where the stars of the more than 50 daily performances are 2,000 animals — whales and elephants, dolphins and tigers, lions and chimpanzees. **Bay Meadows Racetrack** offers Leland Stanford's favorite pastime, thoroughbred horse racing. And the **Coyote Point Museum for Environmental Education** has fauna and flora dioramas and a "hands-on" ecology theme overlooking the Bay.

er-ski
obatics at
ine World
ca USA.
ht,
li Estate,
odside.

— **Belmont** features **Ralston Hall**, the 80-room mansion of 19th Century financier William Ralston, on the grounds of the **College of Notre Dame**. An Italian villa, it has continental furnishings and a gallery of opera boxes overlooking a ballroom.

— Menlo Park, Palo Alto, and finally San Jose.

The Pacific Coast

The most scenic route in the Peninsula is State Highway 1, winding from **Pacifica**, a west San Francisco suburb, to Santa Cruz in the south. Though less dramatic than the cliffside reaches of the Monterey Peninsula, this leg of State 1 is an enchanting day's drive, boasting two vintage lighthouses — **Pigeon Point** near Pescadero (west of San Jose), the second tallest lighthouse in the United States; and **Montara** in the north, where a youth hostel is open in a nearby building.

The largest town along the San Mateo County coast is **Half Moon Bay**, population 7,800, a farming community settled nearly 130 years ago by Portuguese and Chilean immigrants. Half Moon Bay has a homey Victorian downtown, restaurants, gift shops, roadside produce stands and a cozy 1860s country inn, the **San Benito House**. The town is especially known for its "Great Pumpkin Festival," held each October. A spirited event, it includes a Halloween parade and a giant pumpkin weigh-in contest won recently by a hefty orange orb of 375 pounds (170 kilograms).

Deep-sea fishing boats take passengers out daily from the harbor at **Princeton-by-the-Sea**, a small fishing village and art gallery enclave just a few miles north of Half Moon Bay. The largest party-boat companies also offer a full schedule of sightseeing trips. One of the most popular is a whale-watching tour to the offshore **Farallon Islands**; fortunate travelers find themselves in the midst of a herd of gray whales migrating south from the Bering Strait (between November and February) or returning from Baja California with newborn offspring (in March and April).

A special coastal spot is **Año Nuevo State Park**, 20 miles (32 km) north of Santa Cruz near the San Mateo-Santa Cruz county line. Here, whiskered and roly-poly elephant seal pups are born in

Soaring over the salt beds near Redwood City.

January, when entire seal families are visible from lookout points along the beachfront. So popular with sightseers are these seal families that the beach does get crowded. It is best to call Año Nuevo State Reserve beginning October 1 for information and reservations.

Down the middle of the Peninsula, skimming the handsome, high coastal hills, is Interstate 280, California's last new freeway and the most expensive in the state. Off the Cañada exit is the **Pulgas Water-Temple**, a serene and odd Greco-Roman structure built in the 1940s over the terminus of the Hetch Hetchy aqueduct, carrying water from the Sierra Nevada to the pastoral **Lower and Upper Crystal Springs reservoirs** visible from the highway.

Nearby is the glamorous **Filoli** (named for the words "fight," "love" and "live"), a large Georgian brick manor with 16 acres of formal gardens. Once the home of a wealthy shipping family, the property is still in private hands but is open on a limited basis for tours. In the spring, it is necessary to call months in advance for reservations. Late summer is less crowded. Filoli is closed November 15 to February 15.

orful
racters
Pumpkin
stival,
f Moon
.

The Way to San Jose

San Jose was the first pueblo to be founded in Northern California by the Spanish, in 1777. It is today one of the fastest growing cities in the United States and the fourth largest city in California with a population approaching 700,000.

Until 1956, the San Jose area was providing America with half its supply of prunes, but agriculture has gone the way of modern technology. The orchards of three decades ago have now sprouted single family homes, condominiums and industrial parks grown from the microchip.

San Jose is a busy, fast-paced city, with all modern conveniences including major hotels, nightclubs and no fewer than 100 shopping centers. Sightseeing is minimal in metropolitan San Jose, although three major wineries are located within the city limits and all offer free tours and tastings — **Almaden, Mirassou**, and **Turgeon and Lohr**.

For entertainment of a more eccentric bent there is the red-roofed, sprawling, touristy but nonetheless fascinating **Winchester Mystery House** in down-

town San Jose. It was built in convoluted stages by Sarah L. Winchester, who inherited the fortune of her father-in-law, the famed gun manufacturer. Sarah was a spiritualist' who believed that she would live as long as she kept adding to her house. Sixteen carpenters worked on the mansion for 36 years, adding stairways that lead to nowhere and doors without rooms.

The spiritual realm is also the basis for the **Rosicrucian Egyptian Museum** and planetarium. A recreated walk-in tomb of 2,000 B.C. and the West Coast's largest collection of Egyptian, Babylonian and Assyrian artifacts are contained within the building, which draws a half-million visitors annually. There is no admission fee. The Ancient, Mystical Order Rosae Crucis is an international philosophical order said to have been established 3,400 years ago.

Other attractions include 150-acre (61-hectare) **Kelley Park**, with its open-air **San Jose Historical Museum**; the **New Almaden Mining Museum** featuring 19th Century mercury mines, 11 miles (18 km) south of San Jose; **Saratoga's** authentically Japanese **Hakone Gardens**; and the outstanding **Foothill**

College Electronics Museum in the Los Altos Hills. The original **Mission Santa Clara de Asis** (1777) is now the focal point of the **University of Santa Clara** campus; it contains some fine 19th Century paintings and the original mission gardens.

For youngsters in particular, the most exciting attraction in the San Jose area is **Marriott's Great America**, located off the Bayshore Freeway near **Sunnyvale**. A theme park drawing upon five venues of old America (Hometown Square, Orleans Place, Yankee Harbor, Yukon Territory, and Midwest Livestock Exposition and County Fair), it has live stage shows, arcades, snack bars and gift shops. But it is perhaps best known for its wild rides like "The Demon," a scary roller coaster, and "The Edge," a frightening 2½-second fall.

Bugs Bunny and Daffy Duck can be seen wandering through Great America, but not all is rosy in this make-believe world. There are rumors that the park will be sold, perhaps in the next few years. The cause: Great America sits within shouting distance of Silicon Valley, and industrial park developers are making bids for the land.

Winchester Mystery House, San Jose

116

San Francisco Bay Area

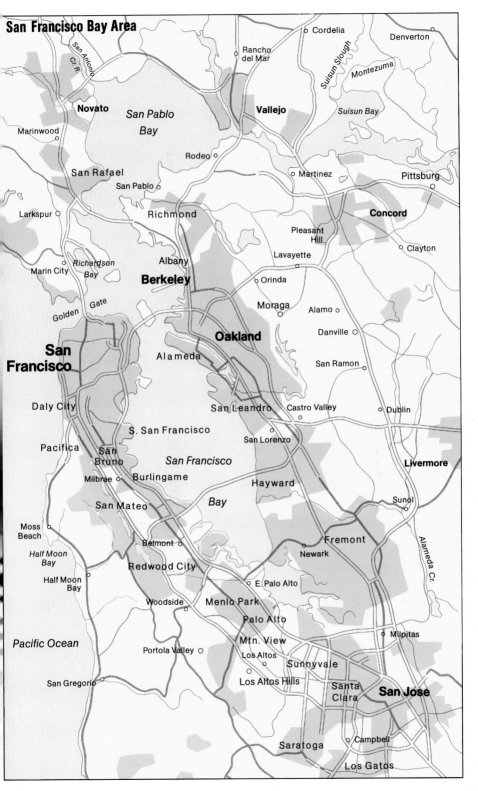

San Antonio Cr. R.

Cordelia

Denverton

Rancho del Mar

Suisun Slough

Montezuma

Novato

San Pablo Bay

Vallejo

Suisun Bay

Marinwood

Rodeo

San Rafael

Martinez

Pittsburg

San Pablo

Larkspur

Richmond

Concord

Pleasant Hill

Clayton

Lavayette

Marin City

Richardson Bay

Albany

Orinda

Berkeley

Moraga

Alamo

Golden   Gate

Oakland

Danville

San Francisco

Alameda

San Ramon

Daly City

San Leandro

Castro Valley

Dublin

Pacifica

S. San Francisco

San Lorenzo

San Bruno

Livermore

Milbrae

Burlingame

San Francisco

Hayward

Sunol

San Mateo

Bay

Moss Beach

Belmont

Fremont

Half Moon Bay

Newark

Half Moon Bay

Redwood City

Alameda Cr.

E. Palo Alto

Pacific Ocean

Woodside

Menlo Park

Palo Alto

Milpitas

Portola Valley

Mtn. View

Los Altos

Sunnyvale

San Gregorio

Los Altos Hills

Santa Clara

San Jose

Saratoga

Campbell

Los Gatos

OAKLAND AND THE EAST BAY

The preposterously ambitious idea of building a bridge linking Oakland and San Francisco was first put forth a few years after the Gold Rush by one of San Francisco's most beloved eccentrics. Joshua Norton, who proclaimed himself "Emperor of These United States" in 1859, used to keep his subjects in stitches with ridiculous ideas for civic improvement. When he proposed the **Bay Bridge**, they were slapping their knees for days.

But after World War I, when ferries were hauling 60,000 commuters a day between the two cities, the California State Department of Public Works decided to heed the emperor's advice. By 1936, the span was complete, 4½ miles (7.2 kilometers) along with another 3½ miles (5.6 km) of approaches. The bridge is partly suspended from enormous cables, but on the Oakland side of **Yerba Buena Island**, where the floor of the bay is too soft for cable anchorages, it is heavily trussed. Driving on the lower deck is nothing special, but the trip back to San Francisco on the upper deck is so spectacular, it's a wonder a day goes by without a pile-up caused by rubbernecking.

"The Mysterious East Bay" is San Francisco columnist Herb Caen's condescending name for the wilds of Alameda and Contra Costa Counties, the butt of a thousand San Francisco in-jokes. Beleaguered, bush-league **Oakland** can never seem to live down Gertrude Stein's infamous quip, "When you get there, there is no there, there." And **Berkeley** is still Berserkeley to those who remember the student wrangling of the Sixties.

Yet snotty San Francisco sighs nostalgically for the shipping business the Port of Oakland — now the second largest container port in the world — has long since wooed away. Once-shabby Oakland is very much a city on the way up, pouring millions of dollars into urban redevelopment. And Berkeley, though still lovably quirky, is now a hotbed of student rest: the University of California has metamorphosed into Preppy Heaven.

Back in the days when the Spanish crown rewarded its faithful soldiers with New World real estate, Don Luis Mario Peralta was given 44,000 acres (17,800 hectares) of prime East Bay land shaded by lovely old live oaks. In the spirit of the woolly West, squatters wrenched Peralta's land away, founded a city that was chartered in 1852, named it after the oaks, and gave birth to descendants who cut the trees down and built skyscrapers.

Socially, Oakland may be one of the most interesting cities in the country; block by block, it is certainly among the best integrated. Its population is 47 percent Black, 38 percent White, most of the rest Asian and Hispanic. The city owes much of its new vitality to the Black capitalists who have taken over the city's political life in recent years. The city council is dominated by Black members and many city department heads are Black. In 1977, Lionel Wilson, Oakland's first Black mayor, was elected with the help of the radical Black Panther Party (now defunct) and the Democratic left. But once elected, Wilson was quick to form alliances with much more moderate political elements — both Black and White businessmen with redevelopment money to spend.

119

Six new buildings have recently shot up in the downtown area, including a new convention center. Yet the redevelopment work is far from complete. The downtown area is a crazy mixture of vacant lots, ratty old buildings and spanking new skyscrapers. The neighborhoods are another kind of crazy quilt. In the business area, at places like the new **Hyatt Regency Hotel** on Broadway, members of the city's well-heeled Black bourgeoisie promenade in designer outfits. In **Montclair**, a mostly White residential area, spiffy redwood houses cling to the hills. In **East Oakland**, below MacArthur Freeway, the city's poor live in small stucco houses. In **West Oakland**, the oldest part of the city, now almost all Black, an enormous amount of federal money has been spent on restoring graceful Victorians and building parks.

Lakes and Other Landmarks

Oakland's most obvious landmarks are the **Tribune Building**, with its distinctive tower; the **Oakland City Hall**, with its wedding cake cupola; and, in the hills above the city, the five-towered, white granite **Mormon Temple**. Also visible from the Nimitz Freeway, for those driving toward the airport, is the **Oakland-Alameda County Coliseum Complex**, former home of the late lamented Oakland (now L.A.) Raiders football team and current home of the city's beloved baseball A's. And there's a natural landmark — **Lake Merritt**, a saltwater tidal lake in the center of the city. Visitors can skim across the lake in a replica of an old-time paddlewheeler and then take the kids to **Children's Fairyland** at **Lakeside Park**, seven acres of nursery-rhyme fantasies with live animals as part of the scenery.

Within walking distance of the lake are two wonderfully contrasting architectural delights — the **Oakland Museum** at 1000 Oak St. and the **Paramount Theater** at 2025 Broadway. The museum is a modern stunner, built on three levels. The Hall of California Ecology, devoted to natural sciences, is on the first level; the Cowell Hall of California History is on the second; and the Gallery of California Art occupies the third. For devotees of the art deco form, the Paramount, considered the

The Bay Bridge to Oakland.

120

masterpiece of architect Timothy Pflueger, is a treat.

Oakland's version of Fishermen's Wharf is the tediously pedestrian **Jack London Square** and **Jack London Village.** The author of *The Sea Wolf* and *Call of the Wild* might not be impressed were he alive to see it. Here are the overpriced restaurants, the T-shirt shops, the ever-so-adorable souvenir emporiums found in tourist traps anywhere. At least there is a view of the Oakland estuary. The **First and Last Chance Saloon** where London himself (an Oakland native) used to belly up, and a log cabin he's supposed to have occupied in the Klondike, are the main attractions.

Housewives Market at 9th and Clay Streets is off the beaten track, but might be the ultimate Oakland experience. It's a cavernous warehouse full of small stands and shops, a bit like the marketplaces of Third World countries. Its primary delight is a meat counter which sells every part of every animal — including raccoon — considered edible by practically anyone.

Not only does Oakland have a lake in its middle, it has another in its northeast corner — and not just a lake, but 48 acres (19 hectares) of land for picnicking, hiking, bicycling and jogging. This is the **Temescal Regional Recreational Area**, one of the 41 parks of the East Bay Regional Park District. During the summer, visitors can swim or just lie on its sandy beach and watch Oakland's rainbow of humanity at play.

Berkeley Bizarre

The mighty **University of California** is now spread over nine campuses throughout the state. It is considered one of the greatest universities in the world, outranking all other American universities in number of Nobel laureates. But it began as a humble prep school operating out of a former fandango house in Oakland. It was then called Contra Costa Academy and at one point, with only three students enrolled, its housekeeping staff got so worried about their paychecks they set up a tavern right in the academy. The housekeepers' rationale was typical of post-Gold Rush times: "Whatever did not succeed in 2½ months in California would never succeed."

The school's founder, the Reverend Henry Durant, quickly closed the tavern and recruited more students. He had 50 by 1855. The school acquired a charter as the College of California and eventually merged with the state's not-yet-organized university at its current site north of Oakland. In 1866 the new college town was named for Bishop George Berkeley, an 18th Century Irish philosopher who had written a poem that caught the fancy of a member of the naming committee — a poem about a new golden age of learning in America.

When the city of Berkeley incorporated in 1878, it had a population of only 2,000, but the town grew very fast as the university developed and as thousands of San Franciscans moved to the East Bay after the earthquake and fire of 1906. However, it was the Free Speech Movement of 1964 that put it on the map, for better or worse.

The issue was an administrative order limiting partisan political activities on campus. But the movement's real importance was in kicking off the snowballing campus rebellions of the Sixties. For several years thereafter the campus was a smoldering center of protest and politics. It ignited again in 1969, when students once more took to the streets to stop the university's expansion in an area they wanted to preserve as a "People's Park." They won, after a fashion, though the violence led to the death of an onlooker. After People's Park things cooled down.

Though the students are once again bent over their textbooks, Berkeley is still a carnival of quixotic politics. In local elections, slates of liberals face slates of ultra-liberals, happily splitting hairs over rent control, traffic control and tobacco control. Berkeley was one of the earliest cities to adopt an anti-smoking ordinance and its anti-auto regulations are not to be believed. In fact, driving in Berkeley can be an adventure without a map, for traffic barriers to discourage cars in residential neighborhoods can turn the bewildered out-of-towner into a rat in a maze. The best plan is to keep to the main streets, or "arterials" — or better yet, simply to park and walk in the university area. (A car is a *must* for the hills).

On the approach to Berkeley, two buildings catch one's eye. On a hillside

White-shi defender haul dow the ball carrier in a college football at UC Berkeley.

toward the south is a fairy-tale white palace. That's the **Claremont Resort Hotel**, finished just before the Panama Pacific Exposition of 1915. The other landmark is a tall, thin, pointed structure, the university's belltower. Its official name is **Sather Tower**, but it's known to all simply as the "Campanile" because it's modeled after St. Mark's Campanile in Venice, Italy.

To get the feel of Berkeley at its liveliest, the visitor should walk down Telegraph Avenue from Dwight Way to the university. Here students, townspeople and "street people" pick their way between rows of shops and stands of street vendors offering jewelry, pottery, plants and tie-dyed everything. On a good day, the atmosphere is rather like that of an Eastern bazaar. A half-block east of Telegraph Avenue on Haste Street is **People's Park**, a terrific example of an idea that didn't work out. Like the dozens of winos and weirdos who call it home, the park is neglected, unkempt and unloved.

Just south of the campus, on Bancroft Way, is the **University Art Museum**, designed by Mario Ciampi. Across Bancroft, on the campus proper, is the **Lowie Museum of Anthropology.** An elevator takes visitors to the 200-foot (61-meter) high observation platform of the Campanile. The seismographic station, where earthquakes are measured, is in the **Earth Sciences Building**. The university's **Bancroft Library**, with its collection of rare books and early California manuscripts, is one of the finest in the world.

In the hills above the campus is the **Lawrence Hall of Science**, a wonderful science museum; nearby are the university's amazing botanical gardens, 30 acres (12 hectares) containing more than 50,000 plants. Though 5,000 rare rhododendrons bloom here in April and May, the succulent garden may be more impressive still. Its 2,000 spooky-looking plants, some cacti twice as tall as the tallest man, are set in a sort of giant bowl in the hillside, forming as weird a landscape as can be seen on this planet.

Higher still, along winding Grizzly Peak Boulevard, is **Charles Lee Tilden Regional Park**, probably the most interesting of the East Bay parks. It contains more than 2,000 acres of eucalyptus, madrona and oak-covered hills

efreshing rnoon ne remont el in the land hills.

with hiking and horse trails, picnic areas, tennis courts and a golf course. It also offers heart-stopping views of the entire bay, from the Peninsula to Marin County.

Oddly enough, the town most people remember for campus riots has gone so straight in one area, it out-trendies Marin County. Berkeley has become the focal point of California *nouvelle cuisine*, devoted to artfully elegant but simple dishes using the native bounty of fresh ingredients. **Chez Panisse**, on Shattuck Avenue, is considered by some the best restaurant in Northern California.

Just north of Berkeley is **Albany**, where connoisseurs of racetracks can take in **Golden Gate Fields**. South of Berkeley and Oakland are a lot of light industrial towns. There are interesting period houses in **Hayward** (the 1886 **McConaghry Home**, 18701 Hesperian Blvd.) and **San Leandro** (the 1897 **Casa Peralta**, 384 W. Estudillo St.). **Fremont** offers **Mission San Jose** (established 1797), which has a small museum. On the Bay near Fremont is **Coyote Hills Regional Park**, a 1,021-acre (413-hectare) wildlife sanctuary with Indian shell mounds and a reconstructed Indian village. In nearby **Niles**, more than 450 movies were filmed between 1910 and 1915, including *The Tramp* starring Charlie Chaplin.

Contra Costa County

Contra Costa ("opposite shore") County, east of **Alameda**, is mostly made up of bedroom communities peopled with San Francisco commuters. Some of the towns, like **Orinda** and **Moraga**, are rather plush; others, like **Walnut Creek** and **Concord**, are rather ordinary. The towns themselves aren't of much interest, but the countryside has a rough Western splendor: the famous "gold hills" of California roll in all directions.

These hills are dear to the native's heart, but may be an acquired taste. Their charm is sometimes lost on visitors with the narrow-minded idea that grass ought to be green. Actually, the hills are green for a few fleeting weeks in the very early spring, frequently starting in February, but the grass dies quickly at the end of the rainy season, leaving the hills a light yellow. As the

Mount Diablo.

124

summer progresses and the sun gets hotter, the color deepens to a rich gold — or so it seems to those with vivid imaginations. By August, the hills seem ready to burst into flame. And they frequently do. In September, when it's even hotter, grassfires are common.

The jewel of Contra Costa is **Mount Diablo**, far and away the highest peak in this region. Because there are no other mountains for miles around, the breadth of the view from the summit is unsurpassed anywhere in the world except from Africa's Mount Kilimanjaro. Kilimanjaro has an elevation of over 19,000 feet (5,895 meters), Diablo only 3,849 feet (1,173 meters). Yet from Diablo, made a state park in 1931, it is possible to see parts of 35 of California's 58 counties.

At different elevations on Diablo, the temperature, rainfall and wind exposure are so different that the vegetation varies widely. A drive up the mountain can lead through several different environments. For those with time to stay, there's picnicking, hiking and camping.

Adventurers can return to the material world at **Hilltop Mall** in Richmond. Designed by architect Avner Naggar,

the mall looks plain from the outside, but it's quite flashy inside with spiraling, purple-carpeted ramps, vast conversation pits, a fountain, an ice-skating rink and a Charles Perry sculpture.

Those who feel more ambitious can continue on Interstate 80 to **Crockett**, a colorful old company town for workers at the **C&H Sugar Refinery**, and then take the **Carquinez Scenic Drive** to **Port Costa**. The drive along the Carquinez Strait is possibly the prettiest in the county and the town of Port Costa is certainly the most charming. Its well-kept Victorian homes are tenanted by artists, it's said, though antique dealers must live there as well — antique shops seem to be Port Costa's main industry.

Nearby **Martinez** has a sight that must have the famous conservationist, John Muir, spinning in his grave. Muir was a naturalist and author who helped found the Sierra Club and who fought long and hard for the establishment of national parks and the preservation of nature. The 17-room Martinez mansion in which he lived has been established as the **John Muir National Historic Site**. It is open to the public. The travesty is that it now practically abuts a freeway.

H Sugar nery, ckett.

MARIN: HOT TUBS AND WILDERNESS

Marin County has a reputation, at least in the Bay Area, as the mecca of hot-tub hedonism. The stereotypical Marin resident is newly affluent (having made his money in computer software or video tapes), cosmopolitan, artsy and politically liberal. On the dark side, he is intellectually shallow, narcissistic and self-indulgent, often found in his lush backyard glade soaking in his tub and imbibing a bone-dry Chardonnay or some other mild hallucinogen. His hauntingly beautiful female counterpart is golden-limbed and sun-buttered, to be found reading her tarot cards over bean-curd soup, behind the stained-glass windows of her redwood cottage.

This stereotype has some validity, as a visitor may discover if he listens in on a couple of Marinites conversing in Psychobabble:

"Martha isn't centered yet, but our dyad is processing through her ego block with some pre-orgasmic body work," says one.

"I can resonate to that," replies the other.

But this should not dissuade the eavesdropper from his visit. The residents may sometimes be a bit phony and self-centered but they can also be friendly and amusing, and while they do guard their habitats and privacy, they often throw open their homes and hot-tubs to the gentle visitor who uses the right approach.

Aside from its inhabitants, Marin County has a panoply of good bars, restaurants, public baths and other amusements that are democratic in the sense that social status is determined strictly on the basis of good cash and credit cards.

What is generally less known about Marin, even locally, is that the county offers some of the premier outdoor experiences in Northern California. Right on the northern lip of a metropolitan area numbering some 5 million, there are tens of thousands of acres of pristine coastline, unspoiled redwood groves and mountain meadows, untrammeled by development and looking pretty much as they did on Day One. This green belt offers an outstanding opportunity for hikers and nature lovers, particularly those who like to mix a little sybaritic indulgence with their exercise.

The able-bodied, for instance, can alternate physical activity — be it day walks, strenuous backpacking or cycling — with a lighter regimen of hot-tubs, massage, good eating, good saloons, sailboats and pretty people.

The Scene in Sausalito

With the lighter regimen in mind, the first stop for most Marin visitors is **Sausalito** (a corruption of the Spanish *saucelito,* meaning "little willow"). The waterside shops, the warrens of pricey boutiques, and the houses perched behind them on a steep slope draw inevitable comparisons to Mediterranean *villes* of the Riviera. The main drag, Bridgeway, is thronged on any weekend. The atmosphere is casual. It's usually easy to make new friends.

The best known bar is called the **No Name,** since the shingle outside it has a large blank where a less clever publican would probably cry his own name. The No Name attracts some literary lights and other local celebrities, but in recent times has had to share this trade with

nearby **Pattersen's,** in ambiance almost a clone. Frenzied dancing and a young crowd typify weekend activity at **Zack's,** across the street and a little north. On lazy weekday afternoons, however, Zack's' deck is a good place to lunch while watching boat owners on the dock below sand and varnish their vessels. An older, more established and often very yachty crowd hangs out at **Flynn's Landing,** well known for its fine food.

But while Sausalito's watering holes can be lively, so can its police force. Parking meters are enforced to the minute, and no mercy is afforded persons stopped for drunken driving.

The best way to arrive in Sausalito, and to meet people, is to sail into port aboard a large boat. Alternately, a ferry departs regularly from the foot of Market Street in San Francisco. Operated by the Golden Gate Transit District, these plush, stable and well-maintained boats carry a loyal traffic of commuters from Sausalito and Larkspur (near San Rafael) on weekdays. On the return runs in the afternoons, the bars aboard are open and the home-bound crowd often turns the ferry into a party boat.

On weekends, the ferries sail for the benefit of the tourist trade. They are great fun and are relatively cheap. Another ferry company, Harbor Carriers, operates a run between Tiburon, Angel Island State Park and Fisherman's Wharf on weekends.

Larkspur and Tiburon

If the Larkspur ferry terminal is the destination, it is easily recognized from afar as a strange triangular egg crate that provides a dubious shelter for 2,000 daily commuters. Around the terminal are shops and restaurants housed in newly erected buildings painted to look weathered and salty. The high point of the complex is an excellent bookstore — known in all humility as **A Clean Well-Lighted Place for Books.**

Right around the corner from the Larkspur terminal, on a little peninsula, is the infamous **San Quentin State Prison,** its grounds surrounded by chain fence topped by barbed wire. The buff-colored prison has been the scene of 400 state-sanctioned executions plus numerous informal ones practiced by the in-

An eccentric submarin houseboo offers ar unusual of hillsid Tiburon.

130

mates on each other. The prison is grossly overcrowded, seethes with the potential for violence, and is a national disgrace. Thus, there are no public tours. There is, however, a gift shop at the main gate.

Tiburon is a pleasant enough ferry destination — touristy, but also home ground for the leisured and well-to-do. The establishment of note here is **Sam's Anchor Cafe**; the drill is to sip a gin fizz on Sam's spacious deck while waiting for the return ferry.

Probably the *ne plus ultra* for ferry riders is a trip to **Angel Island,** which can be reached only by boat and is entirely a state park. In the summer, open-air trams oblige sightseers; year-round there are several good hikes. Of particular interest is the trek up **North Ridge Trail** to the top of the island, where there is an unimpeded panoramic view. Another walk winds around to **Camp Reynolds,** which features the remains of a military garrison, including an old schoolhouse and several pre-Civil War officers' homes. A third walk goes to **Point Blunt,** once a dueling ground and site of a famous brothel.

tubs are essential ily vity for ny Marin inty dents.

North to Mill Valley

In getting around Marin County by car, the thing to remember is that U.S. Highway 101, onto which the Golden Gate Bridge debouches, is the north-south spinal cord which ties all communities together. With rare exceptions, off-ramps aand feeder roads are well marked, and most destinations are easy to find.

Heading north from Sausalito, one passes on the left **Marin City,** the nearest thing the county has to a ghetto. The well-kept barracks-like buildings were raised in World War II as housing for shipyard workers. Today they have been renovated as low-income public housing, and their inhabitants are predominantly Black.

Close to Marin City is a giant open-air **flea market** where hundreds of small-change entrepreneurs haggle and dicker with buyers over what they claim will be the best deal those buyers will ever make. The market, open every weekend in good weather, offers an array of merchandise ranging from outright junk to the occasional bargain.

Clinging to the southeastern slope of

Mount Tamalpais, just a few miles north of Sausalito, is the charming town of **Mill Valley.** This community is frequently cited for its Old World charm, secreted just beyond the supermarkets and shopping centers. **Throckmorton Street** comprises the heart of town, and a couple of blocks are all that casual visitors will really want to see, save for those who enjoy peering at the rustic homes hidden among serpentine lanes.

Mill Valley is an ideal base for day excursions to Mount Tam, as the peak rising above the town is best known. Many Mill Valley visitors head first to the **Book Depot,** a renovated railroad station, where they study Freese maps (bound in distinctive orange covers) of the mountain while sipping cups of expresso. Later, returning footsore and weary from the mountain, they may check into the **Physical Therapy Center** on Throckmorton Street for a hot-tub, sauna and hour-long massage treatment. The masseuse accommodates desires for Swedish or Esalen-style massages, but reservations must be made. And after the massage, the town boasts several outstanding restaurants. Alternatively, the **Mill Valley Market,** despite its unpretentious name, features a full line of gourmet foods, bakery goods and excellent wines. On a balmy evening, a visit to the market and a picnic at **Old Mill Park** might be in order.

Mount Tamalpais

Mount Tamalpais is a hiker's nirvana. This mountain, often called the "Sleeping Maiden" because of several voluptuous bumps on her ridgeline, contains 30 miles (48 kilometers) of trails within 6,000 acres (2,430 hectares) and many more miles of hiking in the contiguous watershed lands. On Mount Tam's lower elevations, often shrouded in fog, are stands of virgin redwood. Above, the mountain's chaparral-covered high slopes jut proudly into the sunshine, overlooking San Francisco Bay and the Pacific Ocean.

One of the redwood stands at the base of Mount Tam is not only dark and quiet; it is world renowned. This is the **Muir Woods National Monument.** At the turn of the 20th Century, a not-very-farsighted Marin water district planned to condemn a property called Redwood Canyon, cut the timber on it, and with

Summit winds a the spar meadow Mount Tamalpa

the profits build a dam and reservoir. This scheme so appalled one wealthy Marinite named William Kent that he peeled off a layer of his own bankroll to buy the land. Then, using the provisions of a then-obscure federal law, he deeded the redwood stand to the government as a national monument. President Theodore Roosevelt thought the woods should be named after its benefactor; but Kent modestly declined, giving the honor instead to his old friend, Sierra trekker and naturalist John Muir.

Thus Muir Woods, almost 300 acres (120 hectares) of unrivaled arboreal beauty, came into the public domain. Here the mighty sequoias grow to 200 feet (61 meters) in height, 16 feet (five meters) in diameter, and live to 1,000 years in age. About 1 million visitors a year amble through these rows of giants. Energetic walkers can leave the crowds behind by heading up the steep slope of Mount Tam on the **Ben Johnson Trail,** through deeply shaded glens rife with ferns and mushrooms, past ever-changing groves of bay, tan oaks, madrona and nutmeg.

Possibly the best hike on Mount Tam begins at the **Mountain Home Inn** on Panoramic Highway. It loops around by way of the **Matt Davis Trail** to the **West Point Inn,** a hikers' way station that offers coffee, tea and lemonade on a shady veranda looking across the Bay. A few miles further, along a fire trail, is the 5,000-seat **Mountain Theater,** a Greek amphitheater constructed from rough-hewn stone during the Depression era by Civilian Conservation Corps workers. It is now used for an annual play and for myriad weddings. Another recommended hike is the **Cataract Trail,** which begins from **Rock Springs,** near the Mountain Theater on Southside Road, and proceeds through the Marin Municipal Water District watershed to **Alpine Lake,** a pristine trout habitat. This trail, sidewinding downhill through jewel-like pools, is a great treat but is very steep.

Mount Tam's finest view is best appreciated from the pinnacle of **East Peak.** According to some accounts, on a clear day one can see 80 towns in 20 countries with the unaided eye.

Beyond Mount Tam, Marin County's green belt extends some 50 miles (80 km) to the distant tip of Point Reyes

National Seashore. The coastal country, known as the **Marin Headlands,** offers so many possibilities for walkers that — according to veteran hiker and outdoor writer Margaret Patterson Doss — they could not be exhausted in a lifetime.

Marin Headlands

The Marin Headlands were spared the usual rampant development more or less by accident. In 1850, they came under the protective wing of the Coastal Fortification Act which caused heavy cannon to be implanted to protect the shores from invading fleets that never arrived. By the time the Army relinquished its stubborn grasp in 1972, the conservation movement was wide awake and at the height of its puissance. Would-be developers were thwarted by the creation of the **Golden Gate National Recreation Area.** Now the conscious policy for the headlands and the national seashore is that they will remain forever under-used. In other words, they will remain mostly closed to vehicle traffic. The visitor who wishes to absorb the essence of this remarkable conservation coup will have to do it on foot.

For the non-ambulatory, stellar views can be had by driving up the **Fort Baker Road** which once led to Nike missile sites. To get there, northbound drivers must turn right off U.S. 101 at the Alexander Avenue off-ramp, cut back under the freeway, through a tunnel, then turn right up the mountain. From any of several outlooks, the city of San Francisco spreads out across the channel.

It's a two-mile jaunt to **Kirby Beach,** just below the remains of fortifications left from the Spanish-American War period. Further along the tortuous Fort Baker Road is **Chronkhite Beach** on **Rodeo Lagoon.** this rugged and often misty locale is favored by sunbathers (during appropriate conditions), bird voyeurs (who find the marshes teeming with avian life) and beachcombers (searching for wave-tumbled agate and other stony baubles).

San Rafael and West Marin

North of Mill Valley on U.S. 101 is **San Rafael,** the Marin County seat of government. There is little to interest the casual visitor here, with the possible exception of some of the architecture.

Left, Stins Beach Sta Park. Rig Point Bon lighthouse Golden G National Recreation Area.

134

In addition to fine pioneer mansions, San Rafael is the location of Frank Lloyd Wright's last great architectural achievement before his death — the **Marin County Civic Center.** The structure was designed to connect three isolated hillcrests with a series of gracefully moving arches. Buff in color, with a lick of blue on the roof, the center gives the appearance of a rail bridge leading up to a roundhouse, with a pagoda sticking out of the middle. The effect for many is reminiscent of the Nanking train station.

West of San Rafael, the landscape is gently rolling pasture that has changed little in 150 years. Undulating country lanes pass dairy farms nestled in verdant valleys. This is superb bicycling country; the ride from Novato to Tomales, for instance, has enough hills to make it an enjoyable workout.

By automobile, the most interesting drive follows **Sir Francis Drake Boulevard** west from U.S. 101 near Kentfield. A chain of rich Marin towns eventually lures the traveler to a rugged coastline almost as majestic as Big Sur.

The town of **Kentfield** is standard upper-middle class. **Ross,** the next in

line going west, is a bastion of exclusivity and wealth. The road narrows at this point to two lanes, Ross 'city fathers having refused to widen it for fear of encouraging even more traffic to pass through their reserve. Next come the little communities of **San Geronimo, Forest Knoll** and **Lagunitas,** once hideouts for a counterculture which has now been mostly priced out. Also along the route is **Samuel P. Taylor State Park** in the midst of a redwood grove. Reservations for overnight camping must be made through Ticketron.

Muir and Stinson beaches, at the foot of Mount Tamalpais, are popular among anglers hoping to hook surf perch and rockfish, and among birdwatchers who want to spy such out-of-the-way creatures as the sooty shearwater, brown pelican, Western grebe, killdeer and millet. When the fog pulls back, the beaches also attract sunbathers. They get crowded only when sweltering weather inland drives tract-home lemmings toward the sea.

Near the coast, Sir Francis Drake Boulevard hits State Highway 1 at **Olema.** A left turn here leads around

e beach,
n County
st.

the shoulder of **Bolinas Lagoon,** a 1,000-acre (405-hectare) nature preserve that is one of the least disturbed of the tidelands and a seafood deli for blue herons, great egrets and many species of ducks. The herons and egrets nest in a rookery at the nearby **Audubon Canyon Ranch,** where a special observatory lets bird watchers telescope in on mating and nesting birds. Hikers who base themselves at the ranch may also see owls, foxes, raccoons, bobcats and various deer. There is also a permanent colony of harbor seals at Bolinas Lagoon: they use Kent and Picklewood islands for their pupping and whelping.

The town of **Bolinas** itself is full of quirky xenophobic types who guard their privacy so jealously that road signs pointing the way to their hamlet disappear as fast as they're erected. Although it's a quaint seaside town, there is little of interest to visitors.

Nearby, however, is another "must-see" for the birdwatcher. The **Point Reyes Bird Observatory,** open year round, hosts a resident group of ornithologists specializing in the study of birds' migratory and breeding habits.

To reach the observatory, travelers must turn west off State 1 onto the Olema-Bolinas Road, then right on Mesa Road.

A left turn from this thoroughfare onto Overview Road takes wayfarers to **Duxbury Reef,** often described as a living maritime laboratory. At low tide, the pools squirm with sea anemones, periwinkles, snails, starfish and sea urchins. Friends of the Barnacle, or some other such environmentalist group, have been known to tear up road signs to discourage visitors. Of course, no specimen collecting is permitted in the tidepools.

A little further down Mesa Road from the Duxbury Reef turnoff is the **Palomarin Trailhead,** step-off point for an incredible hike through the southern portion of **Point Reyes National Seashore.** A necklace of six lakes is strung along the trail; three of the lakes, Pelican, Bass and Crystal, are within easy striking distance of the trailhead.

Windswept Point Reyes

Point Reyes is a triangular peninsula separated from the rest of the world by

Fruit-drink vendors Renaissa Faire ne Novato.

the main fissure line of the San Andreas Fault. Geologists say the fault is prying Point Reyes gradually northeastward at an average rate of two inches (five centimeters) a year. The epicenter of the 1906 San Francisco earthquake was a half-mile from where the main park headquarters now stand on Bear Valley Road. On **Earthquake Trail,** visitors can see where the quake moved one stone fence 15 feet (4½ meters).

To get to the park headquarters and most of the trailheads in the National Seashore, drivers proceed up State 1 past the town of Olema to Bear Valley Road. Somehow this wild, foggy, windswept region escaped most of the depradations of man, and the seashore's 65,000 acres (26,300 hectares) remain more-or-less untouched. The parkland is open only to those who are willing to walk or ride a horse. The terrain is varied; much of it is steep. Gloomy forests suddenly open on sweeping meadows. The coast is rockbound with occasional pocket beaches. From atop wind-whipped **Mount Wittenburg** there is another beautiful view. There are three overnight campgrounds in the park for backpackers.

Near the National Seashore Park headquarters is a reconstruction of a **Miwok Indian village.** The round dugout shelters, roofed over with mud-plastered branches, are said to represent the homes of these gentle hunters and gatherers prior to their obliteration by Europeans.

At the tip of the Point Reyes promontory perches a **lighthouse** which warns ships away from the treacherous coast. Before the light began blinking in 1870, more than 100 vessels sank to the bottom of the sea while feeling through the dense fog for the Golden Gate. This is one of the foggiest places in Marin County, and consequently, there is usually no view at all. When there is a view, it is a good place from which to spot migrating whales.

On the northern edge of the national seashore, Pierce Point Road meanders around to several beaches — **Abbott's, Kehoe,** and the most ruggedly dramatic, **McClure's.** These beaches are not recommended for swimming because of the danger of sharks, undertow and rip tides. **Drake's Beach,** on the southern side of the promontory, is somewhat protected from winds.

ses, left,
water
ds, right,
homes
Point
yes
tional
ashore.

THE CALIFORNIA WINE COUNTRY

Standing on the summit of **Mount St. Helena**, which dominates the Wine Country counties of Napa, Sonoma, Mendocino and Lake, a vast panorama stretches for mile after mile below one's feet.

There are the Napa Valley's emerald vineyards, crystal Lake Berryessa, the Sonoma Valley and Jack London's beloved Valley of the Moon, where oak trees dot grassy hills the color of champagne. To the west, the vast Santa Rosa Plain unfurls until cut off by Sebastopol's apple orchards and the redwood groves of the Russian River. The river's great horseshoe bend tacks up to the Alexander Valley's vineyards. Northward, the burgundy-hued Mendocino ridges guard the inland valleys from cool sea breezes. To the east, the sun glints off the waters of Clear Lake. South lies San Francisco.

Volcanic action created Mount St. Helena, the tallest of all Bay Area peaks at 4,343 feet (1,324 meters). (It is not to be confused with Washington state's Mount St. Helens, a very active volcano.) The volcanic legacy is a land of mineral springs, mud baths and basalt to build stone wineries — not to mention a spicy soil perfect for grape growing.

Those who know where to look, and who have a little imagination, can see the entire history of the Wine Country from the top of this generous mountain.

Russian princess Helena Garagin climbed Mount St. Helena, and it was thus named for her, even as the Russian River was christened after the Russian encampment of Fort Ross on the Sonoma coast. From the summit, mountain man George Yount picked his Napa Valley land grant offered by Mexican General Mariano Vallejo; Yountville marks Yount's homestead, where he planted the valley's first vineyard.

Robert Louis Stevenson honeymooned on Mount St. Helena's slopes in 1880; Spyglass Hill in *Treasure Island* is modeled after the peak.

But the real story of the area is written in fermented grape juice. California's winemaking regions run from San Diego to Humboldt counties and into the Sierra Nevada, but the state's finest premium wine grapes grow best in sculptured valleys north of San Francisco. Cabernet Sauvignon and Pinot Chardonnay, the royal couple of red and white wine grapes, thrive throughout the Wine Country. Napa is also famous for Sauvignon (Fumé) Blanc, the white grape of Bordeaux; and Johannisberg Riesling. Sonoma's specialities include Gewurztraminer, the spicy grape of Alsace; and Zinfandel, California's mystery grape now traced to Italian roots.

Little Old Winemakers

Father Jose Altimira, founder of the Mission San Francisco de Solano at Sonoma, and Gen. Vallejo, who colonized Sonoma and Napa counties with land grants to his relatives and friends, dabbled in winemaking. But it was Count Agoston Haraszthy who pushed Sonoma into wine stardom. Haraszthy, a flamboyant Hungarian political refugee, began Buena Vista, California's oldest commercial winery, in 1857. He trekked across Europe to cull wine-grape cuttings for California's growers. Ever restless, Haraszthy migrated to

ceding
jes,
eyards
round a
pa Valley
mestead.
t,
xander
lley grape
kers bring
the
vest.
ht, a
aemaker
rks in
cellars.

Nicaragua, where he was later eaten by alligators.

Charles Krug, a German political exile and protege of Haraszthy, started the Napa Valley's first commercial winery in 1861. Germans, like the Beringer Brothers and the Korbel family, dominated winemaking, while Chinese laborers dug wine cellars and built stone wineries. By the 1880s, Napa and Sonoma valley wines were winning medals in Europe.

In 1881 the Italian Swiss Colony Winery opened, drawing Italian, Swiss and French vintners who grafted Old World winemaking techniques onto America's budding new wine efforts. The long night of Prohibition almost — but not quite — destroyed the wineries; following repeal of Prohibition in 1933. Beaulieu Vineyard's Georges de Latour, the Mondavi family and others began resurrecting winemaking.

In the Sixties, a wine boom began as large corporations marketed vintage-dated varietal wines at reasonable prices, and small, privately owned wineries produced more expensive estate-bottled wines at higher costs. Old-time winemaking families were joined by oil barons, engineers, doctors and actors who revitalized old wineries and opened new ones. By the U.S. bicentennial celebration of 1976, Napa wines were beating French vintages in European tastings.

Strikingly modern wineries — Robert Mondavi, Sterling, Sonoma Vineyards — arose beside century-old stone ones. Creative spirits traded urban strife for country calm and started restaurants, country inns, small "organic" produce farms or shops selling hand-made furniture and pottery.

Crushing and Fermenting

In the spring, the vineyards glow yellow with wild mustard blooms; the grape leaves appear in April. In dusty summer, the vines leaf out with insignificant grape flowers. Dry, moderately warm weather is needed for grapes to mature properly.

Autumn brings the grape harvest, when the air hangs heavy with the scent of crushed fruit. Grape leaves turn scarlet, gold and purple, creating miniature forests of fall colors. Winter rains between November and March provide

19th Cen winemakii "At Work the Wine Presses," P. Frenze

142

the dormancy grape vines need. Vines are pruned to force remaining branches to yield more fruit. One vine can produce one-third of a case of wine.

Wines begin at the crusher, where the juice is freed from the grapes. Red wines are born when the grape skin and pulp go into the fermenting tank; yeast is added to convert sugar to alcohol and carbon dioxide. Grape skins are pressed to extract more juice, then the reds are aged in stainless steel or wooden tanks. The wine is clarified, then aged further before bottling.

White wines are made from the fermentation of the juice alone, drawn off from the grapes immediately after crushing. Yeast is added, and fermentation occurs in stainless steel tanks. Leaving the yeast creates dry wines; stopping the yeast action makes sweeter wines. Champagne, or sparkling wine, begins the same way, then undergoes a second fermentation. The carbon dioxide is trapped within the bottle, hence the bubbles.

Vintages mean less in California than in Europe, thanks to the state's relatively benign climate. For red wine varieties — Cabernet Sauvignon, Pinot Noir, Zinfandel — 1974, 1978 and 1980 were good years. For white wine varieties — Chardonnay, Chenin Blanc, Riesling — 1975, 1977 and 1980 were good years.

Winery visits should be limited to three a day. Most wineries are open between 10 a.m. and 4 p.m. daily. It is a good idea to try a tour (usually one-half hour) and tasting at a large winery, coupled with tasting-room stops at smaller wineries. Many wineries are open by appointment only; for a full list, oenophiles can send a self-addressed, stamped (37-cent) envelope for "California's Wine Wonderland," Wine Institute, 165 Post St., San Francisco, CA 94108.

For those who want to romp across the Wine Country in a Mercedes or doubled-decked London-style bus, imbibe at private sippings, or dine with a favorite vintner, wine-touring services such as California Wine Tours, Sonoma-California Touring or Wine Tours International are available.

Napa County

The **Napa Valley** (*napa* means "plenty" in the local Indian dialect) is compact — wineries, delis, restaurants and country inns lie close together. Although rural, the country's mix of San Francisco socialites, titled Europeans, semi-retired Hollywood screenwriters and producers gives Napa County a genteel, if sometimes slick, aura.

A 30-mile (48-kilometer) thrust of flatland between the pine-forested **Mayacamas Mountains** and the buff-colored **Howell Mountains**, the Napa Valley is pinched off in the north by Mount St. Helena. The valley evokes an ordered, European air, with expanses of vineyards broken by farmhouses, stone wineries and a series of towns spaced along State Highway 29, **"The Great Wine Way."** Strict land-control measures have kept valley development confined to the towns and the freeway south of Yountville, but have also escalated land prices.

A pioneer's description of **Napa** city in 1849 noted "there wasn't any such place. The name had got there somehow, but the city hadn't." Today's Napa, the county seat, isn't a wine town, but it has the county's greatest variety of family-oriented restaurants and lodging, a harvest of Victorian homes, Napa River picnicking and boating sites at **J.F. Kennedy Park**, and sourdough bread at **Sciambra French Bakery.**

South of Napa, the **Carneros Creek Winery** features Chardonnay and Pinot Noir from early-ripening grapes of this fog-cooled region. North of town, **Trefethen Vineyards**, housed in historic **Eshcol Winery**, is noted for Chardonnay and Cabernet Sauvignon. It is open by appointment.

The Wine Country begins in earnest at **Yountville**, for the vineyards abut the village's historic, renovated brick and stone buildings. Yountville's city-park picnic stop is across from George Yount's grave at the pioneer cemetery. Yount got his 11,000-acre (4,450-hectare) Mexican land grant for roofing Gen. Vallejo's Petaluma Adobe, surely one of history's best contracting deals.

Domaine Chandon Winery, next to the California Veterans Home, is French throughout; in deference to Gallic sensibilities, the champagne is called sparkling wine. The winery, owned by Moet and Chandon, makes sparkling wine in the *methode champenoise*; that is, it is fermented in the same bottle from which it is poured.

Adventures can take an early morning hot-air balloon sweep above the vineyards, followed by a champagne picnic. Most flights leave from Yountville. A one-hour flight costs $95 to $110 per person. Four balloon companies operate in the valley; among them is **Adventures Aloft** (Vintage 1870 complex), which has bicycle and moped rentals, too.

Oakville and Rutherford

Within shouting distance north of Yountville are the twin towns of **Oakville** and **Rutherford**. Cabernet Sauvignons from this region are among the world's best. The turf compares to Bordeaux or Burgundy; many of the valley's top vineyards flourish here, including Joe Heitz' **Martha's Vineyard**.

Robert Mondavi, the vigorous promoter of Napa Valley wines, erected his Cliff May-designed, Spanish-style winery in 1966, filled it with the latest equipment, and now makes outstanding Fumé Blanc, Cabernet Sauvignon and Chardonnay. **Mondavi's** newest venture is a Bordeaux-style Cabernet Sauvignon jointly made with Baron Philippe de Rothschild of Chateau Mouton-Rothschild. Educational winery tours start in the vineyards. In summer, there are Sunday afternoon jazz concerts on the lawn.

The ivy-covered **Inglenook Winery**, founded in 1882 by a Finnish sea captain, is seldom crowded. The tasting room is serene; wines sold under Inglenook and Navalle labels include rarely produced Charbono, a tart red wine.

Informative tours at **Beaulieu** ("Bowl-u" or BV) **Vineyards** highlight their Cabernet Sauvignon, French founder Georges de Latour, and Russian-born, French-trained former winemaker André Tchelistcheff, who pushed post-Prohibition Napa Valley to international fame. Rutherford's eastern hills holds **Auberge du Soleil**, perhaps the most famous restaurant in the valley.

Chardonnay lovers stop at **Grgich Hills Cellars** to taste the team efforts of Croatian-born Mike Grgich and Austin Hills (of the Hills Brothers coffee family). Modern **Franciscan Vineyards'** spacious tasting room and optional tour make it a fine day's-end wine-tasting stop for Chardonnay, Charbono and sparkling wines. Reservations must be

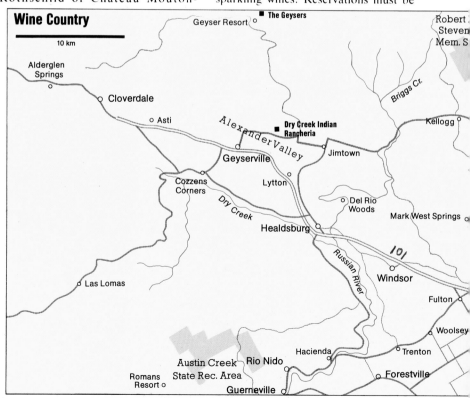

Wine Country

10 km

Geyser Resort   ■ The Geysers

Robert. Steven Mem. S

Alderglen Springs

Cloverdale

Asti

Alexander Valley

■ Dry Creek Indian Rancheria

Kellogg

Geyserville

Jimtown

Cozzens Corners

Lytton

Dry Creek

Del Rio Woods

Mark West Springs

Healdsburg

Russian River

101

Windsor

Las Lomas

Fulton

Woolsey

Hacienda

Trenton

Austin Creek State Rec. Area

Rio Nido

Forestville

Romans Resort

Guerneville

↑ Mustards

inery's sum-
tings of their

trio of fami-
thin walking
— **V. Sattui**
Sutter Home
century ago
in San Francisco; today it offers a tasting room, deli and shady picnic area.
Across State 29 is **Ernie's Wine Ware-**
house, where local vintages càn be compared with the best of Bordeaux. Informal Heitz Cellars has some of Heitz'
prized Cabernet Sauvignon for sale; tast-
ers sip the less expensive wines. Sutter
Home Winery's Zinfandel comes from
Sierra Nevada grapes, offered in a
wooden winery building that's the oldest left in the valley.

The 40 Wineries of St. Helena

St. Helena, the Wine Country's capital, is noted for its 40 wineries, historic
stone buildings, picnic parks, chic
shops, pricey restaurants, country inns
and low crime rate. The **Silverado**
Museum is stuffed with Robert Louis
Stevenson memorabilia — first editions

of his work and souvenirs of his global
jaunts.

South of town, the **Martini Winery**,
run by one of the valley's oldest winemaking clans, offers reasonably priced
wines (Cabernet Sauvignon to sherry)
in an unpretentious setting. Wine and
soap mix at **Spring Mountain**
Vineyards, planted in the hill country
west of St. Helena. CBS' *Falcon Crest*
soap opera is filmed at the winery's
Miravalle mansion, built in 1885 by
playboy Tiburcio Parrott.

A trinity of giant wineries — **Berin-**
ger, **Christian Brothers** and **Charles**
Krug — lie north of St. Helena. Jacob
and Frederick Beringer started their
winery in 1876, modeling the Rhine
House (1883) after their ancestral manse
in Mainz, Germany. They dug limestone caves for aging wine. Today's winery, owned by Nestlé (yes, the chocolate people) features Fumé Blanc and
Cabernet Sauvignon in the mansion
tasting room, spacious lawns and a regal
row of elms fronting the winery.

Christian Brothers' Greystone winery
building was the world's largest stone
winery when erected in 1889 by mining
magnate William Bourn. This white-

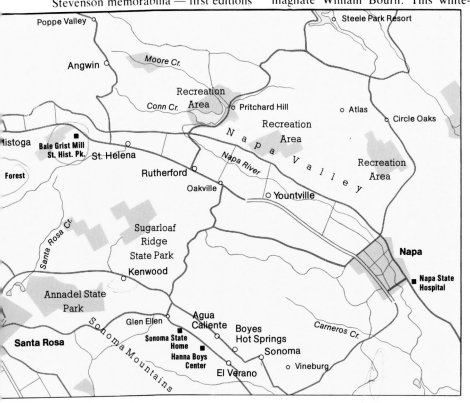

elephant winery changed hands frequently until the Christian Brothers, a Catholic educational order, bought it in 1950. The tour is informal; the tasting room elegant.

Founding father Charles Krug sired Napa's wine industry when he lugged a cider press from Sonoma to squeeze grapes. Today's winery building dates from 1874. Owners Peter Mondavi and sons have an informative, traditional tour, with tastings of Krug and C.K. Mondavi label wines, including Cabernet Sauvignon and Chenin Blanc. Krug's August Moon Concerts present classical productions on the lawn.

Two miles north of St. Helena is **Freemark Abbey**, a winery, restaurant and shopping place. There's no abbey here; the name is an amalgamation of the owners' names. The once-a-day tours are small, a welcome change from larger wineries. The better wines include Chardonnay, Cabernet Sauvignon and Edelwein, a late-harvest Johannisberg Riesling. At the nearby **Hurd Beesway Candle Factory**, visitors can watch candle-making from dripping to scenting.

Three miles north of St. Helena is the **Bale Grist Mill State Historic Park**. The mill, built in 1846 by Dr. Edward Bale (Gen. Vallejo's physician and Charles Krug's father-in-law), recalls the days when the Napa Valley was planted chiefly in wheat. Bale's *Rancho Carne Humana* ("Ranch of Human Flesh") was named when Bale misunderstood the Indian words for the area.

Two champagne cellars, **Hanns Kornell** and **Schramsberg**, are close to **Bothe-Napa Valley State Park**. Kornell, a refugee from Nazi Germany, resurrected a historic stone winery to make his German-style *methode champenoise* champagnes. His speciality is Sehr Troken, a dry variety. Tours are excellent. Schramsberg, open by appointment, is almost unchanged from the day when Jacob Schram invited Robert Louis Stevenson into the cool champagne cellars to taste 18 different vintages of wine.

Sterling Vineyards — part-Greek monastery, part-fantasy — reigns over the upper valley atop a knoll. For a fee, a tram whisks visitors 300 feet (91 meters) up for a self-guided tour. The tram fee is applicable toward purchase

Beringe
Brothei
Winery
St. He
left, the
Rhine l
and rig
winetas

146

of Cabernet Sauvignon, Sauvignon Blanc and other wines.

Calistoga to Lake Berryessa

Unwanted side effects of the Wine Country's *dolce vita* can be doused or steamed away with **Calistoga** water or the mineral and mud baths of this long-standing resort town eight miles (13 km) northwest of St. Helena.

Sam Brannan, the merry Mormon who started the burg, felt the town's spas could outrival New York's Saratoga. At a banquet, Brannan mistoasted the town, calling it "the Calistoga of Sarafornia." The name stuck. A Calistoga mud bath starts with a soak in a mixture of gritty, warm volcanic ash, peat moss and mineral water; this is followed by a mineral-water bath, sauna and blanket wrap. Massages are optional.

A quick walk about town reveals a kaleidoscope of onion-domed Russian churches, the **Sharpsteen Museum** with dioramas of pioneer Calistoga, Sam Brannan's gingerbread-trimmed cottage, and shopping in the **Calistoga Depot** (1868), California's oldest re-

maining railroad depot. It's also possible to sail over the valley in a glider propelled by swirling winds swept off Mount St. Helena, courtesy of the **Calistoga Sailing Center.** A short glide for two costs $42. A **geyser** on Tubbs Lane spews heated mineral water 60 feet (18 meters) skyward about every 40 minutes.

Visitors can reserve a formal Chinese garden for a picnic at **Chateau Montelena**, a revived century-old winery making Chardonnay and Cabernet Sauvignon. Robert Louis Stevenson started his marriage, restored his health, and seriously began his literary career in a miner's cabin on Mount St. Helena's slopes, now encompassed as the **Robert Louis Stevenson State Park.**

The Silverado Trail

The **Silverado Trail** parallels State 29 between Napa and Calistoga, then joins with the highway as the route into Lake County's resort and wine region. Built as the road from Mount St. Helena's cinnabar mines to Napa's river docks, today's Silverado Trail is an elevated, two-lane road above the valley floor offering motorists and bicyclists vistas, uncrowded wineries (most with picnic tables) and hidden valleys in the Howell Mountains.

South from Calistoga, **Cuvaison Winery** is a good stop for Zinfandel. Deer Park Road leads to **Angwin**, a Seventh-Day Adventist community built around **Pacific Union College**, with a hearty selection of natural foods at the **College Market.**

A popular stop is **Rutherford Hill Winery**, an ark-like structure with picnic grounds and Chardonnay, Cabernet Sauvignon and Zinfandel wines. **Stag's Leap**, a rocky promontory where a 16-point Roosevelt elk plunged to its death, overlooks **Stag's Leap Wine Cellars** and **Clos du Val Wine Company.** Stag's Leap winemaker Warren Winiarski made the French jump when his 1973 Cabernet Sauvignon took first place over Bordeaux wines in a 1976 European judging.

The tragedy-ridden Berryessa family lost sons and soil in the Mexican War; today their Napa County land grant is a warm-water nirvana. **Lake Berryessa** can be reached via State 128 from St. Helena or State 121 from Napa. Fishermen can pull in trout, bass and catfish aboard a rented houseboat. Sailors, waterskiers, campers and swimmers have their choice of seven resorts around this lake, which has more shoreline than Lake Tahoe.

Lake County

New, bold and friendly, **Lake County's** visitor-seeking wineries are scattered along State 29 as it wraps around **Clear Lake**, California's largest natural lake. (Lake Tahoe lies partly in Nevada). Besides producing Cabernet Sauvignon, Zinfandel and Sauvignon Blanc grapes, Lake County is famous for Bartlett pears and walnuts.

The first stop for travelers northbound from Napa County is **Guenoc Winery**, on Butts Canyon Road near **Middletown**. This reborn winery once was owned by British actress Lillie Langtry, companion to the Prince of Wales, later King Edward VII. Langtry started the winery to gain California residency for a divorce to remarry an attentive lover housed on a nearby ranch.

Kelseyville's orchard country surrounds **Konocti Winery**, where one can imbibe Cabernet Sauvignon or Johannisberg Riesling while toe-tapping to bluegrass music on Sunday afternoons. Konocti puts on a Fall Harvest Festival every October.

Clear Lake's alpine, sun-warmed waters attract bass and catfish fishermen, waterskiers, boaters and swimmers. Resorts ring the lake; or campers can pitch a tent in **Clear Lake State Park** at the foot of conical **Mount Konocti**, an extinct volcano. **Konocti Harbor Inn's** marina rents boats, and the *Konocti Princess* riverboat offers frequent trips, including moonlight cruises in summer.

Sonoma County

Sonoma is not one place, but many. It is a patchwork of country roads, towns, orchards, ridges and hills. U.S. 101, the Wine Country's only freeway, traverses the north-south length of **Sonoma County**, entering the county near **Petaluma**. There, travelers can pick up Camembert or Brie at the **Marin French Cheese Factory** or see Gen. Vallejo's **Petaluma Adobe**, the state's grandest *hacienda*. The freeway runs through Santa Rosa, Healdsburg (gateway to the Alexander, Dry Creek and Russian River valleys),

and Cloverdale on the Mendocino County border.

Sonoma's population is also diverse — Bay Area commuters in the south of the county, gays and counterculture people along the Russian River, retirees in the Sonoma Valley, plus a smattering of ranchers and farmers.

The **Sonoma Valley** is steeped in wine, literary and political history. *Sonoma* is a Patwin Indian word meaning "land of Chief Nose" after an Indian leader with a prominent proboscis. Gen. Vallejo romanticized it as the "Valley of the Moon" and author Jack London took up the call with a book of the same title about frazzled urbanites rejuvenated by clean country living. State 12 runs the length of the valley, passing through the towns of Sonoma and Kenwood. Glen Ellen, Jack London's old haunt, lies off State 12.

Father Altimira founded California's last mission, **San Francisco de Solano**, in 1823. Vallejo set up the town in 1835, making **Sonoma** the northernmost outpost of a Catholic Spanish-speaking realm that, at its peak, extended all the way to the tip of South America.

On June 14, 1846, a ragtag American

Cablecar at the Sterling Winery, Calistoga

group staged the Bear Flag Revolt by storming Vallejo's Sonoma home. The Americans set up the California Republic and made a crude banner with a bear that the Mexicans derided as looking like a pig. This one-flag, one-month republic was soon replaced by the American government; the Bear Flag is today California's state flag. Count Haraszthy's winemaking innovations at **Buena Vista Winery** a decade later forced Californians to recognize the state's vinicultural potential.

The **Sonoma Plaza**, largest in California, today dominates the town. Several restored adobes and the **Sonoma State Historic Park** — Mission San Francisco de Solano, the **Sonoma Barracks** and General Vallejo's home — ring the Plaza and nearby streets.

Sandwiched among this history are enough culinary stops to put the town on the Weight Watchers hit list. Jack cheese, California's only native cheese, can be sampled at the **Sonoma Cheese Factory**, a good picnic supply stop. **Vella Cheese Company** is just off the Plaza, while the scent of sourdough bread lures passers-by inside the **Sonoma French Bakery**. More than 60 sausage

varieties fill the counters of the **Sonoma Sausage Factory**. Every September, there's a harvest festival at the Plaza.

Two blocks from the Plaza stand **Sebastiani Vineyards**. Some of these vineyards date from mission days; Sam Sebastiani is the third generation to run the winery.

East of Sonoma, **Hacienda Wine Cellars** and Buena Vista Winery both are connected with Haraszthy. Hacienda's vineyards contain the count's plantings; today he might recommend the Hacienda Gewurztraminer, Cabernet Sauvignon or Chardonnay. Culture buffs can pick up tickets at the winery for Buena Vista's summer classical concert series.

The Gundlach and Bundschu families have been involved in winemaking for over 125 years; **Gundlach-Bundschu Wine Cellars'** Zinfandel, Cabernet Sauvignon and Merlot are especially good.

Nearby, the super-expensive, beautifully decorated **Sonoma Mission Inn and Spa** offers elegant exercise and tasty meals.

"I would rather be ashes than dust," Jack London told a reporter only two months before his death at age 40. London's "fast-lane" living, from worldwide romps to his 1,000-word daily writing output, took its toll. London's storybook cottage, where he wrote many of his 51 books; the ruins of his arson-destroyed **Wolf House**; his grave; and the museum of memorabilia inside his widow's home are part of the **Jack London State Historic Park**. The surroundings, high in the **Sonoma Mountains**, form an invigorating mixture of history, picnicking spots and hiking trails. The **Glen Ellen** exit off State 12 leads to the park.

The **Valley of the Moon Winery** occupies part of Senator George Hearst's 19th Century vineyards. Today those vineyards produce a fine Zinfandel. **Grand Cru Vineyards**, a tiny, tucked-away winery born during the wine boom of the Sixties and Seventies, has picnic sites plus fine Gewurztraminer and Chenin Blanc.

Near Glen Ellen is **Beltane Ranch**, today a bed-and-breakfast inn. It was once owned by Mammy Pleasant, a former slave who held sway in 19th Century San Francisco with voodoo and anti-racist activities

North on State 12, visitors come to two wineries in **Kenwood**, and an old

; the er": the rser at istoga.

resort town with outdoor mineral-spring pools at **Morton's Warm Springs**. Small, friendly **Kenwood Winery** features Zinfandel, Cabernet Sauvignon and Chenin Blanc. Chardonnay lovers head for **Chateau St. Jean** with its pseudo-medieval tower and fine Johannisberg Riesling.

Famed botanist Luther Burbank picked **Santa Rosa** as "the chosen spot of all the earth" to create his plant experiments. He developed more than 800 new plants, including myriads of fruits, vegetables and flowers, yet relished few of them except asparagus. Today visitors can tour his home (in summer) and gardens (all year) in the heart of Santa Rosa.

An unfinished freeway, State 12 bisects Santa Rosa, the county seat and Wine Country's largest city (population 83,000), with a wide selection of reasonably priced motels and restaurants. Santa Rosa's trinity of adjoining parks form a 5,000-acre (12,000-hectare) urban oasis with a children's amusement park and lake in **Howarth Park**; camping, picnicking and boating in **Spring Lake Park**; and hiking and equestrian trails in **Annadel State Park.**

Northern Sonoma Wine Country

U.S. 101's four-lane, 32-mile (51-km) stretch between Santa Rosa and Cloverdale whisks travelers past several large roadside wineries and numerous small, family-operated wineries. Side trips into the Alexander, Dry Creek and Russian River valleys reward wayfarers with more wineries amid rolling hills and forests, bike paths and Russian River resorts.

Sonoma Vineyards (Windsor Winery) wines and **Piper Sonoma Cellars'** sparkling wines lie just a cork-pop away from each other. Sonoma Vineyard's cruciform structure holds a tasting room with a rich wine roster, including Cabernet Sauvignon and Chardonnay. Outdoor summer concerts are held in the winery's Greek Theatre. Piper Sonoma Cellars, the creation of Sonoma Vineyards' winemaker Rodney Strong in conjunction with Piper-Heidsieck, French champagne makers, pours Brut and Blanc de Noir in the spacious tasting room.

Healdsburg, 16 miles (26 km) north of Santa Rosa, is a Russian River town centered around a small plaza where,

Bicyclists relax by Silverado Trail.

each May, visitors can sample local wine, food and entertainment at the Russian River Wine Festival. **Madrona Manor**, a renovated Victorian mansion, has lodging plus a dining room featuring dishes culled from local produce and meats.

Just beyond the hamlet of **Geyserville** is **Geyser Peak**, one of the Wine Country's oldest and largest wineries. The Trione family, new owners, make Gewurztraminer and Cabernet Sauvignon with Geyser Peak and Summit labels. **Pedroncelli Winery**, on Canyon Road, is an informal stop for low-priced red and white wines.

Fun-lovers dress in costume, make their own movies, or indulge in parties and sports at **Club Sonoma**, a "summer camp for adults" in the Geyserville hills. The nearby **Italian Swiss Colony Winery** at **Asti** is currently closed, but comedian Pat Paulsen has his winery tasting room in Asti village. **Cloverdale's** informal wineries include **Bandiera's** roadside tasting room and **Cordtz Brothers Cellars'** picnic tables under ancient oak trees.

Mountain man Cyrus Alexander left his name to the spacious **Alexander Val-**

ley that produces nearly one-half of Sonoma County's wine grapes. The soil, deposited by the Russian River, produces Cabernet Sauvignon, Chardonnay, Zinfandel, Gewurztraminer and Riesling grapes. State 128 leads through the valley.

Dry Creek Valley, Sonoma County's most rural wine valley, is noted for Zinfandel. Two places to try it are David Stare's **Dry Creek Vineyards** and **Lytton Springs Winery.**

For generations, the lower **Russian River**, or (simply) "The River," has meant rocky beaches, swimming, canoeing, fishing and cavorting beneath the redwoods, with nary a passing glance at wineries, except for **Korbel**. But the Russian River Valley, between Healdsburg and **Guerneville**, today is home to a half-dozen new wineries.

There are several routes to the Russian River resort region, centered around Guerneville. The River Road exit off U.S. 101 north of Santa Rosa winds past **Mark West Vineyards**, a haven for white wine lovers. Stalwart Korbel, America's largest producer of *methode champenoise* champagne, with its ivy-covered brick walls and lush garden, is an idyllic spot to learn about champagne making. The Bohemia-born Korbels raised tobacco, published a magazine and logged redwoods before settling down to make their sparkling wine.

Many of the river's resorts eater to gays, although a number of family-oriented resorts are found also. **Fife's, The Woods** and **The River Village** are the more popular gay resorts, while **Northwood** and **Southside Resort** welcome families. Guerneville's **Johnson's Beach** is like an old swimming hole back home, except for rental canoes and a concession stand. There are hiking, camping and horseback riding in the **Armstrong Redwood State Reserve's** virgin redwood forest or the grassy hills of **Austin Creek State Recreation Area.**

State 116 runs between Guerneville and **Sebastopol**. A good midpoint stop is the **Russian River Vineyards**, a winery-restaurant known for Chardonnay. **Iron Horse Vineyards**, open by appointment, also makes noted Chardonnay.

Westside Road, a curvy, scenic route between Guerneville and Healdsburg, offers **Hop Kiln Winery**. Its red wines, such as Zinfandel and Petite Sirah, can be tasted inside the stone-and-wood

hop kiln, once used to dry hops for brewers. Close to Healdsburg is **Mill Creek Vineyards**, with a tasting room inside a reproduction of (surprise) a mill.

Mendocino County

Mad, marvelous Mendocino, with its rugged coastline and redwood groves, is thinly but diversely populated with fishermen, loggers, artisans, apple growers, marijuana farmers, innkeepers and latter-day hippies, all somehow coexisting. A score of new wineries have sprung here in the wake of the wine boom of the Seventies. The warmer **Ukiah Valley**, encompassing U.S. 101, compares to Tuscany in Italy, while the fog-cooled **Anderson Valley** resembles the Franco-German Alsace region. Mendocino's wineries are informal; many have picnic tables and shorter hours in winter.

NEVER GOT THERE '88 — Most of the wineries are located off U.S. 101 near **Hopland** and **Ukiah**, the county seat and best spot for dining and lodging. To reach the Anderson Valley, travelers must take State 128 north out

of Cloverdale. This is also a good route to the Mendocino Coast.

Hopland, named for hops once raised here for brewers, today has four wineries. **Milano Winery**, best for Zinfandel, is south of town. **Fetzer Winery** has a tasting room in **Hopland Station**, a restored schoolhouse, with a Mendocino artisans' cooperative. The Station hosts several wineland festivals, complete with country music and barbecued wild boar.

North of Ukiah stand a trio of well-established California wine names. **Cresta Blanc Winery**, born a century ago in Alameda County, features Zinfandel, sherry and sparkling wine. The **Parducci** family has been making wine in Mendocino County for three generations, almost single-handedly keeping viticulture alive in the region. Besides having the area's most instructive tour, their low-priced wine roster includes Chardonnay, Chenin Blanc and Sauvignon Blanc. Another Alameda County transplant, **Weibel Champagne Cellars**, boasts a tasting room shaped like an inverted champagne glass. Weibel's is known for Green Hungarian (a fruity white) and Brut Champagne.

Nearby is Black Bart's old haunt, the restored **Palace Hotel** in Ukiah. Bart, a genteel bandit, left poems with his victims such as this:

> *I've labored long and hard for bread*
> *For honor and for riches*
> *But on my corns too long you've tread*
> *You fine-haired sons of bitches*

Bart only robbed Wells Fargo stages, and he was eventually unmasked as Charles Bolton, San Francisco bon vivant and former Wells Fargo clerk.

Candid Indian portraits can be seen at the **Sun House**, the Ukiah home of artist Grace Hudson. There's swimming, fishing, waterskiing and camping at nearby **Lake Mendocino**.

NEVER GOT THERE EITHER

Compact, countrified Anderson Valley offers roadside apple stands, three wineries and "Bootling," a **Boonville** dialect created from English, Scotch-Irish and Indian words to confuse outsiders. Among Boonville's places for "bahl gorms" (good eats) is the excellent **Boonville Hotel**; the owners raise most of their own meat and produce, and a look at their garden is worth a special trip.

Left, roadside stop in Mendocino County. Right, enjoying Cabernet Sauvignon near Ukiah

152

SACRAMENTO, THE STATE CAPITAL

No one should get the idea that Sacramento is a city.

There are more than 1 million people living in and around Sacramento, but it's still not a city, at least not in the sense that San Francisco is a city. In fact, when Sacramentans talk about going to "the city," they mean San Francisco.

No, Sacramento is the ultimate cowtown, a nice, big, prosperous, comfortable, tree-shaded cowtown.

The town grew up where the Sacramento and American rivers join, where steamers from San Francisco disgorged passengers who continued overland to the gold fields. Sacramento was the western terminus of the Pony Express, then of the Transcontinental Railroad. It remains a transportation hub even today — those whose travel plans don't include Sacramento might still end up there.

Sacramento is located just north of the upper reaches of the maze of water-

ways and low-lying islands called the Delta. It was the southernmost site that could be expected to stay relatively dry during the winter floods that plagued the amazingly fertile 150-mile (240-kilometer) long **Sacramento Valley** before the present flood-control system was built.

Sacramento's central area and surrounding residential neighborhoods offer tree-lined streets with spacious, lush parks and whole blocks of neighborhoods where the residents keep their yards trim, green and cascading with flowers. This is no accident: Sacramento's city charter promotes the greenery by forbidding the installation of home water meters.

To anyone who has driven out of San Francisco on a 55-degree (Fahrenheit; 13°C) summer day and stopped in 85°F (29°C) Sacramento, it is a blazing furnace. But Sacramento's summer is pleasant, all in all. Humidity is low, it seldom rains, and the prevailing wind is a marine breeze from San Francisco Bay that cools the nights. Sacramento's most unpleasant weather is the wintertime tule fog, which can block out the sun for days or weeks on end, leaving

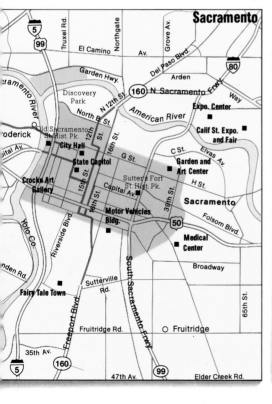

the thermometer stuck at 42°F (6°C)

Sacramento started out as John Sutter's New Helvetia Colony. Sutter, a German Swiss, had the dream of founding an independent state in the wilderness between Oregon and Mexican California. In August 1839, his party sailed up the Sacramento River past the present site of Sacramento, then up the American River a mile or so to land near the knoll where he built his fort. The colony thrived until January 1848, when James Marshall walked into the fort with his gold find from Sutter's sawmill in the hills to the east. Sutter's workers left for the goldfields, squatters grabbed his land, and Sutter died in 1880 in Washington, D.C., attempting to defend his land titles.

What emerged from the Gold Rush was Sacramento. It became the state capital in 1845 after San Jose, Vallejo and Benicia all had a brief reign. Since then, technology and fashion have left their marks, but a rather distinct image of the Sacramento of old can still be detected beneath the town's modern veneer.

A visit to Sacramento should start at the beautifully restored **Capitol** building surrounded by 40-acre (16-hectare) **Capitol Park**. This manicured arboretum has a vast collection of California flora and examples of plants from every climate and continent on Earth. It is popular for brown-bag lunches; the passing parade includes anything from briefly clad, headset-wearing roller skaters to down-and-out bums to state officials and office workers. The big, fluffy blue-gray squirrels are cute to a fault and shameless beggars.

Across 10th Street from the Capitol is the **State Library**. Its California department is vast. The ornate, polished building is an example of a public work erected as a monument to a prosperous society.

Other "don't-miss" attractions include the **Old Governor's Mansion** (15th and H streets), **Sutter's Fort** (between 26th, 28th, K and L streets) and the **Indian Museum** on the fort grounds. There is a bronze plaque at 29th and B streets next to an insulation company yard, marking the point where Sutter first came ashore to found his colony.

The premier public amenity in Sacramento for joggers, hikers, bicyclists, bird watchers, fishermen, rafters, swim-

The Gold Rush riverport in 1849.

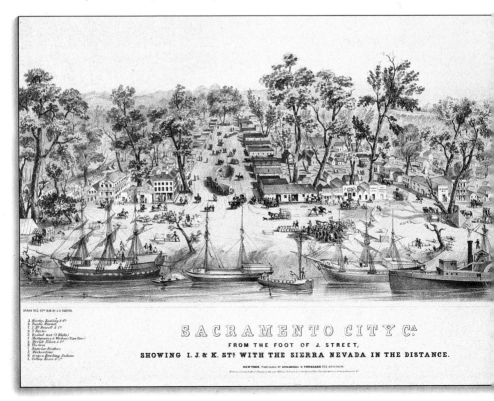

SACRAMENTO CITY Cᵃ

FROM THE FOOT OF J. STREET,

SHOWING I. J. & K. STˢ WITH THE SIERRA NEVADA IN THE DISTANCE.

mers and sunbathers is the **American River Parkway**. It stretches from **Discovery Park** on the Sacramento River to **Numbus Dam**, 23 miles (37 km) up the American River. The best beach is **Paradise,** next to **Glen Hall Park** at the end of Carlson Drive. (Carlson runs north from the **California State University** campus on J Street.) Rental rafts are available from roadside stands near the river on Sunrise Boulevard.

And then there is **Old Sacramento**. It is Sacramento's old west end, the riverfront, terminus of the Pony Express and Transcontinental Railroad, restored and sanitized for the visitor. The **California State Railroad Museum** and attendant attractions of Old Sacramento State Historic Park are well worth some time; rail buffs spend days there. A couple of interesting stores in the old town are a few doors from one another on K Street: **Ramsey's Hats**, which seems to offer every possible style of hat or cap, and the **Solar Syndicate**, a store with an eclectic line of goods in the *Whole Earth Catalog* mode ranging from flour sacks to cast-iron stoves.

Anyone visiting the old town ought

also to visit the **Crocker Art Museum** (2nd and O streets) both for the ever-changing exhibits and the gracious, pleasant feel of the building.

The Sacramento Valley

Surrounding the city of Sacramento is the Sacramento Valley. Drained by the Sacramento River, it is the northern third of California's great Central Valley. (The southern two-thirds are drained by and named for the San Joaquin River). Agriculture is the No. 1 industry in California, and the bulk of it is carried out in this vast valley. Roadside fruit stands offer an opportunity to sample these riches. Life holds few experiences to equal the sensations that go with consuming an almost-liquid, tree-ripened, softball-sized Fay Elberta peach on a hot August afternoon near **Marysville**. The small stands that offer produce from only the owner's fields have fresher products at lower prices, since they are exempted from a state law requiring all farm products to go through a licensed packing shed.

For traveling through this country, the freeways — Interstate 5 north-south

*refronts
Old
cramento.*

JOAN DIDION: 'IT'S JUST GONE'

EDITOR'S NOTE: Joan Didion, who is equally well regarded as a journalist (Slouching Towards Bethlehem, The White Album, Salvador) *and as a novelist* (Play It as It Lays, A Book of Common Prayer), *is one of the most well-known California-born writers. She was brought up in Sacramento. In an interview for this book, she reflected on her hometown.*

I was born in Mercy Hospital on J Street. For a time we lived in town, on U Street, and then, after World War II, we moved to the country — it was the country then, it's not any more — out toward Carmichael. We lived in a surplus mess hall that we turned into a house. It was mostly one room, but a very large room. We had 10 acres with a lot of oak trees.

There were still a lot of farms and ranches then. Just across the American River from town was the Horst Ranch, where they grew hops. Now that ranch is a subdivision called Campus Commons or something. The ten acres on which we lived is a subdivision, too.

Later, we moved to a house further in, off Fair Oaks Boulevard. My parents are still there. It's a quiet neighborhood; there seem to be more houses than people. It's a good place to walk.

Sacramento was hotter when I was growing up than it is now. I know that sounds like something a very old person might say about a hometown, but it's actually true. When the big dams went on the river, it got cooler in Sacramento. In the summer, we tried to go swimming in the afternoons; we didn't have a pool but we knew a few people who did. Or we swam in the rivers. The trick was to stay wet all afternoon, then jump in an open car — we had a Jeep — and get home before your bathing suit dried, or almost, just as the sun was going down.

People didn't have air-conditioning in those days, so all the houses were dark, the curtains closed, the windows closed. When the sun went down, we opened up the house. I remember the summer evenings in Sacramento. It was as if the whole world opened up. There was a sense of infinite possibilities.

I had no sense of Sacramento as a political town. Once a year we'd go down to the State Capitol to see the legislature in action, if we couldn't get out of it. My best friend's father was a lobbyist, and once a year her mother would have a tea for all the legislators' wives, and we'd serve at it. I did go down to see the redone Capitol last year, and it really looks terrific. They did a good job.

I have been in Old Town (the tourist-oriented reconstruction of Old Sacramento) a few times. It's strange the way the freeway just sort of ends right next to it. I remember once going down with my mother and my daughter, Quintana, on a very hot Saturday afternoon. Quintana was wearing a big hat of my mother's to keep the sun off, and a little dress, and there was nothing open. It was very quiet. She walked ahead of us on these wooden sidewalks. I remember thinking about my father's great-grandfather, who operated a saloon down there when it wasn't "Old Sacramento" but "Sacramento City," the real thing, a frontier river town. And there was my daughter, walking down this back-lot Western street. It was a peculiar collision of generations. Or cultures. Or something.

Really, I think I visit Sacramento frequently just to be with my parents; I enjoy being with them. It's certainly not a sense of coming back to a hometown. I can't even find my way anymore, there are so many streets that don't go where they used to, so many highways with numbers instead of names.

In *Slouching Towards Bethlehem*, I wrote an essay about Sacramento ("Notes From a Native Daughter"), and there's a line in there: "All that is constant about the California of my childhood is the rate at which it disappears." That was written almost 20 years ago. I must have had a sense then that there was something there to disappear. Now, it's just gone.

and I-80 east-west — are the main routes. But there are plenty of minor routes that tend to be more interesting: to the north, State Highway 99 or 70; to the Gold Country, State 70,20 or 49; to the Delta and the Bay Area, State 160; to the Wine Country, State 128, 16 or 20.

Heading up State 70, about 45 minutes from Sacramento is Marysville, an old gold camp and river-steamer port on the Feather and Yuba rivers. At the toe of the Yuba levee downtown, the public may visit the **Bok Kai Temple**, maintained by a full-time caretaker employed by the local Chinese societies (*tongs*). The shrine's central deity is Bok Kai, whose province is spring rain and fruitful agriculture. Every March, Marysville conducts a Bok Kai Festival and parade. Never in 103 years through 1983 had it failed to stop raining for the loud, gaudy parade with its dragons, lion dancers and fireworks.

Further north on State 99, about one hour from Sacramento is a mountain range jutting from the center of the valley. These are the **Sutter Buttes**, a beautiful place to hike in spring and fall. (Landowners won't let visitors in

without a guide: contact Allan Sartain in Davis, (916) 756-6283, for information about tours). North and west of the range is the **Buttes Sink**, a low-lying area where an amazing collection of waterfowl gathers every winter. It is not uncommon to see a flock of 100,000 snow geese all take to the air at once. Best viewing is at **Gray Lodge**, west of **Live Oak** and **Gridley**.

Off I-5 north of **Willows** is the old **Blue Gum**, a popular restaurant and motel that, though nothing fancy, managed through a fine reputation to survive being bypassed by the freeway several years ago.

About two hours' drive north of Sacramento is **Chico**, a pleasant farming and state college town founded by Gen. John Bidwell about the time Sutter was founding Sacramento. Bidwell's greatest legacy is **Bidwell Park**, some 2,000 acres (800 hectares) of magnificent oak woodland along Big Chico Creek right in town, with hiking trails, swimming holes and picnic spots among the towering valley oaks.

North of Chico on the way to Red Bluff is **Vina**, where **Our Lady of New Clairvaux Trappist Monastery** is lo-

cated. This was once the ranch headquarters of 19th Century rail baron, governor, senator and university founder Leland Stanford. Visitors may call at the monastery, where monks work as modern-day farm hands in the orchards. In Stanford's time the property was one of the world's largest vineyards.

The downtown area of **Red Bluff**, three hours, now, from Sacramento, still has the feel of a Western movie set. Red Bluff was the head of navigation during the river-steamer days, and the splendid old mercantile building with the clock tower was headquarters for shipping wool and hides.

An adventurous traveler can cross the Coast Range from Red Bluff, but the trip shouldn't be attempted in bad weather nor in a car not sturdy and well-equipped. Accommodations — even stores and gas stations — are primitive and hard to find.

The Delta Region

In the spring, these Coast Range hills offer probably the best wildflower display in California. In a good year it could be the best in the world. The best of the best is **Bear Valley**, reached by a good gravel road that winds north past the resurrected spa of **Wilbur Springs** from State 20 at its intersection with State 16. Highway 16 north of **Woodland** passes through the **Capay Valley**, a sleepy backwater of orchards and hayfields. On Saturdays and Sundays, travelers can get good barbecue at **Slaughter's** in **Guinda.**

The Capay Valley is a branch of the Sacramento Valley that departs west of Woodland and **Davis** and north of **Winters**. From Winters, State 128 up **Putah Creek** is a pleasant alternative route to the Napa Valley, and there are numerous county roads branching off through the hills to hit the Wine Country at different spots.

Winters and **Vacaville** are about the limit of the Sacramento Valley's rich growing area. Orchards thrive around those towns, and at Vacaville on I-80 is the **Nut Tree** restaurant, which got its start decades ago as a fruit stand on the transcontinental highway. It's a good, if expensive, place to have lunch. But more, it's a study in what can happen when a fruit stand is *really* successful — an amazing, sprawling conglomeration of commercial enterprises that even in-

Sunset o
the
Sacrame
River.

cludes a miniature railroad and a full-size airport.

Southwest of Vacaville begins the San Francisco Bay area urban sprawl, but spread out to the south and east is the vast Delta region. Through a series of small bays, the rivers of the Central Valley flow into San Pablo and San Francisco bays at the **Carquinez Strait.**

At **Crockett**, right on the strait beneath the huge freeway bridge, is a fish restaurant and a small marina from which sturgeon fishermen set forth. (The California record sturgeon, 468 pounds [212 kilograms], was landed here in July 1983). The restaurant serves delicious sturgeon that the waiters say comes from Oregon. It is illegal to sell California sturgeon.

Just east of Crockett, the trains of the Transcontinental Railroad — after it was extended past Sacramento — crossed the strait on a ferry between **Benicia** and **Port Costa.** The remnants of both elaborate ferry slips can still be seen. Today there are interesting antique shops and restaurants in both towns, and in Benicia, where the Army once had its main West Coast arsenal (Lt. U.S. Grant once did time in the guard-house), some of the historic buildings enjoys a good reputation.

East from here lies a vast, mysterious region with more than 1,000 miles (1,600 km) of sleepy sloughs and quiet channels winding among man-made islands of rich farmland that lie below sea level behind levees. Much of the area is accessible only by water. The Post Office must serve the heart of the region by boat.

It is possible, however, to get a good look by car. Along State 160, the river road between Sacramento and **Antioch**, is **Locke**, a quaint Chinese community of dark, shadowy alleys and narrow streets between tall, rickety wooden buildings. On Locke's main drag, **Al's** is a popular bar and restaurant. Downriver at **Rio Vista**, the **Point** is a good place to eat and watch the river traffic.

Maps show numerous ferries in the area. All are free, and all are quaint affairs. For maximum quaintness, visitors might try the **Liberty Island** ferry or the three-way job serving **Webb, Bradford** and **Jersey** islands. To really see this region, one must rent a houseboat from one of the dozens of outfits in the area.

...seboat g in Delta.

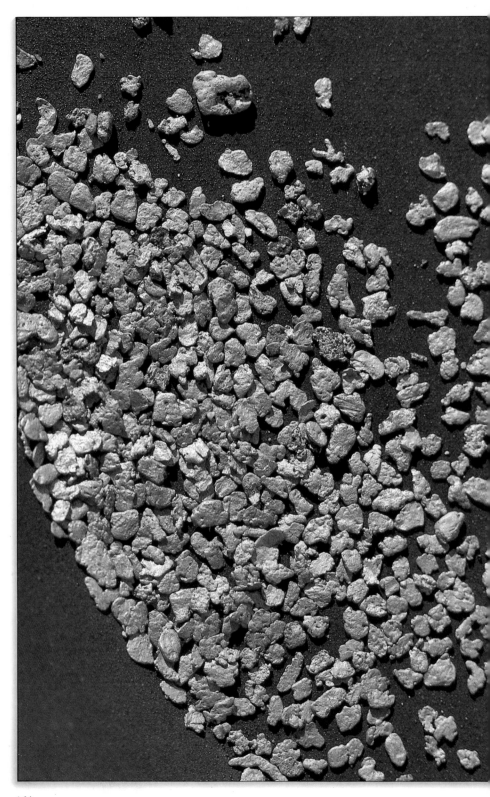

EXPLORING THE GOLD COUNTRY

There may have been an end to the Gold Rush, but it was not because they ran out of gold.

No, they merely ran out of the gold that was lying around on top of the ground. As the holes got deeper and more dangerous, the work got harder and slower and more expensive, until finally it was no longer cost-efficient to dig.

Geologists say there is at least as much gold in the Mother Lode today as was taken out in the previous century. Latter-day gold miners say the 7 million pounds that the old-timers got was only 10 percent of the wealth nature deposited there. Either way, there is a good deal left — and quite a few people are looking for it.

Take Bob Metzler, for instance. On and off since 1948, he has been working away at the tiny vein of gold that strings this way and that through a quartz deposit behind his home in the canyon of the **Merced River** below Yosemite Val-

ley. The interesting thing is that, even though he is now old enough to retire and probably could afford to live somewhere closer to a shopping center, he shows no sign of giving up. There is something about gold and there is something about the Gold Country.

There is also another gold rush going on, from Mariposa to Nevada City — real estate. The traveler up State Highway 49, the Gold Country's major arterial, is likely to see more real-estate signs than ghost towns. The modern miner is competing for land with the housing developer rather than with the claim jumper.

It Happens Every Spring

In the lowest of the Gold Country foothills, spring begins as early as March. The roadsides from the Central Valley towns of Sacramento, Stockton and Fresno are crowded by wild mustard, an edible green plant that adds tang to a salad and which covers the beef-cattle grazing land with miles of yellow blossoms. In the spring months, a succession of wildflowers moves up the hills and turns entire mountainsides blue and

what
miners
e for:
nuggets.
w, 19th
tury
ng
niques.

purple with lupine and brodiaea. There are larkspur and popcorn flowers, purple vetch and baby blue-eyes, and the maroon of the red bud, a flowering bush. In 'the canyon of the Merced around Metzler's, there are times in the spring when a fresh, new, unnamed waterfall appears every few hundred yards for miles. The waterfalls last until native California poppies bloom, usually in June.

It was the water, long ago, that washed the gold out of the rocks and left it in the gravel and sands for the '49ers. But Bob Metzler is unwilling to wait for the water. He fires up the old air compressor that runs the tools and drills holes back in the dark end of the mine tunnel. Once in a while, he packs the holes with dynamite and makes some rubble. Then he carries the rock out of the tunnel in his wheelbarrow. There is, when he is lucky, a little bit of gold in the wheelbarrow full of rock. To get it out, Metzler somehow has to crush the rock and wash it free of the metal. Gold mining is, and generally always has been, a hard way to make a living.

What is not so hard is making a living off those who themselves are looking for gold. The names of rich men who history remembers from the great California Gold Rush tend to be those of retail merchants. Levi Strauss made the trousers that stood up to the rigors of panning. Phillip Armour sold miners meat. Mark Twain and Bret Harte wrote about them. Joaquin Murietta became famous as a bandit, not as a miner. John Marshall, who actually found the first flakes of gold, died impoverished and almost forgotten.

The Bandit and the Senator

Metzler's stake is near State 49 and just past **Mariposa**, the southernmost of the old gold towns and a good place to begin a tour. Mariposa is cattle and timber country now, as is much of the Mother Lode. It enjoys a substantial business as a recreation area for city folks and can be reached by car or, curiously, public transportation. Amtrak trains from San Francisco and Oakland are met in Merced by a bus that takes tourists to Yosemite, with a stop in Mariposa. The state's oldest functioning courthouse is in Mariposa,

20th Cen fortune hunters p for gold near Mariposa.

along with a large mineral collection from all over California and an especially nice place for lunch, the **Gardenia Cantina**. The **Gold Coin**, a saloon, is in the center of town; those who stop by late on a weekend evening might see a good fight. The modest prices for food, drinks and lodging in Mariposa astonish city visitors.

The country around here was home to Murietta, the Mexican bandit with a Robin Hood reputation. The story is that he was wrongly abused and beaten by Anglo miners and took revenge by settling into a life of robbing them. Modern historians, an unromantic lot, have suggested that there may never have been an individual Joaquin, which shows it can be a mistake to pay too much attention to modern historians.

There is no such argument about John Charles Frémont, who lived just north of Mariposa in **Bear Valley** in the mid 19th Century and owned virtually the whole place, including the gold beneath the ground. It was Frémont, with major help from Kit Carson, who scouted and marked many of the important routes into California through the mountains. He was also the first senator from the new state of California in 1850 and the first Republican candidate for U.S. President — four years before Abraham Lincoln.

From his Bear Valley home, Frémont watched the substantial profits of his mine eaten up by lawyers and overhead. Today in Bear Valley, there are the ruins of his house, a store, the Odd Fellows Hall and the **Bon Ton Cafe**, a pleasant place to eat.

The drive to **Coulterville** involves a tortuous hairpin descent from the rocky, scrub-covered country where the Bear Valley mines are, to the Merced River and back up the other side. It is exactly the kind of road the highway engineers don't like and will try to replace, so today it is a treasure of sorts. Many other such stretches of State 49 have been bypassed or bridged but between Bear Valley and Coulterville there is a chance to see what the country was like when the miners worked it — tough, hot in the summer, demanding and beautiful. There are many mines along the road, few of them now operating. Both open and closed mines are dangerous, for different reasons. A gold mine should never be visited without an invitation.

At the bottom of the Coulterville grade is another creation of the engineers — **Lake McClure**. Where there once was the Merced River, the town of Bagby, a railroad to Yosemite and a number of mines, there is now a lake. It is intended for irrigation and electricity. It also can be fished for rainbow and brown trout, bluegill, bass and catfish.

Coulterville itself is so picturesque that it seems as though it might have been built on a Hollywood backlot and shipped up piece by piece. It is not scarred by a freeway like some Gold Rush towns and it is still a bit dusty. The 25 bars of the old days are gone but travelers can still get a cold beer at the **Jeffrey Hotel**, whose original adobe walls are three feet thick.

As the road north of Coulterville dips into the valley of the **Tuolumne River**, travelers can't miss seeing the **Moccasin** plant of San Francisco's Hetch Hetchy hydroelectric system on the right. It provides water and some power to San Francisco, but the cost is high. A dam above Moccasin has destroyed the beautiful Hetch Hetchy Valley, thought by many early explorers to be second in beauty only to the Yosemite Valley itself.

Further along State 49 is the near-ghost town of **Chinese Camp**, which actually has a post office, a few hardy residents, and a little life yet. There were Chinese miners by the thousands during the first Gold Rush — and enough some years later to make for a second gold rush when the great labor gangs that built the trans-continental railroads were disbanded. The second time around, many of the old surface deposits were painstakingly reworked for a second profit.

Of the ghost towns, already abandoned when he visited the Gold Country in 1864, Mark Twain wrote: "You will find it hard to believe that here stood at one time a fiercely flourishing little city of 2,000 or 3,000 souls. ... In no other land, in modern times, have towns so absolutely died and disappeared, as in the old mining regions of California." In Chinese Camp there were 5,000 miners at the height of the Gold Rush.

Sonora, named for the Mexican state from which many of its first '49ers came, is a city again, one that may be losing a struggle with the real-estate developers. The edges of town are now built out with strings of small shopping centers. Beyond are the homes on one-acre lots that burden the community's water and sewage facilities and pack its streets until traffic stops. But all this development has happened because Sonora is beautiful ... and it still has an enjoyable downtown. Especially recommended is the **Gunn House**, a private home now operated as an inn.

The Mother Lode And Jumping Frogs

In the 1870s there was a pocket mine at the north end of Sonora where the operators found a vein of nearly pure gold and recovered, they say, $160,000 worth of gold in one day. It was part of *La Veta Madre*, "The Mother Lode," from which the legends sprang. It is the kind of story that keeps miners at work, back there in the dark tunnels.

The real treasure of Tuolumne County these days is **Columbia**. Just a few minutes north of Sonora and just off State 49, this old town has been restored as a state park and is as good a place as can be found to learn about the Mother Lode that was. For those who have traveled in the Eastern United States, Columbia can be compared to Williamsburg, Virginia, another restored historical town.

Columbia once had a population of 15,000, 50 saloons, competing daily newspapers and at least one church. Nearly $90 million in gold was taken there in 20 years. Much of restored Columbia is closed to automobiles these days, but the quiet majesty of the town itself is worth parking and walking. There are shops, theaters, a museum, and best of all, the splendid **Columbia City Hotel**, open for meals and overnight lodging. The hotel is operated as a laboratory for local junior-college students of hotel management. Around Columbia, as in many of the Gold Country towns, there are several rock or gold shops whose proprietors may be willing to teach visitors where to look for gold and perhaps even how to look for it.

Back on State 49, still headed north, a sign indicates the summit of **Jackass Hill**. It is named for the animals so central to gold prospecting and it is the place where Mark Twain lived in 1864. The Twain cabin has been reconstructed around the original hearth.

During the time Twain lived in the cabin, he heard and wrote what is possibly his most famous yarn, "The Celebrated Jumping Frog of Calaveras County." The actual jumping frogs were supposed to have been a bit north in **Angels Camp** — and they still are.

Angels Camp still harbors the **Angels Hotel** where Twain is said to have heard the frog story. Better yet, each May the community holds a jumping-frog contest that attracts thousands of people to the area — so many, in fact, that about the only way to actually see a jumping frog is to enter one's own in the contest. Any frog more than four inches (10 centimeters) in length is eligible. The wiser course may be to avoid Angels Camp during the week of the frogs. Twain would have.

Most of what Twain and others of the time saw between Columbia and Angels Camp has been drowned by modern engineers. The **New Melones Dam** now floods the **Stanislaus River** and creates a lake that goes far above the 1840s crossing at **Parrot's Ferry**. Instead of the fine picnicking and whitewater rafting of just a few years ago, there is now a high-speed highway bridge and an artifi-

Youth displays nugget f at Colur

168

cial lake providing water for irrigation and flood control.

Black Bart and Kit Carson

From the Angels Camp area, a detour leads up into the mountains to **Murphys**, a Gold Rush period town that is enough off the track to be a natural museum. The **Mercer Caverns**, well worth a visit, are in this area. Further up State 4 is **Calaveras Big Trees State Park**, a magnificent stand of sequoias.

San Andreas is another town whose present is a triumph of development interests, but whose past is alive with romantic echoes. Black Bart, a real stagecoach bandit, was tried here in 1883 for some of the 28 robberies he allegedly committed. Bart was a San Franciscan with expensive tastes and little income. So he instituted a series of polite, bloodless robberies of the gold-laden stages in the Mother Lode. His shotgun was always unloaded and no one was ever hurt. Nevertheless, he served six years in San Quentin prison. Then he disappeared.

In good weather and no hurry, the drive from San Andreas to **West Point** on the Mountain Ranch and Railroad Flat roads is beautiful. West Point was so named because it marked the terminus of a Kit Carson attempt to cross the Sierras. Now it has just a few hundred residents and a historical marker.

In recent years there have been attempts to reopen some of the 500 old mine shafts around West Point. A few of them now crush ore and even welcome visitors. Those who stand in the mouth of a mine shaft, even in mid summer, can see their breath condensing in the cold air seeping up from thousands of feet beneath the ground. The techniques of mining today in deep rock mines really differ very little from those used by the '49ers. In fact, the gold pan and sluice boxes being used by weekend miners are essentially the same tools as were in use 100 years ago.

From West Point, travelers can loop back west to **Mokelumne Hill**, a town that once was so rich its gold claims were limited to 16 square feet (about 1½ meters square). According to legend, the lust for wealth ran so high that there was a murder a week here for more than four months. On a more benign note, Mokelumne Hill is the site of

the founding of the **E Clampus Vitus Society**, a group devoted to good deeds and good times. The Society is still around and active, and generally has an entry in any parade or fair in the Gold Country.

Ten miles (16 km) up the road is **Jackson**, now mostly a modern retail center. The definitely un-modern **National Hotel**, on the narrow main street in the center of town, is open for meals and drinks. The **Wells Fargo**, nearby, has partisans for its bar and for its dinners. Just north of Jackson itself is a vista point on the highway which looks back into a scene that might be an old sepia-tone photograph. Dominating the picture are the huge tailing wheels of the **Kennedy Mine** which, with the **Argonaut**, was open and making money until World War II. The surface of both mines can be visited.

Volcano and Bed Bug

While much of the town of Jackson has become a modern outpost, its surroundings are still peaceful and pleasant. State Highway 88, one of California's most beautiful major roads,

runs through the town toward **Carson Pass**. Just a few miles east of Jackson on State 88 is **Indian Grinding Rock State Park** with more than 1,000 Indian grinding holes, mortars in bedrock granite worn deep by ancient Indian women making acorn meal. Next to the park is the turnoff to **Volcano**, which is not volcanic but which is pretty and picturesque. Volcano has an old hotel (the **St. George**) and an older cannon (**Old Abe**, a Civil War period relic). Just beyond Volcano is **Daffodil Hill**, which has to be seen in the spring to appreciate the name.

On the other side of Jackson is **Ione**, and getting there can be half the fun. One of the smaller county roads off State 49 covers the 10-mile distance. In Ione, the **Bed Bug Hotel** is a good place for a meal or a snack. No one is saying whether the name scares off potential overnight guests. The brooding castle just outside of town used to be the **Preston School of Industry**, where judges sent bad boys for reform.

Next stop on State 49 is **Sutter Creek**, the kind of town with which a casual visitor can fall in love. In fact, vacations or weekend sojourns in places like this

"Sam's T on U.S. Highway in El Dor County.

have encouraged many Californians to pack up and move to the Gold Country. There are several romantic inns and quaint restaurants. For daytime touring, there is **Knight's**, a working foundry more than a century old. There are also the remains of the **Union Mine**, the hole that made Leland Stanford wealthy.

Fiddletown is a six-mile (10-km) side trip off State 49 north of Sutter Creek. A ranch nearby offers wagon-train trips complete with meals and campfire sing-alongs. The Fiddletown area has a number of wineries, some open for tasting and tours. Signs in Fiddletown and **Plymouth** direct travelers to vineyards like those of **D'Agostini, Amador Foothill** and **Montevina**.

Placerville Gold

From Sutter Creek to Grass Valley, about 75 miles (121 km), the countryside surrounding State 49 is mostly a commuter suburb for Sacramento. There are big Safeway supermarkets and rush hours and cable television. In fact, in the Auburn area, and again around Grass Valley, State 49 suddenly and inexplicably becomes a freeway. Nonetheless, there are things to do and watch for along the way.

Poor Red's in **Eldorado**, a town just south of Placerville, has a reputation for barbecued ribs and chicken. It's a plain place with plain prices to match. **Apple Hill**, just above Placerville on U.S. Highway 50, has made a cooperative business of marketing apples. In the fall the whole countryside smells of cider. Bushels of fruit sell for under $8.

Placerville itself was once called Hangtown because of the chosen and frequently used method of executing the guilty. It was the nexus of wagon, mail, Pony Express and telegraph routes and consequently was a busy and exciting place. In the mid 19th Century, Philip Armour was the butcher, Mark Hopkins was the grocer, and John Studebaker built wheelbarrows. All three of these men went on to establish great American business empires.

Placerville now lies on the main routes from the Bay Area and Sacramento to the ski resorts and the gambling casinos of Lake Tahoe, and not a lot is left of its history beyond the crooked streets. Placerville may be the

the
zy Horse
on,
ada City.
it, Indian
ding
k State
near
kson.

only town in America with its own gold mine, however. The **Gold Bug Mine**, north of town, is in a public park and is open for inspection.

North of Placerville on State 49 is **Coloma**, the birthplace of the Gold Rush. There is a state historic park now at the spot where in 1848 John Marshall found the yellow metal that made California. He was building a waterway for John Sutter's lumber mill when he was distracted by gold. The state has reconstructed the mill, though not exactly at the same place, since the **American River** has changed its course in the past century.

For those who don't want to spend all their time meditating on history, Coloma is a pleasant place for a raft trip. A number of companies offer one-day and longer trips down the American River.

Auburn, at the junction of State 49 and Interstate 80, is so much a part of the Sacramento economy today that there is a proposal to link the communities with a light rail commuter service. The population of the Auburn area, roughly unchanged since the 1880s, will double by the year 2000 — retirees, city people looking for a quieter life, commuters and workers in the emerging electronics industry are moving into the area.

The **Placer County Museum** in Auburn is counted as one of the best in the mountains, with collections of native Indian materials as well as gold-mining paraphernalia. Nearby is the colorful and unusual **Firehouse**.

Auburn is a good place to jump off for a visit to Lake Tahoe (up I-80) with a return via State 20 from near **Emigrant Gap**. State 20, the old Tahoe-Pacific Highway, is one of the California's great drives. It returns to join State 49 in the Nevada City-Grass Valley area.

Grass Valley was the center of the deep mines; there are several splendid places to get a sense of what they were like. Some of them, including the **North Star**, have shafts that go hundreds of feet below sea level. The shafts are now closed and flooded. The **Nevada County Museum** in the town of Grass Valley is a good one. The **Empire Mine State Park**, east of town, is the site of a mine that produced $100 million worth of gold before it closed in the mid 20th Century.

Grass Valley is now the center of high-technology industry, most notably the manufacture of equipment for television broadcasting. Consequently, Grass Valley is once again a name recognized around the world, just as it was 125 years ago.

Nevada City North

Nevada City is as quaint as Grass Valley is up to date. It is the kind of place that attracted city people early. They busily converted the old factories and miners' stores into restaurants, museums, antique stores and theaters. There are a couple of pleasant bars — **McGee's** and **Cireno's** — and the **National Hotel** still puts up overnight visitors in rooms tastefully furnished with antiques.

Ten miles (16 km) north of Nevada City there is a large state park at the old **Malakoff Diggings**, a place that generated one of the very earliest pieces of environmental legislation. Visitors to the Malakoff mine can see the effects of hydraulic mining, a method of gold extraction in which high-powered streams of water are directed from cannons at the side of the mountain. This method was effective, but it devasted the mountain, and waterways were clogged with mud as far away as San Francisco Bay. The technique was banned in 1884 but the scars, only slightly healed by time, are still awesome.

It's an hour's drive from Nevada City to **Downieville**, a fitting end to a tour of the Gold Country. The country here is higher, cooler and much less crowded than further south. From **Camptonville**, midway along the route from Nevada City, the lovely **Henness Pass Road** veers off into mountains. In good weather, it is a lovely side trip. There are a number of campgrounds a few miles out toward the pass.

Downieville itself is a picture nearly perfect. It is a tiny and remote place hemmed in by steep hillsides, a place where growth is not just undesirable but would be well-nigh impossible. The population is not more than 500, but there are few places to stay and to eat for a few lucky people.

The real Gold Country is fading fast, a victim of the predictable ravages of a century's worth of time. Like the glittering nuggets themselves, the real Gold Country is hard to find — but it's certainly worth seeking.

An old r
reflects
days of
what-mig
have-bee

LAKE TAHOE: THE NO. 1 RESORT

Mark Twain called it a "noble sheet of blue water lifted 6,308 feet above the level of the sea" but that's because he came for the scenery and not to catch Liberace at the cocktail show.

Actually, when Twain wrote those words about **Lake Tahoe** in *Roughing It*, the year was 1872, the horse was the preferred way to make the trip, and the lake was as pure and sparkling as the silver being dug out of the nearby Comstock Lode.

These days Lake Tahoe's blue waters are sometimes green with algae and its blue skies brown with smog. Many tourists seem more intent on the indoor attractions (roulette wheels and craps tables) than outdoor ones (sun, water and winter snow). No fewer than three McDonald's restaurants perch on its shores, keeping company with hundreds of other fast-food outlets, motels, condominiums, video arcades and, at last count, two miniature golf courses.

Nonetheless, Lake Tahoe — a 200-mile (320-kilometer) drive from San Francisco — is still the place city folks usually mean when they speak of going to the mountains for the weekend. Only a few miles from the furious bustle of the Nevada casinos are wilderness, hiking trails, hidden lakeshore caves, snow-covered backroads ideal for cross-country skiing and quiet beaches that look much the same as when Twain dug a toe into them.

Tucked into a high valley between the Sierra Nevada and the Carson Range, Lake Tahoe (elevation 1,923 meters) is a glacially carved lake ringed by mountains that rise more than 4,000 feet (over 1,200 meters) above the water. It is 22 miles (35 km) long, and 12 miles (19 km) wide.

Indians and Settlers

Despite the popularity of *Bonanza*, America's most popular television show of the Sixties, Lake Tahoe has never lav adjacent to "The Ponderosa," the fictional 19th Century Cartwright ranch. This has not, however, prevented a goodly number of Tahoe establishments from calling themselves "Ponderosa," including a flower shop, a glazier and a delicatessen.

The area's real story, however, would probably get equally high ratings. It involves explorers, cannibalism, silver and gold fever, the construction of a trans-Sierra rail line (the biggest engineering feat of its day), forestry and mining, the Winter Olympic Games and, these days, lots of bickering between developers and conservationists, with the developers seeming to win most of the big ones.

It was in 1844 that explorer John C. Fremont scrambled to the top of 10,100-foot (3,078-meter) **Stevens Peak**, gazed down on the lake, and proclaimed himself the lake's discoverer. That must have come as a surprise to the Piute, Lohantan and Washoe Indians who had been living there for hundreds of years. The Indians hunted deer, fished for trout and, in general, did a lot of other things for survival that today's visitors do for recreation.

Two years after Fremont, things grew considerably more grim. A party of 82 settlers from Illinois, led by George Donner, became snowbound while trying to pass through the Sierra Nevada about 20 miles (32 km) north of the lake. The Donner Party, as it came to

eding
s, skier
s down
slopes
eavenly
y.
afloat
IcKinney
Right,
e-armed
it at a
n Lake
e casino.

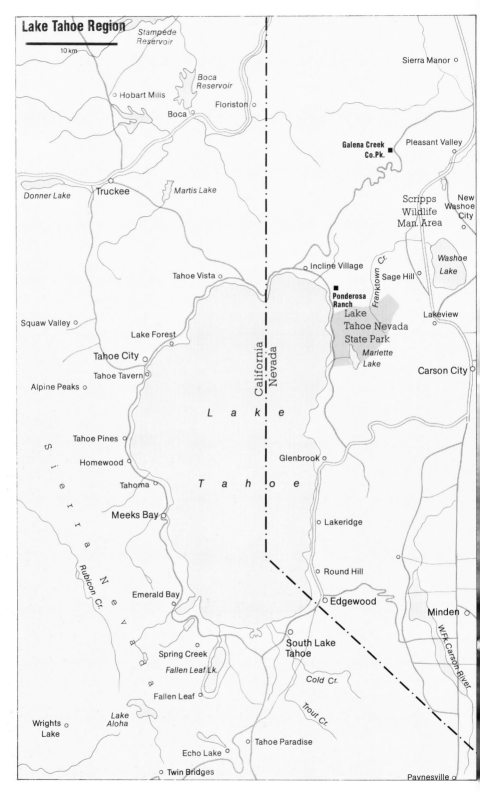

Lake Tahoe Region

10 km

Stampede Reservoir

Sierra Manor

Boca Reservoir

Hobart Mills

Floriston

Boca

Galena Creek Co.Pk.

Pleasant Valley

Donner Lake

Truckee

Martis Lake

Scripps Wildlife Man. Area

New Washoe City

Incline Village

Washoe Lake

Tahoe Vista

Franktown Cr.

Sage Hill

Squaw Valley

Ponderosa Ranch

Lake Tahoe Nevada State Park

Lakeview

Lake Forest

Tahoe City

Marlette Lake

Carson City

Tahoe Tavern

California Nevada

Alpine Peaks

L a k e

Tahoe Pines

S i e r r a

Homewood

Glenbrook

Tahoma

T a h o e

Meeks Bay

Lakeridge

N e v a d a

Rubicon Cr.

Round Hill

Emerald Bay

Edgewood

Minden

Spring Creek

South Lake Tahoe

W.Fk. Carson River

Fallen Leaf Lk.

Fallen Leaf

Cold Cr.

Wrights Lake

Lake Aloha

Trout Cr.

Echo Lake

Tahoe Paradise

Twin Bridges

Paynesville

be known, ate twigs, mice, shoes and finally its own dead in order to survive. **Donner Pass**, now the route of Interstate 80 over the crest of the Sierras, is named in its honor.

Along the south shore of the lake today runs U.S. Highway 50, the old overland route — connecting Salt Lake City with Sacramento — that brought settlers to California. In 1859, more than 3,000 covered wagons and stagecoaches passed by the lake, bound for the valley and farmlands below. The next year, for the first time, a young man on horseback sped along the lakeshore carrying a sack of tissue-paper letters. It was the inaugural run of the Pony Express, which cut in half the time required to send a letter from coast to coast. It was, however, no match for the railroad which was to follow by the end of the decade.

In the mid 1860s, the sound of 16-pound (7.2 kilogram) hammers rang through Donner Pass as tens of thousands of laborers, many of them low-paid Chinese immigrants, struggled to pound rail spikes and lay the first transcontinental railroad track. In 1869, the Central Pacific line, of which the

trans-Sierra stretch was a portion, met the Union Pacific line in Utah and travelers could finally forsake the rigors of covered wagons and stagecoaches.

Modern Uses and Abuses

In the years that followed, the beauty of the lake became the area's drawing card to tourists. Campers, hikers, fishermen and skiers came for the spectacular alpine setting, clear water and pristine skies. In the Forties, at Sugar Bowl west of **Truckee**, developers erected a cable lift to enable skiers to forsake the drudgery of climbing back up hills, and the area's ski industry was born. In 1960, the Winter Olympic games were held at Squaw Valley. 10 miles (16 km) north of **Tahoe City**, despite a meager snowfall that threatened for a time to call the whole thing off. The Lake Tahoe area now has a dozen major ski areas, although weekend skiers, waiting in 30-minute lines for a ride to the top of the hill, probably think there are still too few.

Legalized gambling, among the lake's biggest attractions, is also among its biggest problems. One-third of the lake lies

in the state of Nevada, the only place in the United States (outside of Atlantic City, New Jersey) where casino gambling is legal. High-rise casinos — looking more at home in San Francisco's financial district than amidst the jewel of the Sierras — are a main cause of the growing traffic jams, smog, noise, lake pollution and sewage problems.

Since 1972, development at the lake has been governed by the Tahoe Regional Planning Agency. For years, critics charged it was a rubber-stamp for every hotel, casino and taco stand looking for a home. In 1980, reacting to increasing pressure and deterioration of the lake, Congress expanded the agency, changed its charter to make the approval of new developments more difficult, banned the construction of new casinos and hotels, and restricted the expansion of existing ones. In 1982, California voters approved an $85 million bond act to buy environmentally sensitive lands and spare them from development. Some said the changes came just in time, others said it was far too late.

The fight over the lake's future continues. The water is no longer clear enough for a fisherman to drop a silver dollar into the lake and see it sparkle 100 feet (30 meters) down. In 1983, clarity at the lake was measured to a depth of only 25 feet (eight meters). Charles Goldman, professor of limnology (the study of lakes) at the University of California at Davis, warned that the lake will lose all its clarity and become deprived of oxygen within 40 years unless stricter controls are undertaken now.

The Rush to the Slush

Recreation is the lifeblood of the lake and in winter that means downhill skiing. On Friday nights, the weekend exodus from the Bay Area begins. Tens of thousands of cars with skis strapped on their roofs like sections of picket fences stream up I-80 or U.S. 50 toward the lake. They bring tire chains that they don't know how to install, sunscreen lotion that they forget to apply, and pairs of gloves of which they will invariably lose one half. Their car bumpers are plastered with stickers that say "Go For It"; many of them will scream the same noxious phrase with consider-

Truckee River fly fisherman right, hoping to snare another brown trout left.

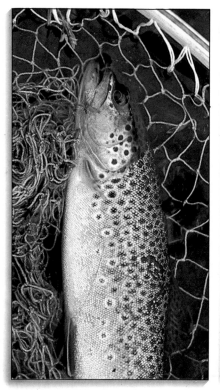

able vigor as they whiz down a ski slope at a speed twice as fast as they can control. Many of them will return home with plaster casts, courtesy of their own recklessness and the dozens of orthopedic doctors whose offices are conveniently located at the base of the slopes.

The largest ski areas are **Squaw Valley**, at the northwest side of the lake, and **Heavenly Valley**, on the south side. Each has more than two dozen ski lifts and terrain to satisfy skiers of every ability, including no ability. These days, skiers need to bring with them as much money as gamblers — the price of a daily ticket at the major resorts was, at last count, $22. All resorts have stores at which skis can be bought or rented, as well as ski schools stocked with dozens of instructors with straight teeth and bent knees.

Heavenly Valley is the favorite ski area for those who like to duck into the casinos at night, as it is located at **South Lake Tahoe**, the busiest part of the lake and just across the state line from Nevada. For all their commotion, the casinos can actually come in handy for skiers in the evening — most offer all-you-can-eat buffet dinners for $5 or so, to lure customers to the gambling tables. The buffet of preference is to be found at **Harrah's**, followed by those at **Caesar's Tahoe**, the **High Sierra** and **Harvey's** hotels. There's no law, however, that says a person can't just visit the dining room, eat his fill after a tough day of skiing, and depart with his fortune still in his pocket.

In general, though, gambling and skiing don't seem to mix, which is why the majority of skiers prefer the northern half of the lakeshore on the California side, particularly the area around Tahoe City. It's quieter, cleaner and the selection of ski areas is better. In addition to Squaw Valley, skiers can choose **Alpine Meadows, Sugar Bowl, Boreal Ridge** and **Northstar**. The latter caters particularly to families — its gentler slopes keep most of the show-offs away. Boreal, perched on the edge of four-lane I-80, is perhaps the easiest to reach. Sugar Bowl is the matriarch, having been around longest. Alpine Meadows is preferred by experienced skiers, as the runs rated "expert" make up 40 percent of the terrain — the highest percentage in the Sierra.

iquil
ting on
erald Bay.

Skiing is easy to learn and difficult to master. It should not be undertaken by anyone reluctant to fall down. A candy bar or wineskin containing stronger refreshments is invaluable. The novice skier should have the foresight to include one or the other among the gloves, hat, lip balm, sunscreen lotion, goggles and extra sweater he must somehow find room for in the pockets of his parka.

After the lifts close, skiers usually retire to a bar with a fireplace. In any given bar are apt to be 100 skiers and only one fireplace, so it is usually impossible to get a ringside seat. These spots will be taken anyway by non-skiers who have been planted in them for hours, pretending to have just arrived from the slopes. They can be spotted easily: they are the ones with energy.

Cross-country skiing, which is more like a hike in the woods that a flight down a mountainside, is attracting more and more people each year. It can be done on any snow-covered back road or meadow, or at Nordic ski-touring areas with maintained ski trails. The skis are longer and narrower, the uphill stretches can make the legs ache, but the silence and solitude are blessed.

Summertime Exploits

In the summer, camping, swimming, fishing, hiking and boating take over, and none of them requires a parka. Marinas at South Lake Tahoe and **Zephyr Cove**, Nevada, offer daily cruises of the lake aborad large vessels, including an authentic paddlewheel steamer. A daytime cruise on the *M.S. Dixie*, departing from Zephyr Cove, costs $8 and takes 2½ hours; evening cruises include dinner or cocktails and cost more. The new boat on the block is the 140-foot (43-meter) *Tahoe Queen*, an authentic steam paddlewheeler that can carry 500 passengers. Both boats cruise through spectacular **Emerald Bay State Park**, an isolated, tree-lined wilderness tucked into the southwest corner of the lake.

The independent-minded can rent motorboats and rowboats for their own exploring, or even waterski boats. If the latter is the choice, visitors are advised to stick an exploratory toe into the lake before signing any papers — Lake Tahoe can be very cold.

Hikers and backpackers usually head for **Desolation Wilderness**, a lake-studded area west of Emerald Bay. Nearby is the **El Dorado National Forest** Visitor Center, offering orientation programs and guided walks. A wilderness permit must be obtained for backpacking in Desolation Wilderness — it's a popular place that frequently fills to capacity in summer. The **Granite Peak** area is also good for backpacking, and Emerald Bay, **D.L. Bliss** and **Sugar Pine Point** state parks are excellent for short walks and picnics.

Trout fishermen have good luck in the **Truckee River** and the river basin at the north end of the lake. The town of Truckee abounds with sporting-goods stores that offer more shiny devices to catch the unsuspecting than DeBeers Limited.

On any summer weekend, joggers and bicyclists take to the roads ringing the lake. The 75-mile (121-km) circle makes a strenuous one-day bike ride, or a leisurely two-day trip.

Getting to Lake Tahoe is easy and, thanks to the many casinos seeking to lure fresh blood from the Bay Area, inexpensive. The drive from San Francisco takes four to five hours in good weather and light traffic. Chains should always be carried in winter, and drivers should be prepared to either lie on their backs in roadside slush to put them on, or to pay $10 to hire one of the "chain monkeys" who cluster on the side of the road during every storm.

A cheaper way to the lake is by bus. Buses run all day from throughout the Bay Area to the pleasuredomes at South Lake Tahoe, offering substantial rebates on the bus fare to passengers once inside the casino. There are also frequent flights to airports at South Lake Tahoe and **Reno**, Nevada.

Probably the most spectacular way to get to the lake is on Amtrak's daily cross – country train, the *California Zephyr*, which leaves Oakland shortly before noon and arrives in Truckee in time for dinner. The train follows the same trans-Sierra route carved so laboriously in the 1860s and the view from the high windows of the lounge car can make a person forget the sound of the kid banging the piano, one of which Amtrak has seen fit to install in every lounge car. Passengers may also disembark in Reno just in time for the dinner show.

In the tr
of Olymp
champior
Squaw V

YOSEMITE AND
THE HIGH SIERRA

When plans were being made for Queen Elizabeth II's state visit to California in 1983, the monarch insisted on a three-day vacation stopover. Not Palm Springs. Not Santa Barbara. Not the Napa Valley wine country. What she wanted most of all, she told her advisors, was to see **Yosemite Valley**.

For the waterfalls. Nowhere else in the world are there so many big falls in such a small area, including 2,425-foot (739-meter) **Yosemite Falls**, the highest in North America. When Ice Age glaciers scoured out eight-mile (13-kilometer) long, mile-wide Yosemite Valley they left behind several smaller hanging valleys on either side, high but not dry, conduits for free-leaping torrents whose very names suggest their variety: **Ribbon, Bridalveil, Silver Strand, Staircase, Sentinel, Lehamite, Vernal, Nevada, Illilouette**.

For the rocks. "Great is granite," wrote New England clergyman Thomas Starr King in 1878, "and Yosemite is its prophet." As the prehistoric ice flows melted and retreated they exposed the colossal building blocks of the Sierra Nevada, shaped and polished into scenery on a grand scale — **El Capitan, Cathedral Rock, Three Brothers, Royal Arches, Half Dome, Clouds Rest**. In the daredevil world of technical rock climbing, from Austria to Australia, there is only one true mecca, Yosemite Valley.

And for all the rest, the meadows and forests and wildflowers, the birds and deer and bears, the myriad conjunctions of animate and inanimate that make the Valley, in writer Edward Abbey's words, "A place where a man should count himself lucky to make one pilgrimage in a lifetime. A holy place."

From Indians to Autos

A holy place is exactly what Yosemite (say "yo-seh-mih-tee") Valley was to its original inhabitants, the Ahwahneechee Indians. Because of Yosemite's isolation, the tribe managed to keep its mountain paradise a secret from White men until 1851, a full year after California attained statehood, when the U.S. Cavalry arrived and herded the Ahwahneechees across the Sierras to a barren reservation near Mono Lake.

As with much of the American West, subjugation of the Indians paved the way for settlement. During the decade following its "discovery," Yosemite Valley was fenced, farmed and logged by homesteaders. Visitors, drawn in increasing numbers by newspaper and magazine accounts of Yosemite's marvels, were appalled to find cow pastures instead of mountain meadows. In 1864, public pressure on the California legislature resulted in the Yosemite Grant, the first attempt in the nation's history to preserve a natural scenic area from commercial exploitation.

There are many who will argue today that the attempt has failed. With thousands of hotel rooms and campground sites, restaurants, supermarkets, liquor stores, gift shops and even a jail, Yosemite Valley has become the textbook example of overdeveloped parkland. In a controversial, decade-long planning effort, the U.S. National Park Service spent millions of dollars trying to determine what to do about degradation of the Yosemite environment; the principal recommendation, elimination of the private auto from the

eceding
ges, the
semite
lley in
ter.
ft, a
redevil's
proach to
summit
Sentinel
ck. Right,
s daring
itors
dy a map
walking
utes.

Valley, seems unlikely to be implemented before the year 2000, if ever.

In the meantime, roads in the east end of the Valley near **Mirror Lake** have been restricted to shuttle buses, bicycles and pedestrians. A convoluted one-way traffic pattern almost everywhere else makes driving a truly masochistic experience, especially in summer.

Exploring the Valley

Luckily, visitors can park their cars in one of the Valley's large parking lots and make use of the free shuttle buses. Because Yosemite Valley is so flat and compact, nearly all its biggest attractions are most easily seen by combining shuttle-bus rides with short walks on well-maintained trails. Visitors can also arrange guided horseback trips through the Valley stables, near **Curry Village** (the first large developed area on the Yosemite loop road). Bicycles may be rented at Curry Village and **Yosemite Lodge**, and several bikeways make two-wheeled travel by far the most efficient choice of locomotion for visitors and residents alike.

Unless one has only a few hours to spare, it's a mistake to simply ride the shuttle-bus loop and assume all the high spots have been hit. In most cases, bus stops are merely staging areas for exploration of nearby meadows, waterfalls and historic sites.

Preeminent among the latter, just a five-minute walk from the Yosemite Lodge shuttle stop, is a marker commemorating the site of John Muir's cabin. A Scottish sheepherder who first visited the Valley in 1868, Muir explored the Sierras throughout the 1870s, carrying little more than a blanket and a bag of flour. For Muir, Yosemite and the surrounding high country amounted to a "vast celestial city, not clothed with light but wholly composed of it." In the mass media of the time, he railed against the state's management of the Yosemite Grant, arguing instead for a much larger park under federal stewardship. Today, Muir is acknowledged as the father of the national park idea, and the Sierra Club, which he founded in 1892, is the most influential conservation organization in America.

John Muir's idea of wild-country comfort was a supper of unleavened biscuits and a bed of pine branches. Those whose own tastes are less spartan won't be disappointed by the range of accommodations in Yosemite Valley. Lodging runs the gamut from wood-frame canvas tent cabins at Curry Village to the palatial Presidential Suite atop the grand old **Ahwahnee Hotel**. In general, Curry Village offers the least expensive rooms, with Yosemite Lodge occupying middle ground and the Ahwahnee targeted for big spenders and royalty.

Yosemite by the Seasons

In summer, Yosemite Valley's singular concentration of natural beauty has its far less felicitous human analogue, complete with overcrowded campgrounds, traffic jams and hour-long waits in cafeteria lines. Although the Valley comprises only eight square miles (21 sq km) of the park's 1,189-square-mile (3,080-sq-km) area, it plays host to more than 90 percent of all Yosemite's overnight visitors. The surest way of seeing Half Dome without an enveloping wreath of smog is to plan a visit during the off season, September through May.

Autumn brings a rich gold to the

Yosemite Falls.

leaves of the Valley's oak trees, and the sun's lowering angle etches the granite domes and spires into sharper relief. Nights are cool, mornings apple-crisp. It's a good time to focus binoculars on rock climbers, lured back to Yosemite's great walls by mild daytime temperatures. Autumn also brings herds of wild deer, migrating through the Valley en route to winter forage in the Sierra foothills. An early-morning stroller may not see another soul on his way through a meadow in October, but chances are excellent he'll see at least half a dozen deer, bounding fleet and silent through the golden grass like dancers.

Yosemite Valley is emptiest of all in winter, when most of the action shifts to the ski resort at **Badger Pass**, 21 miles (34 km) away and 3,000 feet (900 meters) higher. Badger's gentle pine-fringed slopes offer few challenges for accomplished skiers, but prove ideal for family groups and novice-to-intermediate skiers who don't mind the 45-minute commute by car or bus from the Valley. In the Valley, the Yosemite Mountaineering School at Curry Village offers instruction in nordic (cross-country) skiing, as well as beginning

and advanced rock climbing, and an outdoor ice-skating rink boasts views of Glacier Point, Half Dome, and the frozen remnants of Yosemite Falls.

Spring is the favorite season of many Yosemite residents. Wildflowers carpet the meadows, and the roar of wild water resounds throughout the Valley. The force of the runoff is such that most of the waterfalls are unapproachable; gale-force winds and drenching spray enliven the normally placid one-quarter mile walk from Yosemite Lodge to the base of Yosemite Falls. But on full moon nights, the deluge is well worth braving for tantalizing glimpses of rare lunar spray bows. Popularly called "moonbows," these ethereal silver arches shimmer softly with the colors of the spectrum and reach heights of 200 feet (60 meters), only to dissolve into formless mist with a puff of wind.

The Other Yosemite

Seeing Yosemite when the crowds have gone home is the best way to experience the sublime tranquility that inspired the words of John Muir and the photographs of Ansel Adams. But even

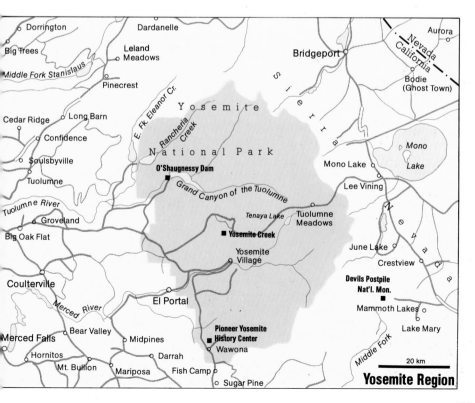

Yosemite Region

on the Fourth of July there are several routes of escape from the Instamatic Army. To the south, State Highway 41 climbs 9.3 miles (15.0 km) to **Chinquapin** junction, where a 15.5-mile (24.9-km) paved road departs for **Glacier Point.** From this famed viewpoint, 3,200 feet (975 meters) above the floor of Yosemite Valley, the entire park comes into unforgettable stomach-clutching focus. Directly below, the meadows, forest and waterfalls of the Valley appear in dollhouse scale, dwarfed by the awesome verticality of the huge northside cliffs and domes. No less compelling is the 80-mile (129-km) vista to the east and south, a panorama of lakes, canyons, waterfalls and the rugged peaks of Yosemite's High Sierra. Close at hand are the granite steps of the **Giant's Staircase,** where Vernal and Nevada falls drop the raging waters of the **Merced River** 320 and 594 feet (98 and 181 meters) respectively.

From Glacier Point, Half Dome is the most prominent landmark, a great solitary stone thumb thrusting skyward. Park rangers are accustomed to one question more than any other: what became of Half Dome's other half? The surprising answer is that the dome never had another half of solid rock, only slabs of granite on the sheer north face that were peeled away like onionskin by advancing glaciers during the Ice Age. At the height of glaciation, 250,000 years ago, Glacier Point itself lay under 700 feet (213 meters) of ice, and interpretive markers explain how the 2,000-foot (610-meter) thick Merced and Tenaya glaciers ground down from the high country to merge near Half Dome and quarry out Yosemite Valley. The mighty glacier formed by their union filled the Valley to its brim, and extended down the Merced canyon as far as **El Portal**, 15 miles (24 km) to the west.

Twelve miles (19 km) south of Chinquapin, at **Wawona**, stately forests of sugar pine, Jeffrey pine, and red and white fir fringe lush meadowlands along the South Fork of the Merced River, where dozens of pioneer families established homesteads before Yosemite National Park was created by Congress. For visitors, the century-old **Wawona Hotel** offers shaded verandas overlooking wide, rolling lawns, fine dining and a pastoral golf course surrounded by

The Valle floor in early autumn.

weathered split-rail fencing. Once an important overnight stopover for visitors en route to Yosemite Valley by stagecoach, Wawona today is a picturesque backwater offering, more than any other developed area in Yosemite, an invitation to linger, the longer the better.

Mariposa and Tuolomne

Five miles (eight km) south of Wawona, just inside the park's southern boundary, a short side road leads to the **Mariposa Grove** of giant sequoias, a 250-acre (101-hectare) preserve containing more than 500 mammoth redwood trees. It was here that John Muir slept under the stars alongside President Theodore Roosevelt, and persuaded the chief executive that the ancient forest should be added to the infant Yosemite National Park. The Mariposa Grove's largest tree, the **Grizzly Giant**, is at least 3,800 years old, with a height of 200 feet (61 meters) and a girth of 94.2 feet (28.7 meters). The best way to experience the big trees is to walk: leave the pavement and wander at random among trees that were already giants when Christ walked the Holy Land.

If Wawona and the Mariposa Grove are Yosemite's Black Forest, **Tuolumne Meadows** is its Switzerland. Reached by an hour's drive north from the Valley on the scenic **Tioga Road**, and situated at 8,600 feet (2,620 meters) above sea level, Tuolumne is the gateway to an alpine wilderness encompassing, in John Muir's words:

> ... innumerable lakes and waterfalls, and smooth silky lawns; the noblest forests, the loftiest granite domes, the deepest ice-sculptured canyons, the brightest crystalline pavement, and snowy mountains soaring into the sky twelve and thirteen thousand feet arrayed in open ranks and spiry pinnacled groups partially separated by tremendous canyons and amphitheatres; gardens on their sunny brows, avalanches thundering down their long white slopes.

Perhaps not surprisingly, familiarity with such an array of natural wonders is not gained easily; the only way to see the more remote areas of the Tuolumne backcountry is to hike, with all creature comforts carried in a backpack that may

rt Dome
e
nne

Road.

tip the scales at 50 pounds (23 kilograms) or more. A less arduous alternative, at least on some of the smoother trails, is to arrange a horsepacking trip through the Tuolumne stables, run by Yosemite Park & Curry Company.

Tuolumne is also the site of **Tuolumne Meadows Lodge**, central star in the summer constellation of High Sierra Camps. Arranged roughly in a circle, about nine miles (14½ km) apart, these six permanent tent camps provide lodging, meals and hot showers to hikers and horsepackers on the High Sierra Loop trail. Elevations of the camps vary from 7,150 feet (2,180 meters) to 10,300 feet (3,140 meters), and a night of acclimatization in Tuolumne is recommended before departure. In a typical year, camps are open from June 15 through September 1, with advance reservations essential. Wilderness permits, available free of charge at park ranger stations and visitor centers, are required for *all* overnight trips in the Yosemite backcountry.

Sequoia and Kings Canyon

It is tempting to dismiss **Sequoia** and **Kings Canyon** national parks as Yosemite without Yosemite Valley. Judging from park visitation figures, many California travelers do just that. In any given year, 2.5 million visitors converge on Yosemite; the comparable figure for Sequoia/Kings Canyon is barely 400,000. (Although Sequoia and Kings Canyon parks were established separately, their adjoining areas are administered as one unit). Even though 7,000-foot (2,130-meter) deep Kings Canyon exceeds Yosemite Valley in sheer vertical relief; even though the sequoia forests of the southern park are larger and more numerous than Yosemite's groves; the absence of waterfalls and striking rock formations make them pale alongside their more celebrated northern cousin. The result is a national park bereft of the most common national park headaches — traffic jams, overcrowding and crime — reason enough for solitude-seeking vacationers to beat a path to the entry station.

Much more so than Yosemite, Sequoia/Kings Canyon is a wilderness park, with only two developed areas near its western boundaries. The backcountry extends east across the west slopes of the Sierras as far as the crest of the range, encompassing the headwaters of the Kern and San Joaquin rivers and the highest Sierra summits, including Mount Whitney. Ironically, a majority of the park's mountain trails are most easily reached from trailheads out of Lone Pine, Big Pine and Bishop on the Sierra's east side, a 250-mile (400-km) drive from park headquarters near **Three Rivers**. As in Yosemite, wilderness permits are required for overnight backcountry camping.

The most scenic approach to the Kings Canyon section of the park, State 180, begins in the sprawling agricultural city of **Fresno**. A 52-mile (84-km) drive through the Sierra foothills leads to the **General Grant Grove**, a stand of massive 3,000-year-old sequoias notable for the wide-open parkland around their bases.

Thirty-eight miles (61 km) past the Grant Grove (where campground sites are available by advance reservation), State 180 drops into Kings Canyon at **Cedar Grove**. In contrast to Yosemite Valley, this gaping chasm is V rather than U-shaped; the smaller flow of the **Kings River** has yet to deposit enough alluvium to level out the canyon's floor.

Backpac dwarfed natural giants, Kings Canyon.

Cedar Grove offers idyllic camping and fishing alongside the placid waters of the Kings, and rustic lodging is also available. Two trailheads lead north and east toward the High Sierra, but the 6,500-foot (1,980-meter) climbs on south-facing (and therefore sun-broiled) slopes are only for the fit and experienced.

After backtracking to the Grant Grove, visitors can proceed into the park's Sequoia section by following State 198 south for 28 miles (45 km) to **Giant Forest**. A short nature trail here leads to the **General Sherman Tree**, believed to be the earth's largest living thing. California's coastal redwoods (*sequoia sempervirens*) are taller than the Sierra subspecies (*sequoia gigantea*), but in terms of girth and overall volume the mountain redwoods come out on top.

Hotel rooms, restaurants, a grocery store and a visitor center make Giant Forest the closest approximation of an urban center Sequoia/Kings Canyon has to offer. Three campgrounds lie a few miles farther south on State 198. The road continues southward past good camping and boating at **Lake Kaweah**, and drops back into the San Joaquin Valley at **Visalia**, 50 miles (80 km) from the park boundary.

The Eastern Sierra

Approached from the west, through the foothills of the Gold Country and on into Yosemite or Sequoia/Kings Canyon, the Sierra Nevada begins gently. Low, rolling hills studded with oak trees give way to higher hills blanketed with pines, which in turn give way to an accelerating crescendo of granite domes, spires and ridges, culminating in the 13,000 and 14,000-foot (4,000-meter) peaks of the crest.

But there is nothing gradual about the Sierra when approached from the east, up U.S. 395 from Southern California. On the east side, the mountains of the crest drop precipitously nearly 10,000 vertical feet (3,000 meters) in the space of a few miles, a single great front nearly 200 miles (320 km) long. From **Walker Pass** at the southern end of the range to **Tioga Pass** on the eastern Yosemite boundary, not a single highway cleaves the scarp, the longest contiguous roadless area in the United

The large living thing giant sequoias, Sequoia National Park.

194

States outside Alaska.

For geologists, the eastern Sierra presents the classic example of a fault-block mountain range: in essence, a huge chunk of the earth's crust that has been detached and uplifted on one margin so the entire mass tilts moderately toward the other. What this means for hikers, fishermen and horsepackers is instant wilderness, a vast alpine playground accessible from Owens Valley on the east side by 10-mile (16-km) drives and two or three-hour walks. And even for the most sedentary travelers, the drive up U.S. 395 presents the Sierras in all their majesty, jagged peak after jagged peak, glacier after glacier, the rugged heart of what John Muir called "The Range of Light."

Owens Valley

Driving north from Los Angeles, the dramatic scenery begins on the shores of **Owens Dry Lake**, near the hamlet of **Olancha**. To the left, the tawny, unforested peaks of the southern Sierras rise abruptly, cresting in granite pinnacles 12,000 feet (3,650 meters) high. To the right, across the wide, shimmering lake bed, the softer, more rounded contours of the somewhat lower **Inyo Range** dissolve into black and purple foothills. These are the portals of **Owens Valley**, deepest in America, "The Land of Little Rain."

The vegetation here is hardy desert flora — scrub oak, mesquite, sagebrush. The few trees there are — twisted, wind-stunted, widely spaced — serve only to accentuate the land's stark severity. By the time Pacific rain clouds reach here their moisture is spent, dropped on the coastal ranges and the Sierras' long west slope; in sight and indeed in the shadow of eternal snows, Owens Valley and the Inyos receive fewer than 10 inches (250 mm) of precipitation per year.

Owens Lake, however, owes its current status not to what scientists call a "rainshadow," but to the city of Los Angeles. The lake is in fact a sink with no outlet, a great catchment for all the water drained by the Owens River from the short but tumultuous streams on the Sierra's east slope. As recently as 80 years ago, steamships plied its azure waters, bearing silver ore from the great lode at **Cerro Gordo** in the southern

195

Inyos. The silver went to Los Angeles, and at one time accounted for a third of the city's commerce; when the ore ran out, the water followed. In 1905 and 1906, through deception and outright fraud, city officials purchased hundreds of thousands of acres bordering the Owens River, with the intention of diverting its entire flow south through an aqueduct. Completed in 1913 and augmented by a second diversion in 1940, the project transformed the irrigated orchards and croplands of Owens Valley into desert, turned prosperous communities into ghost towns, and poisoned forever the attitudes of those who decided to stay. Only two percent of the land in Inyo County remains in private hands; the rest belongs to Los Angeles and the federal government.

Just past the northern end of the lake bed, 21 miles (34 km) north of Olancha, State 136 departs east for Death Valley. Located at the junction is the **Interagency Visitor Center** which dispenses maps, information and wilderness permits for the extensive public lands under federal jurisdiction. In winter, the center is a mandatory stop for the latest word on campground closures and road condi-

tions; in the busy summer season, rangers will steer travelers to campgrounds with spaces still available. Unlike the national park camping areas on the west side of the Sierras, many east-side campgrounds do not accept advance reservations, and first-come, first-served is the order of the day.

Mount Whitney

On a patio outside the Visitor Center building, telescopes are trained on the summit of **Mount Whitney**, at 14,495 feet (4,418 meters) the highest mountain in the United States outside Alaska. The telescopes are necessary not because of the distance (barely three air miles away), but because several lower summits on the Sierra crest are much more commanding. A trail leads to the very top of Whitney where portable latrines have been emplaced to cope with the tide of visitors. It's a strenuous three-day hike (two up, one down), but no technical skills are required, and thousands make the trip every summer. The most difficult part of the journey, in fact, can prove to be getting a reservation: many Whitney trail permits

Alpine panorama greets a descending Mount Whitney climber.

are snapped up a year in advance. For reservations, which are free of charge, write Inyo National Forest, Mount Whitney Ranger District, Lone Pine, CA 93545.

In the heart of five-block-long **Lone Pine**, one mile north of the Interagency Visitor Center, Whitney Portal Road turns left off U.S. 395. The Mount Whitney trailhead lies 13 miles (21 km) farther and 6,500 feet (1,980 meters) higher, with several campgrounds along the way. Three miles out of town, side roads branch into the colorful **Alabama Hills**, where weirdly eroded pinnacles and boulders have served as movie sets for countless cut-'em-off-at-the-pass style Westerns. In reality, the intricate topography here sheltered Piute Indians from White settlers bent on wholesale slaughter, and the numerous rock caves also served as granaries for preserving the year's harvest of pinyon pine nuts.

Lone Pine offers passable restaurants and a plethora of modern motel rooms, many with views of Mount Whitney. But the town's most notable commercial enterprise is the **Alpine Skills Institute**, a school and guide service that offers group and private instruction in skiing, mountaineering, and rock and ice climbing. In 1983, Institute co-owner Mimi Vadasz became the first certified female alpine guide in America, and she regularly leads special courses in women's rock climbing, including technical ascents of Mount Whitney (P.O. Box 1027, Lone Pine, CA 93545).

Seven miles (11 km) north of Lone Pine on U.S. 395, two stone sentry buildings with upswept pagoda-style roofs mark the site of **Manzanar**. In 1942, by order of President Franklin D. Roosevelt, all West Coast citizens of Japanese ancestry (including many American citizens) were deprived of their property and interned in several remote concentration camps. **Manzanar**, with 10,000 prisoners, was the largest. Little remains today to remind visitors of Manzanar — just the fading gridwork of tent platforms, the concrete footings of guard towers, and here and there in the drifting sand the fragments of a porcelain doll.

Independence, 16 miles (26 km) north of Lone Pine, is the Inyo County seat and site of the **Eastern California Museum**, one block off U.S. 395. On

exhibit is an extensive collection of Indian basketry and mining camp relics. The Sierra crest continues high and dramatic for the next 30 miles (48 km) northward, reaching an alpine climax in the glaciers of the **Palisades**. Although the Palisade summits are a few hundred feet shy of Whitney, what they lack in height they make up for in technical climbing difficulty.

The Oldest Living Things

The 12-mile (19-km) Big Pine Creek Road to the Palisades trailheads and campgrounds is one of two routes toward high mountains from the area of **Big Pine**. The other road, State 168, heads east, not west, and the mountains are not the Sierra but the **White Mountains** probably America's least-visited high country. Geographically, the Whites and Inyos are a single range, divided arbitrarily by mapmakers at **Westgard Pass** (7,721 feet) or (2,353 meters). But the peaks at the northern end of the range are as much as a mile higher than the Inyos at Owens Lake, and they also play host to bristlecone pines, the oldest living things on earth, trees that were mature at the time of Homer.

To reach them, travelers must drive 12 miles out of Big Pine on State 168. A side road branches left and begins a steep climb that finally tops out at the 12,000-foot (3,650-meter) level. From here, on a clear day, views of the Sierras across the Owens Valley trench take in 100 miles (160 km) or more, from Mount Whitney to southern Yosemite. Pavement ends at the **Methuselah Grove**, 27 miles (43 km) from Big Pine, amidst the least forestlike setting imaginable. The Whites are desert mountains, sere and stony buttresses rooted deep in rolling extraterrestrial uplands; the topography is so resolutely alien that the National Aeronautics and Space Administration (NASA) tested the Lunar Rover here. And the 5,000-year-old bristlecones, it turns out, live as long as they do precisely because the brutal combination of altitude, wind and extreme cold eliminates virtually all animals and plants as competition for an infinitesimal amount of water.

Bishop, 15 miles (24 km) north of Big Pine, boasts what is undoubtedly the highest per capita number of sporting goods stores in the United States, and

ne gnarled ınk of a istlecone ne bears tness to llennia of rvival in brutal mate.

the first decent restaurants north of the L.A. County line (**Whisky Creek** and **Sierra Embers**). The town's main attractions, though, lie outside the city limits in the **Bishop Creek Recreation Area** that begins 10 miles (16 km) out West Line Street. Seven campgrounds, three pack stations, two major trailheads and dozens of lakes and trout streams make Bishop Creek the most heavily visited drainage in Inyo National Forest.

From the beginning of fishing season in late April until the end of hunting season in late November, solitude is in short supply here. This state of affairs is most easily remedied by a day-long walk over **Piute Pass** (11,423 feet or 3,482 meters) into **Humphreys Basin**, an alpine wonderland containing countless rockbound lakes with close-up views of **Mount Humphreys** (13,986 feet or 4,263 meters), among climbers one of the most sought-after and challenging Sierra summits. Guided trips may be arranged through **Sierra Nevada Alpine Guides**, a skiing and mountaineering school operated by renowned extreme skiers Tom Carter and Allan Bard (P.O. Box 1751, Bishop, CA 93514, Tel. 619-873-5617).

North of Bishop, U.S. 395 climbs up through volcanic rock to **Sherwin Summit** (7,000 feet or 2,134 meters) and leaves Owens Valley proper. Two miles north of the village called **Toms Place**, the highway enters **Long Valley**, alongside man-made **Crowley Lake** with its boat ramps and tackle shops. A broad circular depression ringed by mountains, Long Valley is in fact a caldera, the mouth of an ancient volcano, and recent earthquakes and geothermal activity here have convinced scientists that the area may be on its way to emulating Mount St. Helens. Local residents, as might be expected, are crossing their fingers.

Skiers and Devils

Twelve miles (19 km) north of Crowley Lake, a two-mile side road leads to **Mammoth Lakes**, the largest downhill ski resort in America. In winter, Mammoth is where Los Angeles goes skiing, and it is not uncommon to share lift lines with 20,000 other powder hounds. On the plus side, Mammoth offers gourmet dining (at **Roget's** and **La Boulangerie**), wine and cheese shops, and in summer the Sierra Arts Festival. During ski season, the best way to escape the hustle and bustle here is to drive 15 miles (24 km) north on U.S. 395 to **June Mountain**, a smaller, more rustic resort with a European ambience. But while Mammoth often remains open to offer slushball skiing on the Fourth of July, June Mountain is required by the Forest Service to cease operations by April 15.

A summer (not winter) attraction is **Devils Postpile National Monument**, a 30-minute drive west of Mammoth Lakes into the Sierras. About 630,000 years ago, dark molten lava poured through Mammoth Pass and flowed into the deep canyon of the middle fork of the San Joaquin River, where it cooled, solidified and cracked into astonishingly uniform vertical columns. Successive glaciation scraped and polished the tops of the columns into a smooth, tile-like surface. Today, the abrupt geometric pickets of Devils Postpile (80 feet high, one-quarter-mile long) offer mute testimony to the combined power of the twin forces that shaped the entire Sierras — fire and ice. Limited camping is available in summer at **Agnew Meadows**

(just before the monument boundary on State 203) and **Red's Meadows** (just after the boundary); nominally priced mineral baths fed by natural hot springs add a sybaritic touch to the latter. Red's Meadow is also trailhead for the easiest trail crossing of the Sierras, via a corridor between the **John Muir Wilderness** and **Minarets Wilderness** areas.

At **Deadman Summit**, north of June Mountain, U.S. 395 begins a long descent into Mono Basin, once the site of an inland sea and today the focal point of an ongoing controversy over Los Angeles' appropriation of eastern Sierra water. **Mono Lake**, the last remnant of that sea, is the oldest continuously existing body of water in North America, and volcanic islands near the lake's northern shore are breeding grounds for 90 percent of the world's California seagulls.

Since 1940, when Los Angeles diverted Mono's inflow streams, the lake has shrunk in size and has become highly saline, a result which threatens to decimate the gull population by killing the brine shrimp on which the birds feed. To make matters worse, even moderate winds carry corrosive sediments from

Calcified rocks rise from Mono Lake, the oldest body of water North America.

the exposed lakebed into the homes — and lungs — of local residents. Conservationists claim that a minimal water conservation effort in Los Angeles would obviate the need for Mono diversions; the city argues, in essence, that the lake isn't worth saving anyway. No definitive court decisions are expected anytime soon, and in the meantime dust clouds swirl like disembodied phantoms around eerie calcified rock formations on the receding shoreline. Some of the best examples of these unusual towers, called *tufa*, are preserved at **Mono Lake State Tufa Reserve**, seven miles (11 km) east of U.S. 395.

From May until November, or until the first winter snow falls, the town of **Lee Vining** on Mono Lake's western shore is the east entry to Yosemite National Park, via 9,991-foot (3,045-meter) Tioga Pass. From Lee Vining, Tuolumne Meadows is a 45-minute drive away; it takes at least two hours to reach Yosemite Valley. Campgrounds are spaced every 15 miles (24 km) or so, and unlike the rest of the park's sites, are *not* reservable in advance.

North of Mono Lake, the Sierra crest begins to lower, although "lower" in this case still means snowy summits 11,000 feet (3,350 meters) high. Eleven and one-half miles (18½ km) north of Lee Vining, a graded side road leads 13 miles (21 km) to **Bodie State Historic Park**, which offers both an excellent view of the northern Sierras and a fascinating glimpse into the life of a '49ers' boom town. Once the wildest camp in the West, Bodie was home to a ragtag collection of miners and confidence men who made silver fortunes by day and squandered them by night in opium dens, saloons and bawdy houses.

Bridgeport, three miles north of the Bodie turnoff, makes its living from hunters and fisherman, drawn to the **Twin Lakes Recreation Area** 12 miles (19 km) west and south of town. Boat rentals and guide services abound here, and backpackers and horsepackers may arrange trips into northern Yosemite when conditions permit. **Matterhorn Peak** and the **Sawtooth Ridge** mark the park's northern boundary, as well as the end of the true High Sierra; although the range continues another 200 miles (320 km) northward it never again attains such rocky grandeur.

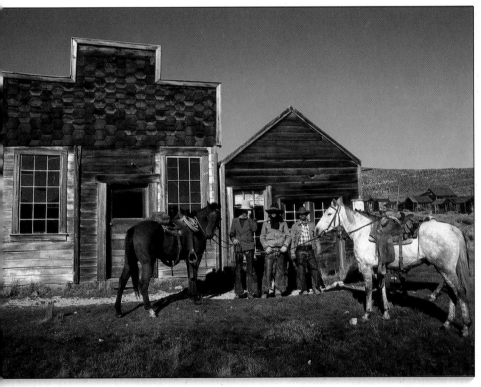

VALLEY OF THE SAN JOAQUIN

The San Joaquin Valley is California's neglected middle child. Stuck between the brash, self-indulgent coast and the awe-inspiring Sierras, the valley suffers the kind of image problem more associated with the American Midwest than the Golden State. Not to be confused with the source of Moon Zappa's musical parody "Valley Girl" (the San Fernando), or even with John Steinbeck's austere collection *The Long Valley* (the Salinas), the San Joaquin endures on its own terms.

Though its name is often mistakenly applied to California's entire Central Valley, the San Joaquin comprises just the southern two-thirds of that 450-mile (720-kilometer) long, 50-mile (80-km) wide basin. It follows the course of the **San Joaquin River**, flowing south to north, to the Sacramento-San Joaquin Delta, where both rivers empty into San Francisco Bay.

Mostly flat and treeless, the valley doesn't at first appear to offer much in the way of attractions. It is experienced by most travelers as something to be passed through quickly on the way to somewhere else. Even the Queen of England got a taste of the valley experience on her California vacation. Interstate 5, running the length of the valley, is the main link between Los Angeles and the Bay Area, and the east-west routes to Lake Tahoe and the Sierras all cross the valley. So the valley can only sell itself by virtue of being in the middle of it all. Fresno, for instance, boasts of being the only community in the United Sates within an hour and a half of three national parks (Yosemite, Sequoia and Kings Canyon).

The San Joaquin *is* known for some unpleasant natural phenomena. Valley fever — a little-known respiratory illness — is spread when strong winds be-stir the spores of a fungus indigenous to the arid soil in parts of the valley and the American Southwest. And in December and January, dense "tule fog" blankets the areas for days at a time, making driving hazardous.

But its second-class status bothers San Joaquin Valley residents very little. The business of the valley is farming, and it succeeds at that like few other spots on earth. The nearby Gold Country mining claims were abandoned long ago, but the valley is enjoying general prosperity. It has become one of the fastest growing areas in the state.

Heaven for Farmers

Agriculture, after all, is California's biggest industry, and more than half of its $14 billion a year in farm goods is produced in the San Joaquin. Fresno County alone accounts for some $2 billion of that, making it the No. 1 farming county in America. The valley's alluvial soil, covering more than a million irrigated acres (400,000 hectares), supports some of the most productive farming in the world. And beneath the soil are deposits of oil and natural gas. Major crops include cotton, grapes, tomatoes, corn, fruit and nuts.

Recently, as population has grown, valley cities have experienced a boom as commercial and manufacturing centers. But it's still the fields and orchards and canneries and processing plants that sustain the area. Employment in the valley is more closely tied to rainfall than to the vagaries of the economy.

This relative stability has drawn a cross-section of people from around the state, with Blacks, Whites, Chicanos, Chinese, Japanese, Filipinos and Armenians represented.

San Joaquin Valley fields were not always peaceful. For years they were the scene of bitter labor disputes as the United Farm Workers Union, led by Cesar Chavez, fought for recognition. Today, however, most large growers have agreed to union contracts.

It is the abundance of that most precious of the state's resources — water that keeps things going and makes the San Joaquin Valley a recreational as well as an agricultural heartland. Aside from the Sacramento River Delta and the mammoth irrigation projects it supports, several of California's great rivers flow through the area — the San Joaquin, the **Stanislaus**, the **Tuolumne**, the **Merced**, the **Kings**, and further south, the **Kern**. Most are renowned for outstanding, and occasionally terrifying, stretches of whitewater rafting.

The San Joaquin is also wine country. It can't match the trendiness, or maybe even the quality, of Napa Valley, but it's got the quantity. San Joaquin Valley is home to dozens of wineries, many of them offering tours and picnic grounds. And all those roadside attractions that have fallen to boutiques, theme stores and amusement parks elsewhere in the state still exist here — canneries, chocolate factories, nut trees, not to mention parks, ranchlands and wildflowers.

It doesn't take long to see that the valley is the lifeline of California. An hour out of San Francisco going east, I-580 crosses **Altamont Pass**, one of the windiest spots on the coast. It is marked by an exquisitely rural sight — a windmill farm, overhead power lines and dairy cows peacefully coexisting. As the descent begins, the highway crosses a branch of the **California Aqueduct**. Almost immediately the freeway is full of trucks hauling double trailer-loads of bottled tomato catsup, or canned peaches or pears. Welcome to the San Joaquin Valley.

Stockton and Lodi

Seventy-eight miles (125 km) east of San Francisco, between I-5 and State 99, is **Stockton**, queen city of the Delta, where the valley is crisscrossed by

California Aqueduct, Merced County.

sloughs and mudflats. A rambling old river city and mining settlement still showing traces of 1910 grandeur, Stockton is the state's oldest and largest inland seaport. The city's most prestigious institution is the **University of the Pacific**, the first chartered university in California. Local eateries reflect the area's diverse population — Chinese, Mexican and American family style. **Xochimilocho** (36 E. San Joaquin Ave.) is a local favorite for good, cheap Mexican food.

Ten miles (16 km) north, on the **Mokelumne River**, **Lodi** is home to the county's **Micke Grove Park and Zoo**, with its gardens, swimming pool, kiddie rides and picnic facilities. **Guild Wineries** on State 12 have a tasting room open year-round. Between Stockton and the **Modesto** area are several major wineries, including **E&J Gallo**, the world's largest independent winery.

There are two ways to travel the length of the valley. I-5 is a fast, flat freeway which gets the traveler from San Francisco to Los Angeles in barely six hours. It guarantees uninterrupted and uninteresting highway driving. One slight detour southwest of Fresno, however, leads 12 miles (19 km) to one

of the valley's most celebrated sights. The oil fields north of **Coalinga** — the little town that survived a devastating series of earthquakes in the summer of 1983 — are an unexpected delight in an otherwise dreary landscape, with oil pumps festively decorated as Indians, animals and mythical creatures.

State Highway 99, the other north-south route, is the valley's main business artery. It is considerably slower than the interstate, but reveals more of San Joaquin's secrets, passing through the valley's most populated areas and some of the best roadside produce stands in the state.

Caswell State Park, reached after a drive through miles of almond orchards, is just off State 99 near the town of Ripon. More than 250 acres (100 hectares) of oak-shaded trails, campgrounds and beaches along the Stanislaus spell relief from the heat of summer, when temperatures close to 100 degrees Fahrenheit (38°C) are common. Though it has more to do with releases from the **Melones Reservoir** than from the melting icepack, even in the dog days of summer the Stanislaus runs cold and deep. The last wild stretch of

e San quin atoes color to acking t.

whitewater, several miles upstream, has been lost to the dam, but the river still delivers fine swimming, fishing and tubing. The park itself offers a glimpse of the natural beauty of the valley 100 years ago, when Indians trapped beaver and fox, and forests covered the valley. **McConnell State Recreation Area**, eight miles (13 km) south of **Modesto** on the Merced River, also offers swimming, fishing, camping and picnicking.

Modesto and Fresno

Like much of California, Modesto is the creation of Leland Stanford's Central Pacific Railroad. The railroad town got its name in 1870 when humble San Francisco banker William Ralston was asked to give his name to the town and declined the honor. To this day, Modesto may be described as unassuming. The Tuolumne River runs almost unnoticed through the southern fringes of town. A turn-of-the-century-vintage steel arch along the main thoroughfare promotes the town's virtues: "Water, Wealth, Contentment, Health."

As in most of the valley, food is king — not eating (one notable downtown restaurant is called **Two Jerks With a Grill**), but producing. A "Gourmet Taste Tour" sponsored by the Chamber of Commerce includes stops at an almond exchange, a mushroom farm, a cheese processor, a Hershey chocolate plant and local wineries.

Halfway between Modesto and Fresno, **Merced** is a major access point to Yosemite. The biggest attraction Merced can call its own may be **Castle Air Force Base**, where lumbering B-52's provide a somewhat chilling context to the **Castle Air Museum's** collection of vintage fighters.

Fresno is the sleeping giant of central California. From a train station by the edge of a wheatfield, it has become a city with 11 freeway exits, rows of highrises and a metropolitan area of more than 300,000. It is the financial and cultural as well as the service and commercial center of the San Joaquin Valley. It is also as ethnically diverse as any city in the state, with large Mexican, Asian, Armenian and Basque communities. Cultural institutions include the **Metropolitan Museum of Art, Science and History;** the **Community Theatre;** and the **Fresno Philharmonic**

Harvestin corn, Ma County.

Orchestra. Two wineries in town offer tours — **Cribari Winery** and **A. Nonini Winery**.

But despite its increasing importance to the cultural and economic life of the valley. Fresno retains the flavor of small-town America. Weekends are likely to be spent watering the lawn, washing the car, and almost certainly watching football on television or at local schools. At night, young people gather in bookstores and theaters as well as on the streets, cruising the city's wide boulevards in classic Fifties style. The early Seventies' Steven Spielberg film classic, *American Graffiti*, was based on this lifestyle; in fact, the movie was focused on Modesto.

As one long-time resident puts it, "People who say there's nothing to do here haven't looked around." **Roeding Park**, right off State 99 in west Fresno, features a number of family amusements — a zoo with more than 1,000 animals; a Playland with rides; and Storyland, a quaint walk-through village where plaster fairytale figures tell their story. **Woodward Park** in central Fresno has a Japanese Garden and a bird sanctuary. But the most bizarre attraction in town is **Forestiere Underground Gardens**, 5021 Shaw Ave. The gardens were the one-time domicile of sculptor-horticulturist Baldasare Forestiere, who singlehandedly carved out the maze of 100 rooms, passageways and courtyards over 40 years.

Fresno is also distinguished by a number of fine restaurants, the best of which is **Harland's**. Its *nouvelle* California cuisine and elegant decor rank with the finest in the state.

The annual rodeo in nearby **Clovis** brings buckeroos together for two days of roping, riding and bronco-busting the last weekend in April. Buffalo roam year-round 40 miles (64 km) northwest at **Safari World** in **Coarsegold**

The San Joaquin Valley has a life of its own. Certainly it is unlike any other part of California. Fig orchards stand between suburban houses, outlying hills reflect brilliant sunsets, the seasons are distinct, and in springtime fields and orchards blossom for miles in spectacular color. It is a place both muscular and subtle, a place where huge packing plants with smokestacks are surrounded by soft fields of new green and autumn yellow.

farmer
ys his
ce.

207

BIG SUR AND MONTEREY BAY

The stretch of Northern California coast from San Simeon to Santa Cruz is one region that does not exist in a state of implicit apology for not being San Francisco. The pace might be slow, but the highly differentiated and individualistic communities which occupy this shore are so busy leading their own lives, the thought of doing otherwise would not occur to them.

Driving north up State Highway 1, the traveler first encounters ruggedly beautiful Big Sur, to which no other coastline in the state can compare. The boutiques and quaint restaurants of Carmel match anything that Union Street can offer. Quiet little Monterey, the former Spanish capital, exists in its own time warp. Santa Cruz is a liberal university community grafted onto a conservative backwater; despite a rocky beginning, their union now shows surprising hybrid vigor. Salinas is a blue-collar agricultural town that makes superficial sophisticates feel properly effete.

Spectacular Big Sur

Big Sur is as much a feeling as it is a place. Those who have been there feel as if they've been to the mountaintop, crawled to the end of the continent, and deliberately put themselves on the last shred of ragged edge.

And part of the attraction is that they *are* on the edge. West of Big Sur there's no more land until Japan. The mountains plunge into the sea. The surf comes booming and crashing over battered rocks to sweep secluded and inaccessible beaches. In the meanwhile, gulls wheel overhead, cormorants wait on white-stained rocks and, further out, big-billed pelicans skim across the water like silent pterodactyls from the distant Pliocene epoch.

Between the two great world wars of this century, convict labor built a narrow, twisting road over the virgin California coastline from the Hearst Castle at San Simeon 93 miles (150 kilometers) north to the Monterey Peninsula. Except for the road itself, it's not much different today than it was then — there are no billboards or streetlights, only occasional scattered mailboxes and, with the possible exception of Big Sur village itself, nothing even recognizable as a town.

The road (State Highway 1) goes back and forth from sea level to 1,000 feet in just a matter of a mile or so with the result that one minute the traveler is shivering in a cold gray mist, sharp with the ammonia smell of salt water and kelp; and hardly five minutes later he is standing on sunny bright hillside, looking out over a billowy white blanket of ocean fog stretching north and south as far as the eye can see. On really hot days in the inland valleys, the rising air currents pull the fog right up the mountainside, turning State 1 into an endless gray tunnel with the fog skimming overhead like an upward flowing waterfall.

The road itself is in no great condition, the blasting needed to build it in the first place having weakened the rock on which it stands. During heavy winter rains, huge chunks of roadway simply slide into the ocean, cutting off local residents for days and weeks at a time.

There are a number of inns, lodges, motels and campgrounds scattered along State 1. There are also places out of sight of the highway where persistent wayfarers can make camp, sip their wine and, high above the crashing surf, listen to the barking of sea lions and the cries of sea gulls as the sun sinks slowly in the west. (One must, however, watch out for poison oak.)

In many ways, Big Sur is still wild country. As recently as the turn of the century, there were girzzly bears roaming the deep redwood canyons in the hills above the coast. Even today, the local men who sip morning coffee at cozy roadside gas station-cafes carry high-powered rifles in the rear-window racks of their pickup trucks — although now they use them mainly for shooting deer and coyotes or punching bullet holes in the "Sea Otter Game Refuge" signs.

Until the end of World War II, Big Sur was mainly populated by ranchers, loggers, miners and such. But following the war, literary people began turning up to live cheaply, grow marijuana in remote canyons, and commune with what long-time resident Henry Miller called "the face of the earth as the creator intended it to look." (Actually, not everyone found it that attractive. Jack Kerouac, for one, couldn't stand

ceding
es, big
at
Sur.
, State
way 1
s a
yon.

211

the solitude.)

By the end of the Sixties, Big Sur had become a cultural fad where neo-agrarian hippies lived off the land (and food stamps), made non-negotiable demands on behalf of the environment and, every dry season, inadvertently set fire to sections of the hills. At the same time, affluent San Franciscans, having discovered that there's nothing like an ocean view to bring out the subtle taste of Brie and Chablis, began arriving by Porsche and BMW in an ever-increasing stream.

The best way to see Big Sur is to drive the entire length. Travelers must beware of bicyclists, most of whom pedal from north to south to enjoy the stiff tailwind. The most compelling part of Big Sur is the coast itself, which in the southern half of the drive is all there is anyway. From **Esalen** north, however, there are additional attractions of quite a different order.

Esalen is located midway between San Simeon and Carmel on the site of an old sulfur hot spring. During the Sixties, it rapidly became the Harvard of the human potential movement, a gathering place for such teachers as Fritz Perls, Alan Watts, Ida Rolf, George Leonard, Gregory Bateson and Abraham Maslow. Today it is an expensive retreat where spiritual seekers ponder Eastern religion, enjoy full body massages, and revel in insights while contemplating the ocean from an outdoor hot tub.

Ten miles (16 km) north of Esalen is the hand-built, charming, always-full **Big Sur Inn,** (reservations must be made well in advance) and a mile beyond that is **Nepenthe,** where Orson Welles once bought a cabin for Rita Hayworth. (She didn't like it.) Today Nepenthe is a striking multi-leveled restaurant/arts-and-crafts boutique where visitors can listen to the music of the Sixties, buy local art, contemplate dramatic sculptures, sip California wine, and watch the restless Pacific beat out its brains against the granite shoreline.

Three miles (five km) further north is **Pfeiffer-Big Sur State Park**, with its tall redwoods and **Big Sur Lodge** (again, reservations must be made early). And at the northern end of Big Sur, just four miles south of Carmel, is perhaps the single best attraction of the entire coast — **Point Lobos State Reserve**, a 1,276-

The Big coastline near And Molera S Park.

212

acre (516-hectare) promontory embraced by cypress trees, tidepools, skin-diving coves, exposed headlands, crashing surf, sea lions, sea otters, harbor seals and, occasionally, killer whales.

Cute and Cozy Carmel

Two chance factors made **Carmel** what it is today — starving writers and unwanted painters fleeing the devastation of the 1906 San Francisco earthquake, and canny developers who, to reduce their real-estate taxes, covered the previously treeless site with a thick carpet of Monterey pines. The result is one of the most endearing little seaside towns on the entire West Coast. When the evening fog rolls in from the bay, the lights inside the cozy little houses, combined with the faint whiff of wood smoke, give Carmel the peaceful feeling of an 18th Century European village. There are no streetlights or stoplights and, except in the immediate downtown area, not even parking meters, sidewalks or curbs.

Although some 3 or 4 million people visit this southern gateway to the **Monterey Peninsula** each year, Carmel has firmly resisted any temptation to yield to used-car lots, fast-food franchises, high-rise buildings and neon signs. The street, the plazas and the quaint little malls attract pedestrians with wine shops and booksellers, antique stores, art galleries and numerous boutiques. The local market offers freshly picked artichokes (from fields barely a mile away), sweet basil, French cheeses, German sausages, liver pâté, and floor-to-ceiling racks of imported and domestic wines. At night, on the side streets, a dozen couples might be dining quietly by candlelight behind dark restaurant windows. In the residential parts of town, the streets meander casually through the forest, sometimes even splitting in two to accommodate an especially praiseworthy pine.

Carmel is such an attractive little community that everyone wants to live there. The predictable result is that even a small cottage sells for upwards of a quarter of a million dollars. Most of the residents are retired, professionals or otherwise well-to-do. As for the starving writers and unwanted artists who founded Carmel ... well, if

ritual
kers find
urfside
ana along
coast
th of
mel.

213

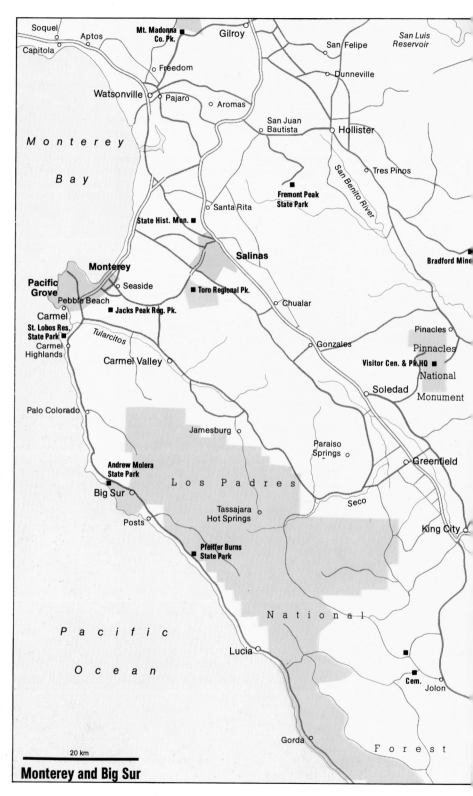

Monterey and Big Sur

they should happen to return, wrote John Steinbeck in *Travels With Charlie*, not only could they not afford to live here, "they would be instantly picked up as suspicious characters and deported over the city line."

In fact, for many visitors, Carmel evokes an ambiguous response. It's cuteness is ultimately cloying. It's not so much a town for active producers as passive consumers, and its restrictive land-use policies have allowed it to slough off less desirable businesses and services onto its less affluent neighbors. Although the city takes great pride in its local artists (and in its own lingering reputation as an art colony), the kind of work turned out by Carmel artists today often runs to images of weatherbeaten barns and crashing surf.

Besides the town itself, Carmel's other main attraction is Father Junípero Serra's **Mission San Carlos Borromeo del Rio Carmelo**, better known simply as the Carmel Mission. Established in 1770, it was Serra's headquarters until his death in 1784. Today it is his tomb: he is buried beneath the basilica floor, in front of the altar. Visitors can see Serra's own small monk's cell as well as 18th Century documents and other relics in the mission museum. It is located on Rio Road at the southern end of Carmel, west of State 1. An annual fiesta is held in late September.

Also worth seeing is poet Robinson Jeffers' hand-built stone **Tor House and Hawk Tower**. Admission is $5; reservations are required.

The **Carmel Bach Festival**, a classical music lover's delight, is held annually from mid July to early August at the Sunset Center on San Carlos Avenue.

The 17 Mile Drive

Just north of the foot of Ocean Avenue is the Carmel Gate entrance to the **Seventeen Mile Drive**, which meanders around the Monterey Peninsula, via the **Del Monte Forest**, to Pacific Grove. Because all the roads in the Del Monte Forest are privately owned, travelers on the Seventeen Mile Drive must pay a $4 use fee to the Pebble Beach Company. The trip is worth it, if for no other reason than to see the big **stone mansion** (looking like something out of a flash of lightning in a dark night on the Scottish Moors) next to **The Ghost Tree** cypress.

ssion San
rlos
rromeo del
Carmelo.

Still, the attitude of the Pebble Beach Company toward tourists seems more than a little condescending. Along their exclusive golf courses are signs every 100 feet or so warning visitors that trespassing on the course is a misdemeanor punishable by a fine and imprisonment. At the famous **Lone Pine Cypress**, a single gnarled and windswept tree near the top of a huge wave-battered rock, the sign on the protective fence reads "No Trespassing Beyond This Point," as if merely being in the forest were a trespass in itself.

The Monterey Peninsula is a mecca for golfers with some 17 private and public courses. Best known of the public courses are **Spyglass Hill** and the semi-public **Pebble Beach**, site of the annual Bing Crosby Pro-Am Golf Championship in January. Those who want to play golf at Pebble Beach should stay overnight in its lodge.

Pacific Grove, home of the migratory monarch butterfly, sits on the northernmost tip of the Monterey Peninsula beyond the Del Monte Forest. Before the arrival of Europeans, native Indian tribes visited Pacific Grove in the hot summers to lounge under the trees and feast on the abundant mussels. abalone and fish.

In 1875, a group of Methodist ministers laid out a tent city on the site and turned it into a religious retreat. Morality was as high as the wooden fence around Pacific Grove. There was a 9 p.m. curfew; bathing suits had to have double crotches; and liquor could only be sold for medicinal purposes. Such rectitude proved contagious, and the town subsequently became a haven for other ethical and religious groups.

During the Depression, John Steinbeck lived in Pacific Grove in a three-room cottage belonging to his father. Although Steinbeck was too poor to afford postage to send out his manuscripts, he didn't go hungry. The soil, he later wrote, was a rich black loam. With a little effort anyone could grow potatoes, lettuce, turnips, onions and kale.

Pacific Grove's ethical-religious traditions still flourish at **Asilomar**, a state-owned conference site with a summer-camp atmosphere nestled in the pines at the north end of the Seventeen Mile Drive. Most visitors come to educate themselves in social, ethical, inter-racial and self-awareness matters. It is not unusual to see conferees hugging on the footpaths or practicing *tai chi* and aerobic dancing on the flagpole green.

Historic Monterey

The history of the people who passed through **Monterey** is the history of California itself — first there were the native Indians, then the Spanish explorers, the Mexican ranchers, the American settlers, the Sicilian fishermen and finally the most ubiquitous and persistent invader of all, the tourist.

Thanks to Steinbeck, the most famous attraction in town is the former Ocean View Avenue, now known as **Cannery Row**. During World War II, Monterey was the sardine capital of the Western Hemisphere, processing some 200,000 tons of the fish a year. As Steinbeck described it then, the street was "a poem, a stink, a grating noise, a quality of light, a tone, a habit, a nostalgia, a dream." When the fishing boats came in heavy with their catch, the canneries blew their whistles and the residents of Monterey came streaming down the hill to take their places amid the rumbling, rattling, squealing machinery of the canning plants. When finally the last

Cannery Row, Monterey

sardine was cleaned, cut, cooked and canned, the whistle blew again, and the workers trudged back up the hill, dripping, wet and smelly.

After the war, for reasons variously blamed on overfishing, changing currents and divine retribution, the sardines suddenly disappeared from Monterey Bay and all the canneries went broke. But as Steinbeck has pointed out, it was not a total loss. In those heady early years, the beaches were so deeply covered with fish guts and flies that a sickening stench covered the whole town. Today the beaches are bright and clean, the air sparklingly fresh. Cannery Row, located along the waterfront on the northwest side of town just beyond the **Presidio**, has become an impressive tourist attraction. Its old buildings have been filled with lusty bars, gaudy restaurants, a wax museum, dozens of shops, a carousel, an arcade and peddlers selling hot pretzels and caramel corn.

In downtown Monterey today the main visitor attraction is **Fisherman's Wharf**. (The real working wharf is two blocks east). Fisherman's Wharf is lined with restaurants, shops, an organ grinder with a monkey at the gate, noisy sea lions who swim among the pilings while barking for fish, and fresh fish markets.

To see the rest of Monterey, a three-mile (five-km) walking tour called **The Path of History** leads past the more important historical buildings and sites. These include the **Customs House**, the oldest public building in California, now a museum; **Pacific House**, a two-story adobe with a Monterey balcony around the second floor and impressive historical exhibits from the Spanish, Mexican and early American periods; **Colton Hall**, a two-story building with a classical portico which was the site of the state's first (1849) constitutional convention; **Stevenson House**, a smaller former hotel where the romantic (and sickly) Robert Louis Stevenson lived for a few months while courting his future wife; and the **Royal Presidio Chapel**, in constant use since 1794. (U.S. President Herbert Hoover was married in a courtyard there.)

The Presidio, founded in 1770 by Gaspar de Portolá, now serves as the **U.S. Army Language School**. Other points of interest in Monterey include the **Monterey Peninsula Museum** of re-

gional art and the **Allen Knight Maritime Museum**, featuring relics of the era of sailing ships and whaling. In mid September each year, the acclaimed **Monterey Jazz Festival** attracts many of the biggest names in contemporary music to the Monterey Fairgrounds.

North of Monterey, State 1 skirts the shore of Monterey Bay, passing the Army's **Fort Ord Military Reservation** and entering **Moss Landing**, the one town on the bay that actually looks like a working seaport instead of a tourist trap. Its landmarks are the huge twin smokestacks of the Pacific Gas & Electric Co. generating plant. There are tuna and shellfish canneries, hundreds of chipped, stained and rusted fishing vessels, and vacant lots filled with weeds, anchor chairs and harbor buoys.

Nonconformist Santa Cruz

Watsonville, the next sizable town north, comes to life on Memorial Day weekend in May when biplanes and other aerial phenomena from all over California drop in for the **West Coast Antique Aircraft Fly-In**.

At the northern end of Monterey Bay — 28 miles (45 km) from Monterey via State 1 — is **Santa Cruz**, a cool, green, redwood-shingled beach town hoisted for the moment on the leftward swing of its own political pendulum. In 1965, when the **University of California** opened its Santa Cruz campus on remote hills high above the city, the intent was to create an Oxford-style university where students could devote themselves to four years of intense semi-cloistered study, uninterrupted by the hue and cry of the outside world.

It was a good idea at the wrong time. What students craved in the Sixties was "relevance," not ivory-tower scholarship. And within a few years their energy and sense of mission had totally transformed what had previously been a quiet backwater town into an activist community. Soon those who went out to dinner in Santa Cruz were shown to their table by a "waitperson" and were entertained by strolling troubadors who sang of their love for redwoods and whales, the latter in Santa Cruz having edged out dogs as man's best friend.

The other distinguishing feature of the new enlightened Santa Cruz was its undiscriminating tolerance. In reaction

Fishing fl[e] at twilight Moss Landing.

cific
astline
rth of
nta Cruz.

to what it saw as the rigidity and conformity of official "Amerika," Santa Cruz became so determinedly tolerant of eccentricity, diversity and even perversity that in the early Seventies it became a hornet's nest of violent crime. In a painful reassessment of what the Sixties had wrought, Santa Cruz's new intellectual community decided that just because conservatives were against crime, progressives didn't have to be for it. And today, Santa Cruz is a peaceful as well as attractive community.

The students may have originally come down off their hilltop campus to demonstrate, but they stayed to open dozens of excellent restaurants, cafes, pastry shops, bookstores and a multitude of shops selling everything from 10-speed bicycles to Japanese kites. In the process, they restored and rejuvenated downtown Santa Cruz, restaining the oak on the turn-of-the-century buildings, polishing the brass, installing stained glass, replacing cement block and aluminum with natural redwood and hanging ferns. Santa Cruz has sparkling clean air in the summer; its only drawback is the torrential winter rain that turns canyons into rivers.

The Santa Cruz **municipal pier** features restaurants, fish markets and fishing facilities. Next to it is a wide white sandy beach. On the other side is the **boardwalk amusement park**, a throwback to an earlier era with its carousel, Ferris wheel, thrilling roller coaster and old-fashioned arcade containing shooting galleries and air hockey, not to mention an unwelcome invasion of chirping, beeping video games.

The **Mission Santa Cruz**, founded in 1791 as the 12th in the chain, has a small reproduction of the original church and a tiny museum. Finally, for those whose interests run to Victorian homes, the chamber of commerce offers information on four short walking tours.

On the bluffs west of the pier on West Cliff Drive, one can look down upon wet-suited surfers waiting in the water for the next perfect wave. And beyond that, in **Natural Bridges State Beach**, a sandstone bridge initially created by the pounding surf is now in the process of being destroyed by the same force.

Six miles (10 km) northwest of Santa Cruz, the settlement of **Felton** attracts train buffs with its **Roaring Camp and Big Trees Narrow Gauge Railroad**. This

late 19th Century steam engine makes five summertime loops a day (once daily in winter) past **Henry Cowell Redwoods State Park**.

On Monterey Bay near Santa Cruz, there's beachfront camping at **New Brighton, Seacliff** and **Sunset** state beaches. But these sites are much in demand and tend to be booked months in advance. Inland sites are frequently available at short notice, as are private campsites and trailer parks. The Santa Cruz County Convention and Visitors Bureau supplies a convenient list.

Inland Monterey County

Just 15 miles (24 km) inland from Monterey Bay, on U.S. Highway 101 between San Jose and San Luis Obispo, is the agricultural center of **Salinas**. Hub of the incredibly rich Salinas Valley, it is known for its vast fields of lettuce and, increasingly, numerous new vineyards stretching out on either side of U.S. 101 as far as the eye can see.

Salinas is also headquarters for Cesar Chavez's United Farm Workers Union. Throughout the Seventies, Chavez fought a bitter series of battles with grape and lettuce growers in an attempt to unionize Spanish-speaking farm laborers. In sharp contrast to the heads of other unions, Chavez lived simply and periodically went on prolonged fasts. While this made him a real hero to California's millions of Chicanos, and a modern folk hero among college students and progressive politicians such as former Governor Jerry Brown, it also earned him the undying enmity of many small farmers who bitterly resented being cast in the role of greedy robber barons.

As a hard-working agricultural town, Salinas doesn't have many tourist attractions outside of the large Victorian house (now converted into a restaurant) where Steinbeck was born and where he wrote his first two books, *The Red Pony* and *Tortilla Flat*. The nearby **Steinbeck Library** has devoted itself to his memory — despite the fact that when he lived in Salinas, Steinbeck was thoroughly condemned for his left-wing leanings. In addition to having a large collection of works by and about Steinbeck, the library also displays a five-foot statue of the Pulitzer Prize-winning author outside the entrance; it makes

The Carm Valley.

him look like an unfortunate cross between V.I. Lenin and a pot-bellied elf.

About 20 miles (32 km) north of Salinas, via State 156, the impressive **Mission San Juan Bautista** has become the focus of a state historic park. The mission, founded in 1797, was the 15th and largest of the mission churches. It still actively serves a Spanish-speaking congregation. Nearby are the **Plaza Hotel** (1813), the **Castro House** (1841) and the **Zanetta House** (1868), plus stables and a blacksmith's shop. A fiesta is held here every July.

Ruins of the **Mission Nuestra Señora de la Soledad** (1791), 28 miles (45 km) southeast of Salinas, and the rebuilt but isolated **Mission San Antonio de Padua** (1771), 67 miles (108 km) southeast of Salinas via **King City**, are also worth exploring.

The town of **Soledad** is the western gateway (via State 146) to the **Pinnacles National Monument**, which might be a good place to make a movie about the first men on Mars. Its 600-foot (183-meter) spirelike projections, flanking a steep central ridge with deep clefts cut by streams, give it a striking, barren, other-worldly quality. It is desolate in the winter, burning hot in the summer. But there are many good hiking trails and fascinating geological and biological attractions in its 16,222-acre (6,565-hectare) area. There is a visitor center at the national monument's eastern entrance, reached via State 25, about 35 miles (56 km) south of Hollister.

Southwest of Pinnacles, deep in the Carmel Valley, **Tassajara** also has an other-worldly quality to it. But this world is quite different, and hardly stark — it's a combination Zen center vegetarian gourmet experience and low-technology hot springs. In the spring and summer, visitors (with reservations) are welcome to use the springs, meditate, prowl quietly around the grounds, or sunbathe in the rocky gorge a mile or so downstream. There are charming cabins for overnight guests and communal meals are extraordinarily good. The only drawback is the tedious 16-mile (26-km) drive down a dirt road at the bottom of a deep narrow canyon in the **Los Padres National Forest**. The Zen Center in San Francisco can provide directions.

sion San
n
tista.

FORESTS AND FISH: THE NORTH COAST

So many people come to visit California's North Coast, that may be its curse. Once there, the traveler wants to stay, looking out over the edge of the Pacific, wearing a mackinaw and a Greek fisherman's cap and living in a weathered dream house. The North Coast is so suitable for vacation, retirement or framing that its salient image is how undeveloped it is compared to the southern part of the state's coast.

The California Coastal Commission, zealous keeper of the belief in beach access for all, has kept architects at bay. The commission was formed in the Seventies after the rest of the state seemed fated to become a 400-mile ribbon of private marinas and ocean-glimpse condominiums housing single secretaries and retired realtors. The only sign of unchecked development on the North Coast is the Sea Ranch, a chic subdivision most notable for its affected desolate purity of design, and the enforced absence of any painted surfaces or backyard vegetable gardens.

Boutique Farmers

North of **Bodega Bay**, most of the Sonoma County coast is a state beach, with comfortable access, plenty of parking, thrilling views, no camping, and appropriate-sounding beach names like **Mussel Point, Salmon Creek, Hog Back, Shell Beach** and **Goat Rock**.

As one travels north on State Highway 1 from Bodega Bay, the prevailing scenery is fog, cypress trees, pines, old barns and grazing sheep and cows — plus slow-moving recreational motor homes struggling with the road's twisting curves and quick ascents. As real estate, this grazing land is so valuable that local ranchers are termed "boutique farmers" because they don't really have to farm; they could sell the land immediately for more money than they'd make in a lifetime farming it.

"I'd rather look at my cows than count money in a bank," said one North Coast dairyman. "If my cows are happy, I'm happy." This same man once owned a chunk of Marin County pasture land that was recently sold for unknown millions of dollars to filmmaker George Lucas for his Skywalker Ranch.

Tourism is the growth industry on the North Coast, overtaking logging and fishing which are both suffering from depression. Although demand for trees and fish is on the increase, the supply is diminishing. The boats in the Bodega Bay salmon fishery, declared an official "economic disaster" in 1983, now remain berthed during the salmon season because it is too expensive to cruise for a product that may not be there. Bodega salmon fishermen sell freshly caught albacore directly from their boats, to recoup losses. The winner in this market may be the camping traveler: fresh barbecued albacore is far better than the deep-fried frozen fish served with professional indifference in tourist cafes along State 1.

The Russian River

In **Jenner** there is a good German restaurant and bar called **River's End**. It is located on a sheer cliff overlooking the Pacific at the mouth of the **Russian River**, about 60 miles (97 kilometers) north of San Francisco. Four miles upriver through rolling green countryside

is **Duncans Mills.** The citizens of Duncans Mills (population 20) apparently voted unanimously to restore this former lumber village to a level of quaintness not achieved since the reincarnation of Williamsburg, Virginia, and they've almost succeeded. Duncans Mills has a riverside campground, and a nice vegetarian-heavy restaurant-bar called the **Blue Heron Inn**.

Four miles farther upstream the traveler arrives at the somewhat frazzled little borough of **Monte Rio**. What Duncans Mills is to a turn-of-the-century country village, Monte Rio is to San Francisco's Haight-Ashbury in the late Sixties — as if by some twisted civic design busloads of zonked-out hippies have been bused to Monte Rio and unleashed to utilize the fronts of all the stores as bulletin boards.

Monte Rio forms a sort of corridor — or gauntlet — to the entrance of the 2,500-acre (1,012-hectare) **Bohemian Grove**, a private Monte Rio for the wealthy and powerful members of the Bohemian Club. Celebrities and politicians such as Helmut Schmidt, Henry Kissinger and several former U.S. Presidents gather here every July for Bohemian Week (actually 10 days); the late President Herbert Hoover called these high jinks "the greatest men's party on earth." Bohemian Week also brings a lot of others to the area, including high-priced hookers and people who want to gawk at the celebrities and politicians and hookers. Some Sonomans actually drive out to Santa Rosa's Sonoma County Airport to catch glimpses of Bohemians stepping out of corporate jets and into limousines.

Guerneville, a raffish summer resort town favored by San Francisco's gay community, is a few more miles inland on State 116. The centerpiece of Guerneville's gay society is **Fife's**, a 14-acre (5.7-hectare) riverside compound that includes three bars, a restaurant, two swimming pools, a campground and an adjacent disco called Drums.

The lower Russian River valley is something of a faded beach resort area, its "glory years" by consensus having passed with the Twenties and Thirties when San Franciscans traveled here by ferry and train to seek a lost weekend. Nowadays, the decay is part of the charm. Some of the best things about the Russian River resort region are the

Fisherm
repairs h
nets.

old roadhouses and tucked-away country inns — vast wooden relics of the so-called boom years.

The best of the genre is **Skippy's Hacienda Inn** on McPeak Road east of Guerneville. Skippy's is undiscovered, unpretentious, un-self-conscious, and so downright unlikely that it may be classifiable as archaeologically important. Bing Crosby once tended bar there and presumably played golf on the abandoned course, since given back to nature. Today the place carries on as a family-style steak-and-seafood restaurant adjacent to the roomy bar, open weekends only.

North Sonoma

Beyond Guerneville, most of the river's 14 miles (22½ km) from **Mirabel Park** to **Healdsburg** are inaccessible by public road. This is perhaps one reason why it is called "the most popular canoe river in the world" by W.C. "Bob" Trowbridge. More likely, Trowbridge calls it so because river canoeists invariably rent their craft from his own ubiquitous summertime canoe-rental stalls.

North of Jenner, State 1 weaves through daily fog, rolling pastures and sudden canyons that drop 1,000 feet (over 300 meters) into the blue and foamy Pacific. The road passes historic **Fort Ross**, a careful reconstruction of the original fort built by Russian traders in the early 19th Century. There are tours, but the best way to see the fort is to stroll through on one's own. The small Russian Orthodox chapel is worth a special stop.

One of the more compelling ways to pass an afternoon in north Sonoma County is to visit the coastal tidepools. At **Stewart's Point State Park**, a popular place for abalone divers, the pools are accessible at most tides, and there is not the risk (present at some North Coast beaches) that the explorer will be swept to a tragic death at sea by what the state's warning signs call "sleeper" waves.

Beyond Stewart's Point, along an especially sunny stretch of coastline called the "Banana Belt," looms the fore-mentioned **Sea Ranch,** probably the first and last subdivision of its kind on the California coast. The Sea Ranch at first appears to be a concentration of weathered barns that are being pro-

California brown pelican, a common sight at coastal communities.

tected by carefully weathered road signs that say "Keep Out." Thanks to the Coastal Commission, these orders may be disregarded. It's worth a quick drive — or walk — to see the Sea Ranch homes that have provided an exercise in style for a number of California's modern architects. Today many of the Sea Ranch units are rented as tourist vacation accommodations.

The major political fight in recent years along the California coast has been over the question of public beach access. The Coastal Commission halted all construction at Sea Ranch until such access was provided. After a court battle and years of stalemate, the issue was settled in 1982 with a compromise. The public can cross private land to get to the beach, but only on designated trails. These routes seem to lead to beaches that can best withstand the usual public abuse — broken glass, paper trash, loud radios, foul language, vandalism and disregard.

The Mendocino Coast

Travelers enter Mendocino County just north of Sea Ranch at **Gualala**, notable for its fine old hotel in the center of town. Fifteen miles (24 km) north, a coastal access path leads to **Point Arena Harbor**, a tiny bayside beach that comprises several dozen weathered mobile homes, two disintegrating and dangerous piers, and the **Arena Cove Cafe** ("short orders"), which also sells bait and fishing tackle and visually is everything one might imagine a battered old shoreline coffee shop could be.

The Coast Guard's **Point Arena Lighthouse** occupies the point of the U.S. mainland closest to Hawaii. Lots of ships have crashed near Point Arena; lots of free literature is available to tell visitors which ships, and where, and what was lost as a result.

Many travelers choose to spend the night in the town of **Mendocino** in a "B&B" — a bed-and-breakfast inn. It is not hard to find one. The B&Bs are proliferating so quickly in Mendocino — 32 miles (51 km) north of Point Arena — that city officials have passed laws prohibiting any new ones from opening.

In a sense, Mendocino is a victim of its own beauty: it's just too lovely to be ignored. A century-old former logging

Sonoma County coastline.

228

village, it's set on a long bluff above a small bay and is full of picturesque Victorian structures. The town is now treading the narrow line between "quaint" and "cute." One inn, for example, has a sod roof. Another is called the **Fools Rush Inn**. "Built in 1877 AD" it says on the entrance to **Heritage House**, a local lodge where the standard accommodations are named "Romeo" and "Juliet."

For a small town with a population under 1,000, Mendocino is hectic. Once the visitor finds (with difficulty) a place to park, he is confronted with restaurants bearing names like **Whale Watch**, and menus listing such delicacies as "Sempervirens Steak" — a "highly seasoned tofu loaf made with whole grains and vegetables and covered with sauteed mushrooms, onions and jack cheese." Travelers can escape from this leisure chic at two nearby state parks, **Van Damme** and **Russian Gulch**, which offer camping, hiking, beachcombing and other quiet pleasures.

The city of **Fort Bragg**, to the north, is the frumpy flipside of Mendocino. It is an unpretentious, blue-collared, beer-bellied rube who greets the wayfarer not with an historical B&B, but with a roadside cafe named Jerko's Koffee Kup. Fort Bragg's love affair with the architectural present (Safeway supermarkets and Payless drugstores) can be a shock to the traveler, like a breath of air freshener.

Some of the best of Fort Bragg's unpretentiousness can be found in **Noyo Harbor**, a sunny inlet lined by docks, charter boats and seafood restaurants. Among them is **Cap'n Flint's**, a simple cafe with plastic tablecloths, paper-napkin dispensers and bottles of McIlhenny's tabasco sauce on the tables. The fish is fresh, breaded, deep-fried and served in a basket with french fries. It represents the best of the North Coast — simple, relaxed and tasty.

Lumberjacks' Hub

The cloud of steam over Fort Bragg is produced by the Georgia-Pacific Corp. lumber mill. As the largest coastal settlement between San Francisco and Eureka, Fort Bragg is an old logging town that hasn't been abandoned, nor does it seem to show the effects of recent mercurial fortunes of the North Coast timber industry. Trucks loaded with fir and redwood logs hurtle along State 1 toward Fort Bragg at the rate of one every two or three minutes. The shoulders of the highway north of the city are strewn with a red fuzz from redwood bark blown off the trunks.

Fort Bragg is the home of the California and Western Railroad "**Skunk Train**," a once-smelly diesel that totes timber and passengers 36 miles (58 km) inland along the **Noyo River** to **Willits**. The Skunk leaves almost every day from the Fort Bragg terminal.

State Highway 1, built before the era of small high-performance cars, is a tortuous two-lane menagerie of BMW drivers and bicycle tourists competing with motor homes and lumber trucks for space. It's not a highway one would want to negotiate after a martini lunch, nor if one were in a great hurry: the pace is often in the 30-mile-per-hour range.

The saving grace of the slow pace is that there is usually a lot to see on State 1. Sometimes, however, the coastal fog is thick and stubborn, especially in summer. South of **Rockport**, it floats ashore in the early evening, a cold, windy blanket covering the auto campers strung along the bluff above the beach.

After Rockport, 28 miles (45 km) north of Fort Bragg, the highway turns inland, merging with U.S. 101 at **Leggett**. But adventurous travelers can explore California's "Lost Coast" by turning left down a dark dirt road near the North Fork of **Cottoneva Creek**.

Redwood Mystique

Much of the mystique of the North Coast is in its tall redwood trees that have survived various attempts by man to transform them into everything from lumber to ashtrays or mulch for suburban rose gardens. Most of California's remaining old-growth redwoods are now protected in parks, where tourists are invited to look up at the trees, to drive through holes burnt or cut through the larger ones, and to buy something made of their wood.

North Coast craftspersons have shown remarkable imagination and creativity with the redwood trinket market. In the hundreds of redwood souvenir shops, one can find in redwood almost everything a person might use

around his apartment, including the apartment itself. At a redwood gift store near **Phillipsville** the traveler may visit a redwood log house — one hollow log — admission $1. "Enter Through Gift Shop," says the sign, which is made of cardboard. The log house is a windowless sewer-sized pipe of redwood bark with a door on one end. Uninhabited, it is held together by steel straps.

But that's only the beginning. Infinite things have been done to sell redwood as a souvenir. There are redwood clocks, tables, cigarette holders, lampshades, hats, purses, paddles, lipstick caddies, watch fobs, salt-and-pepper shakers, statues of gorillas and bears.

Humboldt Highs

Notices tacked to buildings and utility poles all along the North Coast offer "Sinsemilla Tips." Says another bulletin: "Don't get caught with your plants down." The plant in question is marijuana, which has become a multi-million-dollar black market commodity. Until 1981, it was listed in the annual Mendocino County agricultural report as the county's largest cash crop; since then, county officials have chosen not to include the estimated marijuana gross. During the late summer harvest, local and federal police in helicopters, jets and Jeeps dedicate themselves to raids on known dope fields. In **Garberville**, in southern Humboldt County, the weekly newspaper runs a "Bust Barometer," a map on which the week's pot raids are charted. The information is provided by the sheriff.

For sale with the beer, wine and sandwiches in the Garberville delicatessen are books on how to grow marijuana, when to buy gardening and irrigation supplies, and journalism by growers about their adventures — such as buying bat guano. A vandal has taken the time to change a street sign in Garberville from "Left turn only" to read "Left turn on."

For the more civilized sensibility, the **Benbow Inn** south of Garberville is an improbable four-story resort built and furnished in English Tudor style on the edge of the **Eel River**, which here is backed up behind a summer dam to form **Lake Benbow**. The Benbow Inn has an elegant antique dining room and a bar in which the drinks are called "cheers." The juke box is programmed

Left, Aven of the Gia Right, lum mill at Redcrest.

with tunes by Glenn Miller, Tommy Dorsey and Frank Sinatra. The parking lot is full of new sedans with chrome spoke wheels. Reservations are advised.

Avenue of the Giants

North of Garberville a 33-mile (53-km) scenic drive called the **Avenue of the Giants** follows the South Fork of the Eel River through the **Humboldt Redwoods State Park**. The giants — redwood trees, otherwise known as *Sequoia sempervirens* — are tall and sometimes wide. Their size can be marketed: "Drive through a living tree" is the appeal from the Shrine Drive-Thru Tree in **Myers Flat**.

The North Coast shlock market is only a minor distraction along the Avenue, which follows the Eel through small towns from Phillipsville to **Redcrest**. The Eel is wide and wild in winter but in summer it's a clear emerald stream that flows gently north along isolated hot white sand beaches. A swim is *de rigeuer;* swimsuits are optional.

Eventually the Avenue of the Giants can make the traveler wonder about,

even long for, an avenue of the midgets, or possibly a boulevard of the about average-sized. Those seeking to avoid the commercialism, at least for a while, can take the difficult road west from Garberville over the **King Mountains** to **Shelter Cove**. North of this isolated outpost is **Petrolia**, site of the first oil well in California.

An honest glimpse into the spirit of the White man's pre-leisure presence on the North Coast is afforded by **Scotia**, a crisp, neat little company town built entirely of redwood and dominated by the **Pacific Lumber Co. mill,** the largest redwood mill in the world. The mill owns the town. All the town's lawns seem to have been mowed at the same time. There is a visitor's center built entirely of redwood in the style of a classic Greek temple. Redwood logs represent the fluted doric columns. There are no trees growing in Scotia's gardens, nor is there any architectural sign of the 1980s.

Grotto With a Motto

From the moment the traveler arrives, it is obvious that **Eureka** is a good

Carson House, Eureka.

place to buy sewer pipe, lumber, a slab of redwood burl, a life-sized statue of a lumberjack carved from a redwood log, or a fresh fish dinner.

Often shrouded in fog, Eureka (population 24,000) is the largest Pacific Coast enclave in North America north of San Francisco. It is a sprawling, busy industrial place, and it is in that spirit that it prepares its fish dinners. The **Seafood Grotto**, a restaurant on U.S. 101, is also the retail outlet of Eureka Fisheries, which processes 40 million pounds of fresh and frozen seafoods each year. "We Ketch 'em, Cook 'em, Serve 'em" is the motto of the Grotto. The portions are immense. A plate of clams is actually a stack of clams (each the size of a human hand), piled up like pancakes.

Eureka's ubiquitous and impressive Victorian architecture in **Old Town** is highlighted by the **Carson House** at the end of 2nd Street. Visitors can't go inside the house because it is now a private men's club — which makes it seem all the more Victorian. (The little town of **Ferndale**, about 10 miles southwest of Eureka, has a remarkable collection of well-maintained Victorians to excite the architectural connoisseur.) Eureka

is also the location of the North Coast's only institution of higher learning, **Humboldt State University**.

North of Eureka, it's worth getting off the divided four-lane freeway at **Trinidad**, home of the university's **Marine Biology Laboratory**, for a side trip down the lush Patrick's Point Drive to **Big Lagoon**. Here is Sitka spruce forest (a change from redwood), Port Orford cedar, red alder, shore pine, western hemlock, salal, huckleberry, crowberry, blackberry, and in spring a multitude of blooming rhododendrons. Spruce duff produces some of the world's most delicious mushrooms, as well as some of the most deadly. Those inclined to gather the fungus should be sure they know their mushrooms.

Big Lagoon, a county park, is separated from the ocean by a four-mile sandbar. The lagoon is frequently used by sailboarders and kayakers. Well-kept beach cottages border a grassy meadow. Big Lagoon marks a change from the chill of Eureka to a more tepid climate. More people are outdoors, determined to have fun in the sun even when it's foggy.

At **Orick**, the traveler enters **Red-**

herd ing rutting ason, airie Creek te Park.

wood National Park, established in 1968 to consolidate 40 miles (64 km) of majestic forested coastline under federal jurisdiction. A visitor center in Orick gives directions and shuttle-bus information for excursions up **Redwood Creek**, where (8½ miles, or 14 km, southeast of Orick) three of the six tallest trees ever identified on this planet, including the record holder — 368 feet (112 meters) in height — are located. They are clustered in the unimaginatively named **Tall Trees Grove**.

Further north in this 109,391-acre (44,270-hectare) park is **Prairie Creek State Park**, whose heavy rainfall has given rise to the lush **Fern Canyon**, its 50-foot (15-meter) walls green with moss and other rainforest vegetation. Herds of Roosevelt elk browse in the meadows of **Elk Prairie**.

Above the Del Norte County line, just east of the park boundary, a two-mile row of recreational vehicles is parked (they call it "camped") along the thread of beach bordering U.S. 101. They seem right at home beside the **Klamath River** bridge, notable for the four life-sized gilt cement bears which decorate it. (If any of these bears falls victim to the elements or vandalism, extra cement bears are waiting in a field nearby.) Indeed, the Klamath River country may boast one of the highest concentrations of RVs in the United States. Hundreds of them, all carrying salmon fishermen (identifiable by their plaid shirts and baseball caps), congregate here during fishing season.

The White anglers compete with the fishermen of the **Hoopa Indian Reservation** that borders both sides of the river several miles upstream. Salmon-fishing tensions between Whites and Indians have sometimes become violent. The number of lawsuits and countersuits over fishing rights in this area boggles the imagination.

In 1964, the town of **Klamath** was washed away in a flood. That torrent was the result of a cyclonic storm that dumped 40 inches (over 1,000 millimeters) of rain on the Klamath and Eel river basins in just 24 hours. The old site of Klamath's downtown is now a road that disappears into patches of fennel and blackberries.

The new town boasts the most ambitious redwood-souvenir marketing outlet on the entire North Coast — the **Trees of Mystery**. ("The main interest here is some deformed redwoods," wrote one travel writer.) Every motorist who leaves his vehicle in the parking lot has a Trees of Mystery sign wired to the bumper by a fast-working college student. A statue of mythic lumberjack Paul Bunyan and his blue ox, Babe, overlooks the Trees of Mystery souvenir shop, which includes "the largest display of sculptured redwood in the world" and possibly also the world's largest display of small stuffed blue ox toys.

Redwoods and Fog

It is difficult to recommend much of the coastal scenery north of the Klamath, because the odds are one won't see much of it. Certainly, the stands of redwood in **Del Norte Coast Redwoods State Park** and **Jedediah Smith Redwoods State Park**, both extensions of Redwood National Park, are worthy of note. But the foremost fact of life in these environs is fog. In **Crescent City**, one of the principal civic ironies is that someone had the chutzpah to name a seaside restaurant "Harbor View." To be charitable, though, Crescent City — a grim, gray gathering of plain houses and vacant lots around a semicircular harbor — has never fully recovered from a 1962 typhoon which devastated the town.

For the traveler looking for a place to have a pleasant time, the best bet is to head inland to higher and hotter ground. Fortunately, that's easily done. Fifteen minutes east of Crescent City, on U.S. Highway 199 toward Grants Pass, Oregon, the last un-dammed river in California flows gin-clear through the 90-degree (Fahrenheit; 32°C) summer twilight. The **Smith River** is wild; its accommodations are civilized. There's a lodge on **Patrick Creek** with a restaurant and bar. There are clean campgrounds, public and private, under the peeling red madronas. Jagged boulder-lined banks, unrepaired landslides, clear pools, rattlesnakes, good fishing, a great feeling and no redwood souvenirs represent the Smith River.

Souvenirs are unnecessary here. This part of the North Coast, far from the kitsch and the fog, is finally what the North Coast should be — a rich, verdant and peaceful land, a small and secret paradise.

Autumn spectacle Siskiyou County.

THE HIGH NORTH: A STORY IN ROCKS

The key to unlocking the secrets of California's High North is State Highway 299. Running 321 miles (517 kilometers) from the Humboldt County redwoods to the Nevada border, one could easily drive it in two days. But one shouldn't.

Mountainous State 299 should be savored like a fine wine, something this route doesn't offer. The restaurant guides can be left behind; no one undertakes this journey for the cuisine. Weeks could be spent here. At least five days should be allowed.

State 299 is the only paved traverse of the state's isolated north. On its winding, two-lane blacktop trek, it cuts across some of California's least populated wilderness — a remote domain of mountains, valleys, volcanoes, rivers, canyons, basins and, at the end, desert. Other paved roads penetrate the High North, including the north-south Interstate 5, running roughly along the boundary between the Klamath and Cascade mountain ranges. And every journey through here should include side trips up secondary roads. But when it comes to offering visitors the most topographically varied exposure to the region, State 299 is the road to ride.

Geologic Vistas

Most things that happen along State 299 — weather, politics, economics, history — have more to do with boundaries set in rocks than with laws. There is a little farming (cattle, alfalfa, marijuana) and a little recreation (backpacking, hunting, fishing). But lumbering and mining, today as 100 years ago, sustain the region.

The most compelling aspect of this route is its geology. The ideal traveling companion in these parts would be a good field geologist; alternatively, *Roadside Geology of Northern California* by David Alt and Donald Hyndman (Mountain Press) is a respected and easily found volume, lucidly written for the layman. State 299 passes through several major geologic provinces, including the Klamath Mountains, Cascade Mountains and the Modoc Plateau. One should bring camping

equipment, patience and a willingness to stop frequently to inspect roadside outcroppings. In their silent, lithic grammar, the rocks along the highway recall epics of fire, wind, water and ice as dramatic as any told by Homer.

The time to visit is between mid April and mid November. The northern third of California gets two-thirds of the state's precipitation. Winter snows and spring floods make State 299 dangerous; they often close the route altogether. Even under the best conditions, rockslides and heart-stopping curves make driving in this district no experience for the timid, the inebriated or the impatient.

Those who insist on winter travel should bring their own tire chains and avoid the extortionist merchants who would profit from others' troubles. The local police can recommend reputable garages if mechanical assistance is needed. The California Highway Patrol will give current road conditions by telephone: as much of this road is 5,000 feet (1,500 meters) elevation or higher, it is often covered with snow while most of California is sunny.

Home of Bigfoot

Coming from the Pacific Coast, State 299 branches off U.S. Highway 101 at Arcata, north of Eureka, and crosses the low **Coast Range** to the wilderness realm of the **Klamath and Trinity rivers.** These two principal rivers drain the Coast Range and **Klamath Mountains.**

The Klamaths comprise a series of smaller ranges — the **Siskiyou**, the **Trinity**, the **Trinity Alps**, the **Marble**, the **Scott Bar**, the **South Fork** and the **Salmon** mountains. They cover about 12,000 square miles (about 31,000 sq km) of northern California and southern Oregon. **Mount Hilton**, 8,964 feet (2,732 meters), is the highest peak in the region; most vary between 5,000 and 7,000 feet (about 1,500 to 2,100 meters).

The Klamaths are famous as the home of Bigfoot, also known as Sasquatch, the giant humanoid who — according to legend — stalks these mountains. Whether or not Bigfoot really exists, it is an appropriate and cherished myth. There *is* something wild about the Klamaths: with more than 70 inches (1,780 millimeters) of

ceding
es, Lower
High
e, Marble
untain
derness
a. Left,
unt
sta
ers above
hasta City
n.

annual rainfall in some parts, they sustain a lush forest of ferns, hemlocks, pines and spruce. Except for the highest of the Trinity Alps, glaciers are rare, so most peaks retain a raw, jagged quality. River canyons lack the graceful horseshoe shape of their glaciated Sierra Nevada counterparts.

Three national forests contain most of California's Klamaths — Klamath, Shasta and Trinity. Within these forests are more strictly protected wilderness areas. The best-known and most popular is the **Salmon-Trinity Alps Primitive Area**, laced with hundreds of miles of trails for hiking and camping. Ranger stations along State 299 at **Burnt Ranch**, **Big Bar** and **Weaverville**, and on State 3 at **Trinity Center**, will issue fire permits, answer flora and fauna questions, and provide up-to-date information on weather and trail conditions.

About 10 miles (16 km) east of the Trinity River bridge marking the Humboldt-Trinity county line, near the community of Burnt Ranch, State 299 passes just south of **Ironside Mountain** (5,255 feet or 1,602 meters). Ironside's sheer, scenic face is the eroded, exposed tip of a much larger piece of granite — the Ironside Mountain Batholith. About 165 million years old, this batholith is typical of other such intrusions in the Sierra Nevada and Klamaths. Batholiths (see page 00) distinguish the Klamaths from the neighboring Coast Range.

The Warp and Woof Of Weaverville

The Klamath-Trinity is a drainage system that includes hundreds of smaller creeks, lakes and rivers. In high mountain streams, the spring melting of Klamath snowpacks creates a fearsome torrent of a volume and velocity that can move large boulders more than a mile downstream. Recently, some Klamath residents have begun to see money in these currents. Under a recent federal law, local power companies must purchase any electricity generated by small entrepreneurs. With this in mind, some mountain residents have developed small hydroelectric plants — like the one run by Mom & Pop Power Company in Trinity's tiny **Minersville.** Only a few such plants now operate, but others are planned.

For residents of Trinity County, a

Chinese
joss hous
Weavervi

240

"night on the town" usually means a trip to Weaverville, the county seat with a population of 3,500. It saw its glory days during the mid 19th Century, when it was a supply post for Klamath region gold prospectors. Gold hunters still haunt the creeks of Trinity County, but timbering sustains the economy. As is typical in rural California, 72 percent of Trinity County is owned by the federal government, another 10 percent by Southern Pacific Railroad. Although, ironically, no railroads cross the county, Southern Pacific received huge 19th Century land grants here as elsewhere in the West.

Although lumber ranks first, marijuana ranks second in Trinity cash crops. This juxtaposition of enterprises — one traditional, one contraband — is typical of Trinity. Those who go in either of Weaverville's principal Main Street bars, **The New York Hotel** (which isn't) or **The Diggin's**, and mix it up, will soon understand: Trinity County's populace breaks into two groups — natives and those who have come here since the end of the Sixties. Generally, natives tend to be conservative, the newcomers less so.

Despite their differences, Trinitarians share an individualism and a jealous regard for the natural environment. While Trinity often votes conservative in general elections, it also displays an abiding sensitivity to ecological issues — a sort of environmental populism. This is not so much a matter of ideology as one of simple self-interest. Many here hunt their own food and draw water directly from springs, rivers and creeks. (The bedrock of granite and serpentine is too impermeable for aquifers.) So when the county recently tried to stop the federal government from spraying Trinity's woodlands with an herbicide many feared would end up in water supplies, no politicians — Democrat or Republican — openly opposed the grass-roots effort. This closeness to one another and to the land breeds a native suspicion of outsiders.

Visiting motorists should know that Trinity County, like most of California's north, has "open range." Cattle has never been a major part of the economy here, and open range is mostly a symbolic vestige of the region's frontier heritage. Open range means that cattle wander beyond their owner's unfenced

ging
ration,
ity
onal
st.

rangelands. It also means that any driver whose vehicle strikes a cow has just purchased damaged livestock. Hikers must be careful to stay away from creek bottoms on which gold prospectors have staked claims. Likewise, those who come across a sunny patch of marijuana should leave quickly before (a) they are shot at by its grower or (b) they are arrested on suspicion of being its growers.

Weaverville is the site of the **Joss House State Historic Park**, a tribute to Chinese history in California, particularly of the Gold Rush days. The oldest Chinese temple still in use in the state is open daily; tours are available. Nearby is the eclectic **J.J. "Jake" Jackson Museum.** Weaverville is also the gateway to **Clair Engle** and **Lewiston lakes,** part of the expansive **Whiskeytown-Shasta-Trinity National Recreation Area.** A short drive north of town, these lakes were created in the Sixties with the damming of the upper Trinity River. They offer fishing, hiking, boating and camping.

East of Weaverville, State 299 crosses **Buckhorn Summit** (elevation 3,215 feet or 980 meters) then quickly loses altitude. Douglas firs, ponderosa pines and the occasional redwood give way to a drier chaparral environment of manzanitas (whose gray-green leaves look ghostly under headlights) and digger pines.

On its way out of the Klamaths, a few miles past the Shasta County line, the highway skirts **Whiskeytown Lake,** a reservoir for which locals have mixed feelings. Both this lake and nearby Shasta Lake hold waters from the **Sacramento River.** Like Clair Engle and Lewiston lakes, they were part of a huge federal project, completed in the Sixties, that diverted Klamath Mountain waters from the range's east slope. They are now part of the national recreation area.

An extensive system of tunnels, penstocks, dams and aqueducts directs Klamath water into California's Central Valley where it irrigates cash crops for huge agribusinesses. Residents here say they like the lakes but liked even more the wilder, more plentiful waters that once flowed from the mountains. A native businessman put it this way: "We've had our water taken and exported south, our timber cut and our

Marina at Clair Engle Lake.

farmlands flooded. We feel like we've been colonized up here."

There is an information sign by the Whiskeytown dam. Beside it is a button one can push to hear the speech given by President John Kennedy when he dedicated the dam. It echoes across the still lake, with the sure cadences of Manifest Destiny.

Not far from the dam access road, State 299 leads into the town of **Shasta** (population 750), until 1888 the county seat. Now it's mostly a tourist stop: the whole community has been declared a state historic park. A relic of the Gold Rush, it has a courthouse converted to a museum, a restored barn and store.

Conspicuous by their absence along most of State 299, along with traffic lights, are franchise motels and restaurants. According to the marketing strategists, none of the highway's towns has reached that point of development which would warrant franchise food. None, that is, except the sprawling valley town of **Redding** — population 43,500. Redding, it is safe to say, hit the franchise crystallization point a long time ago.

As State 299 metamorphoses into a four-lane highway and straggles into Redding, the fast-food jungle begins: McDonalds, Long John Silver's, Shakey's Pizza and the rest of them. On Market Street, State 299 passes Redding's old **City Hall**, built in 1907, then hitches a brief ride north on I-5. Redding sits at the northern end of the 450-mile (724-km) long Central Valley, and these two miles are State 299's only exposure to the valley. Northeast of Redding, the highway resumes its eastward passage and returns to its two-lane blacktop demeanor.

It Has to Be Shasta

Less than 15 miles (24 km) up I-5 from Redding is one of California's largest lakes, many-coved **Shasta Lake**. A popular resort for fishing, hiking, camping and boating, it comprises the largest section of Whiskeytown-Shasta-Trinity National Recreation Area. As with its counterparts, this reservoir was created by the damming of rivers — in this case, the Sacramento, the **McCloud** and the **Pitt**. Lake Shasta's shoreline stretches for 370 miles (595 km). Visitors can rent houseboats or

even explore the **Lake Shasta Caverns**, an array of underground wonders accessible only by boat or (with difficulty) by foot. Full information is available at the Shasta Dam Area Chamber of Commerce, one-quarter mile west of the Shasta Dam exit on I-5.

North of Lake Shasta is **Dunsmuir** and the granite outcroppings of **Castle Crags State Park,** favored by rock climbers. Above that — some 50 miles (80 km) north of Redding — is magnificent **Mount Shasta,** highest mountain in the California Cascades at 14,162 feet (4,316 meters). Unlike the Sierras' Mount Whitney, which though 332 feet (101 meters) higher is lost among myriad other summits, Shasta stands alone, a majestic monarch dominating the countryside for 100 miles around. This mountain has five glaciers, fine skiing, and an area of 80 cubic miles (333 cubic km). For a sense of its awesome proportions, one should take the scenic highway that winds 7,880 feet (2,401 meters) up its slopes — barely halfway to the top. There's a ranger station on the mountain's western flank in the tiny town of Mount Shasta.

The only town of significant size on I-5 between Mount Shasta and the state of Oregon border, another 55 miles (89 km) to the north, is **Yreka** (population 6,000). The government seat of Siskiyou County, it features a museum with restored buildings from its 19th Century mining past. Just north of Yreka, State 96 heads west, giving access to otherwise isolated stretches of the beautiful Klamath River country. It eventually joins State 299 at Willow Creek in Humboldt County.

The Volcanic Cascades

The Cascades run almost due north from California to Canada's British Columbia. In California, the range runs 40 to 50 miles (70 to 80 km) across; in Washington state more than 80 miles (130 km). Farther north, glaciers dominate the range; here in California, only the highest peaks bear these Ice Age relics. The dominant snow-capped Cascade peaks are young volcanoes. Some, like Washington's Mount St. Helens, are still active. Unlike the Klamaths, the higher Cascade peaks present a sharply vertical profile of high conical peaks surrounded by lower mountains of the 4,500 to 5,000-foot

(1,370 to 1,520-meter) range.

If the Klamaths are a window on preglacial North America, then the Cascades offer another view — one that looks out on the fire and ice of the Pleistocene. Subduction, the melting of tectonic plates as they dive under the continent, continues to nourish volcanic activity here. But it is the condition of that basalt when it returns to the earth's surface that determines the shape, size and duration of the eruptions.

There are three kinds of lavas and four types of Cascade volcanoes. When volcanic rock flows in a molten stream, it is a *lava flow.* If it erupts in solid chunks, it is *lava rock.* If it explodes into molten fragments that solidify before they reach the ground, it is termed *pyroclastic.*

Volcanoes composed entirely of pyroclastics (from the Greek for "fire-broken") are called *cinder cones.* Usually they are steeply conical and indented by a crater from which the lava erupts. Generically named **Cinder Cone** in **Lassen Volcanic National Park** is a textbook example of this type. *Shield volcanoes,* like **Prospect Peak** in the same park, are especially common at sea and on islands — like Hawaii. They are just the opposite of cinder cones: formed from highly fluid lava-flow accumulations, shields are gently sloping and low to the ground.

The *composite,* or stratovolcano, is the classic Cascade volcano. Both Mount St. Helens and Mount Shasta are composite volcanoes. Composites present the most dramatic profiles and are built by an accumulation of both lava flows and lava rock eruptions. Unlike composites, *dome* volcanoes are produced by a single mass of solid rock that has been pushed up through a vent. Like toothpaste squeezed from a tube, the lava is too thick to move away, and it accumulates to form a steep dome atop the preexisting mountain. If a lava dome forms in a preexisting crater, as it did on **Lassen Peak**, it is called a plug dome.

There are few better places to study volcanology than Lassen Volcanic National Park. It is reached via State 36 east from **Red Bluff**, State 44 east from Redding, or State 89 south from State 299 beyond **Burney.** Lassen Peak (elevation 10,457 feet, or 3,187 meters) marks the southern terminus of the Cascade Range, and is one of only two Cascade volcanoes to have erupted in the 20th Century. Until Mount St. Helens blew in 1980, Lassen's 1914-15 eruptions were regarded as the dying gasp of a moribund volcanism. Now geologists are reconsidering accounts by early pioneers and pre-historic Indians of "burning mountains" throughout the Cascade range. Peaks like Shasta, Hood (in Oregon) and Baker (in Washington) are getting a second look. These mountains are geologically very young; the Cascades are still being born.

Much of 108,000-acre (43,700-hectare) Lassen Park lies within a caldera, the giant crater left by the collapse of an ancient volcano. Out of this caldera, Lassen Peak later rose to dominate this expanse of wilderness. But there are smaller volcanoes in the park as well. There is also **Bumpass Hell**, a steaming valley of active geothermal pools and vents. And there are lakes, rivers, meadows, pine forests and fine trails for hiking and camping.

Most of the California Cascades fall within two national forests, Lassen and Shasta. At Shasta's southern boundary lies another prime wilderness, **Plumas National Forest.** These upland woods cover the northern end of the Sierra Nevada and cradle the **Feather River**, one of California's most celebrated wild streams.

Between Redding and Burney, a distance of 53 miles (85 km), State 299 climbs into a gently undulating country of ranches and volcanic debris. The red rocks that litter pastures to the south of the road were deposited by hot mud flows from the eruption of Mount Maidu 7 million years ago. This posthumously named volcano collapsed to form the caldera within Lassen Park.

East of **Bella Vista**, on the south banks of **Cow Creek**, are the ruins of **Afterthought Mine**, a source of zinc and copper from the late 19th Century until the end of World War II.

Just beyond the lumber and livestock marketing center of Burney (population 3,200) is the State 89 intersection. South is Lassen Park; north is Mount Shasta. About six miles (10 km) north is lovely 129-foot (39-meter) **Burney Falls.** Volcanic terrain is inhospitable to rivers, and this state park gives a clear indication why. Before it gets to the falls, Burney Creek disappears into a porous lava flow, but reappears just in time to

Thermal activity at Bumpass Hell, Lass Park.

drop over the spectacular moss-covered precipice.

East of Burney on State 299, in the vicinity of **Fall River Mills**, there are numerous outcroppings of a white, chalky rock. This is diatomite, also called diatomaceous earth. Composed of shells of diatoms, an extinct marine alga, it is a legacy of the sea that once covered the region. It is mined for use in swimming pool filters and cat litter.

The Modoc Plateau

From Fall River Mills to the Nevada border, State 299 runs across the basins and fault-block mountains of the volcano-splattered Modoc Plateau. For much of its route, the highway follows the deep canyon of the Pitt River, the plateau's main drainage.

The Modoc Plateau is a lava plain similar to the Columbia Plateau to the north. In California, the Modoc covers 13,000 square miles (33,670 sq km), taking in all of Modoc County and parts of Lassen, Shasta and Siskiyou counties.

The Modoc doesn't look like a plateau. It looks more like a scrubby basin on which someone left some block-like piney mountains that don't seem to belong. Vestiges of volcanism make up much of the **Modoc National Forest**, which covers 1.97 million acres (797,000 hectares). A pristine example of this volcanic past is **Glass Mountain**, a huge flow of obsidian lava on the forest's western edge.

The focus of any geologic tour of the Modoc Plateau is **Lava Beds National Monument**. A finer example of basalt flows cannot be found than this moon-like landscape of lava flows, columns and caves. (Yes, there are basalt flows on the moon). In one of the caves, a Modoc Indian chief known as "Captain Jack" and his warriors held out against the U.S. Army during the final days of the 1872–1873 Modoc Indian War. This was one of the last such conflicts in American history.

Pahoehoe (smooth) lava flows created the national monument's 300 lava "tubes" — cylindrical caves often only a few feet underground. Some are too small for humans to walk through; others are multi-leveled and exceed 75 feet (23 meters) in diameter. Some of these caves contain prehistoric Indian petroglyphs. There is a visitor center at

Road
ds
ugh Lava
s
onal
ument.

Indian Wells, but no lodging, supplies or gasoline are available. The closest community of any size is **Tulelake** (population 800), about 10 miles (16 km) north on the Oregon state border.

The 46,500-acre (18,800-hectare) national monument lies in Siskiyou County on the western edge of the Modoc Plateau. From State 299 east, travelers should turn north near the **Canby** ranger station and proceed on State 139 about 40 miles (72 km) via **Tionesta.**

Eagles and Geese

In the region surrounding Lava Beds National Monument are three national wildlife refuges — **Tule Lake** (north), **Lower Klamath** (northwest) and **Clear Lake** (east). More than 1 million waterfowl populate these lakes in the fall; there are also significant numbers of bald eagles in January and February. Dirt roads within the protected areas offer access.

Another refuge, the 6,000-acre (2,420-hectare) **Modoc National Wildlife Refuge**, lies a few miles south of the county seat of **Alturas**, at the confluence of the North and South forks of the Pitt River. Located on the Pacific Flyway, it provides nesting for Canada geese, ruddy ducks, green-winged teal and other native and migratory fowl.

Elsewhere in Modoc National Forest, however, there is extensive hunting of these same waterfowl, as well as other game birds, deer and antelope. Trout fishing is popular in the occasional streams. More universal recreations are hiking and camping.

Between Canby and Alturas, a distance of 18 miles (29 km), State 299 crosses part of a higher, rocky central plateau known as the **Devil's Garden.** This high country, covered with pines at its highest elevations and sage and junipers at its lower ones, is the legacy of one of the Modoc's more recent lava flows.

Alturas (population 3,000) is a farming center with a history dating to the mid 19th Century. Its **Modoc County Museum** has a 500-year collection of firearms plus exhibits of regional Indian artifacts. Of greater interest, however, may be its marvelous Basque restaurant — the **Brass Rail.**

Here, at 4,400 feet (1,340 meters) altitude, away from the Cascade rain-shadow, the terrain is dry and vegetation sparse. Annual precipitation is less than 12 inches (300 mm). Summer temperatures often exceed 100°F (38°C); in the winter, they often drop below 0°F (minus 18°C) and snow covers the ground. Cattle graze on a brown-and-purple landscape; alfalfa is the cash crop.

East of Alturas, State 299 rises into the **Warner Mountains**, which form the boundary between the Modoc Plateau and the even more arid high-desert country of the **Great Basin.** Pine forests, rivers and streams cover the Warner range. And while some of its peaks reach almost to 9,900 feet (3,000 meters), most of it is half that high. It's a gently rolling upland that's great for hiking and camping. But outdoorsmen should be reminded to bring water purification tablets: extensive cattle ranging makes these pills essential.

There is a small ski resort at **Cedar Pass**, elevation 6,305 feet (1,922 meters). Then the highway drops down into **Surprise Valley** and the hamlet of **Cedarville**, population 800. Cedarville has ailanthus trees, poplars and a single pay telephone. Not a building exceeds two stories. Except for the automobiles, VISA stickers on shop windows and a Bank of America branch, this town could still be slumbering peacefully in the 19th Century.

Cal Heryford, 41, grew up here. He left only once, to go to school in Idaho. He came right back. He'll sometimes take time out from his work at the gas station and tell visiting motorists why he lives in Cedarville. He will talk of the Modoc and the basin and range country east of here. What he says could be echoed by all those who live along the shoulders of State 299, a road that dies in the Nevada desert, at the state line, just a few miles from here.

"I'll tell you why," says Heryford. "Because, in the winter, I can get in my snowmobile and go east of here for hundreds of miles and not see another person. In addition to this gas station, I trap coyotes: I clear 10 to 15 thousand (dollars) a year at it. I love it here.

"We were in San Francisco not long ago, and a friend of mine said, 'You know, you're living a life that most people just dream about.' He's right: I don't have to go to Alaska to find unspoiled wilderness. I've got everything I want right here."

Angling in
Springs
Creek nea
Drakesbad

THE GOURMET'S SAN FRANCISCO

Everyone who lives in San Francisco feels sorry for anyone who doesn't. Other cities may have great museums, great theaters, great industries; San Francisco has great food. While the citizens of everywhere else scurry through life frowning over profits, worrying about losses, and generally taking the business of living very, very seriously, San Franciscans devote themselves to the things that really matter. In fact, the life of the city is so dedicated to the pursuit of good eating that preparing food has become its major art form.

It has always been this way. When San Francisco was nothing but a shanty town filled with houses made of paper and men with dreams of gold, a historian wrote, "No people in the world live faster or more sumptuously than the people of San Francisco." That was in 1853, long before California's rich land had been tamed and tilled, long before anyone had even thought of planting crops.

In those days, vegetables and fruits were brought from the Sandwich Islands, apples and pears from Chile, and basic necessities like cheese, butter and eggs were shipped around the horn from the Atlantic coast. Cured foods came from as far away as China, and ice was towed down the Pacific coast from Alaska. At a time when most Americans were grateful for a burned piece of beef, San Francisco was already priding itself on its international cuisine. During the first flush of the gold rush, those who struck it rich spent their money on food.

Pioneer Gourmands

The **Poulet D'Or**, the city's first French restaurant, opened in 1849, was soon renamed The Poodle Dog by miners who couldn't wrap their tongues around the French vowels. By 1855 reporters noted that San Franciscans had a choice of "American dining rooms, English lunch houses, French *cabarets*, Spanish *fondas*, German *wirtschafts*, Italian *osterie* and Chinese chowchows." San Franciscans chose them all, reveling in the diversity of their restaurants. By the turn of the century, the city became known as the "American Paris." When the earthquake leveled San Francisco in 1906, more sober Americans muttered darkly that the city was only getting its just deserts, and prophesized that this would teach the snooty city to be more temperate in its appetites.

How wrong they were! San Francisco restauranteurs set up trestle-tables and served meals amidst the rubble. Dinner over, they cheerfully set about the business of rebuilding. It takes more than an earthquake to dull the appetites in San Francisco, probably the only American city which has had a mayor known primarily for the quality of his cooking. (Mayor Tilden was so jealous of his culinary secrets that it was not until after his death that his recipes were published in 1907.)

Mayor Tilden is long gone, but a taste of the past lingers on in some old San Francisco restaurants. There's **Jack's** on Sacramento Street, tables nudging one another in the masculine clutter of its downstairs dining room, blithely unchanged after all these years. The menu remains much the same; and as one eats the sweet, tiny Olympia oysters (which filled the local waters until a greedy populace ate them almost into extinction), the fat mutton chops accompanied by hash brown potatoes and followed by thin jelly-filled French pancakes, it is easy to imagine the sound of horse-drawn carriages just outside the door.

When Mayor Tilden was in the mood for a piece of fish, he went to **Sam's** or **Tadich's** with their old wooden booths and spartan interiors. Generations of San Franciscans have known that the city's finest fresh fish comes to these old establishments, and lines have stretched out their doors at every mealtime for the past 100 years. San Franciscans do their best to hide this information from the non-native. Only tourists eat at Fisherman's Wharf. The locals head inland when they want grilled native petrale sole, or crab Louis, or the locally invented "hangtown fry" (an omelette of oysters topped with bacon, which reputedly came by its name when it was requested by a thief just before he met his end on the rope).

If Mayor Tilden wanted some excitement, he went to Chinatown. He couldn't have eaten at the **Far East Cafe**, because this last-remaining old-style Chinatown restaurant did not open until 1915, but the places he frequented were undoubtedly hung with the

Preceding pages, lobster and vegetables, the ingredients of a Big Sur seafood feast. Left, the Crown Room buffet at the graceful old Claremont Hotel in Oakland.

same exotic Chinese chandeliers and decorated with the same ornately carved wood. The Far East is the only Chinese restaurant where guests can still take a booth, pull the curtains and eat chow mein in complete privacy. When they need a waiter, there's a bell to ring. Even today, it is easy to imagine that just beyond the curtains lies a Chinatown of opium dens and *tong* wars.

'We Might as Well Eat'

If the earthquake failed to turn San Francisco into a sober, serious city, Prohibition came along to give it another try. With one bar for every 100 inhabitants, San Francisco may have been the most bibulous city in the States, and the advent of Prohibition was certainly a severe blow to the citizens. Many of the bars also served lavish free lunches that offered every kind of food to be found in the city. (So much free caviar was served at these bars that the native sturgeon population was entirely decimated.) But even Prohibition could not put a damper on the spirits of San Francisco. When alcohol was outlawed, local people shrugged their shoulders and said, "We might as well eat."

The city threw itself into an orgy of eating that continues to this day. Prohibition ended; times changed; and while other Americans, seduced by convenience, celebrated the glory of fast food, frozen food and fad food, San Francisco stubbornly stuck with fine food. San Franciscans proudly claim that the Coca Cola Company does not consider this a good city for them, and when the local paper noted that San Francisco has more restaurants per capita than any other city in America, natives shook their heads and said the paper had missed the point: that San Francisco has more *good* restaurants than any other American city.

San Francisco once boasted the only restaurant in America serving pizza. Lupo's has since changed its name to **Tomasso's** but very little else has changed since they opened in 1936. The restaurant still uses the same oak-burning oven that gives the hearty Italian food its deliciously smoky quality. San Francisco had the country's first Cantonese restaurants, and then, much later, its first northern Chinese restaurant, the **Mandarin**, now in Ghirardelli Square. It had the first Japanese restaurant in the west, **Yamato**, considered extraordinarily exotic when it began serving *sashimi* (raw fish) in 1931. The city had German restaurants, Indian restaurants, and restaurants representing almost every country — but now it has something else. San Francisco has invented a style

of cooking uniquely its own.

San Franciscans, raised on this cross-cultural stew, began to feel that all these foods belonged to them. They ate so much *sushi* and *pasta* and *dim sum* and *pâté* that they began to regard them as part of their native cuisine. For a long time, diners could go into the kitchens of Italian restaurants and find Chinese chefs at work, or discover that their favorite classic French cuisine was prepared by a Japanese chef. But all that suddenly changed. Local chefs rebelled against the idea that French food belonged in French restaurants, Chinese food in Chinese. Assuming the lead role of a new juggling act, they began experimenting trading tastes from culture to culture, mixing ingredients, and using unorthodox tech-

niques. A brand new cooking style was born which has been labeled "California cuisine."

The Revolution in Berkeley

This was happening all over the city, but nowhere with more passion than across the bridge in Berkeley. Once known as a hotbed of student rebellion, Berkeley is now the "gourmet ghetto." One short stretch of Shattuck Avenue makes the reason blatantly clear. At 1517 is **Chez Panisse**, a restaurant

Adopted tastes and indigenous styles are both part of the San Francisco eating experience. Left, a Japanese chef prepares *sushi;* and right, a label for famed sourdough bread.

opened in 1971 by a young chef who had no formal training other than a lifetime of good eating. The restaurant started simply as a typical little French bistro but when the cooks tired of trying to imitate the food of France, the revolution began. They began to use local products only, making freshness the highest virtue.

The restaurant encouraged local farmers to grow special vegetables for them, and had them raise animals to careful specifications. They encouraged foragers to bring them wild mushrooms, and small-time fishermen to sell their catch. Armed with these wonderful ingredients, they began experimenting and inventing. The result was food unlike anything ever tasted before in America. The strictly French food became

pi River. Next door the nation's first *charcuterie*, **Pig by the Tail**, tempts passers-by with great clouds of herb-scented, olive oil-laden steam. Down the street the **Cheeseboard** offers warm bread and an astonishing assortment of cheeses, while the fish store next door sells crab, fish and *sushi*. Around the corner, the **Produce Market** has oranges and coconuts and mushrooms of all shapes tumbling through its aisles.

Just across the street are an Italian bakery, **Il Fornaio**; a bakery devoted exclusively to chocolate, **Cocolat**; a kosher deli and a store selling freshly roasted coffee so enticing that there is always a long line. And this is just the beginning. In the other direction are a *charcuterie* devoted to chicken, **Poulet**; a barbecue stand; another bakery; an Italian

less strict, and the menu suddenly sported dishes like *ravioli* made of new potatoes and garlic, or a simply grilled lobster. Local oysters were being farmed, for the first time in years, and they became a part of the menu. Thus successful, the restaurant had a second-floor café with an old-fashioned oven added to it, and pizza was elevated to *haute cuisine*. The menu became even more international.

The local response was electric. Across Shattuck Avenue from Chez Panisse, the **Berkeley Co-Op** supermarket sells a heady mixture of such international foods as *tortillas*, eggroll wrappers, *phyllo* dough and *matzoh* balls. The store does more business than any other supermarket west of the Mississip-

grocery store; and a couple of Chinese restaurants mixed in for good measure. Anyone still not convinced that this is an insatiable city, should consider that this is but one of four major gourmet areas in a city of only 100,000.

The availability of these foods makes Berkeley's restaurants special. Some of Chez Panisse's chefs have set up on their own, creating eclectic combinations of ingredients. At the **Santa Fe Bar and Grill** cooking its unconstrained by normal rules, borrowing flavors from every culture. Offerings include fried black-bean cakes with *salsa* and sour cream, *fettucine* with smoked duck, grilled snapper with spicy peanut sauce, and grilled lamb chops with roasted garlic and lime sauce. At the **Fourth Street Grill**, diners can savor classics like caesar salad mingled with Creole gumbo, *linguini* with fresh oysters, or tuna with mango-pineapple sauce.

Experimental Tastes

The same experimental spirit prevails on the other side of the Bay. At **Hayes Street Grill**, fresh fish, grilled over mesquite, is served slightly undercooked and accompanied by sauces ranging from a French *beurre blanc* to Italian *pesto*, Mexican *salsa* or Indonesian peanut. At **Café Americain**, the choices include grilled fish, mussels steamed with ginger, pizza, pasta or a plain old hamburger. All this, and a good wine list!

But San Francisco's most unique restaurant is undoubtedly **Green's**, run by members of a Zen sect who serve strictly vegetarian fare. The restaurant grows its own vegetables, served so fresh they still have the taste of the earth. The Chez Panisse-trained chef takes her inspiration from many places, offering grilled marinated *tofu*, *linguini* with wild mushrooms, salads made with *feta* and olives and topped with flowers. The waterside restaurant is surprisingly elegant, and while the waiters may have shaven heads, they are knowledgeable about their fine wine list.

The city's potpourri of food fare does not end in the restaurants. On any street, people can be seen munching and feasting as they stroll. Many people sit in the parks, eating loaves of sourdough bread stuffed with salami and cheese, happily aware that both the bread and the meat are unique products of the city. (When researchers tried to produce sourdough bread outside of San Francisco, it was a complete flop. Some say this has to do with the weather, but the more romantic say that sourdough simply loses heart when taken out of San Francisco.) Ice cream stores are everywhere, and it is not unusual to see people driving along the streets with one hand on the wheel and the other wrapped around an ice cream cone. What makes San Francisco such a wonderful town for walkers is that they can move through the city literally tasting the neighborhoods.

The taste in North Beach is sweet but bracing, the flavor of cappucino being slowly

savored in the sunshine of one of the old coffee-houses. This Italian neighborhood is not as young as it once was, and it is mostly the older people who remain, firmly set in their ways. **Gloria Sausage Company** still makes sausage like it did when it first set up business 60 years ago, and the dark interior of the store has a friendly, old-fashioned feeling. At the **Cuneo**, **Liguria** and **Italian-American** bakeries, the ladies hand over *grissini*, *focaccia* and *buccelato* with a few gracious words of Italian.

Two popular Bay Area restaurants: left, kitchen staff prepares a vegetarian meal at Green's (Fort Mason); and right, a chef makes bread at Chez Panisse (Berkeley).

The flavors in Chinatown are stronger and more aggressive, not unlike the shops themselves which are pushed out onto the sidewalks, making it even more difficult to walk through the already crowded streets. Grant Avenue is filled with tourist shops and restaurants, but a block towards Stockton there is an entire street dedicated to the art of eating. Whole ducks and pigs hang in shop windows, invitingly glazed. Women stand in the fish stores poking at the gills, examining the eyes, prodding the crabs to see if they're alive. Inside are tanks of live catfish and cages filled with frogs and turtles. Weekends see trucks pull up, piled high with cages of angrily squawking ducks and quail and chickens, and lest anyone be prompted to pity, one truck sports a stern sign saying:

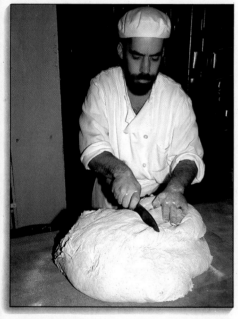

"All inside is not for pet." Onlookers can step into one of the *dim sum* houses or noodle stands for a quick, cheap bite to eat if all this bustle invokes hunger.

Salsa and Sashimi

Out in the Mission the mood is more light-hearted, the aromas spicier, and the music decidedly Latin. On 24th Street, the *taquerias* flash invitations to warm *tortillas* filled with grilled meats and chili-laden *salsas*, as the low-riders' big cars cruise the streets with their bellies close to the ground. The small bright *panaderias* offer sweet cakes, as well as brightly colored cookies and breads shaped into strange bewitching animals as

vivid as anything on the murals for which this neighborhood is known. This is the sunny side of the city, and such tropical fruits as mangos, papayas, pineapples and guavas seem almost at home here.

In Japantown the scents are brisker and saltier. Although this scene is in the heart of the city, so much fish is sold that the streets have the briny scent of the sea. In the stores are huge, deep-red chunks of tuna sitting next to the blue-white flesh of albacore, and the pale tan of buttery yellowtail brought all the way from Asia. Spread out all around are the various roe — the dull mustard-colored sea urchin, bright-orange salmon roe and the flashy red eggs of flying fish which are as fine as sand. These stores, with their rows and rows of lovely crackers and their plastic-wrapped tubes of noodles, vegetables and bean cake, are as neat and quiet as the old ladies who push their shopping carts before them, giggling softly as non-Asians try to decipher the writing on the packages.

But if there is one street in San Francisco that is a true amalgam of all the influences that are felt in this city, it has to be Clement Street. The food shops and restaurants here are so densely packed, they have elbowed almost every other kind of business off the street. There are almost 100 restaurants in a one-mile area, with as many cheese shops, bakeries and grocery stores sprinkled in among them. At the top of the street, at Arguello, is a health-food emporium, followed immediately by a fine French restaurant, an Irish pub and a pizza stand. By the time the street slows to a halt, at its far end dwindling into one of the city's stodgiest residential neighborhoods, most of the major world cuisines have been represented. It would take weeks to eat in all the restaurants, but those who do would sample Russian *pelmeni*, Chinese *bao*, Indonesian *satay*, American barbecue, Japanese *teriyaki*, Vietnamese crab rolls, Viennese pastries, Philippine *lumpia*, Lebanese *shish kebab*, Spanish *paella*, Thai fish cakes, Italian *gnocci*, and would end up in **Bill's**, one of the last restaurants on Clement, where hamburgers and old-fashioned milk shakes are served.

Although the food in all these places could not be more different, the restaurants share a certain quality: they are patronized by people who joyously taste, eat and argue about food as if there were no more important things to do on earth. The truth is that in a city which revels in the joy of eating, and where people take time for all the scents and smells and savory delights of life, there isn't.

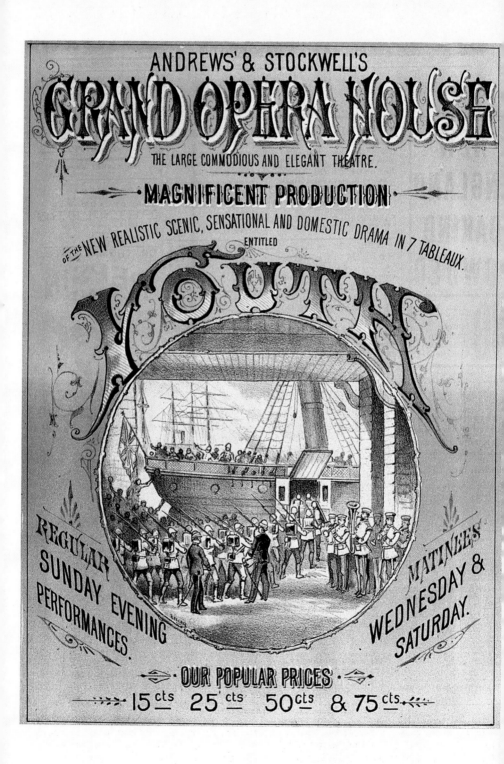

BAY AREA ARTS: A CULTURAL PRIMER

Rome in its first hundred years was still a haven for outlaws who plundered their women from the Sabines. Paris, a century after its founding, consisted of half-naked Gauls in wicker huts, while Athens was a collection of potters, farmers and earthen shrines. San Francisco on the other hand, after a mere century of existence, glittered with operas, symphonies, museums, parks and theaters.

Civilization did not evolve in the San Francisco Bay Area; it was carried here, in partial bloom, by hordes of go-for-broke prospectors, would-be millionaires and assorted bold *caballeros*. The development of the arts in such a milieu is anything but normal. But three shaping influences have always been present.

The first great uniqueness lies in the settlers themselves. "It was a splendid population," wrote Mark Twain, "for all the slow sleepy, sluggish-brained sloths staid home." Such adventurous temperaments did not balk at shipping an entire opera company halfway around the world, performing a symphony in a brothel, or supporting 20 newspapers in a town of 100,000. Many were professional men, city-bred and literate. San Francisco had the highest percentage of college graduates of any city in the nation. This general character — educated, daring, resistant to fetters — informs Bay Area's artists right up to the present.

A second major factor is money. The city's got it; the region was founded on it. To find, acquire, quickly multiply and lavishly spend it was the goal of all who came. And wherever great wealth accompanies an appetite for civilization, the arts are in for a boom. Symphonies, operas, universities, museums and theaters have seldom had trouble with funding. Throughout its history San Francisco has financially supported the arts on a level unsurpassed by any other city in America.

"San Francisco," wrote author Richard Henry Dana, "is the sole emporium of a new world, the awakened Pacific." This is the third factor. The Bay Area has been, from its inception, a busy world port. Goods, peoples and ideas from everywhere have found

Preceding pages: The Truth Company, alternative artists, present a lifelike rendition of the Golden Gate. Left, a 19th Century opera bill. Right, a mime at Ghirardelli Square.

their way here. And in a region where wealth and expectation outstripped actual goods and services, everything that arrived was welcomed. Perhaps no other city in the world has been as freely, almost thoughtlessly open to outside influences as San Francisco has been.

The most unique of these influences, by effect of geography, has been the Far East. Seen at first as a source of cheap labor, Asian countries have come to exert a spiritual influence through the depth and ancientness of their civilizations. There is

not a local art from that hasn't been affected in some way by the ideas and artifacts of India, China and Japan.

These elements combining over the last century have created a wondrously profuse art scene. It would be ingenuous to pretend that many great masterpieces have been produced or that the depth of critical thought and cultural tradition is on a level with London or Paris. San Francisco has no ancient, marmoreal legacies, no thousand-year-old schools nor memories of empire to hold sacred. Still, to have reached near-parity with the artistic centers of the world in a mere 100 years is a feat of no mean energy and daring. Imagine what can be accomplished when the city finally grows up.

261

Literary Lambasters

You couldn't *shanghai* a *hoodlum* before San Francisco produced writers, nor offer a *blurb* to a *beatnik*. These words, now minted into international usage, were first coined in the Bay Area. They reveal something of the region's literary origins — independent working class, anti-establishment — and something of its style — naturalistic, free-wheeling and bold.

The first writings produced by a new city are its newspapers and journals. In this as in much else, San Francisco was flamboyantly prolific. Such lambasters, romancers and dialectologists as Mark Twain, Bret Harte and Ambrose Bierce got started in the 1860s writing for the city's multiple journals. The local reading public was avid for information but even more devoted to criticism and satire. They had not crossed an entire continent to pay homage to Eastern gentility.

It was a basic assumption of California readers, wrote Mark Twain, "that a man who has served a lifetime as a dramatic critic on a New York paper may still be incompetent, but that a California critic knows it all, notwithstanding he may have been in the shoemaking business most of his life or a plow-artist on a ranch."

Social criticism was expected to be caustic. In a city founded by independent laborers and tradesmen, individual justice was a public passion, muckracking an admirable genre. The affinity that binds most Northern California writers is sympathy for the plight of the worker. Henry George, whose world-acclaimed *Progress and Poverty* formulated the rights of all people to the use of the earth, was an impoverished printer in San Francisco. Several early members of the Bohemian Club, founded in 1872 as a gathering place for writers and artists, were socialists. Jack London came out of the canneries of Oakland and wrote with passion about the proletariat. His friend and fellow naturalist, Frank Norris, learned his anti-capitalism at the University of California (Berkeley). Nobel laureate John Steinbeck portrayed the lives of migrant workers, and Upton Sinclair found the best atmosphere for his socialist beliefs in the free-labor spirit of California. Even Dashiell Hammett, creator of Sam Spade and a San Francisco literary landmark, was communist enough to be attacked by the House Unamerican Activities Committee.

It is no less revealing of the ironies produced by this region that many of the works of these early socialists were published by the *Argonaut Review*, a political arm of the

Southern Pacific Railroad; that Frank Norris himself was an inveterate dandy; that Jack London's name has become surrealistically linked to fancy restaurants and tourist shops; and that the Bohemian Club is now the quite exclusive domain of America's most powerful business and political leaders. California is as large as all contradiction.

None of these writers, with the exception of London and Steinbeck, were born in California. The most common literary experience here is coming from someplace else. John Muir, the poet of Yosemite, was from Scotland. Robinson Jeffers, who sang of the towering, craggy-faced beauty of Carmel, was born in Pittsburgh. Robert Louis Stevenson, Sinclair Lewis, Eugene O'Neill, Henry Miller, Jack Kerouac, Wallace Steg-

ner, Czezlaw Miloz and many others have lived here for a time and produced major work.

Some came for the weather and money. But many came for the political and artistic freedom of a region where "do your own thing" is a native expression. The beat movement of the Fifties was centered in the bookstores and coffee shops of North Beach. Poets Allen Ginsberg, Kenneth Patchen, William Everson, Kenneth Rexroth, Gary Snyder and Lawrence Ferlin-

Bay Area art is often avant-garde. Left, a sculpture exhibit at the Museum of Modern Art. Right, a creation of Chip Lord (foreground), co-founder of the Art Farm.

ghetti spoke for a movement that questioned all authority and sought meaning through an inner voice.

"San Francisco," wrote Robert Louis Stevenson, "keeps the doors to the Pacific." And through those doors in the last 30 years has flowed a wealth of Eastern thought and teaching. Perhaps the aspect of the beat movement most specific to the Bay Area was that of Zen Buddhism. The writings of Alan Watts in the Sixties did much to popularize the tenets and practices of Zen. Many local writers, such as Ginsberg and Snyder, have sojourned in Asian countries. Translators, schools and bookstores devoted to Eastern philosophy are scattered throughout the Bay Area and the largest Zen monastery in America is located in Carmel Valley.

and they exist in one place. This is why it takes so many centuries to develop a Rome or an Alexandria.

Still, as San Francisco has proved, a city can create a formidable reputation for itself if it doesn't mind spending the money. In 1871, 23 local artists organized the San Francisco Art Association. They offered exhibitions in a loft in a market "pervaded with the aroma of fish and the sound of the butcher's cleaver." It didn't take long before they could move to a better neighborhood, for wherever man builds mansions, there is a demand for art. Capital accrued. Society settled. Tastes were acquired.

By the 1890s art was becoming a social concern. The Art Association moved into a Nob Hill palace donated by a wealthy pa-

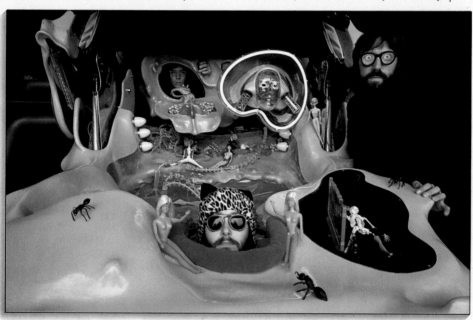

Although San Francisco lacks the publishing clout of New York, writers, editors and booksellers here have always done good trade. The libraries of U.C. Berkeley alone, with the numerous bookstores that surround it, offer as large a concentration of delights for the bibliophile as any square mile in the country.

The Visual Arts

A person can read *Moby Dick*, listen to Bach, or watch Shakespeare in a thousand different places, but unless he goes to Paris he will never see Notre Dame. The visual arts are the most resistant to duplication and dissemination. They reside in their artifacts

tron. A Midwinter Fair was held in Golden Gate Park and its flamboyant neo-Egyptian Exhibition Hall became the nucleus of what is today the De Young Museum. The California School of Painting, represented by earth-tone technicians such as Thomas Hill, Alfred Bierstadt and William Keith, specialized in gangantuan mountain gorges, vast Yosemite landscapes and sylvan meadows.

In 1915 the huge Panama-Pacific International Exposition brought paintings and sculpture to San Francisco from all over the world and 19th Century French aestheticism was placed upon the palate. The earlier landscape painters were referred to as "the brown sauce school" and European influence was courted. In the 1920s Bernard

Maybeck's Palace of the Legion of Honor went up, devoted primarily to French art. The Oakland Museum continued to build its definitive California collection and in the Thirties the San Francisco Museum became America's second museum of modern art.

With museums and schools established, artists were attracted. Money, weather and U.C. Berkeley brought out people like Diego Rivera, Clifford Still and Mark Rothko. Public murals as well as abstract expressionism became regional traditions. They even inspired a personalized and painterly counter-movement, "Bay Area Figurative," led by David Park and Elmer Biscoff. Bay Area art in the Sixties and Seventies produced examples of every form — pop and op art, junk sculpture, minimal art and con-

In 1946, Ansel Adams started the world's first professional photography courses at The California School of Fine Arts (now the San Francisco Art Institute). This attracted such fine photographers as Edward Weston, Imogen Cunningham and Dorthea Lange. The same institute offered the first courses in film making. From the experimental films and psychedelic poster art of the Sixties to the current movement of photorealism in painting, the camera has had a profound influence on Bay Area art. Performance art, that newly born genre of space, art and performer, is another innovation in which San Francisco rivals New York as a world leader.

Perhaps the chief characteristic of Bay Area art is simply the number of people taking part, especially in the crafts. Know-

ceptualist landscape. Because the major museums do not promote local work, dozens of smaller galleries have opened in the last 20 years to encourage and market Bay Area artists.

All this buying, building, exhibiting and importing are necessary, but locating an indigenous artistic strain can be like trying to trace a thread through an arras. Taste among the pioneers was more primal. Inflated with wealth from the Gold Rush, San Francisco produced the most extravagant collection of bar-room nudes this nation has seen; and these popular forms, too old or too new to have been shaped by modern European art, reveal the region's greatest originality.

ledge and respect for wood, clay, stone and cloth are traditional to this region. Carpenters, designers, printmakers abound. There are more potters and jewelry makers in Berkeley than in any 10 Indian pueblos. Robert Arenson, Peter Voulkas and other ceramists are internationally known.

It may be in such locally inspired forms of photography, poster art, dollmaking and ceramics that the Bay Area eventually defines a truly regional style, distinct from outside influences.

Left, a Japanese drum troupe performs at the State Fair in Sacramento. Right, a stage performance by the Children of Light, one of the Bay Area's many new theater groups.

Music and Opera

The hundreds of thousands who flooded this region in the 1850s brought their instruments with them. Music halls went up immediately, as plentiful and as popular as brothels. Orchestras and choral societies played alongside *mariachi* bands and minstrel shows. Amateur groups organized around national instruments and styles. But opera was the most universal form and greatest passion of the populace.

There were always several operas running and every performance was reviewed and discussed. Fire brigades escorted their favorite divas while European troupes made San Francisco a regular stop on their tours. On Christmas Eve 1910 a five-street-deep

crowd, largest in the city's history, assembled in front of the *Chronicle* building to hear their favorite soprano sing Verdi.

The tradition lives on. Today the San Francisco Opera engages the greatest stars and mounts some of the most lavish productions in the world. Opening night of the opera season is the social event of the year on the West Coast. In a metropolitan area one-third the size of New York, there are no less than seven full-scale opera companies.

Symphonic music was heard throughout the 19th Century with Fritz Scheel, later to be the founder of the Philadelphia Orchestra, the leading force. Under Pierre Monteux, the San Francisco Symphony (founded in 1923) became one of the major orchestras

in America. The San Francisco Ballet, over 50 years old, is also rich and well respected, especially under current director-choreographer Michael Smuin. The opera, ballet and symphony are in fact the only ones in the country regularly assisted by public money. Private support is substantial as evidenced by the new $28-million dollar Davies Hall, Oakland, San Jose, Sacramento and Marin also have fully professional symphonies.

But the real profligacy is in the breadth and variety of classical music. There are more concerts per capita than in any other city in the country; one critic calls it "an unreasonable profusion." Chamber music is particularly well served. The San Francisco Chamber Orchestra, the Oakland Symphony Players and dozens of highly polished groups provide a constant variety from baroque to Bartok.

Contemporary music came to the Bay Area in the Fifties when world-famous composers Darius Milhaud at Mills College and Roger Sessions at U.C. Berkeley taught and inspired a new generation of musicians and composers. Today groups such as The San Francisco Contemporary Music Players and the Kronos String Quartet regularly present contemporary work, while festivals of new music occur every year. For the delicately specialized, The Early Music Society sends out a monthly calender that allows lovers of medieval madrigal, chant and motet to attend a concert nearly every day of the week.

Amidst all this European influence one mustn't forget the 19th Century female violinist who rose between musical numbers and demonstrated her "talent and strength of muscle" by doing leaps, splits and somersaults. California gold imported the finest talent touring the world but its indigenous style was always "early raucous" and "popular pioneer." This, in many ways, remains the case.

The region's earliest musical invention was the minstrel show. The honky-tonk reached its apotheosis on the Barbary Coast while the folk-music revival of the Fifties flourished here. Out of this openness to popular forms and divergent lifestyles emerged a remarkable cultural revolution in the late Sixties.

The psychedelic rock and hippie movement was based, like no other movement before it, on a new kind of music. The concerts and light shows staged at the Fillmore, Avalon and Family Dog auditoriums became a standard by which an entire generation would define its ultimate musical experience. Groups like the Grateful Dead, the Jefferson Airplane and Credence Clearwater Revival generated a powerful enthusiasm for rock 'n' roll while serving as an alternative to the establishment's notion of worth and decorum. One hundred thousand swaying devotees would gather at great open-air concerts, dancing topless in the sun, and combining various drugs like colors on a palette. In time, it became a national movement co-opted by commercial interests. But it remained centered in the high and liberated zone of San Francisco Bay.

The Theatrical Tradition

It's not uncommon to find an opera, symphony or museum over 100 years old. But a theater company that survives 10 years is getting to the edge of venerability. The power of the theater is not in how long it lasts but in how easily it can be started. A tent, a pennywhistle, a painted face and presto, it's show business.

Eternal verities presented on a shoestring are ideally suited to frontier boom-towns, and from 1850 to 1906 scores of melodeons (theatre-bar-music halls) were built, burned down and rebuilt in San Francisco. The bill of fare at these pleasure palaces ran the gamut and aimed to please: jugglers, acrobats, minstrels, strippers Shakespeare and melodramas. At some houses, like the successful and infamous Bella Union, champagne and female companionship could be purchased with the program. This Barbary Coast low-life tradition has never fully died out. Through the various years of burlesque, to the sex shows and porn parlors of today, San Francisco has remained boisterously committed to giving an audience whatever it thinks it wants.

By 1870 the fabulously wealthy had become a class. Connected to the East Coast by rail and desirous of sophistication, they supported more refined and professional entertainments. Traditional stock companies were formed and such was the local support that stars and touring companies from England as well as America came here for extended stays. Edwin Booth, John Drew, Ethel Barrymore, Henry Irving, Ellen Terry and Sarah Bernhardt played many times in San Francisco. So did Lola Montes, Marie Dressler and Harry Houdini.

Then came the convulsion. The 1906 earthquake and fire destroyed every theater in the city but one. Forced to start again from scratch, producers found capital hard to raise. High-society money was going into

symphonies and museums. The motion picture, that amazing new invention, was sweeping the country and driving performers from the boards. Incredibly, live theater ceased to be a vital force in the Bay Area from 1906 to 1960.

In 1959, Herbert Blau and Jules Irving founded the Actor's Workshop, dedicated to an "impossible theater" in which constant experiment and engagement were the goals. They declared that theater belongs to actors and directors, not to producers and promoters. A few years later the American Conservatory Theatre (A.C.T.) was opened. Its aim was to become a fully professional repertory company; today, its training school is one of the largest and most respected in America. Berkeley Repertory, San Jose Repertory and the London School of Dramatic Arts in Berkeley serve similar large-scale, traditional functions.

But the greatest effect has flowed from the more experimental premises of the Actor's Workshop. Small to medium-sized companies of every conceivable purpose and style have proliferated to a point bordering on wilderment.

In today's San Francisco, a person who picks up the *Theatre Directory* will discover 87 wildly various companies listed. There are hundreds of performances a week, 76 theater spaces, 12 academic institutions offering theater degrees as well as 65 acting schools and teachers.

Productions range from agitprop and *commedia dell' arte* to lavish *al fresco* stagings of Shakespeare, from avant-garde physical and environmental pieces to the consolation of jugglers and clowns. There are ethnic-based, *noh*-influenced, mask, feminist, one-act, mime and gay theaters.

Accompanying all this has been the development of a strong modern dance movement led by the Margaret Jenkins Company and the Oberlin Dance Collective. Zellerbach Hall in Berkeley has become a regular stop for the best touring dance companies in the world.

If the styles of performing arts vary so much, the same can be said of the quality. There are many enthusiastic amateurs. On the other hand, there are a handful of groups — The San Francisco Mime Troupe, El Teatro Campesino and George Coates Performance Works, to name three — which are world-class at what they do.

Masterpieces of "junk art" beautify the mud flats of San Francisco Bay near Oakland. Artists use any and all materials.

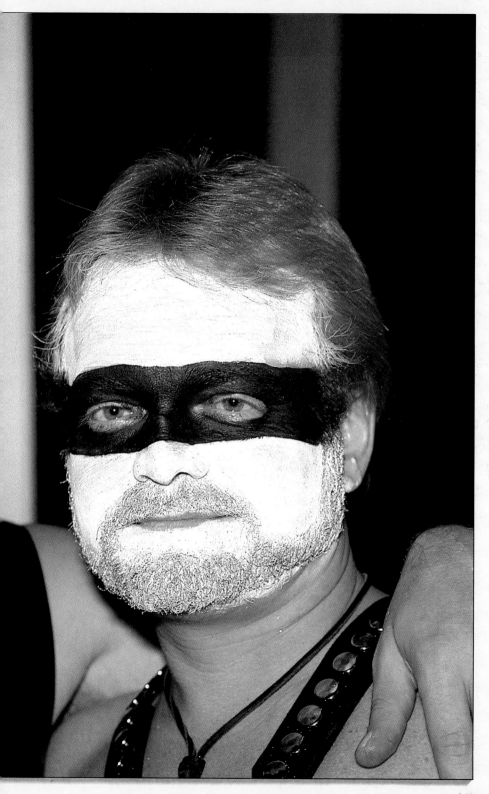

THE GAY COMMUNITY OF SAN FRANCISCO

They've rioted in the streets, refurbished entire neighborhoods of once-decaying Victorian homes, wielded the most powerful voting bloc in local politics, built a substantial business community and, altogether, given San Francisco its current international reputation as the world's gay mecca. The brash emergence of the city's out-front, unabashed and sometimes volatile gay community undoubtedly represents the most significant sociological development in San Francisco since the days of the beatniks and the hippies.

No one knows the exact number of gays living in San Francisco, although city officials speculate endlessly, like medieval theologians, trying to tally just how many homosexuals can disco on the head of a peninsula. Say somewhere between 50,000 and 100,000.

Like nearly every aspect of San Francisco history, the transformation of the Gold Rush town into a homophile Oz grew from most unlikely and improbable beginnings.

It started in the waning days of World War II. The U.S. military began systematically purging its ranks of gays, booting out suspected homosexuals at their point of debarkation. For the massive Pacific theater of the war, this meant San Francisco.

The purges created an entire class of men who had been officially stigmatized as homosexuals. Unable to return home and face inevitable shame, they stayed in the Bay Area, socializing in discreet bars or, more often, at intimate soirées. Another migration of professional gays came during the early Fifties in the heyday of the anti-communist McCarthy era, when the federal government drummed thousands of homosexuals out of government jobs.

Local authorities, meanwhile, did not take much of a liking to the idea of gays grouping in the bohemian bars of North Beach. They treated any gathering of more than a few dozen like an armed insurrection. Bar raids, mass arrests and harsh prosecutions of men and women accused of frequenting "disorderly houses" became common.

Still, there were other parts of America which were even less hospitable to gays than San Francisco, where police officers could often have their moral outrage assuaged by a modest payoff. So more and more gays joined their comrades in the Bay Area through the Fifties.

The Origins of Activism

By 1960, gays began moving toward an open campaign for civil rights, a course of action unthinkable a few years before and unprecedented in American history. Ultimately, gays can credit such institutions as the U.S. military establishment and the San Francisco Police Department for this, since the political activism was created largely in response to anti-gay excesses.

It all started humbly enough in 1955 with the formation of the nation's first lesbian group, the Daughters of Bilitis. Then the notion that homosexuals could actually band together in pressure groups, just like normal people, was considered rather novel. But it caught on. Cadres of politically active gays were soon forming with such non-threatening names as the Society for Individual Rights (SIR) and the Mattachine Society, whose then-radical publication timidly asked whether homosexuality was a "disease or way of life" and whether gays should have "rehabilitation or punishment."

In 1961, Jose Sarria, a prominent female impersonator who was sure he was neither diseased nor in need of rehabilitation, got so irate over police raids on his Black Cat bar that he took off his dress and high heels and donned a three-piece suit to run for the Board of Supervisors, San Francisco's version of a city council. Sarria polled a then-astounding 7,000 votes and clued the fledgling gay groups that their future power would lie in the ballot box.

Liberal candidates for the Board of Supervisors were politely seeking gay endorsements by 1964 without seeing their careers destroyed by pious moralists, a breed in short supply in San Francisco anyway. When the 1969 board election came along, so did an attractive 35-year-old political newcomer named Dianne Feinstein. Feinstein, who would later become mayor, campaigned aggressively among gays and later credited the margin of her landslide city-wide victory to gay ballots.

With that, the dam broke and politicians started courting gay voters with enthusiasm

The most visible fraction of San Francisco's gay community is often the most uncharacteristically bizarre. Preceding pages, a "heavy metal" couple. Left, a satanic-looking mime.

once reserved for organized labor or the Chamber of Commerce. Within a decade, most pundits would estimate that one in four of the city's voters were gay, the single most influential minority group in town. Studies have shown that, proportionately, gays tend to vote in larger numbers and give more money to political candidates than their heterosexual counterparts.

Even as Feinstein campaigned at the Society for Individual Rights, the hippie counterculture was in full bloom in the Haight-Ashbury neighborhood. This provided a fertile territory for the gay liberation movement that was sweeping west from New York City on the heels of the leftist anti-war movement. It didn't take long for some of the flower children to question whether the

As this urban phenomenon began drawing national attention, the image of San Francisco as a gay haven became a self-fulfilling prophecy. Media attention drew more gay immigrants, who in turn ballooned the business and political power of gays, which in turn brought more media, enticing still more immigrants.

Drama at City Hall

Castro Street rapidly became the embodiment of the gay drive for acceptance in the late 1970s. In 1975, gay votes elected George Moscone, the first mayor wholly sympathetic to gay concerns. Two years later, neighborhood voters elected Harvey Milk to the Board of Supervisors. Milk, a Castro Street

do-your-own-thing hippie ethos might mean more than wearing love beads, growing long hair and swallowing LSD. It might even mean accepting the tinglings of taboo sexuality. Slowly, a few dozen, then a few hundred gay hippies moved over the hill from Haight Street to Castro Street, a nearby Irish-American enclave gone to seed.

The native working-class Catholics were terrified at the "gay invaders," as they called them, and many panicked, moving out. They left behind a huge, if somewhat dilapidated, stock of quaint 1880s Victorian homes for gay gentrification. The area quickly evolved into the first neighborhood in the nation literally owned and run by gay people, for gay people.

camera shop owner who organized the area's merchants group, became the first openly gay city official in America.

When gay rights surged to the forefront of the nation's social agenda with the Anita Bryant crusade against homosexuals, Castro Street routinely echoed with the chants of tens of thousands of angry demonstrators who massed around the gay bars and marched to City Hall a mile away.

A series of traumatic historical events interceded in the late Seventies to add even

Left, a show of gay pride in a fund-raising tricycle race. Right, a Halloween masquerade in a Castro Street bar. Group identification binds the gay community together.

more drama. In late 1978, former Supervisor Dan White, the city's most anti-gay politician, gunned down Supervisor Milk and Mayor Moscone in City Hall. The city reeled in shock at the crime and a mixed crowd of 50,000 again marched the familiar path from Castro Street to City Hall, silently bearing candles. Six months later, when a jury decided to imprison double-murderer White for only five years, another rowdier mob marched on City Hall, this time sparking the massive gay "White Night" riots which gained worldwide attention.

Such an outburst in other cities might have strained public acceptance of homosexuals, but this wasn't the case in San Francisco. The sheer volume and diversity of the gay population had ensured a legitimization that

no single event, however riotous, could undermine.

This subtle social process that guaranteed the acceptance of gays had unfolded slowly through the remarkable epoch of gay activism. San Francisco had become more than a center of economic or political clout; it had become the center for what truly was a community, in the old-fashioned sense of the world. Gay marching bands, gay American Indians, gay senior citizens, gay Republicans, gay square dancers, gay doctors, lesbian lawyers and even gay Buddhists formed their own organizations. The Lesbian/Gay Freedom Day Parade every June is the city's largest annual event, drawing 250,000 on an average year.

Entering the Mainstream

The gay population is fairly happily dispersed among several major neighborhoods around the city. The sprawling Castro district today features the Young Urban Professionals, a decidely non-hippie generation of prepped-up "yuppies." In the South of Market gay enclave, buckled around Folsom Street, is a fiercer-looking bohemian set with a penchant for motorcycles, black leather and public displays of dominance or submission. Young gay transients in tight jeans hustle unabashedly on Polk Street and in the seedy Tenderloin district, while an affluent pocket of three-piece-suited gay business executives is patched comfortably on the breast of very, very proper Pacific Heights. A large lesbian community has coalesced in East Bay cities such as Oakland and Berkeley where two-women households, unable to garner the higher incomes of two-male partnerships, find less expensive living.

The continuing presence of gays in such large numbers has created a city in which, more than any other, gays have melded into the mainstream. For years, San Francisco has had a gay supervisor, a growing number of gay police officers, schoolteachers, congressional aides and bureaucrats, as well as an acknowledged lesbian and a gay man serving as full-fledged judges on the Municipal Court. Gains for which gays once struggled are now a matter of course.

The Eighties have also brought a significant calming effect on the once-turbulent gay community. Angry rhetoric has cooled as activists who once railed against the establishment have become a part of the establishment themselves.

The advent of serious health problems — notably acquired immune deficiency syndrome (AIDS) — has also toned down the once-lusty nightlife. Conventional values on dating and courtship are taking hold, even though enough revelers remain to give the city some of the wildest gay bars on earth.

The raucous marches have thinned, as there are fewer and fewer local injustices at which mass anger could be directed. The experience of San Francisco in the past two decades, in the sense, has illustrated the great irony of the American gay rights movement. Once the major goal of that movement is achieved and discrimination is all but eliminated, the entire issue of whether one is gay or straight becomes irrelevant. San Francisco seems set on proving that a successful gay movement is programmed to self-destruct.

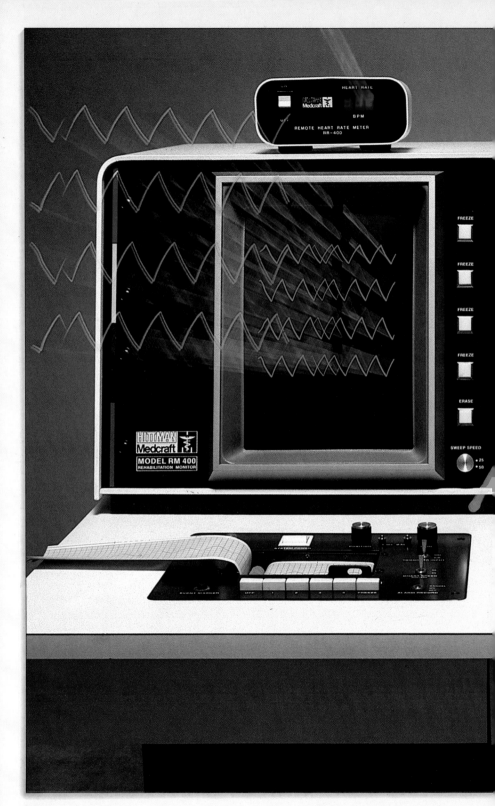

PLAYING 'THE GAME' IN SILICON VALLEY

The young entrepreneurs and would-be entrepreneurs of Silicon Valley talk about "the game." The game is called start-up. Its rules are simple. It can be played by any number of adults. The object is to become rich as Croesus.

The player starts by working for one of the big firms: IBM, Intel, National Semiconductor, Motorola or the like. After a few years, he quietly leaves his job, taking along a few colleagues, promising them a chance to play the game together. He also takes what he has learned, perhaps in the form of secret documents, better still as memorized information.

Funded by venture capital, the player sets up a new company. His ex-employer sues for theft of proprietary information and for predatory hiring; he counter-sues, charging anti-competitive practices and violation of the laws against monopoly. After working 80-hour weeks for a few years, he eventually goes public, selling stock of the company on the open market. Investors, their enthusiasm pumped up by years of big electronics successes, eagerly snap up the entire offering in a few hours, driving the price per share to astronomical heights. Having kept a large chunk of shares himself, the player is now a multimillionaire.

The game is often played with chips, though not the kind found in casinos. These chips are tiny flakes of an element called silicon. They have been transformed, through a manufacturing process, into integrated circuits, microscopic grids of electronic components — transistors, diodes, resistors and capacitors. These are the working parts of computers, communications devices, video systems, radar installations, space satellites and a host of sophisticated weapons systems, as well as digital watches, microwave ovens and electronic toys. The chips themselves are so small, yet so powerful, that they are more like spirits than machines.

A crystal of silicon is on display in the electronics museum at Foothill College. Looking fresh from the refining process before being sliced into the wafers from which chips are made, the crystal is a gray cylinder about 10 inches (25 centimeters) long, flat at one end and round at the other. It looks like nothing so much as a giant bullet, aimed at the future.

Not so long ago, when Silicon Valley was

still called the Santa Clara Valley, it was a quiet place covered with fruit orchards, fragrant with plum blossoms and rich earth. In the late summer, the fuzzy, black caterpillars of the salt marsh moth *(Estigmene acroea)* crawled by the thousands across the narrow country roads.

The first European and American settlers arrived in this valley during the 1850s as part of the great California Gold Rush. The newcomers planted fruit orchards and prospered. The valley became the biggest supplier of prunes in the world.

Even then technology played a role. The transcontinental railroad brought access to the eastern market for dried fruit, and later for refrigerated fresh fruit. A new spraying pump was invented. When the Libby, McNeil & Libby cannery opened in Sunnyvale in 1907, it was the world's biggest canning and freezing plant.

But the industry that would supplant all this had already enjoyed its inconspicuous beginnings. In 1899 San Francisco received the first ship-to-shore wireless message ever

High technology can be a colorful subject (preceding pages). The essential microchip, left, is so small that the technician must study it with microscope, right.

sent in the United States. The message was relayed from several miles offshore to the Cliff House, signaling the imminent arrival of the *USS Sherman* carrying troops back from the Spanish-American War in the Philippines.

In the 50 years that followed, many more milestones in the history of electronics were passed in the San Francisco Bay Area, especially in the Santa Clara Valley. In San Jose, Charles Herrold began broadcasting in 1909 on KQW, the first scheduled radio station in the country. In 1910, at the Tanforan race-

In ensuing years, a generation of gifted engineers set the stage for the post-World War II electronics boom. Many of them started out in rented garages with nothing but pluck and an ingenious invention, building their companies from nothing into international corporations. Hewlett-Packard Co. is an outstanding example: founded in 1938 in a garage in Palo Alto by two Stanford graduates, David Packard and William Hewlett, it is now one of the world's largest makers of electronic testing equipment and computers.

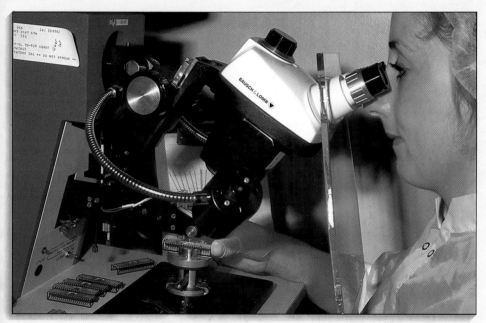

track in San Bruno, the first wireless telegraph message was sent from a plane aloft to a receiver on the ground.

Vacuum Tubes and Transistors

The Federal Telegraph Company, the first American radio firm, was founded in Palo Alto in 1909, bankrolled in part by the president of Stanford University. While working for Federal in 1912, Lee de Forest discovered the use of the vacuum tube to amplify and transmit sounds. This discovery made possible the radio and the long-distance telephone. It was as revolutionary in its day as the transistor and the integrated circuit would be to later generations.

Electronics technology has often advanced in lock-step with the advance of weaponry. The Second World War gave a great impetus to developments in the Santa Clara Valley in the form of hefty government contracts. But the truly momentous development of the Forties took place at the University of Pennsylvania: seeking a superior way to calculate trajectory tables for bombsights and artillery, the first digital computer was built.

This computer, called ENIAC, used 18,000 vacuum tubes. The tubes failed frequently, and when one did it could take hours to locate. Then at the Bell Laboratories in 1948, John Bardeen, Walter Brattain and William Shockley invented the transistor. About the size of a pea, it did everything the vacuum tube had done without the tube's enormous appetite for energy.

Shockley came to Mountain View and founded Shockley Semiconductor Laboratory. That enterprise failed, but some of Shockley's researchers convinced Fairchild Camera and Instrument to let them continue their research. This led, in 1957, to the founding of Fairchild Semiconductor, a "spin-off" company and the first successful semiconductor manufacturer in the area. Two years later, Robert Noyce invented the integrated circuit. (Jack Kilby came up with the same idea independently at Texas Instruments.) Smaller than a cornflake, this "chip" could contain thousands of transistors. It was the start of a new world.

tructure" — the supporting conditions and institutions for this growth. It included research institutions such as Stanford, venture capital firms, colleges and universities to supply trained personnel, and the support of local governments pleased to cooperate in developing prune orchards into industrial parks. Lawyers had to create a new area of jurisprudence for the protection of proprietary information about electronic products.

At some point, all this became self-perpetuating. Computers are built of chips, and computers are used to design new chips. New start-up companies attract venture capitalists who attract entrepreneurs who want to start new companies. As a result, Silicon Valley has become the cradle not only of electronics companies, but of many

Noyce was also the originator of "the game." He left Fairchild and founded Intel where Federico Faggin, Stan Mazor and Tedd Hoff invented the first microprocessor in 1970. A microprocessor has, on one chip, all the working circuitry of an entire computer. The personal computer was suddenly possible. Faggin eventually left Intel to found Zilog and later left Zilog to found Cygnet.

In 1971 the term Silicon Valley was popularized by journalist Don Hoefler. At this point the history of Silicon Valley began to sound like the fifth chapter of Genesis, with one company begetting another in an orgy of start-ups. Concurrently with the multiplication of companies grew the "infras-

kinds of high-technology start-ups. Pharmaceutical companies and the new genetic engineering technology flourish in Silicon Valley, as do laser and telecommunications firms. In the semiconductor market alone, Silicon Valley sales are over $3 billion dollars a year and growing rapidly.

Toxic waste, as might be expected, poses a new problem. The toxic solvents used in manufacturing chips have seeped into the ground water in several locations in the valley and are suspected of causing cancer and

Left, computer fairs are increasingly popular attractions for business and personal consumers alike. Right, a schoolgirl explores a unit adapted for use in her classroom.

birth defects. Rapid growth brings other kinds of poison. San Jose, a sleepy little agricultural town 30 years ago, is now almost the size of San Francisco; it is the fastest growing city in America. Housing is almost impossible to find and when found it is very expensive. Rush-hour traffic, crawling bumper to bumper between San Jose and Redwood City, creates a sickly brown smog that seldom clears.

For all the problems, Silicon Valley retains a vigorous economy and a vital way of life, as can be seen in Cupertino's Valco Center, the area's premier shopping mall. Here the floors are of polished oak and the shops are expensive.

Outside, the broad expressways and roads carry heavy traffic through the blocks of

quiet residential neighborhoods and sprawling industrial parks. The industrial parks themselves, with their manicured turf and carefully planned open space, are parks only in the imaginations of those who have an image to create.

The buildings that house the companies are low, seldom more than two stories and almost never more than four. But they are long, designed to encourage movement of and communication among employees. One of the tenets of Silicon Valley is that progress depends on the sharing of new ideas — even as, paradoxically, the Valley is probably the world capital of litigation over proprietary information.

Inside the buildings, workers dressed in hospital smocks, paper hats and masks bend over microscopes in sealed, dust-free rooms, connecting gold wires, tinier than human hairs, to chips. In other labyrinthine rooms, programmers huddle, each in his or her own cubicle, fingers on keyboards, eyes on video displays. Behind glass, air-conditioned and filtered, squat computers and their peripheral equipment, silent machines in metal cabinets, tape drives, disk cartridges, serpents' dens of cables coiling under the false floors on which they rest.

In the parking lots, basketball and volleyball courts bake in the sun. Employees are treated benevolently in the Valley, where it is often said that they need only walk across the street to find new jobs. Recreational amenities and generous incentives are offered. At higher levels, stock options and company Porches are given. But the volleyball courts are usually empty and the Porches are used to drive to and from work, often seven days a week. The spirit is generous, but very competitive.

Silicon Valley represents the worst aspects of human nature and the best. It is materialistic in its pursuit of Mercedes Benzes and of homes with built-in saunas and satellite-receiving dishes, and in its assertion that all problems will be solved by technology. It is spiritual in its quest for the computer which has no size nor weight and an unlimited power, an ideal worthy of Zen. It is a place where things move so fast that new inventions are obsolete by the time they hit the market, and where the ultimate goal of research is knowledge of the eternal nature of matter and energy themselves.

It has, as its historical imperative, a sense of magic, a quest for gold. Even today, sewage sludge is incinerated in Palo Alto and the resulting ash sold to entrepreneurs. The gold, silver and other metals refined from the ash net the town as much as $1 million a year.

This version of the lotus blossom in the dung heap is reminiscent of the Gold Rush which occasioned the area's first population spurt. As then, the Valley is still a source of great wealth. As then, the salt marsh caterpillar can still be seen (albeit in reduced numbers). The creature crosses the expressways in early September, while in nearby buildings technicians work to create the next generation of computers.

Come spring, some of those caterpillars will emerge as butterflies. Some of those technicians will start up companies and emerge wealthy. So the cycle of life continues; in Silicon Valley, the dollars and the electrons continue to flow.

THE GREAT OUTDOORS

California is, in most ways, two very different states. Certainly this is true if one considers how California residents relate to the outdoors.

In Southern California, outdoors is where the car is. If a person has enough time and gas, the automobile will eventually bring him face-to-face with nature. In Northern California, outdoors is often literally that — outside one's door. An hour's drive, at most, from even the most urban landscape will get one to the edge of wilderness.

In Southern California there is Disneyland; in Northern California there is Yosemite National Park.

In Southern California there are warm nights, phosphorescent ocean waves, barbeques and swimming pools; in Northern California there are wood stoves, picnic baskets, solitary walks along a foggy coast, trout fishing and long soaks in outdoor hot tubs.

In the south, except for the fires and floods that periodically sweep the canyons clean and except for the vast expanse of the tawny-pink Mojave Desert, nature has been paved and tamed. In the north, environmentally conscious residents have kept their territory green.

The Sierra Club was formed in San Francisco by John Muir; early environmentalists made Yosemite Valley the nation's first protected area; the Coastal Preservation Act of 1972 has kept the Northern California coast relatively free of condominiums and shopping malls. On the northern edge of San Francisco lies the largest and most visited urban park in the world, the Golden Gate National Recreation Area.

Ask a Northern Californian why he doesn't move to Los Angeles where there might be more jobs, more professional opportunities, more art and glamour, and chances are he'll say he stays for aesthetic reasons. San Francisco is the prettiest city in the country, not the most exciting, or the most challenging, or the most real. It is a city for lovers and pleasure seekers.

There are, of course, outdoor activities all Californians share — sports that require mild weather, offshore breezes, or proximity to the ocean. Softball, surfing, tennis and

golf are year-long statewide activities. So are more exotic adventure sports — sailboarding, hang gliding and skydiving in particular. All California closets hold a cache of sporting equipment; garages shelter backpacks and dirt bikes; cars roll out of town Friday nights towing boats and trailers, filled with sleeping bags and fishing poles. One out of every three households has some kind of recreation vehicle. Home, they say, is where the heart is, and the heart of California is outside, under the sky and stars; in the bosom of nature herself.

Pacific Playground

The Pacific Ocean in the north is too cold to swim comfortably unless it's one of those rare summer days when the breezes come from the east. It is also full of sharks, undercurrents and large waves.

But these inhospitable elements have their advantages: they keep coves and beaches free from snack bars and volleyball courts. The thing to do on an often-foggy beach in Mendocino, or Carmel, or Point Reyes, is to walk. The waves come in from Japan, the currents sweep down from Alaska, the surf snarls and foams on the rocky shores. It is a thrill to sit in a storm on the edge of a cliff and watch the pounding surf, hear the sounds, inhale the smells, and feel the tingle of spray. There are lessons to be learned from the seagulls and pelicans, sliding so surely and easily through the brisk winds; there is poetry in the patterns of sea foam.

Many secluded coves along State Highway 1 wait to be discovered and walked upon. Agile sun-seekers can scramble down a rocky cliff and bask in the golden rays, protected from the wind by a rock. Then they can break out their bread, cheese, book and wine, and look for driftwood and tidepools.

Tide-pooling is fun anywhere the rocky reefs aren't too close to large populations of schoolchildren with buckets. Turban snails, sea urchins, anemones and starfish can be found right in plain sight. Those who take the time to explore small, still pools at minus tide just might find fire-engine-red sponges spreading like a dazzling carpet across the underside of a ledge, or a spangled mat of bulbous, gooey tunicates swirling amidst soft green moss and crusty spots of lichen. The seaweed lapping gently in the water may be dusty rose, irridescent blue, kelly or sage-

Preceding pages, fishing at Lake Merced, a bit of wilderness in the southwestern corner of San Francisco. Left, a giant sequoia forest in Yosemite National Park.

brush green. Tucked in small hollows of the rock are tube worms and chitons, small fish and tiny eels. In the stillest part of the water, where the pool is deep and calm and never completely dry, the explorer might even find a nudibranch — a day-glow colored snail without a shell, bobbing about like a tiny, tropical fish.

The best places to tidepool are Point Lobos and Pescadero Point in Carmel; Tomales Point and Duxbury Reef just north of San Francisco; Sea Ranch, Salt Point and MacKerricher State Park further up the coast. But anywhere can be good, provided there are exposed rocks and a minus tide.

More active water sports include diving, sailboarding and deep-sea fishing; detailed information on these is contained in this

way to understand their attraction is to go out to meet them. Lucky whale-watchers end up in the middle of a pod, with the whales playing, breaching, swimming and diving right under the humans' noses. And there may be a breathless moment, a still point, when the whale has taken a dive and not yet surfaced. There is no time quite as thrilling as when it explodes out of the water right next to the boat.

Whale-watching boats leave regularly in season from Half Moon Bay, south of San Francisco. Lest sojourners be disappointed, however, the ocean can be rough and cold and boats don't always manage to get close to the whales. Sometimes they don't even spot them at all.

volume's "Guide in Brief."

But the most exciting of the ocean's treasures is not a fish, not the surf, and not even a romantic, isolated cove. It is the whale, that most munificent and benign of all large mammals.

Watching the Whales

Whales are visible offshore all along the California coast from December to April when they migrate almost 12,000 miles (19,000 kilometers) from the Arctic to the coast of Baja California to spawn and then swim back again with their young. They can be seen with binoculars from just about any point jutting out from the coast. But the best

Mountain Magnificence

The mountains are California's other treasure and the best of them lie in the northern part of the state. There are the coastal ranges, which run from the rugged Big Sur Mountains nearly to the Oregon border. There are the Klamath Mountains, 12,000 square miles (31,000 sq km) of sparkling blue lakes, clear running streams, pine and redwood forests, and little-used hiking trails. The Klamaths include the pristine Trinity

Left, the big one that got away; whale watchers sometimes must be satisfied with a glimpse of the gray whale's tail. Right, cross-country skiing near Mammoth Mountain.

Alps, jagged, preglacial peaks which contain perhaps the finest trout fishing in the state in the Fall and Hat creek areas.

At the southern tip of the Cascade Mountain range — which begins at the Canadian border and stretches through Washington and Oregon — are the great volcanic mountains of the north, Mount Shasta and Lassen Peak. Shasta, at 14,162 feet (4,316 meters), totally dominates the surrounding area. A volcanic cone reminiscent of Japan's Mount Fuji or East Africa's Mount Kilimanjaro, the mountain can be climbed from all sides (an overnight adventure for the experienced only). Lake Shasta, at its foot, is a very large and beautiful lake with good fishing and, even better, houseboats for rent.

Lassen Peak (10,457 feet or 3,187 meters)

The pride and joy of California alpinists, however, are the mighty and wondrous Sierra Nevada. Not only are the Sierras long (400 miles, 640 km); they are high, beautiful and benevolent. Summer in the Sierras rarely sees serious storms, and winters are tame enough for the truly adventurous to traverse the mountains' breadth on skis.

Backpackers' Paradise

The Sierras offer so many outdoor activities, it's hard to know where to begin. The environs of Yosemite and Kings Canyon/Sequoia national parks and of Lake Tahoe have been discussed elsewhere in this book. But they represent only the beginning.

One of the great wonders of the Sierras is

is an active volcano which last erupted in 1914-15. It has hot sulfur pools bubbling up from its slopes and steam wafting from vents in the rocks. Lassen Peak is only a moderately strenuous walk from the trailhead off the road. The whole area is a national park with all accompanying amenities, including ranger talks and guided hikes.

A third range at the northeastern tip of the state, the Warner Mountains, is tiny but isolated and hence full of wildflowers and wildlife. Although these mountains are low (their highest peaks are under 10,000 feet, no more than 3,000 meters), they are rugged, with few trails and fewer signposts. Best of all, they offer solitude even at the height of the summer season.

the ease with which they can be entered on foot. Anyone who can carry a pack and climb over a pass can, in one day, be in a world of high tundra meadows, sparkling clear-water lakes and weathered whitebark pines. The Sierras are high — Mount Whitney, at 14,494 feet (4,418 meters), is the highest point in the entire United States outside Alaska. The scenery above tree level is a feast of color, texture, design and light.

Barren summits rise above lush green forests, and the landscape is stippled with a thousand blue-green lakes. Lush carpets of yellow, purple, white, blue and pink wildflowers border tiny streams and fill huge high mountain meadows; glacially polished gray granite rock glistens after a rain and turns pink and orange in the last moments of twilight. Silver ribbons of water spill from lakes and connect the huge water systems, forming the canyons, marking the divides, flowing from one small lake to another down the rocky belly of the classic Sierra formation, the glacial cirque. Eerie snow-covered peaks and desolate rock and scree-filled alpine basins are within a day's walk of cozy forests and fishing lakes.

Hundreds of miles of backpacking trails sprawl all over the Sierras. They include the famous John Muir Trail, which runs 250 miles (400 km) through the heart of the high country from Yosemite Valley south to Whitney Portal; and the Pacific Crest Trail, which runs from Canada to Mexico. Both can be reached from numerous trailheads on the Sierras' eastern and western slopes.

Trailheads on the west slopes are typically found at 5,000 or 6,000 feet (about 1,500 to 1,800 meters) elevation. Cedar Grove trailhead in Kings Canyon National Park and Mineral King, further south, go the deepest into the back country. The western slopes offer beautiful lakes, forested trails and good fishing.

On the east side of the range, trailheads at 10,000 feet elevation are no more than an hour's drive from U.S. Highway 395 on the desert floor. Tioga Pass (State Highway 120) is the most scenic way to cross the Sierras by car (although it is closed in winter); it offers access to Tuolomne Meadows, a perfect base for hiking a high-country loop. The easiest pass into the high country is Piute, a half-day walk from North Lake and Humphrey's Basin. Desolation Valley, south of Lake Tahoe at the northern end of the Sierras, is a fine destination for a quick backpack trip from the San Francisco Bay Area.

Unfortunately, since the 1960s, when all of California seemed to take to the outdoors with backpack, the Sierras have suffered from overpopulation during the summer season. This presents three hassles for the backpacker: *Giardia*, a dysentery-carrying amoeba, has turned up even in remote mountain streams (hikers are advised to boil water before drinking or carry iodine); dead wood for building campfires is gone so one must carry a good stove; and reservations to backpack in popular areas must be made in advance. (Write "Backpacking Reservations" at the appropriate national park or forest; addresses are listed in the Guide In Brief.) Most areas also have a few permits set aside on a first come, first served basis. To get them, backpackers should show up early in the morning at a visitor's center in the area of their planned trip.

The only backpacking accessories that can be rented are tents, crampons, ice axes and sleeping bags. Freeze-dried food is obtainable at most mountaineering stores, but good fly fisherman can catch their dinner. Rainbow trout are unbeatable; knowledgeable anglers bring a frypan and a little oil and garlic.

The best time to backpack varies with the winter snowfall, but generally speaking the mountains open up in May and June, and high-country trails are free of snow by July. The weather holds good until October and sometimes later. September, although dry, is the time to go as it is least crowded. Wildflowers are out in June, July and August.

Lovers of snow and the soft, sensual silence of a black-and-white alpine landscape

go into the mountains in winter for ski touring, cross-country and downhill skiing. (See the Lake Tahoe chapter and the "Guide in Brief" for details.)

Scaling Rock Walls

Veteran rock climbers undoubtedly already know that Yosemite Valley offers the finest rock climbing in the world. During spring and fall months, hundreds of climbers' from all over the world scale its huge granite

Left, gleeful outdoor enthusiasts rafting on the American River near Sacramento. Right, a warning to wing-wary wayfarers in the Sacramento River Valley near Marysville.

walls. Yosemite's faces and spires, walls and peaks (El Capitan, Half Dome, Lost Arrow, Sentinel Rock) have created an entire style of climbing using friction holds and smooth cracks. Yosemite is the place where the first big-wall techniques were formulated and practiced.

Sheer determination and practice, coupled with innovations in hardware (the nuts and bolts that secure man to rock), have improved rock climbing so much over the past two decades that walls once climbed only by death-defying crazy men are now climbed by college kids with a minimum of skill. And women rock climbers have learned to supplement brute arm strength with a confident combination of balance and technique.

California climbers are now in the minority in Yosemite, Observers with binoculars, sitting in a meadow and watching the slow progress of a big wall climb, hear shouts bounce off the rock in Japanese, German, French and Spanish.

Beginners can learn to rock-climb at The Yosemite Mountaineering School. More advanced climbers may hire an instructor to guide and climb with them. Equipment, including climbing shoes, can be rented inexpensively from the school.

The climbing season runs from May through October, but from mid July to mid September, when the walls get unbearably hot, climbers move up to Tuolumne Meadows at 8,000 feet (2,400 meters). The climbing school moves up there, too.

Climbing, at least at beginning and intermediate levels, is fairly safe — most time is spent learning knots, piton placement and techniques for becoming firmly attached to the rock. There is an enormous satisfaction, however, that comes from having attained vertiginous heights, having overcome wobbly knees, and having managed to stand on a quarter-inch foothold, grasping an invisible-to-the-naked-eye finger crack.

Whitewater Thrills

River rafting is the newest outdoor activity in the state, and commercial river-rafting companies have sprung up like mushrooms after an autumn rain. Companies offer trips in six-man paddle rafts or larger oar boats with a professional oarsman doing all the paddling. Some of the river trips, in high water, are dangerous, but most people love the thrill that comes from plunging nose-first into frothy rapids, taking waves in the face, oaring, bailing or simply hanging on. Most commercial river trips also allow time for lounging on sandy river beaches, exploring the side canyons by foot, and feasting on delicious camp food cooked by the river guides themselves.

River trips range from one day to one week, and are best in late spring or early summer. Riding whitewater is a little like riding a roller-coaster, only instead of mechanical propulsion, there is the unimaginable force of tons of rushing water.

For super thrills, the Forks of the Kern is the trip to take. The Kern River flows from the Mount Whitney area east of Bakersfield and is a Class V river (60 gradient feet per mile; 11.3 gradient meters per kilometer.) The Forks has some of the feel of the high Sierras and is rather remote. Rafts and supplies must be carried three miles in from the road by mules.

The Tuolumne, northwest of Yosemite Valley, may be California's most beloved stretch of whitewater. A good Class IV (plus one Class V rapid), it is currently threatened by a dam. The South Fork of the American River near Placerville in the Gold Country is probably the most popular rafting trip for first-timers. It is well-traveled, fast and fun.

Other raftable (and kayakable) rivers are the lower portion of the North Fork of the Yuba, from Goodyear's Bar to the State Highway 20 bridge; the Upper Klamath, runnable year-round; the Trinity River; and the Merced and Salmon rivers. Friends of the River, a San Francisco environmentalist group, can provide information on any of the 40 commercial river rafting companies. (Call 415-771-0400.)

Bird-watching Bliss

California has the highest concentration of waterfowl in the United States as well as large numbers of hawks, falcons and pheasants. The best place to see ducks, sandhill cranes, snow geese, tundra swans, herons and egrets is in the Sacramento National Wildlife Refuge off Interstate 5, 1½ hours north of Sacramento. Self-guided auto tours are conducted through the refuge, which is on the flyway for waterfowl migrating in the winter.

The southwest corner of the San Francisco Bay (near Palo Alto) is also on the flyway

and will soon become a national refuge. Other good Bay Area birding spots are Audubon Canyon Ranch in Bolinas (Marin County), Point Reyes (Marin County) and Coyote State Park (south of Oakland on the Bay).

In Modoc County, at the northeastern tip of the state, migrating birds are abundant, making it the best place in the state for duck and goose hunting. At any one time in Tulelake National Wildlife Refuge, thousands of waterfowl can be seen eating, flying and nesting. During the fall, however, the migration is phenomenal, with a peak migration population of more than 1 million. The Klamath Basin, almost 1 million acres, supports the largest concentration of waterfowl

on the North American continent. It is a staggering experience to go there just to hear the incredible sound of tens of thousands of geese crying.

Steaming Sulfur

Northern California is the land of sulfur hot springs. Some are simple and natural, others offer the latest in massage and other forms of body manipulation.

Hot Creek, near Mammoth Lakes just west of U.S. Highway 395, has the most beautiful setting of any spring. Hot Creek is a sizable river flowing east from the Sierras into the high rolling desert. A hot spring bubbles right into the stream. It's crowded, especially during ski season, but it's free. Nearby, in Red's Meadow, a Sierra trailhead, are inexpensive mineral baths.

Grover Hot Springs, just outside Markleville, south of Lake Tahoe and close to Heavenly Valley skiing, is managed by the U.S. Forest Service.

Wilbur Hot Springs, 25 miles (40 km) from the town of Williams, is more of a spa than a spring. It's also an anthropological curiosity, a true remnant of the Sixties with soft-spoken, long-haired proprietors and a hotel with a communal kitchen.

In Calistoga, in the heart of the Napa Wine Country, are several establishments offering hot pools, massages and mud baths. But for a full-fledged world-class spa experience, travelers might consider Sonoma Mission Inn and Spa in Sonoma. Very expensive, very luxurious, it is a good place to get in shape and relax.

Not everyone has the time, money or inclination to brush up on skydiving techniques or spend a week in a snow cave. But everybody in Northern California can at least step outside and — better yet — take the time to explore, savor and really see. Almost one-half of the state is owned by the federal government and much of its land is protected. More people participate in outdoor recreation in California than in any other state.

Visitors should consider doing as the natives do. Run along a beach, strap on a backpack, paddle down a river on a raft, watch birds on the Pacific Flyway or whales on the Pacific waves. Most of these experiences are free. They are also priceless.

Left, Windsurfing in the waves off Santa Cruz. Right, hang-gliding over the Pacific surf south of San Francisco. Following pages, golfing on the eastern flanks of the Sierra Nevada north of Lone Pine.

GUIDE IN BRIEF

Traveling to Northern California

By Air

San Francisco International Airport (SFO) is the major gateway for foreign travel. More than 20 million passengers fly into the airport each year and most of the international airline companies that serve Northern California land at SFO. The foreign international carriers include Air Canada, British Airways, Canadian Pacific Air, China Airlines, Civil Aviation Authority of China, Japan Air Lines, LTU International, Lufthansa German Airlines, Mexicana, Philippine Airlines, Qantas Airways and Singapore Airlines. Twenty other major air carriers operate at SFO — see notes in **Transportation** section of this Guide in Brief for more information on air travel.

By Sea

Cruising into San Francisco Bay is a luxurious and expensive way to arrive. A cruise from Sydney, Australia, to San Francisco can cost from $2,000 to $5,000. Two steamship companies, the American President Lines and the Lykes Brothers, have regular routes from the Orient (Australia, Japan, Hong Kong, Taiwan) to San Francisco. Each ship, however, carries only 12 passengers. Twenty-seven steamship lines and eight cruise lines include San Francisco in their itineraries as one of their international ports-of-call. Cruise lines into Northern California from the Far East and Europe include General Steamship, Holland America, Princess, Royal Viking, Sitmar, Star and Delta (from South America). Contact the steamship company's office in your city, or make arrangements through a travel agent.

By Bus

Greyhound and Trailways bus companies provide service to Northern California and throughout the area. Greyhound has its own San Francisco terminal at Seventh and Mission streets while Trailways is one of the several bus companies in Trans Bay Terminal at First and Mission streets.

Many bus terminals tend to be in the "problem areas" of towns, and San Francisco is no exception. When venturing from any terminal at night, don't take solitary walks; exercise caution when traveling to and from stations; take a taxi or a city bus.

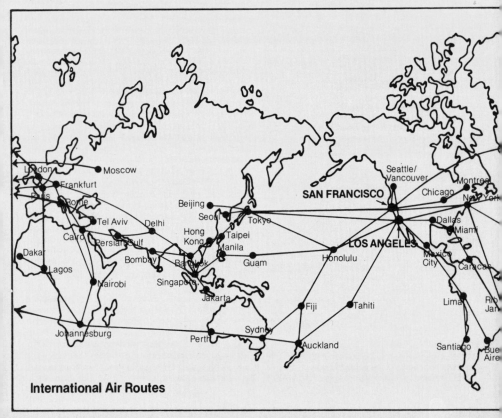

International Air Routes

By Train

Amtrak is the passenger line that offers leisurely service from coast to coast. All trains coming into Northern California end up at the Oakland Depot, an art deco terminal in a warehouse district. Free bus service is provided into San Francisco. Don't expect to purchase Amtrak's rail passes for unlimited riding in the United States. They must be bought from a travel agent in a foreign country. In San Francisco, any information about Amtrak's train services may be obtained by calling 982–8512.

By Car

Major land routes into Northern California are Interstate 5 and U.S. highways 97, 101 and 395 from the north; the same routes plus State Highway 99 from the south; I-80 and U.S. 50 from the east through Nevada. The official speed limit throughout the state is 55 miles (88 kilometers) per hour. Federal and state highways are well-maintained and policed, with refreshment areas and service stations set up at regular intervals. There are no road fees, but major bridges charge tolls up to $1.

Travel Advisories

Most visitors, upon entering the United States, must have a passport and visitor's visa, and if they are from (or have passed through) an infected area, a health record. Canadian citizens entering from the Western Hemisphere need not have a visa or a passport. Neither do Mexican citizens who possess a border pass.

At the Nevada, Oregon and Mexican borders, the State Department of Food and Agriculture inspects all produce, plant materials and wild animals to see if they are admissable under current quarantine regulations. To avoid a lengthy inspection, do not bring any agricultural products into California.

Since visitors to California can encounter problems exchanging foreign currency, the use of American-dollar traveler's checks is advised. When lost or stolen, most traveler's checks can be replaced and they are as acceptable as cash in most stores, restaurants and hotels. Banks will readily cash large amounts of traveler's checks.

In most states, a sales tax is added to retail goods. California charges 6½ percent sales tax, but they don't tax all goods. You're a genius if you can understand the logic behind the tax laws; most people simply memorize them. There is a tax on books, for instance, but no tax on magazines. If you buy a hamburger and eat it in the restaurant they will tax you, but if you eat the hamburger in your car they cannot tax you. If you fail to make sense of these laws, you will be in the same boat as the natives.

Getting Acquainted

State Song and Nickname: *California, Here I Come* and "The Golden State."
State Flower: Golden Poppy
State Motto: "Eureka! (I have found it!)"

Climate

Northern California has two kinds of weather — wet and dry. Generally, the wet season is winter (December through February), and the dry season is summer (June through October); but the fog messes up this simple equation. It hovers around the Golden Gate, often obscuring the bridge. Then it pours in through the Gate and over the coastal hills into the Bay Area during many summer mornings. However, the sun is usually shining in Northern California and the temperature averages a mild 50 to 70 degrees Fahrenheit (10 to 21 degrees Centigrade).

The valleys are the only real hot spots; the Sacramento and the San Joaquin valleys in particular. In summer, it's nice to have an air-conditioned car if traveling through them.

The average daily highs in San Francisco are:

Month	(°C)	(°F)
January	12.8	55
February	14.4	58
March	16.7	62
April	17.8	64
May	19.4	67
June	21.1	70
July	22.2	72
August	22.2	72
September	23.3	74
October	21.7	71
November	17.8	64
December	13.9	57

Clothing

San Francisco's climate is typical of the Northern California coast. Daytime temperatures average in the mid 50s Fahrenheit (10–15°C). Unlike the rest of the country, there is no traditional summer with high temperatures; September and October are the warmest months with the temperature occasionally in the 80s. Coastal fog, common in summer, usually burns off by midday. Most of the average annual rainfall of 20 inches (51 centimeters) falls in the winter, December through February. Umbrellas and raincoats are not necessities, but would be a good idea during these months.

Throughout the year, a sweater or an all-weather coat is recommended. For Bay excursions, visits to windy hilltops in January, or trips to the mountains, you should put on several layers of clothing (including a warm coat). San Francisco is a sophisticated city, but it is also a liberal town, tolerant of all kinds of lifestyles and apparel. The streets are filled with tourists and natives alike dressed in everything from ultra-high fashion to the most casual wear. A few of the finer restaurants still require coats and ties for the men. Women can wear dinner dresses on their evenings out, but should feel comfortable in slacks or pantsuits during the day.

The most important single item of clothing is a comfortable pair of walking shoes. San Francisco is a city best explored on foot.

Time Zones

California is within the Pacific Time Zone, which is two hours behind Chicago, and three hours behind New York City. On the last Sunday in April the clock is moved ahead one hour for Daylight Savings Time, and on the last Sunday in October the clock is moved back one hour to return to Standard Time.

Without Daylight Savings Time adjustment, when it is 12 noon in California, it is ...

10 a.m. in Hawaii
2 p.m. in Chicago
3 p.m. in New York and Montreal
8 p.m. in London
9 p.m. in Bonn, Madrid, Paris and Rome
11 p.m. in Athens and Cairo
12 midnight in Moscow
1:30 a.m. (the next day) in Bombay
3 a.m. (the next day) in Bangkok
4 a.m. (the next day) in Singapore, and Hong Kong
5 a.m. (the next day) in Tokyo
6 a.m. (the next day) in Sydney

Etiquette

It is courteous to show your gratitude for help given to you, and in the service trade nothing is more appreciated than a tip.

The accepted rate for porters at the airports is 50 cents per bag. Hotel bellboys and porters usually get tipped 35 cents per bag or suitcase. A doorman should be tipped if he unloads or parks your car. It is not necessary to tip chambermaids unless you stay several days in a small hotel.

Depending on quantity and quality of service rendered, 15 to 20 percent is the going rate for most other help; taxi drivers, barbers, hairdressers, waiters and waitresses. Make the bartenders happy with 10 to 15 percent. In some restaurants, tips or a service charge is included in the bill if the group is large. No tipping in cafeterias.

Liquor Laws

The legal age for both the purchase and the consumption of alcoholic beverages is 21; proof of age is often required. Alcoholic beverages are sold by the bottle or by the can in liquor stores, in some supermarkets and many drug stores. Alcoholic beverages are sold by the drink (from 6 a.m. to 2 a.m.) at most restaurants, nightclubs and bars. Some of these establishments are licensed to serve beer and wine only. One quart of alcohol may be imported from another country.

Business Hours and Public Holidays

Business hours are 9 a.m. to 5 p.m. from Monday to Friday; banking hours, 10 a.m. to 3 p.m. from Monday to Friday. The biggest banks in Northern California are the Bank of America (with a few hundred branches), Crocker, Interstate, Security Pacific and Wells Fargo. In the San Francisco Bay Area are branches of the Bank of Canton, Bank of the Orient, Barclay's, Dai-Ichi Kangyo, Lloyds, Mitsubishi, Sanwa, and Sumitomo Bank.

Many government agencies close during the holidays listed below. Local banks and businesses may also be closed.

New Year's Day — January 1
Martin Luther King's Birthday — January 15
Abraham Lincoln's Birthday — February 12
George Washington's Birthday — third Monday in February
Memorial Day — last Monday in May
Independence Day — July 4
Labor Day — first Monday in September
Admission Day — September 9
Columbus Day — second Monday in October
Veterans Day — November 11
Thanksgiving — fourth Thursday in November
Christmas — December 25

Tourist Information

When in doubt, use the telephone. The fastest way to obtain assistance is simply to dial "0" for the operator. If operators cannot help, they usually give you the number of somebody else who can be of assistance.

If in San Francisco, the San Francisco Convention and Visitors Bureau can be extremely helpful. Located at Hallidie Plaza, Powell and Market streets, the Bureau is open Monday to Friday 9 a.m. to 5 p.m., Saturday 9 a.m. to 3 p.m. and Sunday 10 a.m. to 2 p.m. (974–6900). The International Visitors Center at 312 Sutter (4th floor) also provides helpful services; from sightseeing suggestions to language assistance as well as the "Meet Americans at Home" program. Open Monday to Friday 9 a.m. to 5 p.m., 986–1388.

Chambers of Commerce

Almost every town in the States has its own Chamber of Commerce. This businessman's association can provide free information about accommodations, dining, shopping, medical facilities and points of interest in the area. To be of further assistance to international guests, most chambers also maintain lists of language translation resources. Chambers of some of the major tourist centers are given below:

Berkeley — 1834 University Ave., 94703 (845–1212).
Concord — 1331 Concord Ave., 94520 (685–1184).
Fresno — 700 "M" St., 93721 (209–233–0836).
Monterey Peninsula — 380 Alvarado St., 93940 (408–649–1770).
Oakland — 1330 Broadway, 94612 (839–9000).
Sacramento — 1311 "I" St., 95814 (916–442–5542).
Salinas — 119 East Alisal, 93902 (408–424–7611).
San Francisco — Visitors and Convention Bureau, Powell and Market streets, 94103 (974–6900).
San Jose — 1 Pasco de San Antonio, 95113 (408–998–7000).
San Mateo — 888 Airport Rd., Burlingame, 94010 (347–7004).
Santa Cruz — Civic Auditorium, PO Box 1476 95061 (408–423–6927).

Transportation

Air Travel

Northern California has landing fields and small-town airports in even the unlikeliest of places and medium-sized airports can be found in Fresno, Sacramento and Reno (Nevada, for Lake Tahoe). Pacific Southwest Airlines (PSA) and AirCal service most of the airports in the region. All three major airports in Northern California are located on the San Francisco Bay: San Francisco, Oakland and San Jose.

Most airlines have both local and toll-free telephone numbers for information and reservations. Look under "Air Line Companies" in the telephone's Yellow Pages, or call (800) 555–1212.

San Francisco International Airport

Located 14 miles (23 km) south of downtown San Francisco on the shore of the Bay near San Mateo, San Francisco International Airport (SFO), the eighth largest airport in the country, has 80 gates served by about 40 airlines. In addition to a dozen international carriers, SFO is served by such major air carriers as American, Continental, Delta, Eastern, Northwest, Pan American, Republic, TWA and United. Regional carriers serving SFO include: AirCal, Alaska, Capitol, Flying Tigers, Golden West, Pacific Express, PSA and Western.

Transportation to and from SFO is provided by Airporter Coaches every 15 minutes, 6 a.m. to midnight, then every 45 minutes from midnight to 6 a.m., from all three SFO terminals to the downtown bus terminal at Taylor and Ellis streets. Fare for the 30-minute ride is $5 (673–2432). Sam Trans, San Mateo County's bus system makes several stops between the airport area and downtown San Francisco; fare is $1.15, call 871–2200 for more information. Other buses in and out of SFO are: Airport Connection (877–0901), SFO-Airporter (877–0345), Marin Airporter (461–4222), Santa Rosa Airporter (707–545–8015), Sonoma County Airport Express (707–526–1360), Amador Stage Lines (916–444–7883), Greyhound (433–1500), and the Handicapped Travelers Association (573–9688). Taxi fares average $20 from SFO to Union Square.

Free shuttle service is provided throughout the airport facilities to all airlines. The parking garage in the center of SFO accommodates up to 6,500 automobiles but can still be full. Valet parking is available, as is long-term (more than six hours) parking. A 24-hour hotline provides information on availability and conditions of all parking areas (877–0123).

Oakland International Airport

On the other side of the Bay is the modern and convenient Oakland International Airport. It is the airport nearest to the Alameda, Contra Costa, Marin, Sonoma, Napa and Solano counties. The airlines that serve Oakland include AirCal, American, Frontier, Pacific Cal, PSA, Republic, TWA, United, Western and World. Oakland Airport has its own travel agency, Tel. 444–4444.

Parking is seldom a problem. The airport is easily accessible from Highway 17, Hegenberger Road exit. There are parking meters for short-term parking (25 cents per half-hour), close-in parking (50 cents each half-hour; $7 maximum per day) and long-term parking ($1 per hour; $4 maximum per day).

Local bus service to and from Oakland is provided by AC Transit (the No. 57 line) which operates from 5 a.m. to 1 a.m. daily. Basic fare is 60 cents (653–3535). Oakland is also served by the Bay Area Rapid Transit system (BART). A shuttle-van links the local BART station with the airport; the ride takes 10 minutes, the fare is 75 cents (465-BART). SFO Airporter provides transportation between the airport and downtown Oakland, the Oakland Army Base, Treasure Island, downtown San Francisco and SFO. Fares are between $4 to $6 (495–8404). Eastbay Airporter provides bus transportation to most East Baycities — from Berkeley, $6, to Livermore, $11 (832–1992).

San Jose Municipal Airport

Currently a city airport, San Jose expects to become an international facility with 30 gates in operation and five terminals by 1986. Fourteen airlines now operate out of San Jose: AirCal, Alaska, American Continental, Pacific Coast, Pacific East, PSA, Republic, Sun World, TWA, United, West-Air, Western and Wings West. The San Jose Chamber of Commerce has an information booth at the airport (408–287–9849).

County transit buses (408–287–4210) and taxis service the airport. Free shuttle buses cover the airport grounds.

Transportation linking the San Jose, the San Francisco and the Oakland airports is provided by Airport Connection (408–730–5555).

Buses

Two major lines traverse the State. Greyhound has its San Francisco terminal at Seventh and Mission streets (433–1500). Trailways shares the Trans-Bay Terminal (First and Mission streets, San Francisco) with other bus companies (982–6400).

Other Bay Area bus lines are AC Transit, serving the East Bay (653–3535); Golden Gate Transit, serving Marin and Sonoma counties (457–3110); SamTrans, serving San Mateo County (761–7000); and MUNI (see notes below), serving San Francisco (673–6864).

Trains

AMTRAK travels the state, making daily stops in Martinez, Richmond and San Jose. Its rail service terminates in Oakland at the 16th Street Station, where free bus service is offered to the Trans-Bay Terminal in San Francisco (982–8512).

Southern Pacific Railroad runs passenger trains between San Francisco and San Jose with several stops along the peninsula. Trains operate between 5:30 a.m. and 12:30 a.m., with frequent commuter service northbound in the mornings and southbound in the afternoons. Fares range from $1 to $4. The Southern Pacific terminal in San Francisco is at Fourth and Townsend streets (495–4546).

Ferries

For commuters and sightseers alike, ferry boats are a convenient and delightful way to cross the Bay. Ferry services are offered from San Francisco to Sausalito and Larkspur on the Golden Gate Ferry Service (982–8834), and the Tiburon Ferry (546–2815). The Red & White Fleet (546–2810) and the Blue & Gold Fleet (781–7877) offer cruises around the Bay.

Taxis

For medium distances of a few miles, taxis are a convenient and reasonably priced alternative to public transportation or walking. The biggest company in the city is Yellow Cab; rates are $1.30 plus $1.20 for each additional mile (626–2345). Other taxi services in San Francisco include City (285–4500), Classic (584–2756), De Soto (673–1414), Luxor (552–4040), Pacific (776–6688), Town (285–1244), and Veteran's (552–1300). Taxis can be called in advance, but in most urban areas, can usually be hailed directly on the city streets.

For long distances, taxis are expensive. A ride from Berkeley to the San Francisco Airport costs between $30 and $40.

Car Rentals

There are dozens of automobile rental agencies throughout Northern California; Avis (800–331–1212), Budget (800–228–9650), Dollar (800–262–1520), Hertz (800–654–3131), and National (800–328–4567). Rental offices are in most cities and at all airports. Basic charges range from $25 to $55 per day; most companies offer unlimited mileage and special weekend rates. Shop around for the best rates and features. Often, smaller local rental companies offer less expensive, more desirable conditions than the large national firms. Be sure to check insurance provisions (usually an extra $5 per day for full coverage) before signing anything. Agencies are listed in the telephone's Yellow Pages under "Automobiles — Rental." Reservations are advised.

Most rental agencies require you to be at least 21 years old (sometimes 25); and to hold a valid driver's license and a major credit card. (Some will take a cash deposit, often as high as $600, in lieu of a credit card.) Foreign travelers may need to produce an international driver's license or a license from their home country. Drivers must abide by local and State traffic regulations.

Motoring Advisories

The speed limit in the state is 55 miles (88 km) per hour. Most city speed limits are 25 to 35 miles (40 to 56 km) per hour.

In addition to street signs advising no-parking hours and special tow-away zones, the color of the curb governs the kind of parking permitted. Red curbs mean no parking at all. Yellow curbs indicate limited stops (usually for trucks only) for loading and unloading of passengers or freight. White curbs, usually found at entrances to hotels and restaurants, are limited to short-term stop-

ping only. Green curbs also indicate parking for limited periods only, usually 10 to 30 minutes. Blue curbs are reserved for the disabled. It is not advisable to ignore any of these signs. Police are strict on illegal parking, summoning tow trucks for vehicles found in No Parking areas or found blocking driveways. You'll need plenty of cash or at least a major credit card to bail your car out. Towing fees and fines are steep.

In San Francisco, parking is often a problem on steep hills. Turn your front wheels into the curb, so that the tire is resting on the curb at an angle that would halt the car from rolling downhill unexpectedly. Be sure to set the emergency brake.

Cable cars and pedestrians *always* have the right of way.

Hitchhiking is not advised. Picking up hitchhiking strangers is also potentially dangerous. Local newspapers regularly recount stories of robbery and rape that began with an extended thumb.

Public Transportation in San Francisco

Every town has a public transportation service geared to its own peculiarities. Santa Clara — with many senior citizens and young children — has a top-notch, low-cost bus system. In Davis — site of a University of California campus — students and town residents alike ride bicycles; almost every major street has a bike path running beside it. San Francisco has its ferries, trolley cars,

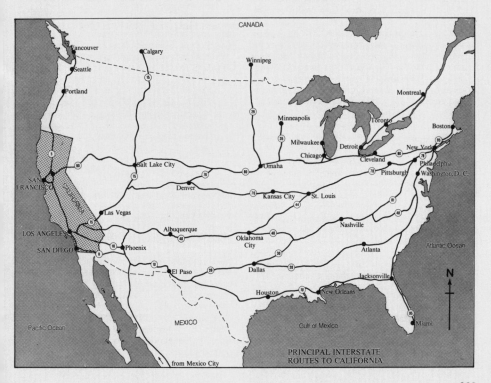

PRINCIPAL INTERSTATE
ROUTES TO CALIFORNIA

cable cars and the BART system (see below).

Bay Area Rapid Transit

The Bay Area Rapid Transit system (BART) is one of the most modern, efficient, and most automated people-moving systems in the world. The sleek, clean, air-conditioned cars carry hundreds of thousands of commuters each day over 70 miles (113 km) of electric track at speeds approaching 80 miles (129 km) an hour.

Often compared to the super-subways of Europe and Russia, BART serves 34 stations in 15 cities Monday to Saturday 6 a.m. to midnight, and on Sunday from 9 a.m. to midnight. Some of its tracks are underground, while others are either surfaced or elevated. Among the underground tracks are those inside the Transbay Tube between San Francisco and Oakland. At 3½ miles (5½ km), this tube is one of the world's longest underwater tunnels.

Everything is automated under the BART system. Yes, there *are* drivers, but do not be fooled. The trains are essentially controlled by trackside relays and a $40-million computer center at the Lake Merritt BART station. There are no cashiers (only vending machines), no ticket-takers (only automated entrance and exit gates) and no conductors (incoming trains are announced on computerized bulletin boards).

Tourists like the BART system and often ride the entire network for a $2 excursion fare (if they enter and leave from the same station). Fun riding should be avoided during weekdays from 7 to 9 a.m. and from 4 to 6 p.m., when trains are jam-packed and riders would be lucky to find standing room.

All stations have wall maps showing nearby tourist attractions, shopping areas, and connecting bus lines; and printed information outlining stations, fares and ticket-buying procedures. In San Francisco, call 788-BART; in other towns, look up the special BART information numbers listed under "Bay Area Rapid Transit" in the directory's white pages.

Cable Cars

Undergoing massive restoration, San Francisco's unique cable cars are expected to be running again by June 1984. The routes will remain unchanged; from Powell and Market streets to Columbus and Chestnut streets and to Beach and Hyde streets, and along Sacramento from Drumm to Larkin. Fare is $1 (558–2301).

The Cable Car Barn Museum contains models, photos, relics of the city's earliest transit system, and the very first cable car. Open daily 10 a.m. to 6 p.m. Call Four Embarcadero Center at 474–1887.

Municipal Railway

The San Francisco Municipal Railway (MUNI) is responsible for all buses, streetcars and cable cars in the City. Streetcars are underground in the downtown area. To board them, enter from BART stations. Fare is 60 cents (exact change is necessary) with no extra charge for a transfer. Buses run frequently; service on some lines is 24 hours (673–6864).

Accommodations

Grand Hotels of San Francisco

The large hotels of San Francisco are particularly well-suited to the international traveler. Many hotels (for example, the classic old hotels sitting atop Nob Hill) are attractive landmarks in their own right. They are usually situated in established areas of the city, with easy access to tourist sites and public transportation. The concierge on duty at most of the finer hotels arranges your theater tickets, tours, telex, seats at sporting events, limos with bilingual drivers, and airline reservations. He recommends restaurants, can speak foreign languages and helps exchange money in a dozen different currencies.

Listed in the appendix are the large hotels in San Francisco. They each have at least 400 neat, clean and modern rooms with air conditioning, color TV and room phones. Parking, restaurants, coffee shops and bars are standard facilities. Their rates range from $75 to $175 per night, double occupancy, with an average rate of about $100. Rates vary from season to season so be sure to call or write to verify rates and make reservations.

Small Hotels of San Francisco

For those not impressed by the stylish glamour (with matching prices) of the grand hotels, the small hotels are a good alternative.

Providing basic comforts with a personal touch, these small hotels are popping up in areas not "central" to the city; in Noe Valley, Golden Gate Park and Russian Hill. At least once a month, another renovated hotel is opening its doors to the public. In expectation of increasing numbers of conventioneers, old fleabags in the Tenderloin and South-of- Market districts are being thoughtfully remodeled.

A few of the current favorites are included in the appendix. It is wise to make reservations well in advance of your trip.

Bed-and-Breakfast Inns

Country inns have become extremely popular in the last decade throughout the United States, especially in New England and Northern California. Most cluster in such scenic areas as the Wine Country, Gold Country, North Coast, and Monterey Peninsula. Being situated in such beautiful rural settings, they do a thriving business with city dwellers in search of a romantic weekend retreat.

Converted from mansions and farmhouses with

five to 15 rooms, these inns offer the traveler a highly individual experience; no two inns are alike, and in most inns no two rooms are alike. Many residents have opened their homes to strangers. For those accustomed to the strict uniformity of large hotels and motel chains, the inns provide a warm, hospitable and quaint alternative.

Many inns have shared bathrooms and only a few have televisions or telephones in the rooms. Most include breakfasts with the room rental; hence, the name, bed-and-breakfast inns.

Prices vary from inn to inn and could be anywhere between $20 to $80 per night. Call or write in advance — the inns are particularly popular on weekends and in the summer. In fact, so favorable has this country inn concept become that small intimate bed-and-breakfast inns are even popping up all over urban San Francisco to compete with the large hotels.

The listing in the appendix contains only the larger and more established inns. Most cost around $40 per night, double occupancy. All serve breakfasts, from coffee and croissants to hearty, full-course meals.

If the idea of selecting and locating the most suitable inn out of the hundreds does not appeal to you, then you can pass on this chore to an agency ... for a small fee of course.

American Family Inn (2185A Union Street, San Francisco 94123, Tel. 931–3083) helps locate accommodations throughout the state, from turn-of-the-century to contemporary lodgings, specializing in places that permit pets and rooms with kitchen facilities.

Bed and Breadfast International (151 Ardmore Road, Kensington 94707, Tel. 525–4569) has hundreds of referrals from $22 to $85 per night.

Home Suite Homes (1470 Firebird Way, Sunnyvale 94087, Tel. 408–733–7215).

Visitors Advisory Service (1516 Oak Street, Suite 327, Alameda 94501, Tel. 521–9366) specializes in accommodations offered by private homes in the immediate Bay Area, as well as short-term rentals of apartments and homes.

Motels

If you are traveling by car and if you don't intend to spend much time in your lodgings other than sleeping, motels are the best solution. Whether set along busy Lombard Street in San Francisco or along a river bank in a remote Northern Californian town, most motels provide parking lot space within paces of your room.

Degree and quality of accommodations vary, but most motels are bare bones. A restaurant or coffee shop, swimming pool and sauna are often found on the premises. Room facilities would include a telephone, TV and radio but do not hesitate to ask the motel manager if you may inspect a room before agreeing to take it.

Other than their accessibility by auto, the other attraction of motels is their price. Motels in San Francisco range from $50 to $80 per night, double occupancy. They are less expensive in the outlying areas, usually $25 to $50.

The major chains provide reasonable and reliable accommodations, and all have toll-free telephone numbers for making and confirming reservations. The biggest chains include Best Western, Hilton, Holiday Inn, Hyatt, Marriott, Ramada, Sheraton and Travel Lodge. Call (800) 555–1212 and ask the information operator for the chain of your choice.

Hostels

Northern California has a chain of more than 20 hostels up and down the Pacific coast, from Jedediah Smith Redwood State Park at the Oregon border down to John Little State Beach. All the hostels are along the shoreline; many are located inside old lighthouses. Hostels are clean, comfortable, *very* inexpensive ($5 per night) and although suitable for people of all ages, they are definitely for the "young at heart."

Beds are provided in dormitory-type rooms. Hostelers carry their own gear (knife, fork, spoon, sheets or sleeping bag, towel, washcloth) and are expected, following breakfast each day, to take 15 minutes to help at such communal tasks as vacuuming, sweeping, chopping firewood and stoking the fireplace.

Hostels are closed daily from 9:30 a.m. to 4:30 p.m., so most guests fill their days with nearby outdoor adventures. Reservations are highly recommended.

Two hostels are actually restored lighthouses: **Point Montara** (near Half Moon Bay) has several rooms and bathrooms, in addition to a large Victorian residence built on the grounds in 1880 (728–7177); and **Pigeon Point** (near Pescadero) can accommodate up to 50 guests (879–0633).

San Francisco is home to the largest hostel in the country, located in a century-old Army dispensary on a bluff at Fort Mason. There are 21 bunk rooms, 11 of which are set aside for families (771–7277).

The oldest hostel in the West (opened in 1937) is the **Hidden Villa Hostel** in the Los Altos Hills on the San Francisco peninsula. Rustic cabins, holding up to 45 people, are nestled throughout the 1,500-acre canyon site (941–6407).

The **Sanborn Park Hostel** in Saratoga is a historic log cabin built in 1908 and is set in a redwood forest (408–298–0670).

At **Donner Summit** is a mountain ski-lodge hostel with a big sundeck, a large recreation room and private rooms available for $15 (916–426–3079).

Campsites

Campgrounds sprinkled throughout California provide an ample choice of outdoor accommodations for the mobile traveler. They range from primitive areas marked off for tents and sleeping bags, to elaborate facilities with utility hook-ups for home-on-wheels recreational vehicles (RVs), restaurants and planned activities. Many also provide lodgings complete with separate bathrooms, kitchenettes and room service. There are even campgrounds for nudists.

Most state parks, forests, national parks, monuments and seashores offer primitive camping facilities; a place to park your car, a sectioned-off spot under the trees or along the river for sleeping, public rest rooms within walking distance, and outdoor cooking facilities. Fees range from $1 to $4 per site. Most public campgrounds are busy from mid June to early September and are allotted on a first-come-first serve basis. Again, advance reservations are advisable. Call Ticketron by dialing T-E-L-E-T-I-X to make reservations for campsites in selected areas of Yosemite and Sequoia. Additional information may be obtained at the toll-free number (800) 952–5580 or from the individual parks or the National Park Service at 450 Golden Gate Avenue, San Francisco 94102, Tel. 556–4122.

Private campgrounds have blossomed around many of the popular parks and commercial attractions. Costing an average of $5 per person, the grounds usually have sites for RVs, a coin laundry, flush/pit toilets and a play area for the children. Sometimes they also have restaurants, grocery stores and swimming pools. The largest private campground association is Kampgrounds of America with its 600-odd nationwide camps. A list of their facilities costs $1, inclusive of postage and handling. Write to Kampgrounds of America, P.O. Box 30162, Billings, Montana 59114.

Communications

Postal Services

Post office hours in big-city branches and those in smaller towns vary so call or ask your hotel or motel personnel. In San Francisco there are more than 50 postal stations; the main office is at Seventh and Mission streets. For rates and information, call 556–2500.

But generally, postage rates are as follows:
letters inside the United States, or to Mexico and Canada are 20 cents for the first ounce and 17 cents for each additional ounce;
postcards inside the United States, or to Mexico and Canada, are 13 cents;
surface letters to other foreign countries are 30 cents for the first ounce and 17 cents for each additional ounce;
airmail letters to other foreign countries are 40 cents for each half-ounce;
postcards to foreign destinations are 19 cents for surface mail and 28 cents for airmail; and
aerograms require 30 cents postage.
Besides the post offices, stamps may be purchased from vending machines located in hotels, stores, airports, and bus and train stations.
The post offices here provide efficient delivery services. If you do not know where you will be staying in a particular town, you may receive mail simply by having it addressed to you, care of General Delivery at the main post office of that town; picking them up personally. To speed up delivery, be sure to include the 5-digit zip code for all addresses within the States. Information about

zip codes may be obtained from any post office. An overnight delivery service, Express Mail, is also provided by the post office and some private companies; look in the Yellow Pages under Delivery Service.

Telegrams and Telex

Western Union and International Telephone and Telegraph (ITT) will take telegram and telex messages by phone. Other smaller companies offering similar services include Nesco, Promptel, TRT and B-Speedi. Look under "Telegraph Service" in the Yellow Pages of the local telephone directory or call (800) 555–1212 for the toll-free numbers of their offices.

Telephones

Public telephones are located in hotel lobbies, drugstores, restaurants, garages, bars, roadside booths... everywhere. Local calls cost 10 cents and long distance call rates vary from 18 cents per minute to Los Angeles, to 74 cents per minute to New York. These rates decrease after 5 p.m.; and are lower after 11 p.m. before 8 a.m., and on weekends and holidays.

Check the directory for all local numbers or call Information at 411. For numbers outside where you are, dialing must be preceded by the area code, which could be obtained from operator at "0" who will also furnish you with all other general information. For toll-free numbers (where there is no fee for calling), call Toll-Free Information at (800) 555–1212.

For telephone number in another district, call the Information in that district, whose number will be the respective area code preceding 555–1212. There is no charge for this kind of call.

News Media

Newspapers

The major daily newspapers in San Francisco are the San Francisco Chronicle in the morning and the San Francisco Examiner in the afternoon. Over the weekend, the two combine into one large edition. Both papers are competent but without much serious national or local reporting. The Chronicle is known for its columnists, its stylish writing and its often amusing approach to the news. The Sacramento Bee covers state politics in great detail.

In addition, every community produces its own local newspaper. The Bay Area has a number of papers printed in Chinese (available in Chinatown), Japanese (available in Japantown) and other foreign languages.

Newspapers of other countries are available at:
Dave's Smoke Shop (2444 Durant, Berkeley, Tel. 841–7292) sells all local newspapers, many foreign magazines and newspapers including those

from France, Germany, Britain and Italy. Open Monday to Saturday 9 a.m. to 11 p.m., Sunday 9 a.m. to 8 p.m.

De Lauer News Agency (1310 Broadway, Oakland, Tel. 451–6157) sells out-of-town newspapers from about 40 American cities, foreign magazines and many European newspapers. Open seven days a week, 4 hours a day.

Harold's (484 Geary, Tel. 474–2937) is San Francisco's international newsstand, selling papers and magazines from all over the world. Open Monday to Saturday 8 a.m. to 8:30 p.m. and Sunday from 8:30 a.m. to 6 p.m.

Other stores that carry foreign periodicals include:

Eastwind Books & Arts (1986 Shattuck, Berkeley, Tel. 548–2350) sells books, periodicals and magazines (but no newspapers) from Taiwan, Hong Kong and China. All topics in stock; from scientific to philosophical, from classical to contemporary literature. Open Monday to Saturday 10 a.m. to 6 p.m. and Sunday 12 noon to 4 p.m.

Europen Book Company (925 Larkin, San Francisco, Tel. 474–0626) sells European books, foreign magazines, foreign-language dictionaries, travel books; and French, German and Italian newspapers. Open Monday to Friday 9:30 a.m. to 6 p.m., and Saturday 9:30 a.m. to 5 p.m.

T'olodumare Bookstore (4834 Telegraph Ave., Oakland, Tel. 652–9122) stocks African books, journals, magazines and newspapers.

Television

In addition to the national networks and cable TV options, most towns in California have their own local TV station. Complete listings appear in the daily newspapers. In the Bay Area, the major stations are:

Channel 2: KTVU, Oakland (Independent)
3: KCRA, Sacramento (NBC)
4: KRON, San Francisco (NBC)
5: KPIX, San Francisco (CBS)
6: KVIE, Sacramento (PBS)

7: KGO, San Francisco (ABC)
8: KSBW, Salinas (NBC)
9: KQED, San Francisco (PBS)

10: KXTV, Sacramento (CBS)
11: KNTV, San Jose (ABC)
13: KOVR, Sacramento (ABC)

Spanish-language TV stations are more common in the southern part of the state. However, stations in the north include:

Channel 19: KCSO, Modesto/Sacramento
21: KFTV, Fresno
35: KCBA, Salinas
60: KDTV, San Francisco

Radio

Most American radios (in cars, hotel rooms, and hand-held instruments) pick up two frequencies; the AM and FM. FM has fewer commercials and a greater range of programs. The most popular stations in the Bay Area include:

AM:
560: KSFO, popular music, talk shows
610: KFRC, pop
680: KNBR, pop, sports (NBC)
740: KCBS, news, talk (CBS)
810: KGO, news, talk (ABC)
910: KNEW, country-western
960: KABL, easy listening
1220: KIBE, classical
1260: KYA, sixties rock
1310: KDIA, soul
1510: KTIM, rock
1550: KKHI, classical

FM:
88.5: KQED, classical, talk, community affairs including excellent news programs from National Public Broadcasting
93.3: KLHT, light rock
94.1: KPFA, talk, classical, community affairs
94.9: KSAN, country-western
102.9: KBLX, soul
104.5: KFOG, rock, from oldies to New Wave
106.1: KMEL, rock

Cities with all-Spanish-speaking A.M. stations include:
Fremont (KDOS), Fresno (KGST, KSJV-FM, KXEX), Gilroy (KAZA), Hayward (KIQI), Hollister (KMPG), King City (KLFA-FM), Lodi (KCVR), Roseville (KPIP-FM), Salinas (KRAY-FM, KCTY), San Francisco (KBRG-FM), San Mateo (KOFY), Santa Clara (KNTA), Santa Rosa (KBBF-FM), Stockton (KSTN-FM) and Watsonville (KOMY).

Some radio stations run occasional programs in foreign languages lasting from 2 to 20 hours a week. Sunday nights have an international flair at KQED, San Francisco's public radio station (88.5 FM). At 9 p.m., it's the Chinese Community Hour; at 10 p.m., it's Israel Calling; at 11 p.m., it's the Filipino Community Hour; and at midnight it's the Arab Radio Hour. Other stations that air foreign language programs include:

French

KRJB, Monte Rio: 97.7 FM
KUOR, Redlands: 89.1 FM
KUSF, San Francisco: 90.3 FM
KSRH, San Rafael: 88.1 FM
KPLS, Santa Rosa: 97.7 AM
KFJC, Los Altos: 89.7 FM

German

KRJB, Monte Rio: 97.7 FM
KTOB, Petaluma: 1490 AM

Greek

KFJC, Los Altos: 89.7 FM
KRVE, Los Gatos: 95.3 FM
KUSP, Santa Cruz: 88.9 FM

Japanese
KRDU, Dinuba: 1130 AM

KLIP, Fowler: 1220 AM
KSTN, Stockton: 107–3 FM
Italian
KWSD, Mt. Shasta: 620 AM
KUSF, San Francisco: 90.3 FM
Portugese
KLOC, Ceres: 920 AM
KRED, Eureka: 1480 AM
KEAP, Fresno: 980 AM
KSJV, Fresno: 91.5 FM
KSTN, Stockton: 107.3 FM
KNBA, Vallejo: 1190 AM

Health and Emergencies

Hospitals and Doctors

There is nothing cheap about being sick in America. Make sure you're covered by medical insurance while traveling in California. An ambulance costs around $200; an emergency room treatment costs a minimum of $50; and an average hospital bed costs at least $300 per night. If costs are a concern, turn first to the county hospital which gives good service and will not charge patients who are indigent.

Most hospitals in the Bay Area have 24-hour emergency rooms. No matter what your problem is, you usually end waiting longer at these "emergency rooms" than you feel you should but the eventual care and treatment is thorough and professional. The biggest and busiest of the emergency rooms in San Francisco are at:

Children's, 3700 California (386–0830)
Mount Zion, 1600 Divisadero (567–6600)
Pacific Medical Center, 2320 Sacramento (563–4321)
Saint Francis, 900 Hyde (775–4321)
San Francisco General, 1001 Potrero (431–2800)
University of California's Moffitt, 500 Parnassus (666–9000)

Outside San Francisco, the biggest and busiest emergency rooms can be found at:

Alta Bates, 1 Colby Plaza, Berkeley (945–7110)
Highland General, 1411 East 31st, Oakland (534–8055)
Marin General, 250 Bon Air Road, Greenbrae (461–0100)
Mount Diablo, Bacon and East streets, Concord (682–8200)
Stanford University Medical Center, Palo Alto (497–2300)
Valley Medical, 751 South Bascom, San Jose (408–279–5100)

If you need non-emergency medical care, look under "Physicians" in the Yellow Pages. In San Francisco, call the San Francisco Medical Society Referral Service (567–6234), or the Dental Society Referral Service (421–1435).

Pharmacies

Certain drugs can only be prescribed by a doctor. Most modern drugstores stock a variety of drugs and have a pharmaciest on duty.

The stores listed below are open for long hours and have pharmacists on duty:

San Francisco

Hub Pharmacy (1700 Market at Gough, Tel. 431–0068) opens daily 10:30 a.m. to 11:30 p.m.
Mission Geneva Pharmacy, (5125 Mission Street, Tel. 333–5266) opens daily 11 a.m. to 9 p.m.
Rexall Reliable Drug (801 Irving, Tel. 664–8800) opens Monday to Saturday 8 a.m. to 9 p.m.
Walgreen Drugs (1524 Polk, Tel. 673–4701) opens Monday to Friday 9 a.m. to 10 p.m., and Saturday and Sunday 9 a.m. to 5 p.m.

Bay Area

Day and Night Pharmacy (1776 Broadway, Oakland, Tel. 451–3965) opens Monday to Friday 7 a.m. to midnight, Saturday 8 a.m. to midnight, and Sunday 12 noon to 9 p.m.
Long's Drug Store (San Bruno Bayhill Shopping Center, Tel. 873–9522) opens Monday to Friday 9:30 a.m. to 9 p.m., Saturday and Sunday 10 a.m. to 7 p.m.
Marin Town & Country Pharmacy, (Tiburon Blvd & Blackfield, Tiburon), Tel. 388–6300) opens Monday to Saturday 9 a.m. to 9 p.m., and Sunday 10 a.m. to 6 p.m.
Thrifty (345 South B Street, San Mateo, Tel. 342–6264) opens Monday to Friday 9 a.m. to 9 p.m., and Saturday 10 a.m. to 6 p.m.
Walt's Drugs (1600 University Ave., Berkeley, Tel. 845–1445) opens daily 9 a.m. to 10 p.m.

Security and Crime

No California city is in the Top 10 of America's most crime-ridden cities. Only Oakland is in the Top 20. In general, it is safe to walk the streets during the day in any part of Northern California, except those areas mentioned below.

Whenever possible, travel with another person while sightseeing or shopping — particularly at night. Women, especially, should not walk in deserted or poor areas alone. Walking the streets is the best way to enjoy San Francisco, but there are certain sections best *driven* to or through; such as the Western Addition (roughly bordered by Gough, Divisadero, Haight and Golden Gates streets) and Hunter's Point (the peninsula just north of Candlestick Park). Other walking areas for tourists to avoid at night are the Mission District (the small, unlit streets between Dolores, Potrero, 14th and Army streets), the Tenderloin (bordered by O'Farrell, Turk, Market and Hyde streets), East Oakland, as well as the towns of Vallejo, Richmond and East Palo Alto, The area south of Market Street, from the Embarcadero to Church Street, can be unsafe for foot travel late at night; it's much wiser to drive or take a taxi.

If driving, lock your car and never leave luggage, cameras or other valuables in view. Lock them in the glove compartment or in the trunk. At night, park in lighted areas.

Never leave your luggage unattended. While waiting for a room reservation, a cab or a rental car, always keep your property in plain view. Rather than carrying your bags around with you, ask the front desk at a hotel, the hostess at a restaurant, or the security guard at a department store if you could check in your luggage with them. Most hotels provide a storage service free of charge. Never leave money or jewelry in your hotel room, even it is only for a short time. Always turn in your room key at the desk when going out.

Try to carry only the cash you need. Use credit cards and traveler's checks whenever possible and avoid displaying large amounts of cash when making purchases.

Emergencies

In case of an emergency, dial 911 for the police, fire or ambulance service. Other numbers that may come in handy while in the Bay Area:
Emergency Ambulance — 431–2800
Poison Control Center — 666–2845
Suicide Prevention — 221–1423
Coast Guard (search & rescue emergencies at sea) — 556–2103
Federal Bureau of Investigation — 552–2155
San Francisco Fire Department — 861–8020
Weather — 936–1212
Time — POP-CORN

Dining Out

The life of a San Franciscan is dedicated to the pursuit of liberty, happiness and the best restaurant in town. (Read Ruth Reichl's essay on "The Gourmet's San Francisco" in the feature section.)

When you wander down the streets, you can't help but take in each neighborhood's fascination with food — the plucked ducks and live fish in Chinatown, the smells of spaghetti sauce and cappucino in North Beach, and the fishmongers at Fisherman's Wharf.

San Francisco once boasted the only restaurant in America serving pizza and was home to the country's first Northern Chinese Restaurant. Today, there are more restaurants in San Francisco, per capita, than in any other city in the United States.

The restaurants listed in the appendix have been recommended by local food writers and/or the authors who have written our guides to each area. Make reservations whenever possible to avoid disappointment.

Shopping

Malls

Malls are where the middle-class American families shop for clothes, furniture and other everyday goods. Middle-class American family, by the way, is one with two kids, two television sets and two cars. Every city in the state has at least one mall, and every mall has at least one major department store (Sears, Penneys, Macy's) and dozens of smaller specialy specialty stores. Few souvenir shops are to be found in malls.

Stonestown Mall (19th Avenue at Winston Drive) is one of the oldest in San Francisco. It has more than 70 stores, including a large department store and supermarket, two large drugstores, 10 women's fashion shops, 12 men's clothing shops, four shoe stores, two ice cream parlors, a bank and a movie house.

The Embarcadero Center (four high-rise buildings at the foot of the Clay Street) is San Francisco's largest mall. Smack-dab in the middle of the business district, Embarcadero Center is very busy during normal workdays, but uncrowded (except for occasional tourists) on weekends.

The Galleria, 50 fashionable boutiques under a vaulted glass ceiling, is San Francisco's newest mall. Bounded by Post, Sutter, Kearny and Montgomery streets, the elegant Galleria is home to such tony clothing stores as Gianni Versace and Marimekko, and such tasty treat-eries as Godiva Chocolatier and the Old Poodle Dog Restaurant. The shops are open 9:30 a.m. to 6 p.m., from Monday to Saturday.

Theme Shopping Centers

The 1970s saw the advent of themed shopping villages; malls that look pretty with historic setting, housing specialty stores for both tourists and residents. Today, the most popular tourist attractions in San Francisco are these theme shopping centers.

Pier 39 (near Fisherman's Wharf), as its name suggests, is an actual pier and marina constructed primarily with wooden planks which were orginally part of a previous pier. There are more than 100 specialty shops, a dozen restaurants with views of the Bay, and free entertainment by magicians, acrobats, musicians during the summer. Kids love it.

The **Cannery** (at the end of Columbus Street near Fisherman's Wharf) was a fruit canning factory and warehouse before it became home to about 50 trendy boutiques. Nearby **Ghirardelli Square** (900 North Point at Larkin) was a chocolate factory before it became a giant complex of 90 specialty shops and restaurants — three of which are wonderful, if unusual, eating experiences: **Maxwell's Plum** (fashionable dining), **Modesto Lanzonne's** (Italian), and **Gaylord** (Indian).

Other interesting themed shopping centers include San Francisco's **Japan Center**, Sacramento's **Old Town**, and Santa Rosa's recently restored historical center adjacent to the downtown mall.

Shopping Areas

Some of the best shopping districts in the Bay Area are actually a few blocks of business streets surrounded by private residences. These streets are where smart local folks shop.

In San Francisco, the best of these neighborhood shopping streets are: **24th Street** in the Noe Valley (between Castro and Church), with a variety of New York-type shops and small restaurants; **Union Street** (between Fillmore and Gough), famed for its art and antique stores, bars, restaurants and Victorian houses; **Haight Street** (between Ashbury and Golden Gate Park), once a hang-out for hippies, still hip, but now also chic; and **Grant Street** (between California and Pacific) for the ultimate in Chinese kitsch and silly San Francisco souvenirs.

The two gay shopping streets are **Polk Gulch** (between Bush and Jackson) which has antique stores, boutiques, restaurants, and bars in old Victorian buildings; and **Castro Gulch** (between 19th Avenue and Market, and then down Upper Market towards Church) which has colorful restaurants, shops, galleries and, on hot weekends, a veritable parade of good-looking young men.

Union Square marks one corner of the city's smartest shopping district, which extends east from the square down Sutter to Kearny and down Stockton to Market. Within these few blocks are the city's finest stores — Gumps (jade and jewels), Gucci (Italian leather), FAO Schwartz (toys), Brooks Brothers (classic clothing), Tiffany (crystal), Williams-Sonoma (kitchenware) Le Vie du Soleil (French country ware) — and department stores; I. Magnin, Saks Fifth Avenue, Neiman-Marcus, Liberty House, Joseph Magnin, Macy's and Emporium-Capwell. A block from Union Square park is **Maiden Lane**, a cute pedestrian street with boutiques, stationery stores, and an outdoor cafe. At the corner of Post and Kearny streets is the Galleria, (see under "Malls").

Other shopping streets around the Bay boasting boutiques, restaurants and specialty stores include **Solano Avenue** in Albany (between Colusa and Sante Fe), **Piedmont Avenue** in Oakland (between Mac Arthur and Pleasant Valley), **University Avenue** in Palo Alto, and the entire business district of **Sausalito**.

Telegraph Avenue in Berkeley (from Dwight Way to Bancroft Way) is one of the most famous shopping areas in the country. In fine weather, the sidewalks are lined with arts-and-crafts booths, "street people," college students, and shoppers quietly browsing among the bookstores, boutiques, restaurants and record stores. Once home of the Free Speech Movement and political rioting, Telegraph Avenue is now an area offering pizza, frozen yoghurt, and designer-label jeans.

Shattuck Avenue in Berkeley, between Virginia and Rose streets, is known as "Gourmet Ghetto" because of its collection of fine cheese, wine, chocolate, coffee, fish, meat and poultry stores, and innovative delicatessens.

On the Farm

If you want to avoid the "I Left My Heart In San Francisco" coffee mugs and other commercial souvenirs, and return home with authentic made-in-California gifts, take a trip to the farm country. Apple wine, blackberry jam, dried fruits and herbs, fresh honey, jojoba oil ... there are hundreds of products that you can buy direct from the producer, saving yourself money while visiting a real, working farm.

Sonoma County Farm Trails is an association of about 160 agricultural producers; from Buchan (famous for its oysters fresh from Tomales Bay) to the Petaluma Desert (potted cactus) with all kinds of imaginable fruits, vegetables, livestock and wines in between! Free maps and brochures are available at all participating farms, and the Santa Rosa Chamber of Commerce (707–545–1414), or by writing: Farm Trails, PO Box 6674, Santa Rosa, 95406.

Santa Clara and Santa Cruz counties have teamed together in a similar program called **Country Crossroads**. Some 50 farms encourage visitors to pick their peaches, tour their egg ranches, and sample their apples. Maps and information are available at participating farms, from the Santa Cruz Visitors Bureau (408–423–6927), or by writing: Country Crossroads, 1368 North Fourth Street, San Jose 95112.

Flea Markets

Flea markets in the Bay Area are outnumbered only by yard sales. They are held on weekends, admission is generally free, and bargains galore! Sellers range from those old-timers who make a living selling discounted new goods and antiques to people who think they have too much junk in their attic or garage. The most common items at flea markets are used household items, but you can also spot brand-new stereo equipment, designer clothes, farm tools, food, arts and crafts, puppy dogs and stuffed teddy bears. Bargaining is expected. Most of them accept cash only; no checks or credit cards.

Alameda Penny Market, the best of the flea markets, held on weekends at the Island Auto Drive-In, three blocks south of the Alameda Tube from Oakland. Admission is 50 cents (552–7206).

San Jose Flea Market, at 12000 Berryessa Road is one of the largest in the United States. About 2,000 booths fill 40 acres (16 hectares) with every imaginable kind of merchandise. There are shady rest areas, refreshment stands, kiddie rides, and live entertainment. Open Wednesday, Saturday and Sunday. Parking fee $1 (408–289–1550).

Marine City Flea Market at 740 Donahue Street off U.S. 101 in Sausalito is the place to pick up something inexpensive you'll love. Open only on weekends (332–1441).

Other flea markets which deserve mention include the **Castro Valley Market** at 20820 Oak Street in Castro Valley Boulevard (582–0396) and the **Solano Flea Market** at the Solano Drive-In, Solano Way and Highway 4 (825–1951).

Duty Free

Retail goods can be purchased at 30 Geary Street duty-free if you're departing San Francisco for Japan or Vancouver. Call for information regarding duty-free shops to other destinations, 989–3020 or 589–6690.

Tours and Attractions

Alcatraz — A two-hour excursion to this infamous island could be the most worthwhile visit you'll ever make to an American institution. The Red and White fleet ferries you to The Rock and back, transporting you to a time of notoriety and a concept of punishment still practiced in America. For $4.50 (less for kids and seniors), you can see where the Birdman of Alcatraz, Al Capone, and Machine Gun Kelly lived out their sentences. The ferry leaves every 45 minutes between 9 a.m. and 3 p.m. from Fisherman's Wharf, Pier 41 in San Francisco, daily. Park rangers lead a walking tour, covering much of the island and most of the prison. It's a hard walk (physically and emotionally). Wear comfortable shoes and dress for winter (it gets quite cold in the middle of the Bay). Reservations advised (546–2805).

Angel Island — This island in the Bay doesn't have the history of Alcatraz, but it has the view. Pack a picnic and board a Red and White Ferry (four round trips daily) at Fisherman's Wharf, Pier 43 (546–2815); tickets are $5.25 for a round trip. You can also reach and leave the island via Tiburon; the ferry leaves every hour 10 a.m. to 6:30 p.m. The charge is $1.50 each way (435–2131). There's a regular ferry service from Tiburon to Pier 41 at Fisherman's Wharf, $2.75 (546–2810).

Bay Model — This two-acre scale model of the San Francisco Bay and Delta region reproduces the tidal action; flow and current of the Bay; as well as the mixing of salt and fresh water. Computerized slide show and interpretive displays. At 2100 Bridgeway, Sausalito. Open daily, 9 a.m. to 4 p.m. Admission free. (332–3870).

California Academy of Sciences — Many museums in one! The Steinhart Aquarium is home of the third largest fish collection in the world: a tide pool, an alligator swamp, a penguin sanctuary, and a circular fish tank with viewer access in the center. The Morrison Planetarium has educational shows on the constellations and moon phases, as well as entertaining rock-music star shows. The Wattis Halls of Science cover subjects from fossils to space exploration. In Golden Gate Park, San Francisco. Open daily, 10 a.m. to 5 p.m. Admission 75 cents to $2. (752–8268 or 221–5100).

The Exploratorium — Without a doubt, this is one of the best science museum in the world. Visitors are *encouraged* to touch the ever-changing exhibits (more than 500 in all). You shout through tubes and into telephones, you push buttons and twist colored knobs, and in the process, understand complex principles of light, sound, technology and human perception. Leave the kids here all day, and they won't miss you at all. 3601 Lyon Street at the Palace of the Fine Arts, San Francisco. Open Wednesday to Sunday, 11 a.m. to 5 p.m. Adult admission $2.50 (563–3200).

Fort Ross — The fort was established in 1812 on the site of a Russian trading post. Restored buildings include the chapel, stockade and two block-houses. Seeming somewhat surreal as you drive up Highway 1, the fort sits serene and solitary on the Sonoma coast, 10 miles (16 km) north of Jenner. Open daily, 10 a.m. to 5 p.m. Admission $2 per car. (707–847–3286).

Lombard Street — Referred to as "the crookedest street in the world," the one-block portion of Lombard between Hyde and Leavenworth Streets descends in a 40-degree slope. There are stairs, but the fun is driving down the street — very carefully.

Marine World/Africa U.S.A. — This 65-acre (26-hectare) amusement park is home to about 2,000 animals: 50 marine mammals (from dolphins to killer whales), 150 birds (from cockatoos to macaws), 250 land animals (from Bengal tigers to dainty mouse deer), and 1,500 fish (from eels to sharks). Off U.S. 101 in Redwood City, 25 miles (40 km) south of San Francisco. Open daily 9:30 a.m. to 6 p.m. One-price admission ($10 for adults) includes special events, all seven animal shows and about 60 attractions (591–7676).

Marriott's Great America — One of the best amusement parks in United States, Great America features Bugs Bunny and Daffy Duck instead of Mickey and Minnie Mouse. Besides the Demon (a spine-chilling roller coaster), there are Willard's Wizard and The Logger's Run rides, a double-decker carousel, and the world's first triple-arm Ferris wheel. Live musical and theatrical productions, motion pictures and all the thrilling rides your stomach can handle are included in the $14 admission (less for children and seniors). Off U.S. 101 in Santa Clara. Open daily during the summer, 10 a.m. to 8 p.m.; open only on weekends the rest of the year (408–988–1800).

Mormon Temple — A magnificent example of religious architecture, this temple acquaints visitors with the religion of the Latter Day Saints. It offers, on a clear day, a scenic vista of San Francisco. Take the 75-minute guided tour of the gardens and worship houses; last tour at 7:30 p.m. 4780 Lincoln Ave. in the Oakland hills. Open daily 9 a.m. to 9 p.m. Admission free (531–1475).

Mount Tamalpais — Spectacular views of the entire Bay Area can be enjoyed after driving up a winding road to the summit, where there's a 6,000-acre (2,430-hectare) state park. In spring and summer, plays and musical programs are presented in the amphitheater. Six miles (10 km) west of Mill Valley (388–2070).

Muir Woods — This 550-acre (223-hectare) national monument, a magnificent redwood forest, offers six miles of trails. The main trail is an easy stroll and has trailside markers and exhibits. Seven unpaved trails offer greater challenge. The *Sequoia Sempervirens* — the tallest trees in the world are in abundance here. Some coast redwoods are 220 feet (67 meters) tall with diameters in excess of 10 feet! No picnicking, no camping, no pets. 17 miles (27 km) northwest of San Francisco. Take State 1 to Stinson Beach; at Muir Beach, follow signs to the Woods. Open daily 8 a.m. to sunset. Admission free 388–2595).

Roaring Camp Railroad — Ride through redwood forests on this old-fashioned, steampowered passenger train. Disembark to hike or picnic at Bear Mountain, then return to Roaring Camp for a chuck wagon barbecue (reservations required) or a walk through Henry Cowell Redwoods State Park. Four miles west of State 17 in Felton, on Graham Hill Road in the Santa Cruz mountains. Train leaves daily at noon; over the summer and on weekends, there are additional departures. Adult admission $7.50 (408–335–4484).

Rosicrucian Egyptian Museum — A one-of-a-kind historical and spiritual experience is offered here, including assembled ancient Near Eastern artifacts stunning in their range and uniqueness. This is the world headquarters of "The Ancient, Mystical Order Rosae Crucis" and San Jose's largest tourist attraction. Propagandistic efforts are low-key and highlights include a planetarium and a Science museum featuring exhibits about the wondrous early discoveries in mathematics and initial efforts to form a written language. There's also a walk-in tomb. Parkand Naglee Ave. San Jose (408–287–9171).

Santa Cruz Beach Boardwalk — California's first and finest seashore amusement area (established in 1868) offers 24 rides, games, arcades, gift shops, entertainment and a mile-long beach. A magnificent casino, built here in 1907, has been renovated to house two restaurants. The antique merry-go-round dates from 1911. The Giant Dipper is one of the best roller coaster rides in the world. 400 Beach St., Santa Cruz. Open daily 11 a.m. to 10 p.m. Boardwalk is free; fees range from 50 cents to $1 each ride, or an all-day unlimited ticket for $8.50 (408–426–7433).

Seventeen-Mile Drive — This scenic drive from Pacific Grove to Carmel is for all coastal visitors! Points of interest along the way include Seal Rock, Cypress Point and four of the most beautiful golf courses in the country, including Pebble Beach. Bicycling is a great way to enjoy the drive; toll for cars is $4.

Skunk Railroad — Nicknamed for the noxious fumes originally emitted by the ancient steam train, the California Western Railroad travels from Fort Bragg (80 feet — 24 meters — about sea level) to Willits — (1,365 feet or 416 meters). The tabulous 40-mile (64-km) trip passes through groves of towering redwood trees, crossing and recrossing the Noyo River. Round trip takes almost eight hours. Fare $5 to $12 (707–964–6371).

State Capitol — Built between 1861 and 1874 and recently restored, this seat of the state government is known for its fine proportions and lofty dome, 237 feet (72 meters) above the street. The main building contains murals, historical exhibits and statuary; the surrounding park boasts shrubs, trees, and plants from all parts of the world. Free guided tours daily, 9 a.m. to 4 p.m.; East Annex is open daily 7 a.m. to 9 p.m. Bounded by 10th, 12th, L and N streets, Sacramento. Free (916–324–0333).

Television Shows — San Francisco is not Hollywood, but there are two live shows that welcome audiences. *People are Talking*, hosted by Ann Fraser and Ross McGowan, encourages audience participation. Features big-name guests. Be at the studio at 8 a.m.; program airs at 10 a.m., Monday through Friday. KPIX, 855 Battery St (478–KPIX for reservations). *AM San Francisco*, another morning talk show, also airs Monday to Friday. Be at the studio at 8:15 a.m. KGO, 277 Golden Gate Ave, (565–7916).

University of California at Berkeley — One of the oldest and most beautiful college campuses in the state, Cal (as it is affectionately called by students and alumni) occupies 720 acres (291 hectares) in the heart of Berkeley. Guided walking tours of the campus depart from the Student Union (near Telegraph Avenue and Bacroft Way) at 1 p.m., Monday to Friday (642–5215). The University Art Museum features modern and oriental art. 2626 Bancroft Way. Open Wednesday to Sunday, 11 a.m. to 5 p.m. Admission 50 cents to $1 (642–0808). The Botanical Garden contains 8,000 species of plants spread over 32 lovely acres (13 hectares). Strawberry Canyon off Centennial Drive. Daily 9 a.m. to 5 p.m. Free (642–3343). The Campanile, at the center of campus, is 300 feet (91 meters) tall. Elevator to the top costs 25 cents. Daily 8 a.m. to 4:30 p.m. (642–3666). Open to the public, Lawrence Hall of Science is a research center, and a button pusher's paradise complete with learning machines, computer games, an earthquake information center, mini-planetarium, do-it-yourself experimental labs, children's classes and workshops. Centennial Drive on the east (hilly) side of campus. Monday to Friday 10 a.m. to 4:30 p.m.; Thursday to 9 p.m.; Saturday to Sunday 10 a.m. to 5 p.m. Admission $1 to $$2.50 (642–5132).

Winchester Mystery House — Sarah Winchester, heiress to the $20 million Winchester rifle fortune, was somewhat eccentric. A psychic told her she would never die if she built additions to her home continuously. Things got complex: 160 rooms, 2,000 doors, (some opening into empty shafts) 13 bathrooms, 10,000 windows (placed at various levels), 47 fireplaces, blind closets, secret passageways and 40 staircases (some that zigzag to nowhere). Take the 2½-hour, guided tour of the mansion and its gardens. 525 South Winchester Blvd, San Jose. Open during summer 9 a.m. to 6 p.m.; hours vary for the rest of the year. Admission $4.25 to $8 (408–247–2101).

World of Miniature — Homes, shops, offices and entire villages — from Maine to California during 1700 to 1950 — are displayed in perfect one-inch scale reproductions. Some of the exhibits are mechanized. There are also four operating scale model railroads and a cargo ship. 1373 South Bascom Ave., San Jose. Open Tuesday to Saturday 10:30 a.m. to 5:30 p.m.; Sunday noon to 5 p.m. Admission $2 to $4 (408–294–4256).

Young and Restless — The youth movement of the 1960s is older now and therefore moving slower, but it can still be found. Check out "Hippie Hill" near Stanyan and Frederick streets in San Francisco's Golden Gate Park. Everyone there grooves on the grass — playing bongos, throwing Frisbees, smoking pot and letting their hair hang down. The kids are always there, but the crowds are biggest on the weekends (558–4268). Also: Free speech messages and political protests can be heard — especially at lunchtime — at Sproul Hall Plaza on the UC Berkeley campus (642–6000).

Zoos — The best zoo in the state is in San Diego, followed by the L.A. Zoo, and then the San Francisco Zoo. Behind bars are more than 1,000 animals — from ants to zebras. Buzz over to the insect zoo, pet a pet at the Children's Zoo, or just sit around Monkey Island. Work your way over to the Lion Grotto at 2 p.m. and watch the big cats with fangs and ferocious appetites lunch on raw meat. Sloat Blvd and The Great Highway. Daily 10 a.m. to 5 p.m. Admission $2.50 (661–4844).

The lions and tigers are fed at 4 p.m. at the **Oakland Zoo**. Although a fraction the size of the San Francisco Zoo, Oakland has about 350 animals (mostly primates and hoofed animals) and a nifty aerial ride, Skyfari. Highway 580 and 98th Avenue. 10 a.m. to 4:30 p.m. Charge is $2 per car (568–2470).

The small **Fresno Zoo** is located in Roeding Park. Open daily 10 a.m. to 8 p.m. Adult admission $1.35 (209–266–9543).

Micke Grove Park and Zoo features more than 500 birds and 150 animals, including lions, tigers, bears and chimpanzees. 11793 North Micke Grove Road, three miles south of Lodi on Highway 55. Daily, 7 a.m. to dusk. Admission 50 cents per car (209–369–2205).

Sacramento Zoo has an island for monkeys, a pond for otters, a pool for penguins, and a house for reptiles. Beautifully landscaped with shrubs, flowers and trees. 3930 West Land Park Drive in William Land Park, Sacramento. Daily 9 a.m. to 5 p.m. Admission 15 cents to 35 cents (916–447–5094).

Safari World is a wonderful wild animal ranch between Fresno and Mariposa where lions, tigers, camels, hippos, buffalo, zebras and many other exotic creatures roam freely in a natural habitat. 32601 Yosemite Highway, Coarsegold. Daily 9 a.m. to 5 p.m. Adult admission $3.50 (209–683–4474).

National Parks

There are 20 National Park System areas in California. Although they come under a variety of guises (in Northern California, four are called "National Parks," while three are "National Monuments," two are "National Recreation Areas," and one is a "National Seashore"), they are all filled with helpful rangers and park personnel, and more scenic vistas than you can point a camera at. Last year, about 30 million people visited California's National Parks; you'll fare better to visit these areas during the week and in the off-season. For information about accommodations, campgrounds, fishing, horseback riding, backpacking and ranger programs, contact the National Park Service, 450 Golden Gate Ave., San Francisco 94102 (556–4122).

Lassen Volcanic National Park — Home of Lassen Peak, the largest plug dome volcano in the world; hot springs; boiling mud pots; ski areas; and several lakes. 106,000 acres, (43,000 hectares), (between Redding and Susanville) (916–595–4444).

Pinnacles National Monument — Hiking and climbing are favorite activities on the eroded slopes of an ancient volcano with spire-like rock formations rising 1,000 feet (305 meters) above the surrounding foothills. More than 30 square miles (78 sq km), between King City and Hollister. (408–389–4578).

Redwood National Park — This park has two distinct zones: the redwood forest (with its associated vegetation, streams, and rivers) and the coastal zone (with abrupt cliffs, beaches, lagoons and tidepools). 106,000 acres, (43,000 hectares), near Crescent City (707–464–6101).

Sequoia and Kings Canyon National Parks — Here are grand old groves of giant redwood trees as well as Mt. Whitney, the highest point in the contiguous 48 states (209–565–3373). Kings Canyon is a Sierra Nevada wilderness of granite domes, jeweled lakes, tumbling waterfalls and deep canyons. 1,324 square miles (3,429 sq km) east of Fresno (209–335–2314).

Yosemite National Park — Take a scenic walk through the Valley with its leaping waterfalls, rounded domes and towering cliffs, or backpack into the alpine forests. Yosemite, one of the most popular parks in the country, has a spledid hotel, a cafeteria, lodges, cabins and camping facilities. 1,189 square miles (3,080 sq km) in central California on the western slope of the Sierra Nevada (209–373–4171).

Golden Gate National Recreation Area — This vast urban park includes ocean beaches, sand dunes, redwood forests, lagoons, marshes, and many historical buildings. 44,000 acres (17,800 hectares) around San Francisco Bay (556–0560).

Whiskeytown-Shasta-Trinity National Recreation Area — Named after the three major lakes inside the park, this sportsman's paradise offers camping, hiking, fishing, boating, swimming, picnicking, hunting and water skiing. 100,000 acres (40,500 hectares) north of Redding (916–246–1225).

Lava Beds National Monument — Self-guiding trails take you to 20 fantastic caves (including relatively recent lava and ice caves), fumeroles and other volcanic wonders. 46,000 acres (18,600 hectares) 30 miles (48 km) south of Tulelake (916–667–2282).

Point Reyes National Seashore — Colorful cliffs, sandy beaches, languid lagoons, bird rookeries, sea lions barking on the offshore rocks, Point Reyes is the perfect place for an afternoon romance. 65,000 acres (26,300 hectares), one-hour's drive northwest of San Francisco (663–1092).

For information on backpacking permits for these areas, see the "Sports" section of this Guide-In-Brief.

Cultural Activities

The San Francisco Bay Area is a major cultural force not only in California, but in the nation. More artists live in California than any other state, and a great number of them reside in the Bay Area. The galleries, theaters, dance companies, concert halls, museums and bookstores offer something for every interest from the most classical to the most contemporary.

San Francisco is home to the San Francisco Ballet, San Francisco Symphony, San Francisco Opera and the San Francisco Museum of Modern Art; all world-class institutions.

Revivals of old movies, touring companies and dance performances are weekly fare at local colleges an universities. In smaller communities around the state, college, campuses may be the only source of nationally-known entertainers, who tour to teach master classes as well as to perform.

The Sunday *Chronicle & Examiner* "Datebook" (affectionately known as the pink section) is an up-to-the-minute guide to current performances and exhibitions, covering music, theater, dance, museums, galleries, movies and sports for the six counties of the Bay Area. Another excellent resource for cultural activities is *City Arts Monthly*, a free magazine distributed at cafes, bookshops and galleries, and at Fort Mason (474–3914).

Museums

All of the museums listed below feature several changing displays in addition to their permanent collections. Information about current exhibitions can be obtained by calling the museum or from the pink section of the Sunday paper. Admission prices indicated are for permanent collections; changing exhibitions may have additional costs.

M.H. De Young Museum — (Golden Gate Park, San Francisco, Tel. 751–4432). Permanent collections of Africa, Oceania, Europe, the Americas and ancient Egypt, Greece and Rome. Superb touring exhibits. Wednesday to Sunday, 10 a.m. to 5 p.m. Admission $2.

Asian Art Museum (Golden Gate Park, San Francisco, Tel. 558–2993). Nearly 10,000 art objects from China, Japan, India, Korea, Tibet, Southeast Asia. Daily 10 a.m. to 4 p.m. except Wednesdays till 6 p.m. only. Admission free.

San Francisco Museum of Modern Art (McAllister & Van Ness, San Francisco, Tel. 863–8800). Permanent collections include both American and European paintings, sculpture, photographs and ceramics. Quite contemporary. Tuesday to Sunday 10 a.m. to 5 p.m. Thursday evenings until 10 p.m. Admission $3.

Palace of the Legion of Honor (Lincoln Park, San Francisco, Tel. 751–4432). See M.H. De Young Museum with which it shares collections.

Oakland Museum (1000 Oak Street, Oakland, Tel. 273–3402). Permanent collections cover California art, historical artifacts and ecological exhibits, including textiles, decorative arts, sculpture, photography, botany, and geology. All collections relate to California theme. Wednesday to Saturday 10 a.m to 5 p.m. Sunday noon to 7 p.m. Admission free.

Mexican Museum (Fort Mason, Bldg. D, San Francisco, Tel. 441–0404). Pre-Hispanic, colonial and contemporary Mexican art and crafts. Wednesday to Sunday, noon to 5 p.m. Admission free.

Crocker Art Museum (216 O Street, Sacramento, Tel. 916–446–4677). Paintings from early Renaissance to 20th century, sculpture, pottery, textiles. Tuesday 2 to 10 p.m. Wednesday to Sunday 10 a.m. to 5 p.m. Admission $1.

Triton Museum 1505 Warburton Avenue, Santa Clara, Tel. 408–248–4585). California and American paintings and prints. Tuesday to Friday noon to 4 p.m. Saturday & Sunday noon to 5 p.m. Admission free.

San Jose Museum of Art (110 S. Market Street, San Jose, Tel. 408–294–2787). Textiles, regional painting, American Print collection. Tuesday to Saturday 10 a.m. to 4:30 p.m. Saturday & Sunday noon to 5 p.m. Admission free.

Art Galleries

In addition to its museums, the San Francisco Bay Area has an active visual arts scene — from the galleries in the financial district to artists' lofts in the warehouse districts in the South of Market area, Oakland and Emeryville. Unlike museums, the displays in art galleries are for sale. Galleries usually specialize in certain artists and the dealers split the sales price with the artists, taking a hefty commission. Exhibits change frequently in the galleries, and the pink section is the best source for information on current shows.

The galleries are the best place to see the work of contemporary local artists.

Ghiradelli Square, Fisherman's Wharf — Geared to the out-of-towners, this area specializes in highly commercial galleries ranging from mass-produced low-price works of questionable quality to prints by well-known artists.

Union Square — For well-established fine arts galleries. The area around the downtown department stores and boutiques has the most and best galleries. Grant Street is home to the **Fraenkel Gallery** (981–2661); one nearby building (228 Grant) houses the **John Berggruen Gallery** (781–4629), **Fuller Goldeen Gallery** (982–6177) and **Foster Goldstrom** (788–5535). Sutter Street from Keary to Mason has **Braunstein** (392–5532) and **Quay** galleries (421–1958), **Stephen Wirtz** (433–6879) and **George Belcher Gallery** (981–3178). **Paule Anglim** (433–2710) and **Harcourts** (421–3428) are also within an easy walk. Hours vary. Admission, of course, is free.

South of Market — The self-styled avant-garde galleries are scattered in the South of Market district among the warehouses in which many artists have their studios and lofts. Among these are **Southern Exposure** (621–9551), **Modernism** (552–2286), and **Camerawork** (621–1001).

Theaters

Theater performances fall roughly into two groups: touring companies that bring to San Francisco big Broadway productions or major revivals, and Bay-Area-based companies that offer a range of productions from Shakespeare to experimental new works.

The price of tickets, particularly the Broadway houses, can be prohibitive. As a result, **Stubs** on Stockton between Geary and Post (433–7827) does a booming business selling half-price tickets of theatrical and musical performances. Open from noon to 7:30 p.m. Tuesday to Saturday. Stubs accepts cash only. Discount tickets are allowed for current bookings only.

Big Houses

These theaters range in size from about 600 to 2000 seats. Ticket prices vary from $11 to $30 depending on the day and the show. Productions are generally Broadway road companies, although occasionally these theaters will present an already-tested local production. **Curran Theater** — 445 Geary (673–4400). **Golden Gate Theater** — 25 Taylor (775–8800). **Marine's Memorial Theater** — 609 Sutter (771–6900). **Orpheum Theater** — 1192 Market Street (474–3800). **Theater on the Square** — 450 Post (433–9500).

Repertory Companies

These are small houses of 99 to 500 seats. Tickets vary from $6 to $20.

American Conservatory Theater (415 Geary, San Francisco, Tel. 673–6440) is the largest San Francisco resident company. ACT has earned a national reputation for consistently good productions and an unimaginative choice of plays. ACT doesn't take risks with new material, preferring to run uncontroversial pieces by well-established playwrights.

Berkeley Repertory Theater (2025 Addison, Berkeley, Tel. 845–4700) started as a repertory company which grew slowly but steadily in the

1970s until its own theater was set up in 1980. More daring than ACT, the Rep offers excellent productions of contemporary drama. Noel Coward revivals and occasional premieres of better-known playwrights. With 80 percent of its house subscribed by the start of each season, tickets are often sold out.

Berkeley Stage Company (1111 Addison, Berkely, Tel. 548–4782). An opposition to the Berkeley Rep, the Stage Company is experimental only, offering world premieres each season and taking many risks. Its sometimes shakey finances can result in somewhat threadbare productions. The audience is always guaranteed an adventure. 1111 Addison, Berkeyley (548–4728).

The Eureka (2730 16th Street, San Francisco, Tel. 558–9811) stages ambitious, politically oriented plays; many are American premieres of European productions.

The Julian Theater (953 De Haro, Tel. 647–8098) is a neighborhood theater in San Francisco's Potrero Hill community center. It's not unusual to see professional actors together with local amateurs in these productions. The Julian often presents controversial material, dealing with contemporary issues and urban themes.

The Magic Theater (For Mason, Bldg. D, San Francisco, Tel. 441–8822) is a campy, crafty crew that likes to do things that have never been done before. There are occasionally impressive partnerships between the production people and the playwrights — Michael McClure and Sam Shepard premiere many of their plays at the Magic.

The One-Act Theater Company of San Francisco (430 Mason, Tel. 421–6162) is the only one-act repertory ensemble in America. In addition to evening performances, usually consisting of three plays as variation on a single theme, the One Act has started popular Wednesday lunch performances for the downtown crowd.

Dance

The Bay Area has two major ballets. The **San Francisco Ballet** performing at the San Francisco Opera House (Van Ness and Grove in Civic Center, Tel. 621–3838) is 50 years old and well-known for traditional choreography, consistently excellent productions and classical form. Members of the San Francisco Symphony perform with the Ballet. San Francisco was the first ballet company in the country to perfrom the *Nutcracker Suite* as a Christmas event. Season runs December through May.

Across the bay (at Paramount Theater, 2025 Broadway, Oakland, Tel. 465–6400) is a vigorous newcomer challenging San Francisco Ballet's dominance. The **Oakland Ballet's** reputation has been built in the last 16 years on innovational and young dancers who make up in dedication and energy what they lack in classical form. By reviving Diaghilev classics with original sets and costumes, western ballets of Copeland-Loring collaboration, and presenting the work of new California choreographers, Oakland is gaining national attention. Season runs September through December.

The modern dance scene in the Bay Area is quite alive and worth exploring. The **Dance Coalition** (Bldg. C, Fort Mason, San Francisco, Tel. 673–8172) publishes a comprehensive monthly calendar covering all forms of dance in the Bay Area — classical, modern, jazz, ethnic, folk and tap.

For modern and contemporary dance shows, try the **New Performance Gallery** (3153 17th Street, San Francisco, Tel. 863–9834). Founded by two modern dance companies in order to have a house of the right size and dimensions for their own performances, the Gallery has expanded to encompass new works from other local choreographers, experimental pieces from various local companies, and a touring program that brings small new companies to San Francisco. New music and performance art are also presented at the Gallery (863–9834).

Two other performance series are worth noting: **The San Francisco Opera House** is home to visiting national and international ballet companies including the Joffrey Ballet, American Ballet Theater and Stuttgart Ballet, among others. Write or call the box office to receive information about upcoming performances: San Francisco Opera House, P O Box 7430, San Francisco 94120, Tel. 431–1210.

The University of California brings a fine mix of classical, modern and ethnic dance touring companies to its Berkeley campus (Zellerbach Auditorium, Bancroft & Telegraph, Tel. 642–9988) as part of its "Cal Performances."

Music

The classical music lover has a symphony of choices for entertainment in Northern California. In addition to the San Francisco Symphony (the preeminent local orchestra), Oakland, Marin, Berkeley, San Jose, Sacramento and Santa Cruz have resident companies. The Bay Area offers more chamber music groups, per capita, than any other cities in the States, and a wide range of Asian and Indian music offerings as well.

The San Francisco Opera is the largest and most fashionable arts organization in San Francisco, an opera-loving city since Gold Rush days. Locals claim the Opera, the second largest in the States, is the best in the world, and some international stars agree.

Public and private money support the Opera and six other opera companies in the Bay Area with unprecedented enthusiasm.

Oakland Symphony (performs in the Paramount Theater, 2025 Broadway, Oakland, Tel. 465–6400) has a reputation for young, dynamic, artistic direction and solid, popular programming.

Sacramento Symphony (14th & L streets, Sacramento, Tel. 916–0800) plays chamber concerts and an outdoor summer series, in addition to its regular season.

San Francisco Conservatory of Music (1201 Ortega, San Francisco, Tel. 564–8086) offers professional chamber music as well as student recitals in its small intimate Hellman Hall. With graduates like Isaac Stern to its credit, the Conservatory is widely regarded as the best West Coast music school.

San Francisco Opera (Grove and Van Ness avenues, San Francisco, Tel. 431–1210) is perhaps best known for its casting which stems from the loyalty of great, international opera stars. It has successfully revived and restored to its current operatic repertoire a number of little-known masterpieces.

San Francisco Symphony (Davies Symphony Hall, Van Ness & Grove, San Francisco, Tel. 431–5400) plays a summer pops series, a Beethoven Festival and the Mostly Mozart Festival each year, in addition to its regular season.

San Jose Symphony has earned a reputation for strong, accessible programs since 1972 under the direction of maestro George Cleve.

Public Libraries

Every city and town in America has a public library. Libraries vary enormously in quality and service, but a few generalities can be made. The larger cities have library systems, built on a main branch which offers major collections and special services. Neighborhood branches around the city offer smaller collections.

In the larger cities of San Francisco, San Jose, Berkeley, Oakland, Sacramento, the library systems offer services to the blind, deaf and physically handicapped, youth and children's services include special collections and story-telling. In addition, some of these systems offer special local history collections, and foreign language books; and both Oakland and San Francisco have business branches devoted to periodial and book selections on subjects relating to international business.

Use of all libraries is free. Non-residents are not allowed to check out books, but can read all you want inside the building; from reference materials to daily newspapers and foreign-language periodicals. Listing of neighborhood branches can be found in the White Pages of the telephone directory under *city government*. For general information about the main libraries:

San Francisco in Civic Center, across from City Hall, Tel. 558–3191 (open Tuesday to Thursday 10 a.m. to 9 p.m., Monday, Friday and Saturday 10 a.m. to 6 p.m.

Berkeley, Kittredge and Shattuck, Tel. 644–6100.

Oakland, 125 14th Street, Tel. 273–3134.

Sacramento, 8th and "I" streets, Tel. 916–449–5203.

San Jose, 180 West San Carlos, Tel. 408–277–4000.

Bookstores

The prevalence of bookstores, found in every neighborhood shopping district, is testimony to San Francisco's fondness for books. San Francisco's **City Lights** bookstore opened in 1953, is perhaps the most famous making literary history the hub of the beat generation. Owned by poet Lawrence Ferlinghetti, it reflects his obvious interests in its large collection of poetry and small press publications.

Across the Bay in Berkeley, Telegraph Avenue (in the blocks jutting out from the University) is a booklover's paradise. There, amid the coffeehouses, restaurants and street vendors, are located some of the best bookstores in the Bay Area. Here you will find **Cody's,** one of the largest independent booksellers on the West Coast, well-known for its broad selection of both popular and esoteric titles. Down the block are **Moe's, Shakespeare & Co.** and **Half-Price Books,** all specializing in used books, and **Shambala,** known for its religious and occult books.

For special interests the Yellow Pages of the telephone directory are the best guide to bookstores.

Movies

Motion picture theaters can be divided into several groups, each with its own devotees: first-runs, drive-ins, foreign films, and revivals.

First-run movies, fresh from Hollywood, are being screened for the first time. Most American theaters show exclusively first-runs — some showing them at slightly reduced price after the first wave of popularity is over. Most theaters offer afternoon matinees on Wednesday, Saturday and Sunday with discounted ticket prices. Tickets range from $4 to $5 in the evening, $2 to $3 for matinees.

Drive-ins, a fading American eccentricity, are theaters with large outdoor screens. The audience watches the movie from their automobiles and rents a sound box to hear the sound track. Most show first-run films, particularly horror, cowboy, and adventure films. Tickets are priced "per car" rather than "per person".

Only the large cities have theaters that specialize in foreign films, subtitled for American audiences. In addition, universities often screen such classics on campus. In San Francisco these theaters are specially listed in the Datebook (pink) section of the Sunday newspaper. Among them are the **Clay, Lumiere, Bridge** and **Surf** and, in the East Bay, the **Rialto** and the **Elmwood.**

A number of movie theaters in recent years have discovered a solid market for revivals, of old classics. The ticket price for these movie theaters is a couple of dollars less than first-run theaters. Most revival movies are shown on a double bill (two movies for the price of one). In San Francisco the most noted revival theater is the **Castro,** a renovated 1930s movie palace complete with gilded ceiling, balconies and a live organist on weekends. The **Pacific Film Archive** in Berkeley (part of the University of California) takes a scholarly approach to films. Here you will see particularly obscure masterpieces, often in conjunction with lectures by people involved in making them. Other revival houses include the **UC Theater** in Berkeley, the **J Street Theater** in Sacramento, and the **Festival** in Palo Alto.

For a complete listing of current movies, the local newspaper is the best resource.

Performing Arts Centers

Arts organizations like to huddle together to weather the storms, or perhaps to make a bigger splash than any single group can make alone. A

Festivals/Events

For the latest in entertainment and events in the Bay Area, check the pink "Datebook" section of the weekend *Chronicle/Examiner* newspaper, or the calendar sections of the *Bay Guardian, San Francisco* magazine or *California* magazine.

Listings are always subject to last-minute changes. So call ahead to confirm the event. For a daily taped message of special activities in San Francisco, dial 391–2000. This events message is also available in Spanish (391–2122), French (391–2003), and German (391–2004). For gay events in San Francisco, dial 861–1100.

January

Bay Area Music Awards — Known as the "Bammies," these annual awards honor local pop, country and rock musicians. Rub shoulders with the likes of Santana, Grateful Dead, Jefferson Starship, Boz Scaggs and Van Morrison. California Hall, San Francisco (T-E-L-E-T-I-X).

fine example is the **Civic Center** in San Francisco along Van Ness Avenue between Fell and McAllister Streets. The **Louise M. Davies Symphony Hall** (431–5400), **San Francisco Opera House** (431–1210) and **Veterans War Memorial Building** (housing the Museum of Modern Art (863–8800), and the Herbst Auditorium) are lined up along the west side of Van Ness in one majestic row. Behind the Opera House on Franklin is the brand new home of the San Francisco Ballet (621–3838).

Another nest of arts organizations can be found at Fort Mason. Located at the intersection of Marina and Buchanan Streets, it is a converted army base that now houses a number of smaller, innovative arts and environmental groups. Fort Mason is home to the **Magic Theater, Peoples Theater, City Arts Monthly,** and **Dance Coalition,** among others. For information about events at Fort Mason, the central information number is 441–5705.

Both San Jose and Fresno have city-built and municipally-operated centers for major art activities: **Center for the Performing Arts,** 225 Almaden, San Jose (408-288-7469) and **Fresno Convention Center,** 700 M Street, Fresno (209-488-1511).

In Oakland, the **Paramount Theater** at 20th and Broadway (465–6400) is the main performance space for the Oakland Symphony and Oakland Ballet, as well as for touring music, dance and theater groups.

Bing Crosby Golf Tournament — The old crooner has passed on, but his game is still swinging. This world-famous golf classic is The Sporting Event of the year in the Carmel-Monterey area. The first hole is outside the Lodge in Pebble Beach. (408–624–3811).

Faceters Fair — Learn all facets of jewelry making and gem cutting. Seminars teach everything from how to recognize fine gems to where to buy the best. Contests, demonstrations and exhibits. Santa Clara County fairgrounds, San Jose. (408–295–3050).

Fiddler's Contest — We're talking here about bluegrass, swing, classical and Appalachian footstomping music. Each contestant has four mintues to play a hoedown and a waltz. The horsehairs tickle the catgut strings from morning till nightfall, with groups of newfound friends and fiddlers clustering about in the parking lot. Citrus Fairgrounds, Cloverdale (707–894–3495); about 1½ hours north of San Francisco.

Fungus Fair — Take a few tips on mushroom picking and eating from the experts at the Mycological Society. More than 200 types of world mushrooms are displayed, and visitors soon learn how to identify the poisonous varieties. Hall of Flowers, Golden Gate Park, San Francisco. (566–7363).

San Francisco Examiner Games — Sponsored by the city's afternoon newspaper, this is a major indoor track and field meet for amateurs. Both men and women athletes from the States and abroad compete at the Cow Palace. (469–6065).

Shrine East-West Football Game — This annual college classic collects crowds at the Stanford Stadium in Palo Alto. (661–0291).

Snoopy Cup Women's Tennis Classic — Recent years have seen Billie Jean King, Rosie Casals and Virginia Wade compete for the "Queen of the Court" title. Redwood Empire Arena, Santa Rosa. (707–546–7147).

Sports and Boat Show — Now in its 42nd year, this popular show fills the main arena of the Cow Palace south of San Francisco with hundreds of pleasure craft and marine accessory dealers. Kids can test their skills in the batting cage, at the free throw line, and on the football field. Instruction is available at the fly-casting pool and the archery range. One entire hall is filled with recreational vehicles. (469–6065).

February

California Junior Miss Pageant — A bevy of young beauties parade about the Veterans Memorial Building, showing off their good looks and looking forward to being selected as the prettiest miss in the state. Santa Rosa. (707–526–1106).

Chinese New Year — One of the largest Chinese communities outside of Asia celebrates its new year in style. The highlight of the week's festivities is the loud, crowded parade with a quarter of a million people watching the procession of oriental floats, bands, marching units, beauty queens and the block-long Golden Dragon. Other events include the official opening ceremonies the Miss Chinatown U.S.A. pageant and coronation, special art exhibits, and walking tours. Most restaurants in Chinatown are closed during the celebrations (974–6900).

Crab Races — This sporting event is held each year among the inhabitants of the northern coastal community of Crescent City. Dinner follows the race. (707–464–3174).

Dog Show — Sponsored by the Golden Gate Kennel Club, this is one of the last remaining benched shows in the country. Some 2500 prize pooches sit, lie down, heel and shake, inside the Cow Palace over the weekend. Arena shows each afternoon feature canine performers. (469–6065).

Peggy Lee — The stylish singing star's appearance at the Venetian Room of Fairmont Hotel is her traditional Valentine to the city. (772–5163).

Snowshoe Walk — A state park ranger shows willing walkers how to follow animal tracks in the snow. Sugar Pine Point State Park on State 89 near Tahoe City. (916–525–7232).

Tidepool Walks — Led by naturalists at the Fitzgerald Marine Reserve on weekends in February when low tides permit. these hour-long walks illuminate a half-mile of colourful coastline covered with creepy little creatures. Moss Beach, north of Monterrey. (728–3584).

Viennese Ball — An annual Valentine-Day tradition is this evening of great waltzes played by the Berkeley Symphony Orchestra. California Hall, San Francisco. (527–3436).

Virginia Slims Tennis Series — The best women tennis pros compete for $150,000 total prize money. Oakland Coliseum. (635–7800).

March

Camelia Festival — Sacramento honors its official flower with more than 30 separate events, including the Camelia Ball, the Camelia Show, and the Camelia Parade. (916–442–7673).

City Golf Championships — This single golf tournament is the largest in the country. Harding Park and the Lincoln Park Golf Course in San Francisco are crowded on weekends, all month long. (495–5776).

Coin Fair — The 21st annual gathering of coin collectors is no small change. Cathedral Hill Hotel, San Francisco. (776–8200).

Daffodil Festival — Celebrate spring in the city at the 43rd annual Daffodil Festival on San Francisco's Maiden Lane. Thousands of yellow flowers decorate the shops and restaurants off Union Square. Street musicians perform, and mimes hand out free flowers. (981–3333).

Easter Seal Western Festival — This jamboree is one of the largest country-western fairs in the country. There are arts-and-crafts booths, games, clowns, food, drinks, country music, and even a mechanical bull for urban cowboys. Cal Expo, Sacramento. (916–481–5024).

Hangtown Motocross Classic — More than 650 pro and amateur riders from all across the country pull into "Hangtown," which is the name Placerville went by in Gold Rush days. They ride for points, awards and good ol' money. Prairie City Park on White Rock Road. (916–920–1121).

St. Patrick's Day — You'd never know San Francisco was so Irish-till their Day on the Green turns up. How do the Irish celebrate? They drink. Join the merriment and have an Irish coffee at such popular pubs as the Buena Vista (2765 Hyde), Pat O'Shea's (3754 Geary), Abbey Tavern (4100 Geary), or Harrington's (245 Front). Highlights of the holiday include the longest parade the city ever sees (with hundreds of bands, floats and marching units weaving down Market Street), the Grand Ball at the United Irish Cultural Center near the zoo (661–2700), and the Snake Race featuring 80 serpents speeding down a 10-foot course at the Crown Zellerbach Plaza at Sansome and Market. (392–6552).

Whale-Watching Boat Tours — Some sensitive stomachs can get a bit upset out there on the choppy high seas, but what better way is there to observe the annual migration of the California gray whale than from a boat? Daily tours continue through mid May. Pillar Point Fishing Trips; reservations suggested (T-E-L-E-T-I-X).

April

Cherry Blossom Festival — Many citizens from Japan travel to this annual celebration in San Francisco's Japantown, always held on two consecutive weekends in April. Most events are free: martial arts shows, an Akita dog exhibit, taiko drumming, tea ceremonies, and demonstrations in doll making, calligraphy, flower arranging and origami. Hundreds of performers participate in the climactic parade from City Hall to the Japan Center. (922–6776).

Easter Sunrise Service — It happens at the crack of dawn atop Mt. Davidson overlooking San Francisco. Muni has a special bus to the cross at the top. (974–6900).

Fireman's Muster — An authentic bucket brigade, a hand-pumping contest, and a hose-cart race. Non-firemen can participate too; munch on the barbecue or plug into the Sunday parade. Columbia State Park near Sonora. (209–532–1982).

Fisherman's Fantasy — This annual festival in Bodega Bay attracts more than 25,000 visitors to the Sonoma coast to watch the Mardi Grass parade of decorated fishing boats sail the channel. Activities include a bathtub race, kite-flying championships, footrace, skeet shoot and golf tournament. There are also barbecue, art shows and a rummage sale. (707–875–3422).

Folsom Prison Art Show — Inmates present their multimedia artwork (most of which can be purchased) on the last weekend of the month. Larkin Hall, Folson Prison. (916–985–2561).

Junior Grand National — This is the best *little* rodeo and horse show to come each year to the Cow Palace in San Francisco. Events include livestock judging, a high-school rodeo with 700 young riders, Hereford heifer sale, swine, lamb and steer auctions, English and western horse shows. (469–6065).

Rhododendron Festival — The city of Eureka blossoms this month. The Opening Day parade is followed by a dog show, golf and bowling tournaments, a square dance hoedown, carnival rides, and musical entertainment at the fairgrounds, plus a plethora of rhododendron displays around the town. (707–442–3738).

Spring Walks — Strolling through the California countryside is fine on your own, but if you'd like a park ranger to point out the native plants and animals, go take a hike in the East Bay: At the Sunol Regional Wilderness (862–2244), the Black Diamond Mines Regional Preserve near Antioch (757–2620), or the Tilden Nature Area in Berkeley (525–2233).

May

Bay-to-Breakers — This is The Biggie of the footraces; more bodies battle out this race than any other foot fair in the state. Thousands of joggers (and twice as many feet) race 7.63 miles from the Embarcadero to the ocean. (777–7827).

Book Sale — Sponsored by the San Francisco Public Library, this book sale is the biggest in the west. Admission is free, and the used library books sell for cheap. Pick a few well-chosen words at Fort Mason (558–3770).

Bud Wilson Memorial Rodeo — In adddition to the usual cow-roping, bronc-busting rodeo events, there is a $1.98 Beauty Queen contest and a Rodeo Man of the Year award. Folsom City Park. (916–985–2793).

Calaveras County Frog-Jumping Contest — You can get a real kick out of this county fair; hop over to the fairgrounds near Angel's Camp to witness grown-up adults vying over whose favorite frog jumps the farthest. Other events: carnival rides, rodeo, air shows, fireworks and musical entertainment. It's fun and games for the 3,000 frogs and 40,000 humans. (209–736–2561).

Cinco de Mayo (Mexican Independence Day, the Fifth of May) — This is celebrated in San Jose for a whole week. Starting with a flag-raising ceremony at City Hall, there's a parade, fiesta, arts-and-crafts exhibits, and costumed dance performances. (408–275–8506).

Concours d'Elegance — Countless classes of classy cars, from horseless carriages to spiffy sports cars, on display in an elegant environment. Hillsborough, one of the ritziest neighborhoods on the San Francisco Peninsula, welcomes thousands of car buffs to its William H. Crocker School grounds to admire opulent autos (344–2272). And the Silverado County Club in Napa is another appropriate home for a concours, also at the end of this month. (652–9202).

Festival of the Sea — Honoring our maritime heritage are musical performances (shanties, ballads, fishing and folk songs), dances, panel discussions, sailor art demonstrations, lectures, films and children's programs. Aquatic Park and Hyde Street Pier, San Francisco. (771–3488).

Rose Shows — The San Francisco Rose Society's 43rd Annual is one of the best rose shows in the West. There are 1,000 cut roses on display, all kinds and all colors, just for Mother's Day. Hall of Flowers in Golden Gate Park (731–8377). Other rose shows this month include the San Mateo Rose Show in the downtown area (574–4050), the East Bay Rose Society Show at the Lakeside Park Garden Center at Lake Merritt in Oakland (655–3356), and the Luther Burbank Rose Festival in Santa Rosa (707–546–ROSE).

Rowing Championships — Strokers from more than 20 West-Coast colleges compete in this fast-action sport. Redwood Shores Lagoon, Redwood City (592–4170).

Square Dance Festival — There's no getting around this one: square dancing is as close as you can come to a national dance. Watch from the balcony of the San Francisco Civic Auditorium as the whirled turn: hoedowns, round dancing, teen dances, and fashion shows. Be there *and* be square (726–6272).

June

Bicycle Classic — Some 10,000 spectators invade Gold Rush country in the 24th annual Nevada City Bicycle Race. The best bikers in America break away through the Sierra foothills (916–265–9334).

Gay Freedom Day Parade — Gay Pride Week features hundreds of thousands of celebrants and dozens of events throughout the City, especially in the two "gay gulches"; Polk Street and Castro Street. Climaxing the week's activities is the Parade, which lasts four hours, starting at the Ferry Building and whipping down Market Street to City Hall (861–5404).

Miss California Beauty Pageant — Thirty four works of native art are on display at the Santa Cruz Civic Auditorium — young ladies from Crescent City to San Diego. Activities at this seaside resort include a public reception, parade, and the judging competitions. (408–423–1113).

Oregon Shakespeare Festival — One of the best Shakespearean companies in California is in Oregon, in the charming, woodsy town of Ashland, just over the border off Interstate 5. The season is almost six months long (ending November 1) but the pay is *really* the thing during the summer months. There are three stages (including an outdoor Elizabethan theater), nine plays alternating in repertory, and a Shakespearean movie series on Mondays. (503–482–4331).

Ox Roast — On the first Sunday of the month, the bull is burned in the plaza of the quaint, gentrified town of Sonoma; dinner is $7. (707–996–1033).

San Francisco Birthday Celebration — The anniversary of the city is celebrated every year since its founding day with a concert of Spanish and Mexican music and dance in the bandshell of Golden Gate Park, a traditional mass at Mission Dolores, and a civic luncheon at the Presidio Officers Club. (282–8502).

Sand Sculpture and San Castle Contest — Build your own, and win a prize in this 18th annual competition at R.W. Crown Memorial State Beach on Alameda Island near Oakland. The dirty work starts at 9 a.m. (531–9300).

Shasta District Fair — At the Anderson Fairgrounds near Mt. Shasta are concerts, games, food, and the diaper derby; a race where trophies are awarded to the babies (up to one year old) who crawl the fastest. (916–926–4865).

Street Fairs — A San Francisco summer tradition is the neighborhood block party: The street is closed to auto traffic, and booths are set up on the sidewalks for food, fun and games. These three fairs are of a commercial nature, with high quality crafts for sale. Check them out, but be prepared for bruised elbows — as they are popular weekend events for locals and tourists alike. **Upper Grant Avenue Street Fair** brings 200 artists and thousands of shoppers to the foot of Telegraph Hill between Vallejo and Filbert streets. Most shops and restaurants stay open for the fair (982–2229). **Union Street Spring Festival** features the famed Waiters' Race, a show of fashions from local boutiques, a tea dance, and musical entertainment on three stages. More than 250 arts-and-crafts booths line the blocks of Union Street from Gough to Fillmore. (567–3055). **Noe Valley Street Fair** is both commercial and *spiritual*: there are psychic and astral readings, palmists, and tarot card readers. Along 24th Street between Church and Diamond. (974–6900).

Stern Grove — This natural amphitheater, surrounded by redwoods and eucalyptus trees, near

Sloat Boulevard and 19th Avenue is home to the oldest, free summer-music festival in the country. San Franciscans have been coming to the Grove for almost 50 years to enjoy a variety of musical concerts — from Beethoven, ballet, opera and chamber music, to country-western, pops and New-Orleans-style jazz. Concerts start at 2 p.m. every Sunday till the end of August but come earlier with a blanket and picnic basket, and reserve a spot on the glade. (398–6551).

July

Fourth of July — A nation's birthday hardly goes unnoticed. This weekend sees celebrations in every hamlet and town across the country. They range from glorious festivities with large crowds (like "Tapestry in Talent" in downtown San Jose: 408 293–9727) to local feasts (like the salmon barbecue at Fort Bragg on the North coast: 707 964–6353). Most towns have picnics and parades in the day, then fireworks at nightfall. The Presidio is base for most of San Francisco's Independence Day entertainment and fireworks. (556–0560).

Bear Valley Festival — Classical music wafts through the Alpine wilderness east of Angels Camp and Stockton for three weeks, late July to early August. (209–753–2844).

Cable Car Bell-Ringing Competition — Conductors and gripmen compete in this annual, uniquely San Francisco event. Thousands of on-lookers flock to Union Square to listen to the clings and clangs. (392–4880).

California Rodeo — This annual event, since 1911, includes steer wrestling, bareback, saddle-bronc and bull riding competitions, horse races, wild-cow milking and all kinds of horse shows. Salinas. (408–757–2951).

County Fairs — Local fairs are America-in-miniature. Usually lasting one-to-two weeks, county fairs are filled with food, arts-and-crafts and gaming booths, livestock shows, nightly entertainment, carnival rides, horseracing and home economics exhibits. Admission is under $5. Fairs are all-day events.
Alameda County Fair includes a celebrity grape-stomp, wine-making contests and an industrial education exhibitions. Pleasanton (846–2881).
Marin County Fair features a national film festival. San Rafael. (499–6400).
Merced Fair features bluegrass and beer gardens, auto racing, a destruction derby and a rodeo. Merced (209–722–1506).
Humboldt County Fair has brought entertainment and excitement to the quaint old village of Ferndale for over 125 years (707–786–8511).
Napa County Fair is held in Calistoga. There are car races, horse-pulling contests, a parade and a beauty pageant. (707–942–5111).
San Mateo County Fair features a fabulous floral show with hundreds of the best blooms in the state on display. San Mateo. (345–3541).
Solano County Fair features a Farmer's Market, demolition derby, women's and men's rodeos. Vallejo (707–644–4401).
Sonoma County Fair is the perfect event for horsing around in Santa Rosa: daily rodeos, a horse show and parimutuel betting on thorough bred racing. (707–528–3247).
San Francisco Fair and Exposition is the urban alternative to county fairs. In addition to the traditional exhibits (food booths, an outdoor carnival, continuous entertainment), there are "city–fied" contests for the best "come-on one-liner" and the best telephone answering machine message. Moscone Center. (557–1168).

Gilroy Garlic Festival — You've never seen, smelled, or tasted so much stinky stuff. Garlic bulbs are displayed in everything from braids to jewelry, and there are more different, more distinctive dishes to be sampled than you can shake a spatula at! In Gilroy, the garlic capital of the world. (408–842–1625).

Sahara Summer Blackjack Classic — The games are played simultaneously in Vegas, Reno and Tahoe. Hefty prize money; open to all. (800–522–1500).

August

ACC Craft Fair — The largest of its kind on the West Coast, the fair features more than 350 craftspeople, working with ceramics, glass, leather, fiber, wood and metal. Fort Mason Center, San Francisco. (566–0560).

Cal Expo — The state fair displays the best and brightest; from farm and industrial products, to star-studded entertainment. Sacramento. (916–924–2000).

Castro Street Fair — Some people come to see the arts-and-crafts displays; most people come to stare at the gays peddling their wares. San Francisco. (346–2640).

Gravenstein Apple Fair — Sebastopol, a fruit-fertile farm area, gets to the core of the local fare with applesauce, apple pancakes, apple ice cream and apple picking at nearby orchards. Ragle Ranch Park. (707–544–5575).

Renaissance Pleasure Fair — The Blackpoint Forest is transformed into an English village during harvest time, 400 years ago. More than 1,500 actors, musicians, jesters, jugglers, acrobats, dancers and mimes dress in Elizabethan costume and stroll each weekend through the "village". Unusual food, drink, and quality crafts available. Continues through mid September. Novato. (883–2473).

Ringling Brothers and Barnum & Bailey Circus — You've never seen a circus so spectacular as this three-ring show: wild animal acts, terrific trapeze feats, trained elephants and carloads of clowns. Oakland Coliseum (635–7800) and the Cow Palace in San Francisco (469–6065), followed by a week in Fresno. (209–233–8368).

San Francisco Flower Show — The emphasis is on flowers that grow best here in Northern California (begonias, dahlias, roses, fuchias) but many exotic flowers (orchids, African violets, succulents) are also included among the hundreds of flower arrangements, blooms and flowering plants on display. Hall of Flowers, Golden Gate Park. (558–3623).

Steinbeck Festival — The home town of California's World-famous author salutes John Steinbeck with movies, plays, and tours of places prominent in his novels. Salinas. (408–758–7311).

Ugly Dog Contest — Pick the most pathetic pooch when the entire Sonoma-Marin fairgrounds in Petaluma goes to the dogs. (707–762–8428).

Wine Country Music Festivals — Spend a summer eve sitting outdoors among the vines, enjoying good wine and good cheese and great music. Such famous favorites as Benny Goodman, Dizzy Gillespie, Stephane Grappelli, Joan Baez and Sergio Mendes have performed among the grape vines. The two main concert series are sponsored by Robert Mondavi in Rutherford (707–963–9611) and Paul Masson Winery in Saratoga (408–725–4275), but there are also occasional performances at Geyser Peak in Geyserville (707–433–6585), Charles Krug Winery in St. Helena (707–963–7756), Buena Vista Winery in Sonoma. (707–938–8504), and other smaller wineries.

September

Aki Matsuri — Events abound in Japantown during this fall festival: dancing, taiko drumming, tea ceremonies, an Akita dog contest, martial arts demonstrations, musical performances, films, theater, origami, bonsai and flower-arranging workshops, and the popular Food Bazaar. Japan Center, San Francisco. (922–6776).

The Big Fresno Fair is the biggest show Fresno ever sees. The 17 day fair features parimutuel horse racing, musical entertainment, nightly fireworks, logging championships, rodeo, boxing, tractor pulls, livestock shows and auctions, clowns, bands, and agricultural exhibits. (209–255–3081).

Feline Fantasy — One of the largest cat shows on the West Coast features 500 merry meowers of all breeds inside the Cow Palace. (469–6065).

In-the-Water Boat Show — Three hundred sail- and powerboats bob about the Mariner Square Marina on Alameda Island off Oakland. There are free sailboat rides, displays of marine clothing, and plenty of relaxed salesmen. You can learn to yacht at this two-week-long event, a boat-buyer's dream. (436–4664).

Labor Day Festivities — Founded in honor of the workmen of America, this national holiday is held on the first Monday of September. Unions and local organization traditionally sponsor picnics, parades, parties and speeches. Check your local listings. Two unusual labors of love are: the old-time Steam Threshing Bee on a small, family ranch near Red Bluff, 125 miles north of Sacramento (916–385–1389); and the Festival of the Saws, a series of musical concerts and workshops in honor of lumberjacks and carpenters, in downtown Santa Cruz. (408–476–2800).

Nevada State Fair — Horses, cows, sheep, tractors, clowns carnival rides and cotton candy come to Reno (north of Lake Tahoe) for four days. (702–827–4914).

Rubber Ducky Raft Race — 500 rubber and inflatable rafts race around a landfill lagoon in Foster City, south of San Francisco. With all the splashing and crashing of rafts, the 25,000 spectators, clowns, carnival rides and cotton candy come to Reno (north of Lake Tahoe) for four days. (702–827–4914).

Russian River Jazz Festival — Held on Johnson's Beach, right on the river in Guerneville. (707–869–9000).

San Francisco Opera — One of the cultural highlights of the year is the opening of the 62nd fall opera season — hand-in-hand with the new San Francisco Symphony season. War Memorial Opera House and Davies Symphony Hall. (864–3330 and 431–5400).

Scottish Gathering and Games — Thousands of kilted contenders invade the Sonoma County fairgrounds in this annual event. Highlights from the Highlands include caber-tossing, putting the stone, and throwing the 56-pound (25.4 kilogram) weight. Some 200 Scottish dancers and 20 bagpipe bands perform. There's a soccer match and plenty of Scottish foods, crafts and ales. Santa Rosa. (707–528–3247).

Transamerica Open Tennis Championships — The kings of the court compete in this high-stakes annual tournament. Cow Palace, San Francisco. (469–6065).

Barefoot Waterskiing Championships — Skimming the surface of the lagoon at Marine World/Africa U.S.A. are the best barefoot jumpers and trick skiiers in the world. Later in the month, the amusement park provides free milk during the annual Great Milk Carton Boat Race — 240 people-powered boats, constructed from empty milk cartons, racing around the lagoon. No charge to these special events after paying the regular $10 entrance free. Redwood City. (591–7676).

Columbus Day Celebration — Columbus Day is the Italian community's largest and oldest observance. Most activities take place during the first two weeks of the month in North Beach, center of the Italian community. Highlights include: bocce ball tournament, blessing of the fishing fleet, a re-enactment of Columbus landing in the new world, and a spectacular parade. For full schedule, call San Francisco Visitors Bureau (974–6900).

Exotic-Erotic Ball — Halloween Eve in San Francisco is a dress-up affair with strange people parading around. One of the wilder parties is the come-as-you-are ball; be sure to bring a camera (T-E-L-E-T-I-X). You can also find bizarre costumes in the "gay gulches" of the City — Polk Street (round Sutter) and Castro Street (up from Market).

Ghirardelli Square — This shopping complex celebrates its 20th anniversary with free, outdoor concerts and games for the children. San Francisco. (775–5500).

Grand National Rodeo — Professional cowboys and cowgirls ride, rope, and bust broncs in the arena. But there's also the pomp and pageantry of the west's largest horse show, as well as a complete top quality livestock exposition. Held at the Cow Palace, built specifically for the Grand National in 1941. From the end of the month through the first week in November (469–6065).

Healdsburg Harvest Hoedown — Healdsburg heralds the approach of autumn with hayrides, sidewalk sales, a grape stomp and bluegrass music. At the downtown plaza of this quaint, small town. (707–433–6935).

Pumpkin Festival — Each year growers along the San Mateo coast produce up to 6,000 tons of pumpkins. The hassle-free hamlet of Half Moon Bay is home to the World Heavyweight Pumpkin Championship and Pumpkin Festival. Hordes of Halloween merrymakers eat their fill of pumpkin pie, bread, pumpkin candy and ice cream, watch the parade and visit the hundreds of arts-and-crafts booths lining Main Street. (726–5202).

San Francisco International Film Festival — The annual festival features films every night at the Palace of Fine Arts and also at the Castro Theatre. Many events, especially the daytime showings, are free or moderately priced. Highlights are Opening Night (when the stars come out) and the Tribute Series to major moviemakers. (221–9055).

Scarecrow Contest — Some farmers find fun in scaring away birds from their fields with fanciful decoys, which decorate the pumpkin patch outside the Nut Tree Restaurant in Vacaville, north of San Francisco on Route 80. (916–448–1818).

November

Dickens Christmas Fair — Fort Mason in San Francisco is transformed into 19th century London, the Charles Dickens era. Streets are crowded with handmade merchandise and toys for Christmas shoppers; carolers and entertainers cruise through the fair in colorful costumes; hearty foods, beverages appropriate to the season, and a delicious onion soup tempt hungry visitors. Through the end of December. (441–5705).

Fol de Rol — The San Francisco Opera's big, glamorous party is a benefit starring lead perfor-

mers of the current opera productions. Balcony seats are moderately priced. Civic Auditorium. (431–1210).

Harvest Festival and Christmas Crafts Market — Get a taste of 19th Century rural America in a 20th Century city. Craftspeople and entertainers are dressed in period costumes; there's downhome bluegrass music and barbershop quarters; foods, beverages and crafts are representative of the period; there are fashion shows, corn-husking contests and lace-making demonstrations. Brooks Hall, San Francisco. (974–6900).

Ice Capades — The greatest show on ice swishes and swirls, slips, slides and glides into, first, the Fresno Convention Center (209–233–8368), then the Oakland Coliseum. (635–7800).

International Auto Show — The largest assemblage of new domestic and imported cars fills the Moscone Center. There are also antique, classic, prototype and race cars on display. San Francisco. (974–4000).

Karate Championships — This nationally-rated "A" tournament attracts top U.S. competitors. San Francisco Civic Auditorium. (974–6900).

Kool Jazz Festival — Great names in jazz (with styles ranging from traditional to funk) perform at several clubs and concert halls in San Francisco and Oakland. The Bay Area is the last stop on their 20-city tour, so this cool music can get pretty hot and heavy. (T-E-L-E-T-I-X).

KQED Wine and Food Festival — This benefit for San Francisco's public TV station features fine wines donated by 50 wineries and food (from hors d'oeuvres to desserts) prepared by some of the city's best restaurants. Trade Show Center, San Francisco. (864–2000).

December

Department Store Santas — Part of the Christmas tradition is the wink, the pat, the friendly intimacy a youngster gets from a department-store Santa Claus. At the stores suggested here, your child can have a picture taken in the lap of Mr. Claus from free to $4. But the hearty chuckle and Christmas wishes are on the house.

San Francisco Santas: Emporium Capwell, 835 Market Street; I. Magnin, Geary and Stockton; Macys, Stockton and O'Farrell.

East Bay Santas: Bayfair Mall, San Leandro; Eastmont Shopping Center, Oakland; Emporium Capwell, Broadway and 20th Street, Oakland; Hilltop Mall, Richmond; Hink's, Shattuck Avenue and Kittredge Street, Berkeley.

North and South Poles: Serramonte Center, Daly City; Eastridge Shopping Center, San Jose; The Pruneyard, Campbell; The Cooper House, Santa Cruz; Strawberry Town & Country Village, Mill Valley.

Elegant Celebration of Christmas — This decorative show of 80 fantasy Christmas trees and table settings designed by famous film and TV stars is a fund-raiser for the local American Conservatory Theater. There are food booths, a restaurant, a boutique and carolers. Trade Show Center, San Francisco. (673–6440).

Hanukkah Celebration — In San Francisco's Union Square, this Jewish winter holiday lasts for eight days. A massive menorah is kindled each sundown. Highlights include an outdoor concert of Hasidic music, stories from local rabbis, and warm words from Mayor Feinstein and the consul general of Israel. (845–7791).

New Year's Eve Parties — Plenty of parties at the musical clubs and discos around town. Two very different ways to go — Ritzy: The Hyatt Regency in San Francisco (788–1234) hosts a six-room, six-party celebration — ballroom, disco, polka, calypso, cabaret and big-band sounds (Tickets $35); and Country: the downhome Firemen's Ball (707–894–5790) expects farmers, firemen and lumber millers to bring their own hip flasks and fox-trot around the Citrus Fairgrounds up in Cloverdale (Tickets $4).

Nutcracker Suites — Sugarplum fairies twirl, snowflakes dance, toy soldiers battle troops of king-sized mice, and children are awestruck with delight ... with Tchaikovsky's marvelous ballet, the *Nutcracker*. Every year at this time, there are dozens of *Nutcracker* ballets performed throughout Northern California. The **San Francisco Ballet** (at the Opera House, 431–1210) is the biggest and the brightest — with 250 costumes handmade from silk, satin and velvet and a 40-piece orchestra. The **Oakland Ballet** (at Paramount Theater, 465–6400) though not quite as opulent and elegant, is equally enjoyable.

Nightlife

The Bay Area is a young area and has plenty of nightlife — from easy listening to exotic entertainment. The pink "Datebook" section of the Sunday newspaper provides up-to-date details of the week's nightclub offerings and dancing opportunities. The Appendix lists some of the standard, ongoing fare.

For small, funky clubs featuring local talent singing and playing the blues, Oakland-style, it's best to visit West and East Oakland. However, these clubs come and go; the best source of information is the weekly East Bay newspaper, *The Express* (653–7332).

Strip Shows

Certainly San Francisco has more to offer than bare buttocks but visitors are constantly drawn to the neon lights of Broadway, seeking their pounds of flesh. Well, better to stroll along Broadway than through San Francisco's other red-light district, the **Tenderloin** (roughly bounded by Ellis, Taylor, McAllister and Larkin streets).

The strip shows along Broadway are tamer and the drinks more expensive, but the all-round atmosphere and proximity to North Beach makes them more upbeat. The over-priced drinks on Broadway contain more water than alcohol and it takes an interminable amount of time for the performers to take off their clothes. But if this is your idea of fun, then give your regards to Broadway. often find drunks asleep on the sidewalks and prostitutes at work on the street corners.

The Condor. The first club in the country to go topless, the first to go bottomless, and the first in the hearts of its countrymen. 300 Columbus Ave. (392–4443).

Garden of Eden. Its "Naked Love Act" never fully reaches fruition, and its "Naked Women Wrestlers" never really get hurt. 529 Broadway. (397–2596).

Hungry i. The greatest comedy club of the 1960s (spotlighting the likes of Steve Allen, Mort Sahl, Jonathan Winters and Lenny Bruce) now boasts "Amateur Night with College Co-eds." 546 Broadway. (362–7763).

Off Broadway. Male strippers. 501 Broadway. (986–4449).

Sports and Outdoor Activities

There are two ways to be a good sport: You watch it, and You do it.

Spectator Sports

Baseball

The Bay Area is blessed with two major league baseball teams, the **San Francisco Giants** and the **Oakland Athletics** (or Oakland A's, as they are usually called). Over the years, the two teams have scored similar success stories, their yearly attendance is about the same, and their fans are equally fanatic. They both play about 80 home games each year in a lengthy season that lasts from April to October. The main different between the two teams lies in the parks they play in. The Giants bat it out in Candlestick Park (467–8000), a cold, colossal coliseum with whipping winds you won't believe. (Be sure to bring a sweater and windbreaker!) The A's slug it out in the warmer, sunnier, much more mellow Oakland Coliseum (638–0500).

Other than the weather, both teams provide a similarly enjoyable American outing. Prices ($1 to $6) are the same, as are starting times (1:05 p.m. for afternoon games, 7:35 p.m. for evening games), length of games (three, sometimes four hours), and quality of the hot dogs and beer.

Basketball

The **Golden State Warriors** have a ball from late October through the middle of April. The team holds court 41 times during the season at the Oakland Coliseum Arena. Tuesday and Thursday night games start at 7:35 p.m., Saturday night games start at 8:05 p.m. Tickets are $5 to $11 (638–6000).

Football

Baseball may be the national sport but the football games are the ones that are always sold out. The champion **San Francisco 49ers** pass the pigskin in Candlestick Park from early September through the end of December but there's only eight home games so tickets are seldom available. When there are seats remaining, they cost $15 each (468–2249).

College football is not professional, but it is accessible. Stanford University's season runs from September through November; games start at 1 p.m. or 1:30 p.m. (497–1021). University of California at Berkeley has six home games during the season (642–5150).

The most recent football team in Northern California is the **USFL's Oakland Invaders**. There are nine home games in the season (March through July) and seats are often available as late as a few days before the game. Tickets are $11 to $13, Oakland Coliseum. (638–7800).

Horse Racing

Not only can you sit and watch sleek horses out to trot, but you can wager as little as $2 on your favourite filly and win oodles of money ... if you're lucky. Luck (and a love of horses) draws thousands of racing fans to the two Bay Area tracks, **Golden Gate Fields** in the East Bay and **Bay Meadows** on the Peninsula. There are usually nine races a day (five days a week) during the season, and you can gamble as much as you like on any race.

Bay Meadows — The oldest, busiest and one of the most beautiful ovals in the State is located in San Mateo. The thoroughbred horses race from mid September to early February, quarter horses run from mid February to early May, and the San Mateo Fair offers an assortment of horses (thoroughbreds, Appaloosas and quarter) the first two weeks in September. The first race is either at 12:30 p.m. or 1 p.m. and there are special 4 p.m. races on Fridays. The track is open Wednesday through Sunday. Admission $2.50 (general), $5 (club house) and $10 (turf club; dress code enforced). Parking $2–$5 (valet). Off Highway 101 (574–7223).

Golden Gate Fields — The highlight here is the thoroughbred racing, early February through late June, Tuesday through Saturday. Post times and admission are similar to Bay Meadows. Off Highway 580 in Albany. (526–3020).

Participant Sport

Golf

Golf is a year-round sport in California, and just about every town has a municipal golf course.

Rated in the top 10 golf courses of the States.

Pebble Beach in Carmel is California's world-famous championship golf course. Green fees are $75 and everything else about this semi-private club is as expensive. But the setting, along the ruged Pacific Coast, and the course itself are truly beautiful. To make sure you can reserve green time, stay overnight in the lodge. For reservations call (408) 624–3811. If you want some serious lessions, Ben Doyle, the mentor of Bobby Clampett, teaches golf in the Monterrey area, Tel. (408) 624–1581.

Another top golf course in a country club setting is **Silverado Country Club** in Napa, the heart of the wine country. It's a 36-hole course with a Southern Plantation style lodge and separate cabins. Tel. (916) 255–2970.

In addition to private golf and country clubs, San Francisco has four public golf courses: **Harding Park Golf Course** is on Lake Merced (Harding Road off Skyline Blvd); **Lincoln Municipal Golf Course** overlooks Golden Gate Park (Lincoln Blvd. and Clement Street); the **Golden Gate Park Golf Course** (47th Avenue and JFK Drive) and the **Jack Fleming Golf Course** (Harding Road off Skyline Blvd.).

Other notable public courses include **Tilden Park** (Berkeley), **Cypress Point** (Monterrey), **Sea Ranch** (below Mendocino on the North Coast), **Franklin Canyon** (Rodeo), **Mountain Shadows** (Rohnert Park) and **Dry Creek**.

Tennis

Tennis is another year round sport on the West Coast. It's one of the most popular participatory sports in America and, as usual, California leads the nation. There are public tennis courts in every town, usually at the local high schools and parks. In the city of San Francisco alone there are 142 public tennis courts (558–4532). You can reserve one simply by sitting on the sidelines and waiting for a court to open up. It is not rude to ask players what game they're playing.

If you're serious about tennis, and wouldn't mind improving your game while on vacation, check out **John Gardiner's Tennis Ranch** in Carmel Valley. It's the first tennis ranch in the States and offers a tennis clinic for non-members Sunday through Friday. The clinic includes intensive instruction through videotape, gourmet meals, beautiful accommodations, breakfast in bed and general pampering. For reservations and information write P.O. Box 228, Carmel Valley, California 93924. Closed on Thanksgiving and Easter.

Bicycling

A great way to see the state is on the bike. To absorb all of San Francisco's Golden Gate Park, rent a bicycle on Stanyan Street (near Haight) and pedal over to the museums, the Japanese Garden, maybe down to the buffalos and the beach. For longer, more adventuresome outings, borrow a ten-speed (they are difficult to rent) and try to tackle one of these trails outside The City. Take along a windbreaker.

Angel Island offers some of the best views for a cyclist. The terrain, however, may discourage the novice (546–2815).

The Alum Rock Park Trail runs for 13 miles (21 km) near San Jose. Stop alongside the 60-foot waterfall or the old mineral springs marked by rock grottos. The Southern Pacific train service will transport both you and your bike from San Francisco to Alum Rock. (408–259–5477).

A gusty wind is likely to speed your progress across the Golden Gate Bridge. So pedal (carefully) over to Sausalito, browse, grab a bite, and return along the breezy bridge path. The west sidewalk is open weekends and holidays to cyclists.

The colorful coast ride of California has something for every rider. The trail traverses 50 miles (80 km) of spectacular surf and sand, from Santa Cruz north to Half Moon Bay. Begin and end anywhere. The easiest stretch extends from Highway 1 between the tourable Pigeon Point Lighthouse and Pescadero Beach. Or paddle backwards in time along the three-mile Monterrey Path of History, a well-marked route lined with old adobe structures. (408–649–3200).

There's also good bicycling in the wine country, through the foothills of the Sierras to Yosemite Valley; between two beautiful and fairly remote volcanic mountains — Shasta and Lassen; and along the famous (and flat) garden bowl of the United States — the San Joaquin and Sacramento Valleys.

Traveling through the wine country is a little like traveling through southern France. There is plenty of good bread, cheeses, and wine, and restaurants seem to pop up along the roadside like sunflowers.

The bicycling section of the Sierra Club (there are several in the Bay Area) can tell you about good routes, and so can experienced salesmen in the bicycle shops. You need to plan your trip in advance so you can reserve campsites in popular forest areas and parks. For information on the state parks call a tollfree number (800) 952–5580. For a bicycle map of the Pacific Coast, write Cal Trans, 1129 N. St., Sacramento, Ca. 95814. The California Department of Transportation established a Pacific Coast Bicentennial Bicycle Route in 1976 and designated special sections in the state parks for cyclists.

Canoeing

W.C. Trowbridge rents out canoes for an easy, safe but still interesting ride down the Russian River. His headquarters are in Healdsburg, about 1½ hours north of San Francisco. Pack a picnic. One-day-trips cost about $15; you do the driving (707–433–4116). You can also rent canoes right at the river.

Water Slides

At **Oakwood Lake Resort**, water sliding is just one of the water sports to enjoy. With eight slides in all, Oakwood offers tubular shapes for fast, yet safe, sliding at $3 for every half-hour session. For nonsliders, Oakwood provides paddle boats, canoes, and an outdoor roller-skating complex. 874 East Woodward, Manteca. (209–239–9566).

The four water slides in **Milpitas** seem almost as steep as waterfalls; some with 360-degree turns! Pay $2.50 per half-hour sesson, or $8 and splash down all day long. Free parking and changing rooms. 1200 South Dempsey Road. (408–263–6962).

At **Windsor Water Works**, four slides are open daily in the summer. A half-hour session costs $3; the all-day rate is $9 for adults, $8 for children. There's also a pool and picnic area where you can play volleyball or horseshoes. 8225 Conde Lane, six miles north of Santa Rosa. (707–838–7760).

Diving

Diving off the Northern California coast is only for those who are willing to brave large waves and poor visibility. About 80 percent of all divers are in search not of beautiful underworld visions, (the visions are there, although most of the time you can't see them) but of abalone and fish. **Salt Point** is a good place to find abalone, as is **Humboldt Bay** at the northern end of the state; and you can spear ling cod and halibut just about anywhere. Remember that you must have an abalone iron for prying abalones off the rocks and that red abalones must be at least seven inches long before you can take them. The season runs from December through July, excluding the month of April.

Dive shops in the Bay Area rent diving equipment by the day, week or weekend.

Sailboarding

Sailboarding is also for the experienced, since the Northern Pacific is rarely calm. At **Pier 39** in San Francisco, equipment can be rented cheaply by the hour; double the price if you insist on going beyond the breakwater into the San Francisco Bay (where they will insist on escorting you in a boat.) South of San Francisco, **Waddell Creek** in Santa Cruz is a popular sailboarding spot, with the right waves and weather.

Deep Sea Fishing

From **Half Moon Bay**, **Fisherman's Warf**, **Sausalito**, **Berkeley**, **Emeryviline**, **Bodega Bay** and various seaside villages further north, fishing party boats leave on regular schedules in search of salmon, seabass, halibut, rock fish, bonito, shark and albacore. (Look in the Yellow Pages under "Fishing Parties"). The average cost for a full day's fishing is about $30 plus $10 for tackle. Remeber that the Pacific Ocean can be rough and seasickness is often a problem. Also, the weather offshore is usually windy and rarely warm enough for sunbathing.

Ski Touring

Lovers of snow and the soft, sensual silence of a black and white alpine landscape, go into the mountains in winter. Because of relatively mild weather, some say the Sierras may be the best mountans to ski tour in the world. Spring is the best time to ski tour and the most spectacular route is down the central spine of the Sierras on the John Muir trail. This is a sport for the experienced: those with good equipment, good map sense, and the ability to build a snow cave. Unlike the Alps, or the Himalayas, there are few huts in the Sierras where travelers can take shelter from a storm.

Sierra Ski Touring offers guided tours, including the Sierra high route and the White Mountains (east of the Sierras, in the desert) which have perfect intermediate terrain. For brochures, write Sierra Ski Touring, Box 9, Mammoth Lakes, California 93546.

If you want to learn how to ski tour, or cross country ski (see entry below) contact the **Kirkwood Ski Touring Center** one mile south of Kirkwood (a downhill ski resort near Lake Tahoe). Telephone (209) 258-8864.

Cross Country Skiing

Cross country skiing (as it's called when you ski-tour for only a day) is fast becoming popular as an alternative to the long lines at downhill ski resorts, and in the Tahoe Area there are numerous official cross country ski trails offering packed snow and beginning to advanced runs. Most people forego official trails, however, and just take off and hike through the snow to a hill or lake. Not having to pay for skilift tickets makes the price right. Also, cross country skis can be rented at almost every ski shop for about one-third the cost of downhill skis.

Downhill Skiing

Downhill skiing in Northern California is great if you're from the East Coast (where trails are icy and crowded) but not so if you've skied in the Rockies or the long, leisurely trails of Europe. On weekends and holidays most California resorts have long lift lines and many of the trails are frighteningly crowded. During the week this changes and skiing can be spectacular (although deep powder snow rarely lasts).

There are two main ski areas in Northern California — **around Lake Tahoe**, about 3½ hours from the Bay Area, and at **Mammoth Mountain** on the eastern side of the Sierras, about eight hours from San Francisco. For descriptions of the ski areas see our "Lake Tahoe" and "Sierras" section. Lift tickets run about $20 per day.

Fishing

California leads the nation in the sale of fishing licenses. Trout and steelhead run in the upper Klamath near the Oregon Border, and for two of the finest fishing streams in the country, toss a line into **Fall River** or **Hat Creek** in the Burney Basin northeast of Redding. The **McCloud** and **Upper Sacramento** rivers just north of Lake Shasta also offer good, easily accessible fly fishing as does the

Truckee River from Truckee to Pyramid Lake, just north of Tahoe.

fly fishing as does the **Truckee River** from Truckee to Pyramid Lake, just north of Tahoe.

Eagle Lake in the northeastern part of the state has more than 300 Forest Service campsites and hundreds of chances to catch a giant Lahontan cut-throat trout. **Lake Pillsbury**, northeast of Ukiah, has 115 campsites for fisherman and **Lake Siskiyou** near Mount Shasta has more than 200 campsites.

You must have a valid California fishing license to fish in the state, but they are easily obtainable at nearly all sporting goods stores and local offices of the California Department of Fish and Game.

Hang Gliding

There's more hang gliding in California than any other state in the States, due to good, consistent coastal winds. The **Owens Valley**, east of the Sierras, is home of the **Cross Country Classic**, a hang gliding event held every July that attracts enthusiasts from all over the world. Its flight record is 158 miles, and every year more than a few flyers go over 100 miles.

The once-in-a-lifetime flight to make if you are an experienced hang glider is from **Glacier Point**, just above Yosemite Valley. You can jump off the point in the early morning and take a leisurely ride down 4,000 feet to the valley floor below. While falling, you can explore some of Yosemite's famous rock spires and granite walls.

The best site for coastal ridge soaring is **Fort Funston**, just south of the San Francisco zoo. If you need to learn the sport, there are a dozen hang gliding schools in Northern California and the average price for a day's lesson, including equipment, is $50. Look for schools in the Telephone Directory's Yellow Pages under "Hang Gliding."

Soaring

It's possible to get the feel of gliding without actually endangering your life; just plain gliding — being towed up 3,000 feet in a motorless fiberglass airplane and then catching an updraft to 10,000 feet and flying 15 minutes before landing. At the **Calistoga Soaring Center**, 1546 Lincoln Ave., Calistoga 94515, a pilot will take you up over the wine country.

Sky Diving

If falling from a plane with a parachute is your cup of tea, California is for you; there are more drop zones here than any other state. Many of these schools use Accelerated Free Fall, a training technique that allows a student to make his first jump from an altitude of 10,000 feet (3,050 meters). One jump and 10 hours of training costs from $300 to $500.

Falcon Parachute School, 11 miles south of Los Banos and about three hours south of San Francisco, is one of the best loved sky-diving schools in the state. Renting equipment at any drop zone sites costs from $7 to $15.

Group Runs

America is on the run. Jogging has been a fitness fad for years now, and the running shows no signs of letting up. Part of the thrill is the joy of competition; if you'd like to join the race, here are a few of the Bay Area's biggest group runs:

Bay to Breakers — California's largest footrace follows 12-kilometer course from one side of San Francisco to the other. Mid May. (777–2424).

Nimitz Run — There are two scenic courses: a 5-kilometer flat run on Treasure Island, and a 10-kilometer course around Treasure Island and hilly Yerba Buena Island. Mid May. (642–3551).

St. Jude Run for Kids — This 10-kilometer scenic run starts and ends at The Anchorage, 2800 Leavenworth Street. Mid June. (800–632–0512).

San Francisco Marathon — The scenic course takes in the sights of the City while avoiding most of the hills. End of July. (681–2322).

Bigfoot-Bigheart — This 10-kilometer race through Golden Gate Park is a benefit for Catholic Social Service. Mid September. (864–7400).

Bridge-to-Bridge Run — The benefit for Big Brothers & Sisters is an eight-mile run along the San Francisco waterfront. Late September/early October. (951–7070).

Seagull Run — Two races are open — the five-kilometer and the 10-kilometer; both around Treasure Island. Mid October. (765–5088).

Golden Gate Marathon — Sponsored by the YMCA, the full marathon ends at the Larkspur Ferry Terminal in Marin County, and the half-marathon in Sausalito. End of October. (392–4218).

Zoo Run — Some 2,000 runners wind their way through one of the most unusual courses imaginable — 3.5 miles through the San Francisco Zoo. Mid January. (661–2023).

Backpacking

General backpacking information is given in the "Great Outdoors And How To Enjoy It" in the features section of this book. The following information tells you how to obtain a wilderness visitor's permit before you set out for any trip.

To get your permit, write in advance, detailing your plans, to the National Park or Forest Service. If you don't have enough time to write and receive a permit in the mail, you may call the park or forest; most will take phone reservations one week in advance. And if you decide to take a truly last minute trip, or if all the advance permits are taken, you can show up at the Visitor's Center the morning of, or the day before, your trip. The Forest Service saves half of its permits for a first-come, first-served basis, and so do most of the Parks.

Appendix

Accommodations

San Francisco

Grand Hotels

Claremont. Although located in the hills between Berkeley and Oakland, it's an easy 15 mile (24–km) drive into the city from this grand old hotel. The resort boasts a large swimming pool, sauna, whirlpools and 10 tennis courts. Ashby at Claremont, Oakland 94705, Tel. 843–3000.

Four Seasons–Clift. Old, conservative and elegant. Two blocks west of Union Square at 495 Geary, 94102, Tel. 775–4700.

Hilton. Two modern skyscrapers in the City; both have swimming pools and accept pets.

Airport. Spacious grounds at the airport entrance. Off Highway 101. P. O. Box 8355. San Francisco 94128. Tel. 589–0770.

San Francisco Hotel and Tower. 1685 rooms on the edge of Union Square, near the more seedy Tenderloin. Splendid view from Henri's Room at the top. 330 O'Farrell, San Francisco 94102, Tel. 771–1400.

Holiday Inn. America's innkeeper has five large hotels in San Francisco. All but Union Square have swimming pools.

Convention Center. 50 Eighth Street, 94103, Tel. 626–6103.

Financial District. 750 Kearny, 94108, Tel. 433–6600.

Fisherman's Wharf. 1300 Columbus, 94133, Tel. 771–9000.

Golden Gateway. A last resort. 1500 Van Ness, 94109, Tel. 441–4000.

Union Square. The best of the bunch. 480 Sutter at Powell, 94108, Tel. 398–8900.

Hyatt. This chain runs two of the best hotels in the City.

Regency. The huge atrium is a tourist attraction in itself. 5 Embarcadero Center, 94111, Tel. 788–1234.

Union Square. Good food, great location. 345 Stockton, 94108, Tel. 398–1234.

Sheraton. This hotel chain has three very different inns.

Airport. Has a heated indoor swimming pool and whirlpools. 1177 Airport Blvd., Burlingame 94010, Tel. 342–9200.

Fisherman's Wharf. 2500 Mason, 94133, Tel. 362–5500.

Palace. A historical landmark. Its beautiful Garden Court restaurant is an essential stop for a meal. 639 Market, 94105, Tel. 392–8600.

Westin. This hotel chain has two of the best hotels in the city.

Miyako. Only 200 units but its authentic Japanese decor and service attract businessmen and celebrities alike. 1625 Post, 94115, Tel. 922–3200.

St. Francis. Makes up for the Miyako with 1,200 units on Union Square. 335 Powell, 94102, Tel. 397–7000.

Small Hotels

The Canterbury. The attraction here is its restaurant; Lehr's Greenhouse serves decent meals amidst a festival of flowers. 750 Sutter, 94102, Tel. 474–6464.

Stanyan Park Hotel. This recently restored Victorian hotel mixes the charm of antique furniture with the convenience of color TV and direct–dial phones. Located near the main entrance to Golden Gate Park. 750 Stanyan, 94117, Tel. 751–1000.

Bed–and–Breakfast Inns

Bed & Breakfast Inn. Located in two adjoining Victorian rowhouses, this is an Englishstyle pension on Union Street, the center of one of San Francisco's shopping and nightlife districts. 4 Charlton Court, 94123, Tel. 921–9784.

Casa Madrona. Right across the Golden Gate Bridge from San Francisco, this inn has magnificent views of the Bay and features an excellent French restaurant, Le Vivoir. 156 Buckley Ave., Sausalito, 94965, Tel. 332–0502.

Jackson Court. The keynote here is elegance, brass beds, oriental carpets, private telephones and color TVs. Reservations by the week only. 2198 Jackson Street, 94115, Tel. 931–6406.

The Mansion Hotel. With 16 rooms each named after a local historical figure and events ranging from magic shows to concerts, and a garden full of sculpture by Beniamino Bufano, this inn is a real San Francisco experience. 2220 Sacramento, 94115, Tel. 929–9444.

Washington Square Inn. Located in San Francisco's North Beach, this relatively inexpensive inn is within an easy walk of Fisherman's Wharf and Chinatown, the financial district. 1660 Stockton St., 94133, Tel. 981–4220.

Wine Country
Bed–and–Breakfast Inns

Burgundy House. Built as a winery in the 1870s, the inn keeps up the tradition by providing complimentary wine for its guests. 6711 Washington St., Yountville 94599, Tel. (707) 944–2855.

Chalet Bernensis. Located in the center of the Napa wine producing region, the inn began as a private home in 1884. 225 St. Helena Highway, St. Helena 94574, Tel. (707) 963–4423.

Magnolia Hotel. In its checkered past, the hotel has served as a bordello and as a rum-running depot. 6529 Yount St., Yountville 94599, Tel. (707) 944–2056.

Sonoma Hotel. Located on the main plaza in Sonoma, the hotel is furnished with authentic pieces from the 1870s. 110 West Spain St., Sonoma 95476, Tel. (707) 996–2996.

The Webber Place. The staff has earned a reputation for their knowledge on wineries and restaurants of the region. 6610 Webber St., Yountville 94599, Tel. (707) 944–8384.

Sacramento
Hotels and Motels

Best Western Ponderosa Motor Inn. Centrally located, three blocks from the State Capitol and walking distance from Old Sacramento. 1100 H St., 95814, Tel. (916) 441–1314.

Beverly Garland Motor Lodge. Family-oriented with a playground for kids. 1780 Tribute Road, 95815, Tel. (916) 929–7900.

Hotel El Rancho. A resort and conference center with 256 units, most of them with kitchens. Recreational facilities include tennis and racquetball courts, a health club, swimming pool, sauna and whirlpool. 1029 W. Capitol Ave., 95691, Tel. (916) 371–6731.

Holiday Inn Capitol Plaza. A popular resting spot for visiting businessmen, close to downtown. 375 units. 301 J St., 95814, Tel. (916) 446–0100.

Mansion Inn. Opposite the governor's mansion, this hotel features a lovely landscaped courtyard and balconies adjoining most of its 247 units. 700 16th St., 95814, Tel. (916) 444–8000.

Red Lion Motor Inn. The capital's largest hostelry with 448 well-appointed rooms. 2001 Point West Way, 95815, Tel. (916) 929–8855.

Sacramento Inn. Spacious grounds with three swimming pools, a wading pool and a putting green. Adjacent to the Arden Fair Shopping

Plaza. 1401 Arden Way, 95815, Tel. (916) 922–8041.

Vagabond Inn. Walking distance from the State Capitol, close to the Chinese Cultural Center and Old Sacramento. 909 Third St., 95814, Tel. (916) 446–1481.

Gold Country
Hotels

City Hotel. Prior to 1874, the building was a gold assay office, a stage company headquarters, an opera house, and a newspaper office. P.O. Box 1870, Columbia 94310, Tel. (209) 532–1479.

National Hotel. Built in 1852 for the Gold Rush, this beautiful Victorian has 43 remarkable rooms, each one decorated differently. 211 Broad St., Nevada City 95959, Tel. (916) 265–4551.

Motels

Air Wave Motel. This homey haven with rock-bottom prices is within walking distance of downtown Nevada City. Pool. 575 Broad St., Nevada City 95959, Tel. (916) 265–2233.

Northern Queen Motel. A big and modern motel, it has some rooms overlooking the creek, and some two-storey cottages. 400 Railroad Ave., Nevada City 95959, Tel. (916) 265–5824.

Bed–and–Breakfast Inns

Red Castle Inn. This gingerbread mansion evokes the grandeur of the Gold Rush years in Nevada City. 109 Prospect St., Nevada City 95959, Tel. (916) 265–5135.

Sutter Creek Inn. Jane Way, the owner of Sutter Creek, is a legend and inspiration among country-inn proprietors. 75 Main St., Sutter Creek 95685, Tel. (202) 267–5606.

Vineyard House. The winery that originally surrounded the inn produced such famous wines that U.S. President Grant stopped twice to try them. The hotel has a long, fascinating history of suicide, insanity and ghosts. P.O. Box 176, Coloma 95613, Tel. (916) 622–2217.

Woodside Mine. Built as the "American Hotel" in the 1860s, it was originally a stage stop on the Tahoe route. P.O. Box 43, Georgetown 95634, Tel. (916) 333–4499.

Lake Tahoe
Hotels and Motels

Best Western Lake Tahoe Inn. Right on the Nevada state line on U.S. Highway 50, this spacious motor inn (399 rooms) is a short walk from the casinos. Two pools. P.O. Box Eye Eye, South Lake Tahoe 95729, Tel. (916) 541–2010.

Best Western Station House Inn. Two blocks from the casinos and a block-and-a-half from a private lakefront beach. Luxurious rooms off Park-Loop Road. P.O. Box 4009, South Lake Tahoe 95729, Tel. (916) 542–1101.

Best Western Timber Cove Lodge. A lakefront inn near the Heavenly Valley ski resort. Sandy beaches, boat launches, fishing, swimming, water skiing, hot spas. P.O. Box AC, South Lake Tahoe 95705, Tel. (916) 541–6722.

Caesar's Tahoe. Expensive, modern casino-hotel with oversized round beds and five restaurants. On U.S. Highway 50. P.O. Box 5800, Stateline, Nevada 89449, Tel. (702) 588–3515.

Forest Inn. Tasteful, well-landscaped accommodations. Most have kitchens. Minimum stay is two days, and advance reservations are required. On Park Avenue. P.O. Box 4300, South Lake Tahoe 95729, Tel. (916) 541–6655.

Harrah's Tahoe Hotel. Considered by some to be the finest casino accommodation in America. Most of its 540 rooms have panoramic views of both the lake and the mountains. Superb restaurants, shopping mall, theaters, night clubs and heated indoor pool. On U.S. Highway 50. P.O. Box 8, Stateline, Nevada 89449, Tel. (702) 588–6611.

Harvey's Hotel. A recently remodeled casino-hotel, it has a pleasant, woodsy atmosphere. On the U.S. 50 casino strip. P.O. Box 128, Stateline, Nevada 89449, Tel. (702) 588–2411.

Harvey's Inn. A small casino about a mile north of the strip with 124 comfortable rooms. P.O. Box 128, Stateline, Nevada 89449, Tel. (702) 588–2411.

Lakeland Village. A summer-winter recreational resort on a wooded 19-acre lakefront plot. 3535 Lake Tahoe Blvd., P.O. Box A, South Lake Tahoe 95705, Tel. (916) 541–7711.

North Star at Tahoe. 250 units in a mountain setting between Kings Beach and Truckee. Ski tows and lifts in the winter, with equipment rental available. Tennis, golf and horseback riding in summer. P.O. Box 129, Truckee 95734, Tel. (916) 562–1113.

Hyatt Lake Tahoe. Spacious grounds and lovely lakeside location. Fine restaurants and accommodation worthy of the Hyatt name. P.O. Box 3239, Incline Village, Nevada 89450, Tel. (702) 831–1111.

Sahara Tahoe Hotel. Large (540 rooms) casino-hotel on U.S. 50 with 18-hole golf course. P.O. Box C, Stateline, Nevada 89449, Tel. (702) 588–6211.

Tahoe Marina Lodge. Lakeshore chalet apartments. P.O. Box 82, Tahoe City 95730, Tel. (916) 583–2365.

Tahoe Silver Sands Resort. Rustic cottages set among pines on the lakefront. Some fireplaces. Pool, hot tub, sauna, putting green, fishing, sailboat and kayak rentals, playground. On State Highway 28. P.O. Box 109, Tahoe Vista 95732, Tel. 546–2592.

Yosemite
Hotels

Ahwahnee Hotel. Outside is the rugged splendor of Yosemite Park: slim waterfalls, green meadows and granite walls; inside is a warm, wonderful castle complete with a Great Lounge you can get lost in, and the grandest dining room in the country. Make reservations well in advance. In Yosemite Valley, just east of Park Headquarters, 95389 Tel. (209) 373–4171.

San Joaquin Valley
Hotels

Fresno Hilton. This modern hotel on the mall has 200 well-furnished rooms and suites. Dining room and coffee shop are above average. 1055 Van Ness Ave., Fresno 93721, Tel. (209) 485–9000.

Hanford Victorian Inn. Thirteen individually decorated rooms in two restored houses offer charm and intimacy 35 minutes south of Fresno. Furnishings are either antique or handmade. 522 N. Irwin, Hanford 93230 Tel. (209) 584–9286.

Smuggler's Inn. Fresno's finest hotel is a world in itself; sheltered pool and whirlpool on nicely landscaped grounds. 3737 N. Blackstone Ave., 93726, Tel. (209) 226–2200.

Monterey/Big Sur
Motels

Asilomar. This unique resort is located on 105 acres (42 hectares) of pines and sand dunes at the ocean's edge. Rooms range from rustic lodges to large cottages with fireplaces and kitchenettes. Primarily used as a conference center. 800 Asilomar Blvd., Pacific Grove 93950, Tel. (408) 372–8016.

Bide-a-Wee-Motel. Cute, charming and very private cottages reminiscent of a 1930s–style motor inn. Most have kitchenettes. One block from beach. 221 Asilomar Blvd., Pacific Grove 93950, Tel (408) 372–2330.

Doubletree Inn. Adjacent to Fisherman's Wharf and overlooking both bay and harbor, this large (375 units), modern hotel has pool, whirlpool, 2 restaurants, 3 tennis courts and 33 steambaths. Pacific and Del Monte avenues, Monterey 93940, Tel. (408) 649–4511.

Quail Lodge. Nestled on the manicured grounds of the private Carmel Valley Golf Course, this resort has two pools, four tennis courts, golf and clubhouse privileges. Four miles east of downtown Carmel, 8205 Valley Greens Dr., Carmel 93923, Tel. (408) 624–1581.

Ventana Inn. The building is quite contemporary, overlooking thee sea at Big Sur, south of the Monterey Peninsula. Saunas, jacuzzi, and 90-foot (27-meter) swimming pool. Expensive. Very good food. Big Sur 93920, Tel. (408) 667–2331.

Bed–and–Breakfast Inns

Big Sur Inn. This small inn has a long history in Big Sur and is so popular for weekend romantic trips that reservations must be made weeks in advance. Big Sur 93920, Tel. (408) 93920.

Gosby House Inn. During the Victorian era, Pacific Grove was a popular summer retreat because of its clean, refreshing air. The tradition is carried on at Gosby House with its no smoking policy. 642 Lighthouse Ave., Pacific Grove 93950, Tel. (408) 375–1287.

Old Monterey Inn. Built in 1920, this inn is a large mansion modeled after English country homes. All rooms have private baths. 500 Martin St., Monterey 93940, Tel. (408) 375–8284.

Pine Inn. Large for a country inn, it offers 49 guest rooms and four dining rooms in the center of town. Ocean Avenue, P. O. Box 250, Carmel 93921, Tel. (408) 624–3820.

Vagabond House. A poetic hideaway built around a stone courtyard surrounded by flowers — fuchsia, azalea, rhododendron and camellias. 4th & Dolores, P.O. Box 2747, Carmel 94921, Tel. (408) 624–9988.

North Coast
Bed–and–Breakfast Inns

DeHaven Valley Farm. Located on a working 40-acre farm, this inn has a lovely view of the Mendocino Coast and pine forests. P.O. Box 128, Westport 95488, Tel. (707) 964–2931.

The Gray Whale Inn. The inn is named for the gray whales whose annual migration can sometimes be seen from the inn's solarium. 615 North Main St., Fort Bragg 95437, Tel. (707) 964–0640.

Joshua Grindle Inn. Built in 1882, this New-England-style inn features many early American antiques. 44800 Little Lake Rd., Mendocino 95460, Tel. (707) 937–4143.

Little River Inn. The inn is run by the great grandson of Silas Coombs who built the mansion in 1853. Little River 95456, Tel. (707) 937–5942.

MacCallum House Inn. This Victorian mansion offers an excellent restaurant as well as good lodgings. 740 Albion St., Mendocino 95460, Tel. (707) 937–0289.

Eureka
Motels

Bishop Pine Lodge. Cottages secluded in the redwoods; you'll soon resort to taking the foot trails to the beach and forest. 1481 Patrick's Point Dr., Trinidad 95570, Tel. (707) 677–3314.

Decker's Oceanside Lodge. Cozy cottages on 12 acres by the ocean. Closest neighbors are sea lions and whales. Pets permitted. Kitchen units. 3058 Patrick's Point Dr., 4 miles north of Trinidad 95570 Tel. (707) 677–3502.

Eureka Inn. A huge 50–year–old Tudor townhouse which has an excellent primer rib restaurant, rambling garrets, modern rooms and fabulous suites (fireplace, wet bar, jacuzzi). 7th and F streets, Eureka 95501, Tel. (707)442–6441.

Redding/Mount Shasta
Motels

Red Lion Motor Inn. The biggest hotel in Redding and one of the best; large, modern units have balconies and patios overlooking luscious landscapes. 1830 Hilltop Dr., Redding 96002, Tel. (916) 221–8700.

Shasta Inn. A tasteful, modern motel. Inner courtyard has pool and whirlpool. Pets permitted. 2180 Hilltop Dr., Redding 96002 Tel. (916) 221–8200.

Tree House Best Western. The owner, a former lumberjack, took a standard motel and worked wonders in wood. There's plenty of interesting wood panelling and much of the furniture is hand-carved. Adjacent to Interstate 5, Mount Shasta 96067, Tel. (916) 926–3101.

Restaurants

San Francisco

Balboa Cafe. The City's finest California cooking; warm salads, perfect pasta, handsome hamburgers and fresh fish. 3199 Fillmore, Tel. 921–3944.

Caffe Sport. Chaotic and crowded all hours. Campy decor and superb shellfish dishes. 574 Green, Tel. 981–1251.

Camargue. A Paris bistro with a menu that's both original and startlingly simple. House special is a three-course dinner for $12. Closed Monday. 2316 Polk, Tel. 776–5577.

China House. The City's finest Shanghai restaurant. Begin with extraordinary vegetarian pot stickers and end with unusual pancakes with red bean paste. 501 Balboa, Tel. 386–8858.

Donatello. Luxurious and expensive. Excellent pasta, fine carpaccio, good service; the perfect place for a business meeting. Post and Mason, Tel. 441–7182.

Ernie's. Formal decor (crystal chandeliers and velvet walls) and innovative French cooking; both the *nouvelle* and the *ancienne* cuisine. Coats and ties required for men. Very expensive. 847 Montgomery, Tel. 397–5969.

Fournou's Ovens. Order from the oven — a succulent roast rack of lamb, fine fowl or other meat. Award-winning wine list. At the Stanford Court Hotel, 905 California, Tel. 989–1910.

Gaylord. Elegant Indian cuisine. Lovely view of the Bay, especially at lunchtime. Ghirardelli Square, Tel. 771–8822.

Green's. Dinners have to be reserved months in advance. Managed by the Zen Center, the vegetarian fare is gorgeously gourmet. Closed Sunday and Monday for lunch. Reservations for lunch may be made a week in advance; otherwise it's first come first served. Beautiful harbor setting. Fort Mason, Building A, Tel. 771–6222.

Hayes Street Grill. Best place in town for mesquite-grilled fresh fish served raw. French fries are impeccable. 320 Hayes, Tel. 863–5545.

Hunan. From the hearty harvest pork to the fragrant chicken salad, everything is hot (spicy) and delicious. Closed Sunday. 924 Sansome, Tel. 956–7727.

Kinokawa. The most uptown of all San Francisco's *sushi* bars, and one of the best. Expensive. 347 Grant Ave., Tel. 956–6085.

La Rondalla. A perennial favorite with locals who know that they can get inexpensive, filling Mexican food here until 3:30 a.m. daily except Monday. 901 Valencia, Tel. 647–7474.

Le Castel. Classic French cuisine; try anything with cabbage, or the stuffed squab. Closed Sunday. Very expensive. 3235 Sacramento, Tel. 921–7115.

Le Central. Parisian bistro popular with celebrities, especially at lunch. Closed Sunday and for lunch Saturday. 453 Bush, Tel. 391–2233.

L'Etoile. Elegant, exquisite and very expensive, this is where the fancy folk go. The piano

bar is a nightly institution. Dinner only; closed Sunday. 1075 California, Tel. 771–1529.

Le Trianon. Pomp, circumstance and fine food in this conservative bastion of classical French cuisine. Dinner only; closed Sunday. Very expensive. 242 O'Farrell, Tel. 982–9353.

Little Joe's. Large portions, hurly-burly atmosphere and mouth-watering *calamari* and *cacciuco*. Closed Sunday. 53 Broadway, Tel. 433–4343.

MacArthur Park. Something to please everyone: hopeful singles at the long bar in front, grilled fresh fish, tender ribs, decent hamburgers. Closed for lunch on weekends. 607 Front, Tel. 398–5700.

Mai's. Vietnamese, from the Saigon-style shrimp-and-pork-noodle soup to the Hanoi-style anise-and-lemon-flavor soup. 316 Clement (221–3046) and 1838 Union (921–2861).

Mamas. Just plain good food. It's jammed on weekends, so try it during the week. Two locations: on the north side of Washington Square and 1701 Stockton St., Tel. 360–6421.

Modesto Lanzone's. Elegant Italian fare. Dining rooms are filled with art works, the view of the Bay at the Ghirardellii Square location is wonderful. The wine list is exciting, and the line of customers is always long. Closed Monday and for lunch on weekends. Ghirardelli Square, Tel. 771–2880 and 601 Van Ness, Tel. 928–0400.

Osome. Excellent sushi bar plus usual range of cooked Japanese food. Closed Tuesday and for lunch on weekends. 1923 Fillmore, Tel. 346–2311.

Prego. The perfect place for elegant pizza pie, cooked in a wood-burning brick oven. 2000 Union, Tel. 563–3305.

Tadich Grill. Fresh fish and hefty drinks in an atmosphere of male conviviality. Long waiting lines. Closed Sunday. 240 California, Tel. 391–2373.

Trader Vic's. This is the place where the elite meet to greet and eat. Avoid the Chinese dishes and concentrate on the pu-pu appetizers and remarkable rum drinks. Men must wear coat and tie. Closed for lunch on weekends. 20 Cosmo Place, Tel. 776–2232.

Vanessi's. Elegantly Italian in a fun and informal Frisco institution that is almost always open and always crowded. Closed for lunch on Sunday. 498 Broadway, Tel. 421–0890.

Yank Sing. Classiest *dim sum* place in the city serving food unique to Hong Kong and San Francisco. *Dim Sum* are Chinese tea pastries, and are eaten only for brunch or lunch. A very

San Francisco experience. 427 Battery, near Clay, Tel. 362–1640.

Other *dim sum* restaurants: **Tung Fong**, most exotic and inexpensive. 808 Pacific, Tel. 362–7115. **Asia Garden**, huge, noisy and authentic by Hong Kong standards. 772 Pacific, Tel. 398-5112.

Zuni. Simply-cooked California cuisine with dishes made from fresh, local ingredients. The menu varies with the market but it's always good especially the breakfasts. 1658 Market, Tel. 552–2522.

Peninsula/San Jose

Caffe Santa Maddalena. This Italian-style trattoria is great: self-service cafeteria. Good for breakfast or espresso and desserts. Inexpensive. 233 University Ave., Palo Alto, Tel. 322–1846.

Chantilly. From the cobblestone entry to the curtains framing the windows, this small French restaurant evokes the spirit of New Orleans. Closed Sunday and for lunch on Saturday. 530 Ramona St., Palo Alto, Tel. 321–4080.

El Charro. Mexican fare — excellent margaritas and *chilies colorado* — plus some Argentinian steak specialites. Inexpensive. 2169 S. Winchester Blvd., Campbell, Tel. (408) 378–1277.

Emile's Swiss Affair. Dinner only, closed Monday. 545 S. Second St., San Jose, Tel. (408) 289–1960.

Fung Lum. A sumptuous environment for elegant Cantonese dining. Closed for lunch Sunday. 1815 S. Bascom Ave., Campbell, Tel. (408) 377–6955.

Hi-Life. Good barbecued food at reasonable prices. Dinner only. 301 W. Saint John St., San Jose, Tel. (408) 295–5414.

La Foret. On the site of the first adobe hotel in California (built in 1848), this charming old house is graced with tuxedo-clad waiters, traditional continental entrées, fresh mussels and clams, and tempting desserts. Dinner and Sunday brunch. Closed Monday. 21747 Bertram Road, San Jose, Tel. (408) 997–3458.

La Hacienda Inn. Can get a full Italian dinner here at moderate prices. 18840 Saratoga-Los Gatos Road, Los Gatos, Tel. (408) 354–6669.

Liason. Friendlier and more informal than most French restaurants, the menu also features inventive Italian entrées. Closed for lunch on weekends. 4101 El Camino Way, Palo Alto, Tel. 494–8848.

Original Joe's. Home of the famous "Joe's Special" — a tasty sandwich of spinach, ground beef, mushrooms, onions and scrambled eggs. 301 S. First St., San Jose, Tel. (408) 292–7030.

Paolo's Continental Restaurant. Gracious, leisurely service. The homemade pastas are superb. Closed Sunday and for lunch Saturday. 520 E. Santa Clara St., San Jose, Tel. (408) 294-2558.

St. Michael's Alley. The chalkboard menu at this tiny restaurant changes daily. Next door, the Waiting Room serves wines, coffees, and elegant desserts to the accompaniment of local musical talent. Closed for lunch Sunday. 800 Emerson St., Palo Alto, Tel. 329-1727.

Si Amigos. A tiny, narrow place that dishes up warmth and friendliness along with excellent *chilies rellenos, tacos, nachos,* and assemble-it-yourself meals. Inexpensive. Closed Sunday and Monday. 1384 Lincoln Ave., San Jose, Tel. (408) 279-9083.

Vahl's. In the American roadhouse tradition, this Fifties-like eatery dishes up good food (not great) and plenty of it. Closed Monday and Tuesday. Taylor and El Dorado streets, Alviso Tel. (408) 262-0731.

East Bay

Bay Wolf. A lovely little restaurant that serves fine Mediterranean food. Sundeck. 3853 Piedmont, Oakland, Tel. 655-6004.

Chez Panisse. One of the most famous restaurants in the country and one of the best in the Bay Area. The $35 *prix fixe* dinner downstairs changes nightly. In the upstairs cafe, there are pizza, pasta, great salads and reasonable prices. Expect to wait in line at least an hour for a table; no reservations are taken. Closed Sunday. 1517 Shattuck Berkeley, Tel. 548-5525.

Hunan. One of the few restaurants in Oakland's Chinatown serving excellent spicy food. Menus are impressive and amazingly inexpensive, don't forget to ask for the day's specials. You can't go wrong in any Chinese restaurant in this area. 366 Eighth St., Tel. 444-1155.

Fourth Street Grill. Casual dining, with an outdoor area. Fabulous steak *tartare* and the best caesar salad in town. Closed for lunch on Sunday. 1820 Fourth St., Berkeley, Tel. 849-0526.

Le Marguis. The finest French food in Contra Costa county. Dinner only; closed Sunday and Monday. 3524-B Mount Diablo Blvd., Lafayette, Tel. 284-4422.

Narsai's. Mondays and Tuesdays are special dinners, honoring a celebrated chef or a particular country. On other nights, the food is elegant Mediterranean. Excellent service and wine list. Very expensive. Dinner only. 385 Colusa Ave., Kensington, Tel. 527-7900.

Oakland Grill. Airy and attractive, although it is right in the middle of the Oakland produce market. Burgers are big, breakfasts are beautiful. 3rd and Franklin, Oakland, Tel. 835-1176.

Santa Fe Bar and Grill. Restored train station and blues piano provide wonderful atmosphere. The new California cuisine is a taste treat. 1310 University Ave., Berkeley, Tel. 841-4740.

Siam. Always exceptional Thai cuisine, hot and spicy but irresistible. Dinner only, closed Tuesday. 1181 University Ave., Berkeley, Tel. 548-3278.

Union Hotel. American food, cooked from scratch with only the finest ingredients. In the beautiful old Union Hotel. Closed Monday. 401 First St., Benecia, Tel. (707) 746-0100.

Marin

Coquelicot. The decor is simple, the menu ambitious, the $20 prix fixe dinner a bargain. Also, a wide range of a la carte dishes. Closed Sunday and Monday. 23 Ross Common, Ross, Tel. 461-4782.

Epanoui. Daily specials as well as a four-course prix fixe dinner of *nouvelle cuisine* for $21. Tiny and cluttered. Closed Monday and for lunch Sunday. 1550 Tiburon Blvd., Tiburon, Tel. 435-2020.

Maurice et Charles' Bistro. A French bistro with casual formality and consistent fare. Try the fish soup, wild boar or pastry-wrapped sweetbreads. Dinner only; closed Sunday. 901 Lincoln Ave., San Rafael, Tel. 456-2010.

Wine Country

Auberge du Soleil. With a view of the vineyards and creative French cuisine that occasionally attains brilliance, the $34 *prix fixe* dinner is a bargain. Open for lunch and dinner. Closed Wednesday. 180 Rutherford Hill Road, Rutherford, Tel. (707) 963-1211.

Calistoga Inn. Casual, friendly service, large portions and excellent food. Dinner only; closed Monday. 1250 Lincoln Ave., Calistoga, Tel. (707) 942-4101.

The Diner. Plain, old, American breakfasts, lunches and dinners. The malts are made with real ice cream. Inexpensive. Closed Monday, and for dinner Tuesday and Wednesday. 6476 Washington St., Yountville, Tel. (707) 944-2626.

John Ash & Co. California cooking — fresh foods prepared with French and Oriental accents. Closed for lunch Saturday and for dinner Monday and Tuesday. 2324 Montgomery Dr., Santa Rosa, Tel. (707) 527-7687.

Miramonte. Very innovative *nouvelle cuisine* that looks as good as it tastes. Very expensive. Dinner only; closed Monday and Tuesday. 1327 Railroad Ave., St. Helena, Tel. (707) 963-3970.

Provencal. This restaurant is definitely not for those on a diet. Wonderful *pasta primavera, pates, potages* and beautifully cooked fowl. Dinners only; closed Sunday (except for Sunday brunch) and Monday. Very elegant. 18140 Sonoma Highway, Sonoma Mission Inn, Boyes Hot Springs, Tel. (707) 996-1041.

Rose et LeFavour. If you're lucky enough to get one of the 28 seats in this flower-filled restaurant, you'll be pampered all evening. Eight-course dinner is fixed at $40, plus choice of excellent wines. Very expensive. Dinner Wednesday-Saturday, lunch Sunday. Reservations in advance advised. 1420 Main St., St. Helena, Tel. (707) 963-1681.

Sacramento

Alhambra Fuel & Transportation. Good for a late night supper, or a nice dinner and drinks. 1310 Alhambra.

Americo's. Perfect pasta and beautifully executed sauces. 2000 Capitol.

Hong Kong. Good Chinese food from a variety of regions in a converted Western barbecue place that still has the wagon-wheel light fixtures. 5th and Broadway streets.

The Mandarin. Good Szechuan and Hunan Chinese food. Spicy. 1800 Broadway.

Torch Club. A bar with a cross-section of the community. 1612 L St.

Wakano Ura. — An upstairs place in the Japanese district that can be a little noisy with Japanese revelers, although the fun becomes infectious. 2217 10th St.

Zelda's. — Wonderful deep-dish pizza. 1415 21st St.

Gold Country

Auburn Hotel. The family-style fare features 12 courses; from antipasto to dessert with loads of spaghetti, frittata, stuffed pork chop and fried eggplant in between. And the price is right: $8.50. 853 Lincoln Way, Auburn, Tel. (916) 885-8132.

Framastanyl's. Three rooms under one roof. Enter a fireplace-fern bar with the best margaritas in town. Step up and cruise through the old-fashioned dance hall. A few more steps and enter the antique dining room where three meals with a Mexican-Philadelphia-style Italian flair

are served daily. The salad bar is worth the trip up all those stairs. 235 Commercial St., Nevada City, Tel. (916) 265-9292.

National Hotel. The food is standard American fare but the furnishings are strictly Victorian. Carefully prepared breakfast, lunch, dinner, and Sunday brunch. 211 Broad St., Nevada City, Tel. (916) 265-4551.

Lake Tahoe

La Table Francaise. On the outskirts of Reno sits a bastion of French cuisine. Desserts are exquisite. Dinner only; closed Monday and Tuesday. 3065 W. Fourth St., Reno, Tel. (702) 323-3200.

La Vieille Maison. Every dish is flavored with garlic! All meals begin with a heaping bowl of *aioli*. Dinner only; closed Monday and Tuesday. State Highway 267 at River Rd., Truckee, Tel. (916) 587-2421.

Le Petit Pier. Highlights include crisp puff pastry filled with *foie gras* and a fresh black truffle, New Zealand wild boar, and mussels in cream sauce. Dinner only; closed Tuesday. 7252 North Lake Blvd., Tahoe Vista, Tel. (916) 546-4464.

Old Post Office Coffee Shop. During both breakfast and lunch, the place is crowded and friendly. Inexpensive. 5245 North Lake Blvd., Carnelian Bay, Tel. (916) 546-3205.

San Joaquin Valley

Harland's. Creative *nouvelle cuisine*: chicken in a raspberry *vinaigrette* sauce or veal with morels in a lovely lemon sauce. Closed Monday. 2915 N. Moroa, Fresno, Tel. (209) 225-7100.

The Ripe Tomato. Quail and venison are standard menu items; typical specials include duck with apricot-garlic sauce, veal with oysters and mushrooms in vermouth sauce, and lamb with pesto sauce. 5064 N. Palm, Fresno, Tel. (209) 225-1850.

Vintage Press. Fresh food with a European flair. The fish, veal, vegetables and desserts are personally prepared. Closed Monday. 216 N. Willis, Visalia, Tel. (209) 733-3033.

Monterey/Big Sur

Casanova. Emphasis is on seafood served with light sauces, but there are also veal, lamb and beef selections. Breakfast, lunch, dinner and Sunday brunch in a French cottage setting. Fifth Street near San Carlos, Carmel, Tel. (408) 625-0501.

Glen Oaks. Rustic exterior belies elegant dining room filled with fresh flowers and fine music. Large, eclectic menu. Closed for breakfast Wednesday and for dinner Monday. State Highway 1, Big Sur, Tel. (408) 667–2623.

La Maisonnette. Good French food, homemade bread, very moderately priced. 218 17th St., Pacific Grove, Tel. (408) 372–4481.

Maison Bergerac. This Victorian home with just 12 tables requires reservations well in advance. Fastidiously prepared *prix fixe* dinner is $30. Closed Monday. 649 Lighthouse Ave., Pacific Grove, Tel. (408) 373–6996.

Mansion House. Try the homemade cheesecake topped with papaya. Closed for lunch Saturday. 418 Main St., Watsonville, Tel. (408) 724–2495.

Nepenthe. Spectacular view of waves crashing 800 feet below, homemade soups and enormous chef's salads. Tourists and locals mingle comfortably. State Highway 1, Big Sur, Tel. (408) 667–2345.

Ventana. A luxurious and charming resort set back in the woods. Save room for the accomplished desserts. State Highway 1, Big Sur, Tel. (408) 667–2331.

The Whaling Station Inn. Seafood predominates — either grilled or sautéed. Dinner only. 763 Wave St., Monterey, Tel. (408) 373–3778.

North Coast

Albion River Inn. Large beamed dining room overlooks the sea. Hearty fare. Dinner, and weekend brunches. State Highway 1, Albion, Tel. (707) 937–4044.

Cafe Beaujolais. The atmosphere is cozy, the juice fresh, and the omelets, coffee cake and waffles are all wonderful. Breakfast and lunch year-round, dinner May-September. 961 Ukiah St., Mendocino, Tel. (707) 937–5614.

Ledord House. A rustic little house overlooking the sea. Locally grown food is used when available, and always cooked to order. Dinner only. 7051 State Highway 1, Little River, Tel. (707) 937–0282.

Little River Cafe. Each evening sees a different three-course dinner, with a choice of seafood, poultry or meat. The fixed price is $16.50. Dinner only; closed Monday and Tuesday. State Highway 1, Little River, Tel. (707) 937–0404.

New Boonville Hotel. California cooking to the core — fresh, simple, sensitively prepared. All the food has been grown or raised right at the hotel. State Highway 128, Boonville, Tel. (707) 895–3478.

Olema Inn. A restful, restored century-old inn at the gateway to the Point Reyes National Seashore. Closed Wednesday. Sir Francis Drake Blvd., Olema, Tel. 663–8441.

St. Orres. A beautiful restaurant emphasizing French cooking in a Russian-styled hotel. Also serves Sunday brunch. State Highway 1, in Gualala, below Mendocino, Tel. (707) 884–3303.

Sea Gull Inn. Fresh fish, a buttery chicken kiev, assorted veal dishes and a nightly vegetarian special are offered. 10481 Lansing St., Mendocino, Tel. (707) 937–5204.

Station House Cafe. Fresh well-cooked food in a warm, bustling atmosphere. Perfect stop after a day's hiking on Point Reyes Peninsula. Third and A streets, Point Reyes, Tel. 663–1515.

Wellspring. The entire place is handmade and lovely with stained glass, high ceilings and bare wood. The vegetarian fare is creative and very good. Closed Wednesday. 955 Ukiah St., Mendocino, Tel. (707) 937–4567.

Eureka

Cafe Marina. Serves very fresh scampi, scallops and sole. If fish is not your fare, there are scrumptious sandwiches and Italian dishes. Breakfast, lunch and dinner. Woodley Island at the Eureka Marina, Tel. (707) 443–2233.

Lazio's Seafood Restaurant. At Lazio's, also a seafood wholesaler, the fish couldn't be fresher. The Windjammer Lounge is as popular with the locals as the restaurant is with the tourists. 4 "C" St., Tel. (707) 442–2337.

Samoa Cookhouse. Breakfast ($4) includes orange juice, scambled eggs, pancakes, sausage, hash browns and coffee. Hefty lunches ($3.65) and dinners ($7.65) start with soup and salad, end with hot apple pie, and include plenty of homemade bread. Off U.S. Highway 101 across Samoa Bridge, Tel. (707) 442–1659.

Redding/Mount Shasta Area

Tree House Restaurant. The owner, a former lumberjack, added an array of creative wooden carvings to this rustic restaurant. The cocktail lounge is cozy and the food is substantial American fare. Central Mount Shasta exit off Interstate 5, Tel. (916) 926–3101.

Hatch Cover. The menu is varied and good, but the view of the Sacramento River is exceptional. One mile east of downtown Redding at 202 Hemsted Dr., Tel. (916) 223–5606.

Piemont. Piemont is one of the best of the current Italian eateries, dishing up mouthwatering ravioli and rigatoni. For skiiers, hikers and lumbermen, there's American fare: ribs, fried chicken and hefty steaks. 1200 S. Mount Shasta Blvd., Tel. (916) 926–2402.

Night Spots

Comedy

Cobb's Pub. Intimate bar with both the best and the worst comics in town. Nightly shows. Cover varies, free to $5, plus two-drink minimum. 2069 Chestnut, San Francisco, Tel. 563–9658.

Holy City Zoo. The oldest comedy hangout, this 80-seat, funky bar serves beer and a strange brew of comedy. Nightly shows. Cover varies, free to $5, plus two drink minimum. 408 Clement, San Francisco, Tel. 752–2846.

Laughs Unlimited. Nightclub atmosphere provides evening entertainment in Old Sacramento. Shows Tuesday to Sunday (two shows on weekends). Cover $4 to $5. 1124 Firehouse Alley, Sacramento, Tel. (916) 446–5905.

Old Spaghetti Factory. Comedy and improvisation in a funky room off the main restaurant. Varied schedule. Cover varies, free to $6. 478 Green, San Francisco, Tel. 421–0221.

The Other Cafe. Crowd includes hippies from the Haight and students from the medical school. Shows nightly. Cover $1 to $5. 100 Carl, San Francisco, Tel. 681–0748.

The Punch Line. The slickest, most "professional" of the clubs. Shows Tuesday to Sunday. Cover $2 to $6 plus two-drink minimum. 444 Battery St., San Francisco, Tel. 397–4334.

Disco

Disco 2001. Rustic atmosphere. Daily 6 p.m. to 2 a.m. Cover varies free to $4. 2001 Union St., San Francisco, Tel. 567–3121.

Le Disque Alexia. Rich, continental ambiance, in accord with one of the City's fanciest restaurants. No cover. 1001 California St., San Francisco, Tel. 771–1001.

Oz. Beautiful views; strict dress code; very elegant. Sunday to Thursday 9 p.m. to 2 a.m. Friday and Saturday 9 p.m. to 4 a.m. Cover Sunday to Thursday $7, Friday and Saturday $15. Hotel St. Francis, Union Square, San Francisco, Tel. 397–7000.

Palladium. Three dance floors, complete with fog machine and neon lights. Thursday to Saturday 9 p.m. to 6 a.m. Cover $5. 1031 Kearny St., San Francisco, Tel. 434–1308.

Park Exchange. Two dance floors; popular with visitors. Tuesday to Wednesday 8 p.m. to 2 a.m. Thursday till 3 a.m. Friday and Saturday

till 4 a.m. Cover $3 to $5. In the Transamerica Pyramid, 600 Montgomery St., San Francisco, Tel. 983–4800.

Music

Country-Western

Ancient Moose Saloon. Country rock on small dance floor. Live band Monday to Saturday from 9 p.m. to 1:30 a.m. Restaurant. No cover. 450 Bercut Dr., Sacramento, Tel. (916) 446–3012.

Last Day Saloon. an in-spot that's invariably crowded. Some big-name bands. Shows Tuesday to Sunday from 9:30 p.m. Cover $2 to $5 with one-drink minimum. 406 Clement, San Francisco, Tel. 387–6343.

O.T. Price's Music Hall. Country swing. Nightly shows from 9 p.m. Cover varies, free to $5. 3660 Soquel Dr., Soquel, Tel. (408) 476–3939.

Paul's Saloon. Fine, free, friendly bluegrass. Nightly shows from 9 p.m. No cover; one-drink minimum. 3251 Scott St., San Francisco, Tel. 922–2456.

Saddle Rack. A cavernous club with five dance floors, six bars, and one mechanical bull. Nightly shows. No cover. 1310 Auzerais Ave., San Jose, Tel. (408) 286–3393.

Jazz

Bajone's. Unpretentious neighborhood club in the heart of the Mission District. Shows every evening and on Sunday afternoons. Cover varies, free to $2. 1062 Valencia, San Francisco, Tel. 282–2522.

Douglas Beach House. During the week it's classic, country or rock; on weekends, it's always excellent jazz. Cover varies, free to $10. Right on the beach north of Half Moon Bay, Tel. 726–4143.

Erle's Solano Club. Comfortable, cool, very Berkeley-ish. Nightly shows from 9 p.m. Cover varies, free to $8, plus two-drink minimum. 1403 Solano Ave., Albany, Tel. 524–9314.

Earthquake McGoon's. After 23 years tooting his horn, Turk Murphy and his Dixieland Jazz Band are a local institution. Dancing. Nightly shows from 8 p.m. Cover $4 plus two-drink minimum. Pier 39, San Francisco, Tel. 986–1433.

Pier 23 Cafe. Dixieland jazz overlooking the Bay. Shows Wednesday to Saturday from 9 p.m.; Sunday 4 to 9 p.m. No cover; two-drink minimum. Pier 23, San Francisco, Tel. 362–5125.

Vangari's. Contemporary jazz; Thursday to Sunday. Cover $3. Blues night; Wednesday cover $2 to $5. Dancing. 2000 K St., Sacramento, Tel. (916) 448–1723.

Pop

Great American Music Hall. Big stars in jazz, folk, easy rock and comedy perform in this beautiful building. Schedule varies. Cover $5 to $12. 859 O'Farrell, San Francisco, Tel. 885–0750.

Inn of the Beginning. Great dance floor for great shows; rock, blues, jazz, reggae. Shows Wednesday to Sunday from 9 p.m. Cover $2.50 to $7. 85 La Plaza, Cotati, Tel. (707) 795–7622.

The Stone. Everything from Ray Charles to punk has appeared on the Stone's elevated stage. Nightly shows. Cover $1 to $10 with two-drink minimum. 412 Broadway, San Francisco, Tel. 391–8282.

Venetian Room. The classiest, most expensive supper club in San Francisco, this is a regular home to singers such as Tony Bennett, Anthony Newley and Ella Fitzgerald. Big band dancing. Shows Tuesday to Sunday at 9:30 p.m. and 11:30 p.m. Cover $10 to $20. Restaurant. Fairmont Hotel, California and Mason, Tel. 772–5163.

Rock

Berkeley Square. The best New Wave in Berkeley is probably the best in the Bay Area. Nice art-decor but sometimes it gets hot and stuffy. Nightly shows from 9:30 p.m. into the night. Cover $4 to $8 with two-drink minimum. 1333 University Ave., Berkeley, Tel. 849–3374.

Catalyst. Big-name acts on the weekends. Nightly shows from 9 p.m. Cover $2.50 to $7.50. 1011 Pacific Ave., Santa Cruz, Tel. (408) 423–1336.

Earl's. A tiny marble dance floor is the focal point of this weird New Wave club. Recorded music. Food and video upstairs. Wednesday to Sunday from 9:30 p.m. to 4 a.m. Cover free to $3. 310 Pacific, San Francisco, Tel. 981–3402.

Echo Beach. Fancy New Wave. Recorded music. Open Fridays only from 9 p.m. Cover $2. Showplace Design Center, 8th and Townsend, San Francisco, Tel. 864–1500.

I-Beam. Lounge areas and large dance floor. Live and recorded music Monday to Thursday; gay Friday to Sunday. Cover $2 to $5. 1748 Haight St., San Francisco,Tel. 668–6006.

Keystone Palo Alto. Good acts, good dance floor. Performance schedule varies. Cover $1 to $11 with one-drink minimum. 260 California Ave., Palo Alto, Tel. 324–1402.

Mabuhay Gardens. This punk club inside a Polynesian restaurant is so famed it's known simply as the Mab, mockingly as "the Fab Mab." *All* kinds of shows, nightly from 10:30 p.m. Cover $3 to $5 with one-drink minimum. 443 Broadway, San Francisco, Tel. 956–3315.

Old Waldorf. *The* professional performance place: the biggest names in the business. Two shows nightly. Cover $4 to $12 with two-drink minimum. 444 Battery, San Francisco, Tel. 397–3884.

Specialty Houses

Ali Baba. A big band plays ballroom tunes in this large, oval, elegant ballroom. Dance lessons precede the program. Formal dress. Wednesday, Friday and Saturday evenings. No cover. Grand Ave. and Webster, Oakland, Tel. 451–7040.

Ashkenaz. International folk dancing; a different country every night, with a little rock 'n' roll thrown in. Tuesday to Saturday. Cover varies. 1317 San Pablo Ave., Berkeley, Tel. 525–5054.

Beach Blanket Babylon Goes to the Stars ... and Broadway! Stocked with silly sing-alongs, daring dances and crazy costumes, there's no show like this show — anywhere. A *must* see ... if you can get reservations. Tickets $13 to $15. 678 Green, San Francisco, Tel. 421–4222.

Cesar's Palace. The biggest Latin show around, offering salsa at its saltiest. Shows Wednesday to Sunday from 9 p.m. to 6 a.m. on weekends. Cover $3 to $10. 3140 Mission, San Francisco, Tel. 826–1179.

Finocchio's. Fourteen female impersonators attract tons of tourists to North Beach's only-in-San-Francisco cabaret. Shows from 8 p.m. to 2 a.m. Closed Monday and Wednesday. Tickets $5. 506 Broadway, Tel. 982–9388.

Hyatt Regency. In the atrium of this space-age hotel a jazz combo plays every afternoon, classic music every night, and big-band dancing Friday afternoons. No cover. Embarcadero 5, San Francisco, Tel. 788–1234.

La Peña Cultural Center. Films, comedy, ethnic music, dancing, leftist theater ... anything that supports the People. Shows from 7:30 p.m. closed Monday. Cover $2.50 to $5. 3105 Shattuck, Berkeley, Tel. 849–2568.

Plowshares Coffeehouse. The best folk music in the Bay Area. Hear the songs America sings. Fridays and Sundays. Cover $3.50 to $5. Fort Mason, Building C, San Francisco, Tel. 441–8910.

"Strip Shows" from Guide in Brief.

Bookstores

San Francisco Specialty Shops

City Lights. Excellent poetry collection, new and used books. 261 Columbus Ave. Tel. 368–8193.

European Book Company. Book and magazines in French, German, Spanish, Italian and English. 500 Sutter Street, Tel. 981–1666.

Multi-Media Resource Center. Human sexuality, fantasy, psychology and sex education aids. 1525 Franklin, Tel. 673–5100.

Old Wives Tales. Books by and about women; third-world and lesbian literature. 1009 Valencia, Tel. 821–4675.

East Bay

Cody's. Over 50,000 titles in stock; all new books. 2454 Telegraph, Tel. 845–7852.

The Holmes Book Co. Extensive California and America history selections; new and used books. 274 14th Street, Oakland, Tel. 893–6860.

Half Price Books. Magazines (back issues), records, tapes, paperbacks and hardcovers; new and used. 2525 Telegraph, Berkeley, Tel. 843–6412.

Moe's. Art & antiquarian books, used books, new and sale books. 2476 Telegraph, Berkeley, Tel. 849–2133.

Shakespeare & Co. Used books, paperbacks, scholarly books. 2499 Telegraph Avenue, Berkeley, Tel. 841–8916.

Shambala. Astrology, religion, occult. 2482 Telegraph Avenue, Berkeley, Tel. 848–8443.

Other Areas

Bookshop Santa Cruz. 1547 Pacific Ave., Santa Cruz, Tel. (408) 423–0900.

A Clean, Well-Lighted Place for Books. Locations in Larkspur Landing at 2417 Larkspur Landing Circle, Tel. 461–0171; and in Cupertino at 21271 Stevens Creek Blvd. Tel. (408) 255–7600.

Eeyore Books. 554 East Cotati Blvd., Cotati, Tel. (707) 795–8301.

Tower Books. 7830 Macy Plaza Dr., Sacramento, Tel. (916) 481–6600, and 16th & Broadway, downtown Sacramento, Tel. (916) 444–6688.

Foreign Consulates

Argentina
870 Market Street, 982–3050.

Australia
256 Sutter Street, 986–4040.

Bolivia
870 Market Street, 495–5173.

Brazil
300 Montgomery St., Suite 1160, 981–8170.

Canada
1 Maritime Plaza, 981–2670.

Chile
870 Market Street, 982–7662.

Colombia
870 Market Street, 362–0080.

Costa Rica
870 Market Street, 392–8488.

Denmark
1 Market Plaza, 781–1309.

Dominican Republic
870 Market Street, 982–5144.

Ecuador
870 Market Street, 391–4148.

Egypt
3001 Pacific Avenue, 346–9700.

El Salvador
870 Market Street, 781–7924.

Finland
120 Montgomery Street, 981–4656.

France
540 Bush Street, 397–4330.

Germany
601 California Street, 981–4250.

Great Britain
120 Montgomery Street, 981–3030.

Greece
2441 Gough Street, 775–2102.

Guatemala
8870 Market Street, 781–0118.

Haiti
430 Monterey Blvd., 469–5629.

Honduras
870 Market Street, 392–0076

Hong Kong
160 Sansome, 989–5005.

India
540 Arguello Blvd., 668–0662.

Indonesia
351 California Street, 982–8966.

Ireland
681 Market Street, 392–4214.

Israel
693 Sutter Street, 775–5535.

Italy
2590 Webster Street, 931–4924.

Japan
1601 Post Street, 921–8000.

Republic of Korea
3500 Clay Street, 921–2251.

Malaysia
Two Embarcadero Center, 421–6570.

Mexico
870 Market Street, 392–5554.

Monaco
2209 Pacific Avenue, 362–5050.

Nepal
3630 Jackson St., 751–3630.

Netherlands
601 California Street, 981–6454.

New Zealand
1 Maritime Plaza, 788–7430.

Nicaragua
870 Market Street, 391–4738.

Nigeria
369 Hayes Street, 864–8001.

Norway
One Embarcadero Center, 986–0766.

Panama
1880 Wawona Street, 566–4144.

Pan-Asiatic Chamber of Commerce
317 12th Ave., 752–4093.

Paraguay
870 Market Street, 982–9424.

People's Republic of China
1450 Laguna Street, 563–4885.

Peru
870 Market Street, 362–7136.

Phillippines
447 Sutter Street, 433–6666.

Portugal
3298 Washington Street, 346–3400.

Senegal
P.O. Box 850, Mill Valley, 383–8264.

Singapore Tourist Board
251 Post, 391–8476.

Spain
2080 Jefferson Street, 922–2995.

Sweden
1960 Jackson Street, 775–6104.

Switzerland
235 Montgomery Street, 788–2272.

Taiwan
166 Geary, 989–8677.

Tunisia
3401 Sacramento St., 922–9222.

Union of Soviet Socialist Republics
2790 Green Street, 922–6642.

Uruguay
870 Market St., 982–3730.

Venezuela
870 Market Street, 421–5172.

Yugoslavia
1375 Sutter Street, 776–4941.

Further Reading

General

American Automobile Association. *TourBook: California/Nevada.* 1983.

Bailey, John. *San Francisco Insider's Guide.* Berkeley: Non-Stop Books, 1980.

Brant, Michelle. *Timeless Walks in San Francisco: A Historical Walking Guide.* Berkeley: Brant, 1979.

Coleberd, Frances. *Hidden Country Villages of California.* San Francisco; Chronicle Books, 1977.

Delehanty, Randolph. *Walks and Tours in the Golden Gate City.* New York: Dial Press, 1980.

Doss, Margot Patterson. *Golden Gate Park at Your Feet.* San Rafael: Presidio Press, 1978.

Doss, Margot Patterson. *There, There: East Bay at Your Feet.* San Rafael: Presidio Press, 1978.

Doss, Margot Patterson. *A Walker's Yearbook: 52 Seasonal Walks in the San Francisco Bay Area.* San Rafael: Presidio Press, 1983.

Editors of the *Bay Guardian. Free and Easy.* San Francisco: Downwind Publications, 1980.

Editors of *Sunset* magazine. *California Coast.* Menlo Park: Lane Publishing, 1978.

Flashmaps! New York: Flashmaps/Instant Guide Publications, 1983.

Fohrman, Nadine, and Sam Gisburg. *A Jewish Guide to the Bay Area*. Oakland: Hillel Academy, 1978.

Fradkin, Philip L. *California; The Golden Coast.* New York: Viking Press, 1974.

Gentry, Curt, and Tom Horton. *The Dolphin Guide to San Francisco and the Bay Area*. New York: Doubleday, 1982.

Leadabrand, Russ. *Exploring California Byways*. Los Angeles: Westernlore Press, 1972.

Leadabrand, Russ. *Guidebook to Rural California*. Pasadena: Ward Ritchie, 1972.

Levin, Bella, and Dan Whelan. *City guide: San Francisco and Northern California*. San Francisco: Cityguide, 1983.

Madison, Louis. *San Francisco on a Shoestring: The Intelligent Traveler's (and Native's) Guide To Budget Living in San Francisco*. San Francisco: A.M. Zimmerman, 1982.

Matson, Robert W. *North of San Francisco*. San Francisco: Celestial Arts, 1975.

Milne, Terry. *The Ultimate Bay Book*. San Francisco: California Living, 1979.

Metropolitan Transportation Commission. *Regional Transit Guide*. Berkeley: MTC, 1981.

Stanford Research Institute. *Take a Walk Through Mission History: Walking Tours Through San Francisco's Inner Mission*. Palo Alto: Stanford University Press, 1974.

Tavenner, Blair. *Seeing California: A Guide to the State*. Boston: Little, Brown and Co., 1948.

Thomas, Earl. *Back Roads of California*. New York: Clarkson N. Potter, 1983.

Wood, Basil. *The What, When and Where Guide to Northern California*. New York: Doubleday, 1977.

Wurman, Richard Saul. *San Francisco Access*. San Rafael: Presidio Press, 1982.

History

Bagwell, Beth. *Oakland: The Story of a City*. San Rafael: Presidio Press, 1982.

Cole, Tom. *A Short History of San Francisco*. San Francisco: Monte Rosa, 1981.

Editors of *Sunset* magazine. *The California Missions: A Pictorial History*. Menlo Park: Lane, 1979.

Flamm, Jerry. *Good Life in Hard Times*. San Francisco: Chronicle Books, 1976.

Hansen, Gladys. *San Francisco Almanac*. San Rafael: Presidio Press, 1980.

Hart, James. *A Companion to California*. New York: Oxford University Press, 1978.

Johnson, Paul, and Richard Reinhardt. *San Francisco as It Was, as It Is*. New York: Doubleday, 1979.

Lavender, David. *California. A Bicentennial History*. New York: W.W. Norton, 1976.

Lockwood, Charles. *Suddenly San Francisco*. San Francisco: California Living, 1978.

Pettitt, George. *Berkeley: The Town and Gown of It*. Berkeley: Howell-North Books, 1973.

Geography and Natural History

Alt, David and Donald Hyndman. *Roadside Geology Of Northern California*. Mountain Press, 1975.

Brown, Vinson and David Hoover. *California Wildlife Map Book*. Naturegraph Publishers, 1967.

Fisher, Stephen and Anita Rubin. *The Environmentalist's Guide to the East Bay Shoreline*. Self-published, 1973.

Gilliam, Harold and Michael Bry. *The Natural World of San Francisco*. New York: Doubleday, 1967.

Hart, John. *San Francisco's Wilderness Next Door*. San Rafael: Presidio Press, 1979.

Hornbeck, David. *California Patterns: A Geographical and Historical Atlas*. Mayfield, 1983.

Miller, Crane and Richard Hyslop. *California: The Geography of Diversity*. Mayfield, 1983.

Sharsmith, Helen. *Spring Wildflowers of the San Francisco Bay Region*. Berkeley: University of California Press, 1965. (Other titles in this excellent series: *Evolution of the Landscape, Introduction to Seashore Life, Weather of the San Francisco Bay Region* and *Butterflies*.)

Food Guides

Editors of *Bon Appétit* magazine. *America's Best Restaurants: A Reader's Choice Selection of Where to Eat in San Francisco*. Los Angeles: Wilshire Marketing Corp., 1982.

Jutkovitz, Serena. *An Exceptional Approach to Round-the-World Wining and Dining in the San Francisco Bay Area*. San Francisco: Russian Hill House Books, 1982.

Kahn, Judith. *Indulge Yourself: A Guide to San Francisco's Neighbourhood Cafes and Coffeehouses*. San Francisco: Kahn Publishing, 1982.

Levine, Beverly. *Fifty Grand Picnics: Menus and Recipes for the Best Picnic Sites Around the Bay Area*. San Francisco: Chronicle Books, 1982.

Low, Jennie, and Diane Yee. *The Chinese Restaurant Experience: The Best of the Bay Area*. San Rafael: Presidio Pres, 1982.

Metzger, Elizabeth. *The Breakfast Book*. San Francisco: Chronicle Books, 1979.

Meyers, Carole Terwilliger. *Eating Out With The Kids*. San Francisco: Carousel Press, 1980.

Ristow, William. *The San Francisco Bar Book*. San Francisco: Downwind Publications, 1981.

Unterman, Patricia, and Stan Sesser. *Restaurants of San Francisco*. Sausalito: Comstock, 1981.

Shopping Guides

Brazil, Diane. *South Bay Bargain Guide*. San Francisco: Chronicle Books, 1981.

Hudson, Nelly. *Antique Hunting in the Bay Area and Northern California*. Wingbow, 1978.

Socolich, Sally. *Bargain Hunting in the Bay Area*. Wingbow, 1983.

ART/PHOTO CREDITS

Cover	Bret R. Lundberg; model, Teresa Ecrette
Cover, corner	Bret R. Lundberg (mountaineer); Vautier-de Nanxe (TransAmerica Pyramid and Columbus Building)
End paper, front	Lee Foster (seal of the City and County of San Francisco)
1	Vautier-de Nanxe
2-3	Bill Bachman (Scoopix)
4-5	Vautier-de Nanxe
6-7	Lee Foster
8-9	Bret R. Lundberg
10	Lee Foster
13	Lee Foster
14-15	Bancroft Library, University of California, Berkeley
17	Bancroft Library
18	Bancroft Library
19	Bancroft Library
21	Bancroft Library
22	Bancroft Library
23	Lee Foster
24	Bancroft Library
25	Bancroft Library
26-27	Bancroft Library
28	Bancroft Library (lithograph first published by Britton and Rey, San Francisco).
29	Bancroft Library (first published by H.K. Robinson, New York).
30	Bancroft Library (from Ballou's Pictorial Drawing-Room Companion).
31	Bancroft Library (first published by Herrmann J. Meyer, New York)
32	Vautier-de Nanxe
33	Vautier-de Nanxe
34	Bancroft Library
35	Bancroft Library (first published by M. Ullmann, San Francisco)
36	Bancroft Library
37	Bancroft Library
38	Bancroft Library
39	Bancroft Library
40	Bancroft Library
41	Bancroft Library (from The San Francisco Illustrated Wasp).
42-43	Bancroft Library
44	Bancroft Library
45	Bancroft Library
46	Bancroft Library
47	Bancroft Library (from the Associated Oil Co.)
48	Bret R. Lundberg
50	Lee Foster
51	Bret R. Lundberg
52-53	David Ryan
54	Jan Whiting
55	Vautier-de Nanxe
56	Vautier-de Nanxe
57	Vautier-de Nanxe
58	Vautier-de Nanxe
59	Bret R. Lundberg
60	Maxine Cass
61	Courtesy of the San Francisco Chronicle
62	Maxine Cass
63	Jan Whiting
64	Vautier-de Nanxe
65	Jan Whiting
66	Jan Whiting
67	Jan Whiting
68-69	Bret R. Lundberg
70-71	G. R. Russell
72	Vautier-de Nanxe
76-77	Bret R. Lundberg
78	Jan Whiting
79	Lee Foster
82	Jan Whiting
83	Bret R. Lundberg
84-L	Jan Whiting
84-R	Jan Whiting
85	Bret R. Lundberg
86	Bret R. Lundberg
88	Jan Whiting
89	Jan Whiting
90	Lee Foster
92	Bret R. Lundberg
93	Bret R. Lundberg
94	Bret R. Lundberg
96	John Sanford
97	Courtesy of Mayor's Office, City of San Francisco
98	Bret R. Lundberg
99	Bret R. Lundberg
102-L	Jan Whiting
102-R	Bret R. Lundberg
103-L	Vautier-de Nanxe
103-R	Jan Whiting
104	Bret R. Lundberg
105	Jan Whiting
106	Bret R. Lundberg
107	David Ryan
108-109	Bret R. Lundberg
110	Bret R. Lundberg
112	Bret R. Lundberg
113-L	Jan Whiting
113-R	Lee Foster
114	Lee Foster
115	Vautier-de Nanxe
116	Jan Whiting
118	Bret R. Lundberg
119	David Ryan
120	Bret R. Lundberg
121	Lee Foster
122-L	Bret R. Lundberg
122-R	Jan Whiting
123	Jan Whiting
124	Lee Foster
125	Jan Whiting
126-127	Jan Whiting
128	Bud Lee
129	Bret R. Lundberg
130	Bret R. Lundberg
131	Bud Lee
132	Jan Whiting
133	Jan Whiting
134-L	Jan Whiting
134-R	Bret R. Lundberg
135	Jan Whiting
136	Jan Whiting
137-L	Jan Whiting
137-R	Jan Whiting
138-139	Lee Foster
140	Jan Whiting
141	Lee Foster

INDEX

340

342

By Way of Introduction

Continued from page ix

tor to this book. A native of Southern California, she was instrumental in coordinating many aspects of this book's production, from organization and communications to gathering photographic material.

Most historical reproductions came from the archives of the Bancroft Library, University of California, Berkeley. Bill Roberts gave special assistance in obtaining these materials.

The main selection of color maps was produced by cartographers under the direction of Gunter Nelles in Munich, West Germany. Additional maps and charts were drawn by Yong Sock Ming. Apa assistant editor Vivien Loo drew the marginal maps designed to help readers quickly locate destinations cited in the text. She also helped tie together many loose ends in Singapore. Editorial secretary June Foong provided valuable assistance.

Others who helped to make this book possible were John Hennessey and Michael Pera of the San Francisco Mayor's office, the *San Francisco Chronicle,* Cris Lundberg, Linda Carlock, and the various members of Apa's staff in Singapore—including marketing director Yvan Van Outrive, production coordinator Nancy Yap and financial controller Henry Lee.

In any production of this nature, when the work of making a book is completed, the work of getting it to the readers begins. It would be impossible to list all of the thousands of individual bookshop owners, travel agents and special sales representatives whose multiple efforts carry this book into private homes and offices in 30 countries around the world. We wish to acknowledge with thanks their individual and collective contributions. In particular, we wish to thank Michael Hunter, head of the general publishing division of Prentice-Hall Inc., and his team of sales representatives.

To every one, an earthshaking California *thank you.*

—Apa Productions